International Criminal Law and Procedure

International Criminal Law and Procedure

Editor:

Marko Nikolić

Delve Publishing

www.delvepublishing.com

International Criminal Law and Procedure

Editor: Marko Nikolić

708 3rd Avenue, 6th Floor
New York, NY 10017
United States of America
www.delvepublishing.com

ISBN: 978-1-68095-794-5

Library of Congress Control Number: 2016951553

About the Editor

Marko Nikolić

Marko obtained his Master's degree from University of Belgrade - Faculty of Law in 2014. He specialized in Criminal Law, Family Law and Environmental Law. He spent his Master year studying about international child abduction. He is currently employed in Ministry of Defense's Legal Department

Contents

List of Contributors

Wayne Sandholtz
Gould School of Law University of Southern California

David Welsh
Eller School of Business at the University of Arizona

Ron Levi
George Ignatieff Chair of Peace and Conflict Studies, Deputy Director of the Munk School of Global Affairs, and Associate Professor of Global Affairs and Sociology, University of Toronto

John Hagan
John D. MacArthur Professor of Sociology and Law, Northwestern University, and Senior Research Fellow and Co-Director of the Center for Law & Globalization, American Bar Foundation

Sara Dezalay
Research Fellow, Cluster of Excellence "The Formation of Normative Orders," Goethe Universität, Frankfurt am Main

MD. RAISUL ISLAM SOURAV
Department of law, Dhaka International University (DIU), Bangladesh

Venus GHAREH BAGHI
Research Scholar in law, PhD in progress, Faculty of Law in Islamic Azad University, branch of Kazerun, No 159, 7th Boostan St., Pasdaran Ave

T. R. MARUTHI
Assistance Professor of Law, Department of Studies in Law, Mysore University. India

Inger Skjelsbæk
Peace Research Institute Oslo (PRIO), Oslo, Norway

Martin Paul Eve
Professor of Literature, Technology and Publishingat Birkbeck, University of London

Mohammad Rabiul Islam
Atish Dipankar University of Science and Technolog, Dhaka, Bangladesh

Éder **Milton Schneider**
Instituto de Física, UFRGS, Porto Alegre, RS, Brazil

José Roberto Iglesias
Instituto de Física, UFRGS, Porto Alegre, RS, Brazil, Programa de de Pós-Graduação em Economia, Escola de Gestão e Negócios, Unisinos, São Leopoldo, RS, Brazil, Instituto Nacional de Ciência e Tecnologia de Sistemas Complexos, Rio de Janeiro, RJ, Brazil

Karen Hallberg
Centro Atómico Bariloche and Instituto Balseiro - CNEA, CONICET, 8400 S. C. de Bariloche, Argentina

Marcelo Néstor Kuperman
Centro Atómico Bariloche and Instituto Balseiro - CNEA, CONICET, 8400 S. C. de Bariloche, Argentina

Brian Dube
Faculty of Law, Department of Public Law, Midlands State University, Zimbabwe

Lucy Fiske
University of Technology Sydney (UTS) - Faculty of Arts and Social Sciences

Rita Shackel
University of Sydney - Faculty of Law

Karen-Margrethe Simonsen
Department of Aesthetics and Communication, Aarhus University, *Århus* C, Denmark

Admore Tshuma
University Centre, Southend and Thurrock, United Kingdom

Ahmad Hoteit
Dean of Faculty of Letters and Humans Sciences, Islamic University of Lebanon, Western sea, Sue, Lebanon

Issam Ali Khalifeh
Faculty of Letters and Humans Sciences, Islamic University of Lebanon, Western sea, Sue, Lebanon

Kai Ambos
Comparative Law and International Criminal Law, Georg-August Universität Göttingen, Göttingen, Germany

Ignaz Stegmiller
German Agency for International Cooperation GIZ, Phnom Penh, Cambodia

Fatou Bensouda
Children and International Criminal Justice, University of Georgia School of Law, Athens, Georgia

Anne-Marie Slaughter
Dean, Woodrow Wilson School of Public and International Affairs, Princeton University

William Burke-White
Assistant Professor of Law, University of Pennsylvania School of Law. The authors wish to thank Larry Heifer and the participants in the Vanderbilt Law School Faculty Colloquium,

Benoit Mayer
International Law Institute, Wuhan University, Wuhan, China

Katja Ziegler
Sir Robert Jennings Professor of International Law, University of Leicester

Preface

Small number of areas in the law are connected to as much controversy International criminal law and international criminal tribunals. The reason for this is the fact that international activities are always burdened with politics. Because of this we can consider this for scientific field in its infancy and constant development, with often steps back on its way. Meaning and basic principles of justice should be universal but the world will need many more years to come to good, working solutions. Until then we have to work with what we have, and still wander from problem to problem, from one conflict to the next crisis. Hoping that we are all moving to a better future.

In The New Terrain of International Law, Alter presents a panoramic view of modern international courts and argues convincingly that they influence domestic and international politics as never before. Whether the current development of international courts represents a new era or is a temporary golden age will depend on the degree to which the courts serve the needs and interests (both material and normative) of those who live under the legal rules those courts curate? That is the question asked in the Chapter 1. Throughout the world, there is a growing consensus that America has a lack of credibility as a fair and just world leader. War on Terror is critical because terrorism is not a conventional threat that can surrender or can be defeated in the traditional sense. More on this subject is in Chapter two. How institutions such as the International Criminal Tribunal for Rwanda, the International Criminal Tribunal for the former Yugoslavia (ICTY), and the permanent International Criminal Court (ICC) has reshaped how atrocities are handled at the international level is the question of Chapter 3. Chapter 4 will present and contrast the definition of enforced disappearance in respectively national and international criminal law in Bangladesh. It is also shown that the current situation amounts to a continuous violation of national and international customary law and that continued enforced disappearances constitute international crimes and crimes against humanity. Finally, some recommendations will be put forward to bring about an end to the situation. Principle of proportionality indicated to, are that the criminal codes should contain for crime or category of crimes. The Tribunals' Rules of Procedure and Evidence has been given additional directives on sentencing but The ICC Statute, does not provide precise penalties for specific crimes. This subject is further elaborated in Chapter 5. Chapter 6 examines the ways in which principal perpetrators of sexual violence crimes are situated in an international criminal court. It is based on a narrative psychological analysis of the sentencing judgments of the International Criminal Tribunal for the former Yugoslavia. On the other hand, Chapter 7 discuss whether the US should have captured Osama Bin Laden alive and put him on trial, as per the Nuremberg precedent set in the apprehension and subsequent judicial sentencing of Nazi World War II war criminals. In July 17, 1998, 120 states voted to adopt the Rome statute of the ICC at headquarters of the FAO in Rome. The elaborate and complex negotiated instrument, a framework for an international criminal justice system, represented the highest point of a process that began in the wake of the Nuremberg Judgement, when the first time United Nations considered the establishment of an international criminal jurisdiction. This is elaborated in Chapter 8. Chapter 9 study the role of international tribunals, like the International Criminal Court (ICC), as an effective way of reducing the number and/or gravity of crimes against humanity. The term 'crimes against humanity' has been widely used by different people to mean different things. Chapter 10 traces how crimes against humanity as a category of international crimes emerged and its essential requirements and how courts and institutions have developed and interpreted it, since the term crimes against humanity has acquired both a legal as well as socio-political perspective. The rape of women has for centuries been an endemic feature of war, yet perpetrators largely go unpunished. Chapter 11 briefly maps historical attitudes towards rape in war, outlines some analyses and explanations of why rape in war occurs and finally turns more substantively to recent efforts by the international community to prosecute rape as a war crime and a crime against humanity. Chapter 12 investigates the political function of human rights in 16th-century Spain just after the conquest of America. It claims that the study of this period of early globalization is relevant for an understanding of the function of human rights discourses today, at the "end" of globalization. Chapter 13 interrogates conditions by which deeply divided societies such as Zimbabwe can move forward through a recognition paradigm often used by Truth Commissions (TCs). The study is located within a dispute that troubled societies cannot fully reconcile as long as pre-existing grievances are not addressed. Wars, confrontations and conflicts in general, between two or more opposing factions, have always represented a serious threat to the integrity of the cultural heritage located in their territories. Cultural property protection is the subject of Chapter 14. Chapter 15 analyze the so far published selection and strategy papers of the Office of the Prosecutor ("OTP") of the International Criminal Court ("ICC") with a view to their consistency, coherence and comprehensiveness. Nelson Mandela once said: "We owe our children, the most vulnerable citizens in our society, a life free of violence and fear." Chapter 16 contains a speech dealing with this serious topic. More recently, international law has penetrated the once exclusive zone of domestic affairs to regulate the relationships between governments and their own citizens, particularly through the growing bodies of human rights law and international criminal law. Read about this in Chapter 17. International lawyers and international relations scholars certainly have a role to play, along with moral philosophers, in debates on global justice. The expertise of international lawyers could most obviously help to characterize existing norms in international law, thus providing a factual basis for a moral reckoning of international law. International relations theories, on the contrary, may help us to envisage realistic steps toward a more just international law. Chapter 18 covers this topic. Chapter 19 bring one more actual question, whether the EU is utopia that is falling apart or model of accountability and democracy while we finish with Chapter 20 and the dogs of war which are awaken. Dangerous times are in front of us. We need educated and informed people in eternal hope that the bloodsheds will be stopped and people responsible for crimes punished.

Editor
Marko Nikolić

INTRODUCTION

International criminal law is used in cases such as war crimes, crimes against humanity and genocide. These crimes generally are committed against citizens of countries rather than governments, but the crimes are serious enough to cause concern even among nations whose citizens were not targeted. There are no clearly defined parameters in international criminal law, but many nations are able to agree on basic principles of behavior and what is acceptable or unacceptable. When an action is considered to have violated international criminal law, a tribunal — a temporary court — might be established to deal with specific issues. Tribunals have been convened to address things such as the actions of the Nazis during World Word II and genocide in Rwanda.

Many international criminal law tribunals are conducted by the United Nations, an organization of which more than 180 countries are members. The United Nation's International Court of Justice is located in the Netherlands, a neutral country that does not take sides in international affairs. Although tribunals can be held at the International Court of Justice, this is not required.

Perhaps the best-known example in modern history of an international criminal law tribunal is the Nuremberg Trials. After World War II, the international criminal court prosecuted former Nazi soldiers and Nazi doctors. The Nuremberg trials lasted from 1945 to 1949. The indictments at the Nuremberg trials included conspiracy to wage aggressive war, waging aggressive war, war crimes and crimes against humanity.

The Nuremberg trials were held in Nuremberg, Germany. After these international trials came to an end, more Nazi war criminals were tried in the same courtroom, but each of the subsequent trials was held by one country instead of the international community. For example, the United States prosecuted Nazi doctors for cruel medical experiments on children and adults, and Great Britain tried those responsible for running the Bergen-Belsen concentration camp.

Another well-known tribunal was held to address genocide in Rwanda, a country on the continent of Africa. The people in the area belonged to different tribes, and when battling for land and supremacy, one group attempted to completely kill off another tribe. An international criminal law tribunal was convened to address the grievances of the surviving victims of attempted genocide.

What is the International Court of Justice?

The International Court of Justice (ICJ) is the judicial arm of the United Nations (UN). Established in June 1945 by the UN Charter, the ICJ plays an important role in disputes between member countries. The court has the power to both settle disputes and provide advisory opinions; however, its power is somewhat limited as few member states are pleased with the idea of being subject to international, rather than national laws. In some cases, the ICJ has come into direct conflict with the UN Security Council, which has the ability to veto decisions of the court.

The Netherlands is the official home of the International Court of Justice. The only major UN operation not housed in the United States, the ICJ operates out of the famed Peace Palace in The Hague. The Court consists of 15 judges who serve terms of nine years with two opportunities for reelection. The ICJ holds elections on a rotating basis to provide consistency, with one-third of the judges up for re-election or retirement every three years. No concurrently serving judges may be of the same nationality.

The function of the International Court of Justice is to provide mediation between disagreeing nations, and to help sort out complex legal problems that have an international effect. Some experts suggest that the court is most effective when managing issues such as border delineation and water rights.

There are varying opinions on the usefulness of the International Court of Justice throughout the legal world. While technically the judgment of the court is supposed to be binding, it lies within the power of the UN Security Council to oversee consequences for failing to implement court orders. Since the five permanent members of the Security Council each retain veto power over court decisions, any attempt to judge against these members can result in an immediate veto. The United States exercised veto power in the instance of Nicaragua v. United States, when the court ordered that the US pay reparations for illegally assisting in the overthrow of Nicaragua's government. The ability of Security Council members to simply overturn a verdict they do not agree with makes the ICJ appear to critics as only a token puppet version of a judicial entity.

International law is a continuously evolving system; each time a new case comes up, it may be dealing with laws that are effectively not yet written. The International Court of Justice is bound to abide by existing treaties and sources of international law, but at the same time must frequently rely on a sense of fairness and justice in order to get anything done where no laws yet exist. This type of judgment is known as ex aequo et bono, and is the source of much contention, as it relies on the wisdom of the judges rather than actual statutes.

What is international criminal law?

International criminal law is a subset of public international law, and is the main subject of these materials. While international law typically concerns inter-state relations, international criminal law concerns individuals. In particular, international criminal law places responsibility on individual persons—not states or organizations—and proscribes and punishes acts that are defined as crimes by international law. International criminal law is a relatively new body of law, and aspects of it are neither uniform nor universal. For example, some aspects of the law of the ICTY are unique to that jurisdiction, do not reflect customary international law and also differ from the law of the ICC. Although there are various interpretations of the categories of international crimes,[1] these materials deal with crimes falling within the jurisdiction of international and hybrid courts, including the ICTY, ICTR, SCSL, ECCC, and the ICC. These crimes comprise genocide, crimes against humanity, war crimes and the crime of aggression.[2] They do not include piracy, terrorism, slavery, drug trafficking, or other international crimes (whether or not also criminalized in the national laws of BiH, Croatia, and Serbia) that do not amount to genocide, crimes against humanity, or war crimes. International criminal law also includes laws, procedures and principles relating to modes of liability, defenses, evidence, court procedure, sentencing, victim participation, witness protection, mutual legal assistance and cooperation issues. Each of these topics will be addressed in these materials.

How to Distinguish International Law from Municipal Law

International law, a term coined around 1800 by philosopher Jeremy Bentham, refers to the body of legal decisions, rules, and customs that regulate the discourse between nations (e.g., human rights, military intervention, and global concerns such as climate change). Conversely, municipal law governs the actions of individuals and commercial entities within the borders of sovereign states (e.g., civil codes and criminal statutes).

Understand the concept of public international law. When questions and conflicts arise in the relationships between sovereign nations, they are solved under the rules of public international law. This body of law consists of the treaties and legal decisions interpreting those treaties.

- International law assumes that all the parties, as sovereign states, are equals.
- Conflicts arising under public international law can be settled either through diplomatic negotiations or in the International Court of Justice. This is the court of the United Nations. Fifteen judges, elected by the UN General Assembly, use international legal precedent to issue advisory opinions and solve legal disputes between governments.
- The International Court of Justice has jurisdiction in two types of cases. The first is where the two countries agree to submit the conflict to the court. The second is when a treaty specifies the court as the legal authority over disputes

Differentiate private international law from public. When citizens of different states have a legal dispute, there is often a question about what law applies. This choice of law question in civil issues, ranging from contracts to family law, is discussed in the Hague Conference on Private International Law.

- In general, courts will first defer to any contract or agreement clauses that identify what courts will have jurisdiction. In the absence of explicit choice of law language, the court will look to the overall circumstances of the contract, the behavior of the parties in creating the contract (called parol evidence) and if the parties can agree on jurisdiction.

Review the sources of international law. The customary international law is codified in the Vienna Convention on the Law of Treaties. Under this custom, states consistently adhere to certain practices out historical and legal obligation.

Examining the Precepts of Municipal Law

Define municipal law. In common usage, especially in the United States, municipal or municipality, refers to a city or town. However, in the realm of international law, municipal refers to any sovereign entity, including countries, states, counties, provinces, cities, and towns. In short, municipal refers to the internal law of a sovereign government.

Familiarize yourself with the basics of municipal law. There are two primary forms of municipal, or domestic, law. The first is civil law, composed of the statutory law and regulations to administer those laws. Statutes are passed either by the legislative bodies of the state or by popular vote. Domestic law is also formed by the common law, which is law handed down by the lower and upper courts of the country.

- Common types of municipal law are criminal statutes, traffic laws, and government regulations. Basically, municipal law regulates the relationship of citizens with the government.

Understand the enforcement mechanisms of municipal law. Civil and common law are enforced in very different ways. For example, law enforcement agencies, ranging from local police to the federal investigative branches, have jurisdiction over civil criminal statutes. On the other hand, most common law, often called judge-made law, is referred to during legal issues such as contract law or disputes between domestic businesses.

Distinguishing International and Municipal Law

Look at how the laws were created. There are no international statutes. The United Nations agrees on conventions that member nations may choose to ratify and abide by, but there is no international governmental body. International law is created by treaty, by custom, and by agreements between nations. This is in stark contrast to the legislative process that creates the internal municipal laws of nations and states.

- International treaties are legally binding agreements between nations. In a nation like the United States, a treaty is an agreement ratified by Congress. Once it has been ratified, it holds the same status as federal legislation (i.e., statutes). Therefore, treaties can mean different things depending on the nation or international body discussing them. An example of a treaty is the Treaty of Versailles, which was the peace settlement signed after World War I.
- International agreements are usually less formal than treaties, although the international community often sees them on the same level as treaties. In the United States, an international agreement does not need to be ratified by Congress and they are only applicable in domestic law (i.e., they are not enforceable themselves). An example of an international agreement is the Kyoto Protocol, which sets international emissions reductions with the hope of curbing climate change.
- International customs are created when a nation generally and consistently adheres to a certain practice due to a sense of legal obligation. They are not necessarily written down and are the least formal of all the sources of international law.

Study how the laws are enforced. There is no police agency with complete international jurisdiction. Even INTERPOL, the organization with 190 member countries, acts only as a coordination agency, passing information and training to municipal police forces. When there is a dispute between nations, the international law is enforced through treaties, United Nations conventions, and the ICJ.

- In municipal law legal disputes, the case will be decided based either on the civil laws, in the form of statutes, or by the body of common law in the forum state.

Study who the parties are and how they are affected. If the two sides in the legal dispute are sovereign nations, you can assume that international laws, enforcement methods, and dispute resolution will apply. Conversely, if both parties are citizens of the same nation, municipal law enforcement, court systems, and jurisdictional rules will be used to settle the dispute.

- When the citizenship is mixed, such as individuals of different countries or an individual in a dispute with a government of another sovereignty, the courts will look to any treaties, UN conventions, or contracts that may shed light on the jurisdiction before agreeing to accept jurisdiction.

Determine how nations are required to conform to international law. While nations are under a general obligation to follow international law, there is usually a great amount of leeway in how they choose to do so. Nations are generally free to decide how they incorporate international law into municipal law. While different nations handle this issue in different manners, the prevailing position seems to be dualist. Therefore, most nations require the formal integration of international law through the passage of some municipal law.

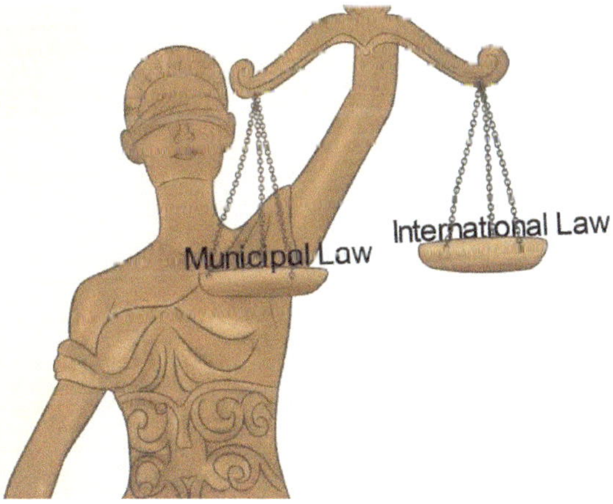

Assess how international law interacts with municipal law. In the international sphere, international law wins out over municipal law. However, municipal law is useful evidence of international customary law and general principles of law. In addition, international law often leaves questions to be answered by a nation's own laws. Therefore, if you found yourself in international court, you might use municipal law to help you decide whether there has been a breach of international law. An international court may even look to municipal law to help them interpret international law.

- In the municipal (i.e., national) sphere, the interaction is more difficult to assess. In general, less formal international agreements and customs are accepted and followed so long as there is no conflict with municipal law. If there is a conflict, municipal law will usually win. However, more formal treaties, so long as they are self-executing (i.e., operate within a nation automatically), are usually seen as being on par with municipal law. However, some nations take different views.

CHAPTER 1

A NEW AGE OF INTERNATIONAL COURTS

Wayne Sandholtz

In *The New Terrain of International Law*, Karen Alter argues that the international courts of today perform more roles and do so with greater effect on world politics than their predecessors did.[1] In theorizing the roles of modern international courts and illustrating their effects on national and international law and policy, Alter has established a new plateau in scholarship on international courts, one upon which many others will surely build.

Alter's agenda is ambitious: she aims to show that "new-style" international courts (ICs) are producing a "judicialization of international relations" that is "diminishing government control over how international legal agreements are understood domestically and internationally."[2] To accomplish that goal, the book offers a theory of the functioning of modern international courts, traces their emergence, maps their empirical terrain, and offers case-study explorations of the effects—both domestic and international—of specific IC decisions. *New Terrain* is a capstone to the major contributions that Alter has made to theorizing international courts and evaluating them empirically for more than twenty years, in research that has extended from the European Court of Justice to international courts in Latin America and Africa.

In the review that follows, I first explore the book's theoretical framework, high-lighting connections to major strands of research on international law and courts and emphasizing the decisive stance *New Terrain* takes toward them. I then turn, in the second section, to three central themes in the book, each of which signals directions for complementary lines of inquiry. The first theme addresses the nature and importance of rule of law cultures, which play a crucial role in international courts "altering politics."[3] A second theme concerns judicial decision-making in international courts, in particular, how inter-national judges might (and probably must) take into account domestic political and legal contexts. The third theme emphasizes the dynamism of normative systems where new-style international courts are at work. The final section offers concluding thoughts.

THEORY

Alter sets out her theory in chapter 2, "International Courts Altering Politics." The chapter is the single best theoretical piece on international courts that I have encountered. Alter stakes out a position as far from that of the international law skeptics as she can make it. The international law skeptics are scholars who, importing simplified versions of "real-ism" from International Relations, argue that international law has no independent effect on the behavior of states.[4] They contend that states comply with international legal obligations not because they are legal but because compliance either serves state interests or is imposed by superior power. The realist view of international courts is that, because international law has no autonomous effect, ICs can only be agents of states, molding their decisions to conform to the preferences of the most powerful states.[5] The contrary view, advanced vigorously by Alter and others, is that under certain conditions, international courts can be trustees of a normative system rather than servants of states.[6] In previous work Alter has contributed to theorizing about trustee courts.[7] In *New Terrain* she qualifies slightly the earlier work, arguing that ICs are most like trustees when they are empowered to enforce legal norms against states themselves.[8]

The debate on whether international courts can be anything more than faithful agents of states has tended to focus on the European Court of Justice (ECJ); the ECJ is also the international court that has been most intensively subjected to empirical analysis for the purpose of determining whether its rulings are systematically shaped by member state preferences.[9] The ECJ is a natural focal point for such research because it is widely seen as having exercised a broadly independent role in shaping EU law and policy and, in fact, as having "constitutionalized" the EU regime.[10] A substantial body of empirical work has shown that the ECJ routinely rules in ways

Citation: Wayne Sandholtz, A New Age of International Courts, http:// digital commons. law.utulsa. edu/cgi/ view content. cgi?article=2981&context=tlr

that the member states oppose and would not have approved through normal legislative mechanisms.[11]

In the most recent round of this debate, Carrubba, Gabel, and Hankla claim to offer quantitative evidence supporting the proposition that the EU member-state governments constrain the ECJ's decision-making by: (1) collectively threatening to override its judgments, and (2) individually threatening non-compliance with those decisions.[12] Both claims have been comprehensively refuted.[13] Carrubba, Gabel, and Hankla mistakenly assumed that the ECJ decisions in their dataset of 3,176 legal issues were all subject to over-ride by a qualified majority vote of the member states, which would make it easier for states to reverse them. In fact, more than ninety percent of the legal issues they include in the analysis could only be overridden by unanimity, which makes the threat of override non-credible.[14] Carrubba, Gabel, and Hankla provided no data on member-state threats of non-compliance and offered no test of their second proposition.[15]

In fact, the European Commission's position, which will virtually always support the expansion and application of EU law, is more likely to predict the ECJ's decisions than are the weighted member-state government positions, in cases where the defendant is a member state.[16] Stone Sweet and Brunell show that in non-compliance cases (Article 258 enforcement proceedings), though the member states rarely (3.2 percent of cases) register a net weighted position supporting the Commission, the ECJ rules against the defendant state more than 90 percent of the time.[17] Non-compliance, in other words, triggers ECJ action; it does not constrain it. In preliminary reference cases (under Article 267, in which national courts refer a question to the ECJ for the interpretation of EU law), when the Commission and the member states (collectively) take opposite sides, the ECJ favors the Commission position more than two-thirds of the time.[18]

Alter has been a protagonist in the debates on the ECJ and takes the question of the Court's independence as settled.[19] On the broader question of whether international courts in general are simple agents of states or whether they can have an autonomous impact on politics and policies, she takes the latter view as her point of departure: "[I]t is more plausible that we accept the possibility that ICs can rule against the preferences of governments and then ask how ICs get governments to then change their behavior."[20] Alter does not claim that ICs are wholly independent of state preferences, nor that state compliance with IC judgments is non-problematic. Rather, she presents a theory of the conditions under which international courts can bring about shifts in state behavior, "in the direction of greater respect for international law,"[21] that is, how ICs can alter international politics.

The problem with existing accounts of the relationship between international courts and national governments is not that they are all wrong, but that they are all right—some of the time. *New Terrain* identifies three existing categories of models. ICs help states to resolve disputes by identifying focal points that are consistent with the preferences of both states (the interstate arbiter model). By judging that certain acts fall outside the bounds of legality, ICs can also generate behavior that is consistent with international law through decisions that motivate other states to impose sanctions-based or reputational costs on the offending state (the multilateral adjudication model). Finally, IC decisions can mobilize and empower both domestic and transnational actors who can bring pressure to bear on governments to comply with the IC ruling (the transnational politics model). Alter's goal is to bring the three existing classes of models together into one unifying framework (she, correctly in my view, does not label it a theory). The unifying framework is a set of inter-locking propositions about how legality, and actors that value legality, can move states toward compliance with IC decisions.[22]

At the center of Alter's argument are "compliance constituencies." Compliance constituencies include actors—primarily state officials—who have the authority to "choose compliance" with international law and with specific IC decisions, as well as broader groups of non-state actors who "support adherence to a specific international law" and provide political backing to officials who pursue it.[23] International courts influence governments through alliances with domestic and international compliance constituencies. Through their decisions, ICs can empower "those actors who have international law on their side, increasing their out of court political leverage. ICs then alter political outcomes by giving symbolic, legal, and political resources to compliance constituencies."[24] The move to see international courts' primary channel of influence as operating through a variety of transnational and domestic allies parallels important lines of research on international norms and law. A durable insight in research on the effects of international human rights norms, for example, is that norm entrepreneurs and activists can bring political pressure on rights-abusing governments by mobilizing both transnational and domestic ac-tors.[25] Human rights treaties exert their most powerful effects through domestic channels, giving domestic actors a source of political leverage (pressure politics) as well as the potential for legal recourse in domestic courts (judicial politics).[26]

By focusing on alliances between ICs and various domestic and transnational actors, Alter shifts the compliance focus away from governments, who are the key actors in realist-inspired accounts. International courts, then, are not constrained to be simple agents of states because governments are not the only effective players when it comes to compliance with IC decisions. Domestic judges, administrators, military officers, and legislators can all, in some circumstances, take action to comply with IC judgments. One implication, of course, is that as international judges craft their rulings they must think about a variety of potential compliance constituencies beyond just national executives. I return later to two issues raised by compliance constituencies: the motivations of compliance constituencies, and the links between international courts and domestic politico-legal contexts.

A second key theoretical anchor for *New Terrain* is Alter's temporal framework for the international litigation process. Once a state violates an international rule or obligation, international courts exercise their influence in three partially overlapping periods or stages. The stages are not meant to represent a strict linear chronology but are analytical constructs that illuminate important mechanisms and processes. Time 1 is the pre-litigation stage, in which most of the action takes place domestically. Both domestic actors (courts, legislatures, prosecutors) and international legal actors bring pressure to bear on national political actors who have the authority to choose compliance with international law. The key is that this takes place "in the shadow of an IC," as litigation looms should the state not rectify its violation of an international obligation.[27] In Time 2, the various actors try to persuade an international court to rule in their favor. If the IC rules against the state, compliance constituencies use "leverage strategies" in Time 3 to pressure the state to comply with the IC's decision. The mechanisms highlighted in the three existing models of compliance with international courts can all operate within Alter's three-stage framework.

Alter makes the bold claim that "new-style" ICs can shift international relations "away from state control in both domestic and international realms."[28] It is the "new-style" qualifier that requires emphasis. "Old -style" international courts were designed simply to help states resolve disputes. Old-style ICs, like the International Court of Justice, continue to function in this mode, and international law skeptics[29] assume that international courts in general are limited to that role. New-style ICs can take on additional roles (administrative review, enforcement, and constitutional review in Alter's typology). These modern ICs are producing a "judicialization of international relations and diminishing government control over how international legal agreements are understood domestically and internationally."[30]

What is new about the "new-style ICs"? Two main features distinguish them: (1) they tend to have compulsory jurisdiction, and (2) they allow non-state actors (international commissions or prosecutors, or private individuals) to trigger litigation.[31] Old-style courts see international law essentially as contracts between states.[32] New- style courts imply a "rule of law conceptualization of the meaning of international law" in which "governments are not above the law" and law creates "obligations regardless of what other states do."[33] The book focuses on twenty-four international courts, selected because they are both permanent and operational.[34] Excluded are quasi-judicial bodies, like the International Centre for the Settlement of Investment Disputes (ICSID), whose panels are *ad hoc* and therefore not permanent, and courts that exist on paper but are non-functioning (like the dispute settlement body of the Organization of Arab Oil Exporting States). Of the twenty-four ICs, twenty-three have at least some new-style features; the sole exception is the International Court of Justice (ICJ).[35] Only six of the twenty-four courts existed before 1989, and of the 37,236 binding judgments issued by the twenty-four courts in contentious cases, ninety-one percent came after the fall of the Berlin Wall.[36]

Europe (in the form of the ECJ and the European Court of Human Rights (ECtHR)) is, as Alter notes, exceptional. The ECJ and the ECtHR have accounted for 33,451, or 90%, of all judgments produced by the twenty-four ICs.[37] But Alter also notes that the European courts started out slowly and that, if compared from the year of their first judgment, the more recent new-style ICs have been about as active as the two European courts in a similar phase of their development.[38] Still, it seems unlikely that other ICs will experience the same conditions that generated the rapid expansion of judicial activity in the ECJ and the ECtHR: the simultaneous and mutually reinforcing growth in legislation, in cases filed, and in expansive judicial decisions, all in the context of strong rule-of-law cultures.

EXPLORING THE NEW TERRAIN

International lawyers and social scientists who follow one or a few international courts may not need to be persuaded that ICs created in recent decades have generated important jurisprudence through decisions that have substantive effects. But *New Terrain* will be useful even for that audience, as Alter presents the broader picture of ICs taken as a whole. The book offers a tour of the empirical territory of modern ICs and an analytical framework for assessing their effects on international and domestic law and politics. *New Terrain* opens multiple questions and provides points of departure for finding ways to answer them. This section explores some of those questions and raises further ones, focusing on cultures of obedience to international law, judicial decision-making, and the dynamism of judicialized systems.

The Commitment to Law and Cultures of Obedience

Underlying Alter's framework is an assumption, or perhaps a commitment to the idea, that at least some actors value legality in itself. It is a crucial assumption, and one that appears almost every time Alter discusses compliance constituencies. It is also an assumption that starkly separates Alter from the international law skeptics, who assume that states decide whether to comply with international law and IC judgments purely on the basis of instrumental calculations of material payoffs. To take a prominent example, Goldsmith and Posner explicitly assume that (1) rules and institutions do not shape interests and (2) rule-following cannot be a state interest.[39]

In contrast, much of the distinctiveness of Alter's account stems from the idea that at least some actors value legality and adherence to law for their own sakes. Alter recognizes that actors are driven by both instrumental and normative motivations.[40] "Some [compliance] supporters will be self-interested, seeking rulings that benefit themselves and their clients."[41] Others support compliance with IC rulings because they "benefit from the international legal system overall."[42] Still other compliance constituencies favor conformance with IC judgments even when they "do not have a dog in the fight," because they "see themselves as rule of law actors."[43] As Alter argues, "[s]upport for the rule of law . . .bring[s] civil society groups and countries that are substantively self-interested together with individuals, groups, and foreign governments that care about correct legal interpretation and the rule of law more generally."[44]

New Terrain does not explore the basis for or the logic of the second category of motivation—the benefits of the international system of rules—and, in fact, it remains largely undeveloped in scholarship on international law compliance. The idea is that specific "games" of international relations are embedded in higher -order or "meta" games, which are about the system of rules itself. Violating the rules in the lower-level game (to gain a temporary trade advantage, for example) could have an economic or political payoff in the short-term, but potentially at some cost in the meta -game if violations undermine the system of rules and the predictability that they bring. Actors may therefore be in a situation of optimizing:

How much selfish breaking of the rules in the lower-level game is possible without destabilizing the framework of rules itself? And do actors think about their interests at both levels? Theoretical development could help explore answers to such questions.

The third motivation—that some actors value legality and the rule of law itself— seems plausible. Many readers will want to accept it. But the book does not attempt to justify the assumption that such a motivation is real nor examine its foundations. Research has addressed the underlying psychology of compliance with law,[45] and the late Thomas Franck argued that international law created through fair and accepted processes exerts a compliance pull.[46] But little work that I am aware of has focused directly on the extent to which people (in governments, courts, NGOs, or publics) in fact view international legality as a sufficient motive or justification for action. Yet the assumption is crucial to Alter's arguments. Alter posits that "some compliance supporters are primarily motivated by their normative commitment to the rule of law and a belief that the IC ruling correctly applies the law."[47] International courts can empower these actors, providing them with legal justifications for choosing policies that conform to IC decisions. IC judgments carry a "presumed authority" that can help compliance advocates "delegitimize" positions that are contrary to the IC's interpretation.[48]

The commitment to legality and the rule of law is especially vital when international courts exercise constitutional review, which consists of "the judicial authority to invalidate laws and government acts on the basis of a conflict with higher order legal obligations."[49] In the new terrain of international law, those higher order legal obligations are to be found in, for example, the EU treaties with respect to the ECJ, the American Convention on Human Rights for the Inter-American Court of Human Rights (IACtHR), and the General Agreement on Tariffs and Trade (GATT) within the World Trade Organization (WTO) Dispute Settlement System. Effective constitutional review by international courts re-quires the existence of "[a] culture of constitutional obedience," which means "a political culture in which any legislative text or government action found to violate higher order law becomes inherently illegitimate."[50] Scholars have studied the development of domes-tic constitutional courts, constitutional review, and cultures of constitutional obedience.[51] However, cultures of constitutional obedience to international law may be, as Alter notes, something quite different.[52] Scholars have made progress in analyzing when and how domestic courts make use of international law and IC decisions,[53] but Alter makes a different argument: that broader judicial cultures of adherence to international law can empower international courts. The book does not explain how to identify cultures of adherence to international law or assess their strength. It does, however, provide some initial signposts for possible directions of such work, noting that national judges are probably crucial to whether domestic cultures of obedience to international law develop.[54] The idea of domes-tic cultures of adherence to international law is a richly intriguing one that begs for research to identify their preconditions, to assess their variation across countries, and to document their effects on law and policy.[55]

Judicial Decision-Making in International Courts

New Terrain depicts international courts affecting domestic law and policy and shifting international relations. The judges who sit on new-style international courts, then, play a pivotal and increasingly important role. Yet how international judges perform that role and how they reach decisions, when they are both partially independent but also legally and politically constrained, remain largely unknown. Though theories of judicial decision-making are quite developed in the U.S. context (especially for the Supreme Court) and are beginning to emerge in other national and comparative settings,[56] we know little about judicial decision-making in international courts.[57]

Alter does not offer a theory of international judicial decision-making, but her arguments reveal a set of important assumptions. Elsewhere she has argued that the multilateral nature of the appointment process for judges on international courts means that international judges are probably more insulated from appointment or confirmation politics than are domestic judges.[58] The assumption that international judges are at least partially independent of national governments underlies the entire argument of *New Terrain*. Delegation to an IC creates "an independent outside actor with the legal authority to say what international law means" and whose "legal interpretations are presumed to be more independent and disinterested compared to self-serving arguments litigating states put forward."[59] ICs are legal actors that reside "outside of the control of litigating states."[60]

A second key assumption is that, in general, judges on international courts will act as trustees of a legal regime and seek to apply its norms. This means that "international judging" is guided in part by "legal facts," namely, "what the law requires."[61] Thus "ICs enforcing international economic rules will tend to promote market openness. ICs enforcing human rights rules will tend to promote a human rights agenda. International war crimes tribunals will tend to condemn state practices that harm noncombatants."[62] Alter assumes that judges on international courts possess both the degree of independence and the underlying judicial preference to uphold international legal rules and apply them even, at times, when doing so contradicts the preferences of important states.[63] These are crucial assumptions that call for empirical exploration.

At the same time, Alter recognizes that "[b]eing a trustee [of international legal norms] does not mean that international judges are entirely neutral or fully independent actors."[64] They are both "legally and politically constrained."[65] Where Alter diverges from the international law skeptics and the IR realists is that she does not see the source of political constraints on ICs as emanating solely from states.[66] Rather, ICs are constrained (or enabled) by the absence (or presence) of domestic compliance constituencies (see the discussion above).[67] Governments, or more narrowly, national executives, are not the only potentially important constituency.[68] The upshot is that, though ICs (like all courts) lack overt means to compel states to comply with their rulings, they are not "beholden to the interests and preferences of governments."[69] The range of IC interlocutors is much broader. ICs can use "their institutional position to aid actors inside and outside of states that share the objectives inscribed into the law."[70] International courts can therefore "work with domestic and transnational interlocutors to either orchestrate compliance or construct counter-pressures that alter the political balance in favor of policies that better cohere with international legal obligations."[71] In other words, the primary constraints on ICs are the availability of compliance constituencies and the ability of the court to engage or empower those actors.[72]

International courts must consequently take into account the degree to which their interpretations of the law are likely to resonate with and lend political or legal support to (primarily) domestic pro-compliance actors.[73] As Alter puts it, "international judges should, and probably do, consider whether or not there is legal and political support for the interpretations they advocate."[74] The point is such a crucial one that it calls for further theoretical and empirical development—work that social science and law scholars should be eager to take up. Alter offers the intriguing speculation, for instance, that the adjustment by international judges "to the realities of their environments" may be most visible in the remedies they order, where judges might enjoy greater flexibility.[75] The case studies in the second half of the book offer examples of remedies that vary in the difficulty of domestic implementation. At one end, the Andean Tribunal of Justice ordered no remedies in the *Peru Exemptions Case*, finding that the violation had already been corrected.[76] In the

Modern-Day Slavery Case, Hadijatou Mani v. Niger, the Economic Community of West African States (ECOWAS) Court of Justice ordered compensation for the victim but did not rule on whether Niger's laws violated international rules, making compliance more likely.[77] At the other extreme, the IACtHR ordered Nicaragua to adopt substantial legal and institutional changes regarding indigenous communal land rights in *Mayagno (Sumo) Awas Tingni Community v. Nicaragua*.[78]

Alter's insight on ICs' potential flexibility with remedies flags the need for much greater understanding of judicial decision-making in international courts.[79] How do international judges weigh the multiple legal and political considerations that arise in the disputes that come before them? In particular, how do IC judges balance two objectives that are often in fundamental tension: one, advancing the international rule of law, and two, garnering support for and compliance with their judgments?

Research has begun to explore that key question. For instance, Stone Sweet and Brunell analyze how international courts expand the reach of international legal norms while navigating the heterogeneous preferences of member states.[80] They argue that international trustee courts employ a strategy of "majoritarian activism."[81] The heart of the strategy is that the court assesses the practice of the states involved in the regime, to gauge the degree of state consensus on the rule in dispute, or even on a more expansive interpretation of it.[82] The practice of a majority of states is a fact relevant to the resolution of the case.[83] The court's decisions will then approximate outcomes that the states might adopt "under majoritarian, but not unanimity, decision rules."[84] When a majority of states has enacted a more expansive interpretation of a norm in their domestic policies and practices, the court can adopt that interpretation in its decision, thereby applying it to all states within their jurisdiction, even the "laggard[s]."[85] For instance, the ECtHR has expanded rights protections for homosexuals through a strategy of majoritarian activism.[86] The strategy allows the court to expand the reach of international legal norms while at the same time ensuring a majority compliance coalition of states.[87] Sandholtz and Rangel Padilla offer evidence that the Inter-American Human Rights System (comprised of a commission and a court) has modulated both the timing and the scope of its fourteen decisions on national amnesty laws in light of domestic politico-legal conditions.[88] The IACtHR has thereby been able to construct an interpretation of the American Convention on Human Rights that prohibits amnesties, but it has done so in a way that increased the likelihood that its rulings would find (in Alter's terms) domestic compliance constituencies.

On judicial decision-making in international courts, *New Terrain* thus raises crucial questions and indicates important avenues to be pursued.

The Dynamics of Law in International Courts

New Terrain forcefully makes the case that international law is inherently dynamic,[89] and that international courts are engines of legal norm change, with consequences for state behavior and world politics.[90] The contrast here is with (mainly) political science approaches to international law and international legal institutions, in which a sense of the dynamism of law and judicialized politics is almost entirely missing.[91] For example, in the "legalization" approach in International Relations, the focus is on the choices and tradeoffs states make in creating international legal rules and institutions.[92] There is no systematic attention to how legal norms evolve through disputes and dispute resolution.[93] The "rational design of international institutions" approach suffers from the same limitation.[94] It offers sophisticated propositions about the tradeoffs states make in setting up institutions to enforce international agreements[95] but has almost nothing to say about what happens once such bodies are adjudicating claims and interpreting rules. The inattention to the dynamics of legal and judicial institutions is traceable to the baseline position for many International Relations scholars that international courts have no independent effect on con-duct or outcomes.[96] Indeed, the field of International Relations has, for the most part, ignored international jurisprudence. Alter offers an important corrective: "[T]he decisions of governments to create ICs . . . are important, but legal practice shapes what institutions become."[97]

Alter contends that "[d]elegation to ICs . . . promotes political change in the direction indicated by the law"—provided that the necessary compliance constituencies exist.[98] The process is dynamic because ICs can "interpret existing laws in unexpected ways," and those interpretations can empower various domestic and transnational actors who will pressure governments to comply with IC decisions.[99] Alter's argument powerfully complements the work that Stone Sweet and others have done over many years to integrate jurisprudential and political analyses and to show empirically how judicial decisions shift the calculations, and hence the choices, of social and political actors.[100] The more judicialization proceeds, the more motivated actors will be to act in ways that are defensible in light of the legal interpretations announced by the court, and the more their decisions will be influenced by the shadow of the court.[101] The more courts are seen as authoritative interpreters of norms, the more violations of the rules will trigger litigation, and the more courts will shape (or reshape) the rules.[102]

In *New Terrain*, Alter makes a compelling argument that these dynamics are emerging around more international courts than most readers will have imagined.[103] She illustrates her claims in the second half of the book with a series of case studies.[104] The case studies analyze the jurisprudence of diverse international courts resolving diverse kinds of claims, and examine their effects on political and policy outcomes.[105] The point of these chapters is not to test a theory but to establish the plausibility of the broader argument that international courts are altering domestic and international politics.[106] Readers' prior beliefs about international courts will probably shape how they judge the cumulative effect of the case studies.

Readers may be less convinced that the framing of the case studies in terms of four judicial roles (dispute resolution, administrative review, enforcement, and constitutional review), or indeed the role typology itself, is crucial to the argument. Of the twenty-four courts included in the book, only six perform just one of the four roles. Of those six, three are international criminal tribunals (the ICTY, the ICTR, and the ICC), which necessarily have narrowly specified jurisdiction. Eight courts (one-third of the total) perform all four judicial roles. Alter notes frequently that the roles often "morph" into one another.[107] The real work seems to be done by the distinction between "other-binding" and "self-binding" functions, which do not map directly onto the four judicial roles.

CONCLUSION

In *The New Terrain of International Law*, Alter presents a panoramic view of modern international courts and argues convincingly that they influence domestic and international politics as never before.[108] She suggests that international law, and international courts in particular, have entered a new era.[109] Turning back the clock to a time when states could choose, case by case, whether or not to be subject to international adjudication "is not a realistic or viable option."[110] The new terrain represents a major shift in world politics, one that is "unlikely to be reversed any time soon."[111]

But does the current state of international courts represent a new era or instead a time that will be remembered as a high point in the judicialization of world politics? Skep-tics might suspect the latter. The two temporary criminal tribunals, the ICTY and the ICTR, are winding down. The International Criminal Court has been unable to secure the arrest of Omar al-Bashir, even though he has traveled to ICC member states that are sup-posed to be committed to cooperating with the Court. The ICC had to shut down its case against President Uhuru Kenyatta of Kenya and faces widespread resistance, if not hostility, across much of Africa. International criminal courts, in other words, may not be poised to expand their role in world affairs. Among the human rights courts, the ECtHR is coping with an overwhelming caseload while the IACtHR continues to be under-resourced and modestly utilized. The African Court on Human and Peoples' Rights has not really begun to function, and there appears to be no prospect of human rights courts emerging in the Middle East or Asia. Among international courts with jurisdiction over trade and economic issues (the largest single category of ICs), the ECJ has by far the largest caseload (18,511 binding rulings), followed distantly by the Andean Tribunal of Justice (2,197 rulings) and the Common Court of Justice and Arbitration of l'Organisation pour l'Harmonisation en Afrique du Droite des Affairs (OHADA) (569 rulings).[112]

The European courts—the ECJ and the ECtHR—are, by any measure, the most effective and influential international courts.[113] Alter argues that the ECJ and ECtHR design templates have been adopted by most other ICs around the world.[114] The question is, can the non-European courts follow not just the design templates but the trajectory of usage and effectiveness of the two European models? Alter provides evidence that many of the non-European courts show activity levels that compare favorably with those of the European courts, *at similar operational ages*.[115]

Whether the current development of international courts represents a new era or is a temporary golden age will depend on the degree to which the courts serve the needs and interests (both material and normative) of those who live under the legal rules those courts curate. Whether that happens will depend on three conditions: first, actors—states, firms, NGOs, activists, and individual persons—see third-party dispute resolution as an effective means to resolve disputes, vindicate rights, and hold authorities accountable; second, international courts effectively meet litigants' needs; and third, compliance constituencies embedded in cultures of adherence to international law keep the pressure on governments to comply with IC rulings.[116] The three conditions are mutually reinforcing. If they develop together, judicialization will proceed.[117] Alter makes the bet that they will.

FOOTNOTES

[1]Karen j. alter, the new terrain of international law: courts, politics, rights (2014).

[2]Id. at 5.

[3]Id. at 32-67.

[4]JACK L. GOLDSMITH & ERIC A. POSNER, THE LIMITS OF INTERNATIONAL LAW (2005). Goldsmith and Posner are probably the most cited exponents of this view, which has, of course, been vigorously contested by other scholars. The literature on both sides of the debate is too extensive to be cited or adequately discussed in this review.

[5]Geoffrey Garrett et al., *The European Court of Justice, National Governments, and Legal Integration in the European Union*, 52 INT'L ORG. 149 (1998); Geoffrey Garrett & Barry R. Weingast, *Ideas, Interests, and Institutions: Constructing the European Community's Internal Market, in* IDEAS AND FOREIGN POLICY: BELIEFS, INSTITUTIONS, AND POLITICAL CHANGE 173 (Judith Goldstein & Robert O. Keohane eds., 1993).

[6]Alec Stone Sweet & Thomas L. Brunell, *Trustee Courts and the Judicialization of International Regimes: The Politics of Majoritarian Activism in the European Convention on Human Rights, the European Union, and the World Trade Organization*, 1 J.L. & CTS. 61 (2013).

[7]Karen J. Alter, *Agents or Trustees? International Courts in Their Political Context*, 14 EUR. J. INT'L REL. 33 (2008).

[8]ALTER, *supra* note 1, at 9 n.8. Alter describes ICs that can apply international rules to states as acting in "self-binding

judicial roles." "Self-binding" refers to situations in which ICs apply rules that are meant to con-strain states themselves. "Other-binding" refers to situations in which ICs extend state power by enforcing legal norms against other states, international organizations, or non-state actors.

[9]Stone Sweet & Brunell, *supra* note 6, at 72 ("To date, the EU is the only international regime on which scholars have designed systematic research to assess whether judicial outcomes are constrained by the threats of noncompliance and override.").

[10]Eric Stein, *Lawyers, Judges, and the Making of a Transnational Constitution*, 75 AM. J. INT'L L. 1 (1981); Joseph H. H. Weiler, *The Transformation of Europe*, 100 YALE L.J. 2403 (1991); J. H. H. WEILER, THE CONSTITUTION OF EUROPE (1999); ALEC STONE SWEET, THE JUDICIAL CONSTRUCTION OF EUROPE (2004).

[11]*See generally* Karen J. Alter, *Who Are the "Masters of the Treaty"?: European Governments and European Court of Justice*, 52 INT'L ORG. 121 (1998); Anne-Marie Burley & Walter Mattli, *Europe Before the Court: A Political Theory of Legal Integration*, 47 INT'L ORG. 41 (1993); RACHEL CICHOWSKI, THE EUROPEAN COURT AND CIVIL SOCIETY: LITIGATION, MOBILIZATION, AND GOVERNANCE (2007); Margaret McCown, *The European Parliament before the bench: ECJ precedent and EP litigation strategies*, 10 J. EUR. PUB. POL'Y 974 (2003); Stacy A. Nyikos, *The Preliminary Reference Process: National Court Implementation, Changing Opportunity Structures and Litigant Desistment*, 4 EUR. UNION POL. 397 (2003); MARK A. POLLACK, THE ENGINES OF INTEGRATION: DELEGATION, AGENCY, AND AGENCY SETTING IN THE EUROPEAN UNION (2003); STONE SWEET, *supra* note 6; Jonas Tallberg, *Delegation to Supranational Institutions: Why, How, and with What Con-sequences?*, 25 W. EUR. POL. 23 (2002).

[12]Clifford J. Carrubba et al., *Judicial Behavior under Political Constraints: Evidence from the European Court of Justice*, 102 AM. POL. SCI. REV. 439 (2008).

[13]Alec Stone Sweet & Thomas Brunell, *The European Court of Justice, State Noncompliance, and the Politics of Override*, 106 AM. POLI. SCI. REV. 204 (2012); Stone Sweet & Brunell, *supra* note 6.

[14]Stone Sweet & Brunell, *supra* note 13, at 206-08.

[15]Instead of testing their hypothesis that the threat of non-compliance constrains ECJ decisions, Carrubba, Gabel, and Hankla test a very different proposition, namely, that "[t]he more opposition a litigant government has from other MSGs [member-state governments], the more likely the court is to rule against that litigant government;" Carrubba et al., *supra* note 12. This allows them to count as evidence in their favor any case in which the balance of weighted member-state observations favors a ruling against the defendant state, even if only one state submits an observation and even if that state is a small one like Luxembourg. Their analysis therefore does not test the claim that the threat of non-compliance by a state that is subject to an unfavorable ECJ decision constrains the Court.

[16]Stone Sweet & Brunell, *supra* note 13.

[17]Stone Sweet & Brunell, *supra* note 6, at 73.

[18]Id. at 75.

[19]Alter, *supra* note 11; KAREN J. ALTER, ESTABLISHING THE SUPREMACY OF EUROPEAN LAW:THE MAKING OF AN INTERNATIONAL RULE OF LAW IN EUROPE (2001).

[20]ALTER, *supra* note 1, at 43.

[21]Id. at 52.

[22]Id. at 42-52.

[23]Id. at 53.

[24]Id. at 19.

[25]Alison Brysk, *From Above and Below: Social Movements, the International System and Human Rights in Argentina*, 26 COMP. POL. STUD. 259 (1993); MARGARET E. KECK & KATHRYN SIKKINK, ACTIVISTS BEYOND BORDERS: ADVOCACY NETWORKS IN INTERNATIONAL POLITICS (1998).

[26]BETH A. SIMMONS, MOBILIZING FOR HUMAN RIGHTS: INTERNATIONAL LAW IN DOMESTIC POLITICS (2009).

[27]ALTER, *supra* note 1, at 55.

[28]Id. at 19.

[29]GOLDSMITH & POSNER, *supra* note 4; Eric A. Posner & John C. Yoo, *Judicial Independence in International Tribunals*, 93 CALIF. L. REV. 3 (2005).

[30]ALTER, *supra* note 1, at 5

[31]Id.; see also Laurence R. Helfer & Anne-Marie Slaughter, *Toward a Theory of Effective Supranational Adjudication*, 107 YALE L.J. 273 (1997).

[32]ALTER, supra note 1, at 6.

[33]Id.

[34]Id. at 70. These courts meet additional criteria included in the definition of international courts employed by the Project on International Courts and Tribunals (PICT). For more information on PICT, please visit http://www.pict-pcti.org/matrix/Matrix-main.html.

[35]Id. at 84 fig.3.2.

[36]Id. at 4, 73-75 fig.3.1.

[37]ALTER, supra note 1, at 72-73 fig.3.1.

[38]Id. at 106-07 figs.3.14 & 3.15

[39]GOLDSMITH & POSNER, supra note 4, at ch. 1.

[40]ALTER, supra note 1, at 64

[41]Id. at 53.

[42]Id. at 22.

[43]Id. at 53.

[44]Id

[45]*See, e.g.*, Jonathan Jackson et al., *Why Do People Comply with the Law?: Legitimacy and the Influence of Legal Institutions*, 52 BRIT. J. CRIMINOLOGY 1051 (2012); TOM R. TYLER, WHY PEOPLE OBEY THE LAW

(2006).

[46]THOMAS M. FRANCK, THE POWER OF LEGITIMACY AMONG NATIONS (1990).

[47]ALTER, *supra* note 1, at 53.

[48]*Id.* at 22.

[49]*Id.* at 282 (citing ALEC STONE SWEET, GOVERNING WITH JUDGES: CONSTITUTIONAL POLITICS IN EUROPE 21 (2000)).

[50]*Id.* at 290.

[51]*Id.* at 291-92. *See also id.* at 291 nn.14-17, 292 n.18 (citing some of the relevant research).

[52]ALTER, *supra* note 1, at 292.

[53]*See, e.g.*, André Nollkaemper, *Internationally Wrongful Acts in Domestic Courts*, 101 AM. J. INT'L L. 760 (2007); ANDRÉ NOLLKAEMPER, NATIONAL COURTS AND THE INTERNATIONAL RULE OF LAW (2011); DAVID SLOSS, THE ROLE OF DOMESTIC COURTS IN TREATY ENFORCEMENT: A COMPARATIVE STUDY (2009); Melissa A. Waters, *Mediating Norms and Identity: The Role of Transnational Judicial Dialogue in Creating and Enforcing International Law*, 93 GEO. L.J. 487 (2005); Melissa A. Waters, *Creeping Monism: The Judicial Trend Toward Interpretive Incorporation of Human Rights Treaties*, 107 COLUM. L. REV. 628 (2007)

[54]ALTER, *supra* note 1, at 292-94.

[55]Analyzing cultures of adherence raises tricky empirical challenges. For instance, it is crucial to devise indicators of the existence of a culture of adherence that are independent of the IC's decision-making. Alter argues that an IC will exercise restraint if it perceives that a domestic culture of international law obedience is lacking, but then IC restraint cannot serve as evidence of the absence of such a culture. For a useful exploration of the multiple ways in which international law and international courts interact with national law and institutions, see Gregory Shaffer, *How the WTO Shapes Regulatory Governance*, 9 REGUL. GOV. 1 (2015).

[56]*See, e.g.*, Ezequiel González Ocantos, *Persuade Them or Oust Them: Crafting Judicial Change and Transitional Justice in Argentina*, 46 COMP. POL. 479 (2014); Ezequiel González Ocantos, The Collapse of Impunity Regimes in Latin America: Legal Cultures, Strategic Litigation and Judicial Behavior (July 2012) (unpublished Ph.D. dissertation, University of Notre Dame); GRETCHEN HELMKE & JULIO RÍOS-FIGUEROA, COURTS IN LATIN AMERICA (2011); LISA HILBINK, JUDGES BEYOND POLITICS IN DEMOCRACY AND DICTATORSHIP: LESSONS FROM CHILE (2007); Alexandra Huneeus, *Judging from a Guilty Conscience: The Chil-ean Judiciary's Human Rights Turn*, 35 LAW & SOC. INQUIRY (2010); DIANA KAPISZEWSKI, HIGH COURTS AND ECONOMIC GOVERNANCE IN ARGENTINA AND BRAZIL (2012); Georg Vanberg, *Establishing Judicial Independ-ence in West Germany: The Impact of Opinion Leadership and the Separation of Powers*, 32 COMP. POL. 333 (2000).

[57]Empirical research on judicial behavior in international courts is sparse. In one of the few existing studies, Voeten shows that judges on the European Court of Human Rights tend to favor their home countries, but that the proportion of cases in which a home-country bias might affect the outcome is extremely small. *See* Erik Voeten, *The Impartiality of International Judges: Evidence from the European Court of Human Rights*, 102 AM. POL. SCI. REV. 417 (2008).

[58]Karen J. Alter, *Delegation to International Courts and the Limits of Recontracting Power, in* DELEGATION AND AGENCY IN INTERNATIONAL ORGANIZATIONS 312 (Darren G. Hawkins et al. eds., 2006)

[59]ALTER, *supra* note 1, at 9.

[60]Id.

[61]Id. at 23.

[62]Id.

[63]Id.

[64]ALTER, supra note 1, at 9.

[65]Id. at 8.

[66]Id.

[67]Id. at 19.

[68]Id. at 18.

[69]ALTER, supra note 1, at 19.

[70]Id. at 20.

[71]Id.

[72]Id. at 18-20

[73]Id. at 66.

[74]ALTER, supra note 1, at 66

[75]Id. at 60.

[76]Id. at 295-98.

[77]Id. at 260-67; Mme Hadijatou Mani Koraou v. The Republic of Niger, (2008) AHRLR 182 (ECOWAS 2008), available at http://www.chr.up.ac.za/index.php/browse-by-subject/379-niger-koraou-v-niger-2008-ahrlr-ecowas-2008.html.

[78]ALTER, supra note 1, at 315-19; The Mayagna (Sumo) Awas Tingni Cmty, v. Nicaragua, Judgment of Aug. 31, 2001, Inter-Am. Ct. H.R., (Ser. C) No. 79 (2001).

[79]ALTER, supra note 1, at 346, 348.

[80]Stone Sweet & Brunell, supra note 6, at 61.

[81]Id.

[82]Id. at 63-64.

[83]Id.

[84]Id. at 64

[85]Stone Sweet & Brunell, *supra* note 6, at 81.

[86]Id. at 79-80.

[87]Id. at 86

[88]ALTER, *supra* note 1, at 19; *see also* Wayne Sandholtz & Mariana Rangel Padilla, Law and Politics in a Trustee Court: Amnesty Laws and the Inter-American System (2015) (Workshop paper) (on file with the UCLA Department of Polical Science).

[89]On the dynamics of international law, see Alec Stone Sweet, *Judicialization and the Construction of Governance*, 32 COMP. POL. STUD. (1999); WAYNE SANDHOLTZ, PROHIBITING PLUNDER: HOW NORMS CHANGE (2007); WAYNE SANDHOLTZ & KENDALL W. STILES, INTERNATIONAL NORMS AND CYCLES OF CHANGE (2009); Terence C. Halliday, *Recursivity of Global Normmaking: A Sociolegal Agenda*, 5 ANN. REV. L. & SOC. SCI. (2009); Terence C. Halliday & Gregory Shaffer, *Transnational Legal Orders*, *in* TRANSNATIONAL LEGAL ORDERS (Terence C. Halliday & Gregory Shaffer eds., 2015).

[90]ALTER, *supra* note 1, at 44.

[91]See generally JUDITH L. GOLDSTEIN ET AL., LEGALIZATION AND WORLD POLITICS (2001).

[92]Id. at 386.

[93]See generally Barbara Koremenos et al., The Rational Design of International Institutions, 55 INT'L ORG. 761, 762 (2001).

[94]Id. at 761.

[95]Id. at 771

[96]Most International Law (IL) scholarship, with the exception of IL "realists" and skeptics, assumes the opposite. Constructivist approaches in IR tend to take international courts seriously.

[97]ALTER, *supra* note 1, at 111.

[98]Id. at 27; see Part II.A supra. The crucial role played by compliance constituencies in Alter's framework underscores the necessity, discussed above, of identifying the factors that produce or foster cultures of international law obedience.

[99]ALTER, *supra* note 1, at 27.

[100]Alec Stone Sweet, *Judicialization and the Construction of Governance*, 32 COMP. POL. STUD. 137 (1999); ALEC STONE SWEET, THE JUDICIAL CONSTRUCTION OF EUROPE (2004); Alec Stone Sweet, *Path Dependence, Precedent, and Judicial Power*, *in* ON LAW, POLITICS, AND JUDICIALIZATION (Martin Shapiro & Alec Stone Sweet eds., 2002); Burley & Mattli, *Europe Before the Court: A Political Theory of Legal Integration*, 47 INT'L ORG. 41 (1993); Wayne Sandholtz, *The Emergence of a Supranational Telecommunications Regime*, *in* EUROPEAN INTEGRATION AND SUPRANATIONAL GOVERNANCE ch. 5 (Wayne Sandholtz & Alec Stone Sweet eds., 1998); Wayne Sandholtz & Alec Stone Sweet, *Law, Politics, and International Governance*, *in* THE POLITICS OF INTERNATIONAL LAW 238-71 (Christian Reus-Smit ed., 2004); Jonas Tallberg, *Paths to Compliance: Enforcement, Management, and the European Union*, 56 INT'L ORG. 609 (2002).

[101]ALTER, supra note 1, at 5.

[102]Id. at 7.

[103]Id. at 3-4.

[104]Id. at 260-67.

[105]Id

[106]ALTER, supra note 1, at 4.

[107]Id. at 38, for example. See also the index entry for "morphing judicial roles."

[108]Id. at 3 4.

[109]Id. at 5-6.

[110]Id. at 30.

[111]ALTER, supra note 1, at 31

[112]Id. at 104.

[113]Id.

[114]Id. at 90.

[115]Id. at 106-07.

[116]See generally ALTER, supra note 1, at 20.

[117]Id. at 4-5

REFERENCES

1. Ab'u al-Waf'a, A. h., *La non-comparution devant la Cour internationale de justice* (Paris, Libr. générale de droit et de jurisprudence, 1986).
2. Abi Saab, Georges, "The Court and the bomb: a case of mutual deterrence?," 7(2) *Transnational Law & Contemporary Problems* 429-57 (Fall 1997).
3. Ago, Robert, "Binding Advisory Opinions of the International Court of Justice," 85 *American Journal of International Law* 439 (1985).
4. Akande, D., "The International Court of Justice and the Security Council: is there room for judicial control of decisions of the political organs of the United Nations?," 46 *The International & Comparative Law Quarterly* 309-43 (April 1997).
5. Alexandrov, S. A., "Accepting the Compulsory Jurisdiction of the International Court of Justice with Reservations: an Overview of Practice with a Focus on Recent Trends and Cases", 1*Leiden Journal of International Law* 89-124 (2001).
6. Alford, N.H., "Fact Finding by the World Court", 4 *Villanova Law Review* 37-91 (1958).
7. Allsebrook, M., *Prototypes of Peacemaking: the First Forty Years of the United Nations* (Burnt Mill, Harlow, Essex, U.K., Longman, 1986).
8. Alvarez, J.E., "Judging the Security Council," 90 *American Journal of International Law* 1-39 (January 1996).
9. American Bar Association Section of International and Comparative Law, *Report on the Self-judging Aspect of the United States' Domestic Jurisdiction Reservation with Respect to the International Court of Justice* (1959).
10. Anand, Ram Prakash, *Compulsory Jurisdiction of the International Court of Justice* (New York: Asia Publications House, 1962).
11. Anderson, D. H., "The Icelandic Fisheries Cases: Professor Jaenicke as Agent and Counsel before the International Court of Justice", *Liber amicorum Günther Jaenicke zum 85. Geburtstag*, pp. 445-463.
12. Arend, Anthony C. (ed.), *The United States and the Compulsory Jurisdiction of the International Court of Justice* (Lanham: University Press of America, 1986).
13. Askew, L.A., "The ECJ, the ICJ and intellectual property: is harmonization the key?," 7(2) *Tulsa Journal of Comparative & International Law* 375-412 (Spring 2000).
14. Audeoud, Olivier, "La Cour internationale de justice et le reglement des differends au sein des organisations internationales," 81 *Revue Generale de Droit International Public* 9451006 (1977).
15. Bastid, Suzanne, *Les problèmes territoriaux dans la jurisprudence de la Cour international de Justice* (Leyde, 1963).
16. Bedi, S. R. S., "African Participation in the International Court of Justice: A Statistical Appraisal (1946-1998)," 6 *African Yearbook of International Law* 181-222 (1998).
17. Bedjaoui, M., "Expediency in the decisions of the

International Court of Justice," 71 *The British Yearbook of International Law* 1-27 (2000).

18. Bekker, Peter H. F., "Recent Developments at the World Court," *American Society of International Law Newsletter*, Mar.-Apr. 1997.

19. Benvenuti, P., *L'accertamento del diritto mediante i pareri consultivi della Corte internazionale di giustizia* (Milano: A. Giuffrè, 1985).

20. Berlia, G., *Jurisprudence des tribunaux internationaux en ce qui concerne leur competence* (Leyde, 1956).

21. Bilder, R., "The United States and the World Court in the Post "Cold War" Era", 40 *Catholic University Law Review* 251 (1991).

22. Bleichert, M.A., "The effectiveness of voluntary jurisdiction in the ICJ: El Salvador v. Honduras {1992 I.C.J. 351}, a case in point," 16 *Fordham International Law Journal* 799-847 (1992/1993).

23. Bloed, A. & P. v. Dijk, *Forty years International Court of Justice: Jurisdiction, Equity and Equality* (Utrecht: Europa Intituut, 1988).

24. Blokker, N., "The 1996 Elections to the International Court of Justice: New Tendencies in the Post-Cold War Era?," 47 *International & Comparative Law Quarterly* 211-223 (1998).

25. Bodie, Thomas J., *Politics and the Emergence of an Activist International Court of Justice* (Westport, Conn.: Praeger Publishers, 1995).

26. Boffi Boggero, L. M., United Nations., et al., *?Está en crisis la Corte Internacional de Justicia?* (Buenos Aires, Editorial Astrea, 1975).

27. Boisson de Chazournes, L. & P. Sands (eds.), *International law, the International Court of Justice and Nuclear Weapons* (New York: Cambridge University Press, 1999).

28. Bosco, Giorgio, *La soluzione delle controversie giuddiche intemazionali nel quadro delle Nazioni Unite* (Padova: Cedam, 1989).

29. Bowett, D. (ed.), *The International Court of Justice: Process, Practice and Procedure* (London: British Institute of International and Comparative Law, 1997).

30. Brauer, R.H., "International Conflict Resolution: the ICJ Chambers and the Gulf of Maine Dispute," 23 *Virginia Journal of International Law* 463-486 (1983).

31. Briggs, Herbert W., "Reservations to the Acceptance of Compulsory Jurisdiction of the International Court of Justice," 93 *Hague Academy of International Law, Collected* Courses (1958-I), pp. 223-367.

32. Brown, Colton, "Enforcement of ICJ Decisions in United States Courts," 11 *Maryland Journal of International Law and Trade* 7392 (1987).

33. Bruggen, E. v. d., "Compulsory Jurisdiction of the International Court of Justice in Tax Cases: Do We Already Have an 'International Tax Court'?," 8 *Intertax* 250-267 (2001).

34. Bufferne, J., "La fonction de la Cour internationale de justice dans l'ordre juridique international: quelques reflexions," 15(1) *Revue Quebecoise de Droit International*, 141-78 (2002).

35. Bulterman, M. K., M. Kuijer, et al., Compliance with Judgments of International Courts: Proceedings of the Symposium Organized in Honour of Professor Henry G. Schermers byMordenate College and the Department of International Public Law of Leiden University (The Hague; Boston: Martinus Nijhoff, 1996).

36. Burmester, H., "Australia and the International Court of Justice," 17 *Australian Yearbook of International Law* 19-37 (1996).

37. Carnegie Endowment for International Peace, Division of International Law, and W. H. Zeydel, *Annotation of the Charter of the United Nations and Statute of the International Court of Justice* (Washington: Carnegie Endowment for International Peace, 1947).

38. Casado Raigon, Rafael, *La jurisdiccion contenciosa de la Corte Internacional de Justicia: estudio de las reglas de competencia* (Cordoba: Servido de Publ. de la Universidad de Cordoba, 1987).

39. Cellamare, Giovanni, *Le forme di intervento nel processo dinanzi alla Corte Intemazionale di Giustizia* (Bari: Cacucci Editore, 1991).

40. Cereste, S., "The International Court of Justice, the International Criminal Court, and the ad hoc tribunals," 17(3) *New York Law School Journal of Human Rights* 911-15 (Summer 2001).

41. Charney, Jonathan, "Compromissory Clauses and the Jurisdiction of the International Court of Justice," 81 *American Journal of International Law* 855 (1987).

42. Churchill, R. R., "The Fisheries Jurisdiction Cases. The Contribution of the International Court of Justice to the Debate on Coastal States' Fisheries Rights," 24 *International & Comparative Law Quarterly* 82-105 (1975).

43. Cilliers, A. C., *"Whither the International Court?" Inaugural Address Delivered before the University of Port Elizabeth on June 18, 1971* (Port Elizabeth: the University of Port Elizabeth, 1971).

44. Chinkin, Christine M., "ThirdParty Intervention before the International Court of Justice," 80 *American Journal of International Law* 495531 (1986).

45. Clemons, H.V., "The ethos of the International Court of Justice is dependent upon the statutory authority attributed to its rhetoric: a metadiscourse," 20 *Fordham International Law Journal*1479-510 (April 1997).

46. Committee for Effective Use of the International Court by Repealing the Self-Judging Reservation, *Report on the Connally Amendment: Views of Deans of Law Schools and Professors of Law, International Law and Related Subjects, in Law Schools, Colleges and Universities* (New York, The Committee, 1961)

47. Connell, B., "A Small Country Applicant: The Immense Task of Proceeding before the International Court of Justice", in: Anghie, A., (ed.), *Legal Visions of the Twenty-First Century: Essays in Honour of Judge Christopher Weeramantry* (The Hague: Kluwer, 1998), pp. 681-699.

48. Cot, J.-P., "À propos de l'ordonnance du 15 mars 1996: a contribution de la Cour internationale de Justice

au maintien de la paix et de la sécurité en Afrique," 5 *African Yearbook of International Law* 115-136 (1997).

49. Ordonnances du 22 juin 1973," 19 *Annuaire français de droit international* 252-271 (1973).

50. Crawford, J., "The Legal Effect of Automatic Reservations to the Jurisdiction of the International Court", 50 *British Yearbook of International Law* 63-86 (1979).

51. Crockett, G. H., "The Effects of Interim Measures of Protection in the International Court of Justice," 7 *California Western Law Journal* 34884 (1977).

52. Crook, J.R., "The 2002 judicial activity of the International Court of Justice," 97(2) *American Journal of International Law* 352-64 (April 2003).

53. Daillier, P., "L'intervention du Secretaire General des Nations Unies, dans la procedure consultative devant la Cour international de Justice," 19 *Annuaire Francais de Droit International*376410 (1973).

54. D'Amato, Anthony, "The United States Should Accept, by a New Declaration, the General Compulsory Jurisdiction of the World Court," 80 *American Journal of International Law* 3316 (1986).

55. Damrosch, Lori, "The election of Thomas Buergenthal to the International Court of Justice," 94(3) *American Journal of International Law* 579-82 (July 2000).

56. Daniele, L., "L'ordonnance sur la demande d'examen de la situation dans l'affaire des essais nucléaires et le pouvoir de la Cour internationale de Justice de régler sa propre procédure", 100*Revue générale de droit international public* 653-671 (1996).

57. Davì, Angelo, *L'intervento davanti alla Corte internazionale di giustizia* (Napoli: Jovene, 1984).

58. David, M., "Passport to justice: internationalizing the political question doctrine for application in the World Court," 40(1) *Harvard International Law Journal* 81-150 (Winter 1999).

59. De Visscher, Ch., *Aspects récents du droit prodédural de la Cour internationale de justice* (Paris: Pedone, 1966).

60. DeWeese, G.S., "The failure of the International Court of Justice to effectively enforce the Genocide Convention," 26(4) *Denver Journal of International Law and Policy* 625-54 (Summer 1998).

61. Delbez, L., *Les principes généraux du contentieux international* (Paris, Libr générale de droit et de jurisprudence, 1962).

62. Dillard, Hardy Cross, "The World Court: Reflections of a Professor Turned Judge," 27 *American University Law Review* 20550 (1978).

63. Dolzer, Rudolf. "Connally Reservation," in Bernhardt (ed.), *Encyclopedia in Public International Law* 1 (1981), pp. 557.

64. Donner, Ruth, *International Adjudication: Using the International Court of Justice, with Special Reference to Finland* (Helsinki: Suomalainen Tiedeakatemia, 1988).

65. Doussis, E., "Intérêt juridique et intervention devant la Cour Internationale de Justice", 1 *Revue Générale de Droit International Public* 55-91 (2001).

66. Dubisson, M., *La cour internationale de justice* (Paris: Pichon et DurandAnzias, 1964).

67. Dugard, J. & E. M. Grosskopf, *South West Africa and the International Court: Two Viewpoints on the 1971 Advisory Opinion* (Johannesburg: South African Institute of International Affairs, 1973).

68. Dupuy, P.M., "The Danger of Fragmentation or Unification of the International Legal System and the International Court of Justice," 31 *NYU Journal of International Law and Politics* 791-808 (1999).

69. Eisemann, P.M., "Les effets de la non-comparution devant la Cour internationale de Justice", 19 *Annuaire français de droit international* 351-375 (1973).— & V. Coussirat-Coustère, et al., *Petit manuel de la jurisprudence de la Cour internationale de justice* 2nd ed. (Paris: A. Pedone, 1980).

70. Elian, G., *The International Court of Justice* (Leiden: A. W. Sijthoff, 1971).

71. Elias, T. O., *The United Nations Charter and the World Court* (Lagos: Nigerian Institute of Advanced Legal Studies, 1989).

72. Elkind, Jerome B., "The Duty to Appear before the International Court of Justice," 37 *International & Comparative Law Quarterly* 67481 (1988).

73. Elkind, Jerome B. "The Aegean Sea Case and Article 41 of the Statute of the International Court of Justice," 32 *Revue des Droits de l'Homme. Droit International et Droit Compare* 285345 (1979).

74. Elsen, Theodor J. H., *Litispendence between the International Court of Justice and the Security Council* (The Hague: T.M.C. Asser Instituut, 1986).

75. Evensen, Jens, "The International Court of Justice Main Characteristics and Its Contribution to the Development of the Modern Law of Nations," 57 *Nordic Journal of International Law*364 (1988).

76. Eyffinger, A. & A. Witteveen, *La Cour internationale de Justice, 1946-1996* (La Haye; Boston: Kluwer Law International, 1999).

77. Falk, R. A., *Reviving the World Court* (Charlottesville: University Press of Virginia, 1986).

78. Falsafi, H., *L'affaire des essais nucléaires devant la Cour internationale de justice* (Neuchâtel: Impr. H. Messeiller, 1978).

79. Fatiþc, A., *Reconciliation via the War Crimes Tribunal?* (Aldershot: Ashgate, 2000).

80. Fitzmaurice, G., *The Law and Procedure of the International Court of Justice* (Cambridge: Grotius Publications, 1986).

81. Fitzmaurice, M., "The optional clause system and the law of treaties: issues of interpretation in recent jurisprudence of the International Court of Justice," 20 *Australian Yearbook of International Law* 127-159 (1999).

82. Fleisch-Hauer, C.-A., "The constitutional relationship between the Secretary-General of the United Nations and the International Court of Justice", Boutros Boutros-Ghali, *Amicorum discipulorumque liber: paix,*

développement, démocratie, vol. 1 (Bruxelles: Bruylant, 1998), pp. 451-474.

83. Fleming, Denna Frank, T*he United States and the World Court 1920-1961*, Rev. ed. (New York: Russell & Russell, 1968).

84. Ford, C.A., "Judicial discretion in international jurisprudence: Article 38(1)(C) and "general principles of law," 5 *Duke Journal of Comparative & International Law* 35-86 (Fall 1994).

85. Garcia Arias D., Luis, *Balance y perspectivas del Tribunal Internacional de Justicia* (Madrid: Real Academia de Jurisprudencia, 1972).

86. Gharbi, F., "Le declin des declarations d'acceptation de la juridiction obligatoire de la Cour internationale de justice," 43(3) *Les Cahiers de Droit* 433-502 (September 2002).

87. Gill, Terry D., *Litigation Strategy at the International Court: A Case Study of the Nicaragua v. United States Dispute* (Dordrecht; Boston: Martinus Nijhoff Publishers, 1989).

88. Gillespie, A., "The 1995 Nuclear Tests Case: the ICJ Fails to Address the Merits of an International Environmental Concern", *New Zealand Law Journal* 195-200 (1996).

89. Giraud, C., "French Nuclear Testing in the Pacific and the 1995 International Court of Justice Decision", 1 *Asia-Pacific Journal of Environmental Law* 125-133 (1996).

90. Giuffrida, R., *La ricevibilità generale nella giurisprudenza della Corte internazionale di Giustizia* (Milano, 1995).

91. Goldie, L. F. E., "The Connally Reservation: A Shield for An Adversary," 9 *University of California Los Angeles Law Review* 277- 359 (1962).

92. Goldsworthy, Peter J., "Interim Measures of Protection in the International Court of Justice," 68 *American Journal of International Law* 25877 (1974).

93. Gomula, J., "The International Court of Justice and administrative tribunals of international organizations," 13 *Michigan Journal of International Law* 83-121 (Fall 1991).

94. Gordon, Edward, "Observation on the Independence and Impartiality of the Members of the International Court of Justice," 2 *Connecticut Journal of International Law* 397426 (1987).

95. Hussain, Ijaz, *Dissenting and Separate Opinions of the World Court* (Dordrecht: Nijhoff, 1984).

96. Hutchins, T., "Using the International Court of Justice to check human rights abuses in World Bank projects," 23 *Columbia Human Rights Law Review* 487-524 (Summer 1992).

97. Irwin, J.C., "An alternate role for the International Court of Justice: applied to Cameroon v. Nigeria {{1996} I.C.J. 13}," 26(4) *Denver Journal of International Law and Policy* 759-73 (Summer 1998).

98. Janis, M.W, "Individuals and the International Court," in: Muller, A.S., D. Raic, J.M. Thuránszky (eds.), *The International Court of Justice: Its Future Role After Fifty Years* (The Hague; Boston: Martinus Nijhoff, 1997).

99. Jennings, Robert Y., "The role of the International Court of Justice," 68 *The British Yearbook of International Law* 1-63 (1997).

100. Kaikobad, K.H., "The Court, the Council and interim protection: a commentary on the Lockerbie Order of 14 April 1992," 17 *Australian Yearbook of International Law* 87-186 (1996).

101. Katz, S. R., "Issue Arising in the Icelandic Fisheries Case," 22 *International & Comparative Law Quarterly* 83-108 (1973).

102. Kebbon, N., "The World Court's Compulsory Jurisdiction under the Optional Clause: Past, Present and Future," 58 *Nordic Journal of International Law* 257-286 (1989).

103. Kennedy, R.F., "Libya v. United States {1992 I.C.J. 114}: the International Court of Justice and the power of judicial review," 33 *Virginia Journal of International Law* 899-925 (Summer 1993).

104. Keith, K., "The advisory jurisdiction of the International Court of Justice: some comparative reflections," 17 *Australian Yearbook of International Law* 39-58 (1996).

105. Koe, A., "Damming the Danube: the International Court of Justice and the Gabcíkovo-Nagymaros Project (Hungary v. Slovakia)," 20 *The Sydney Law Review* 612-629 (1998).

106. Kolb, R., "De la prétendue discrétion de la Cour internationale de Justice de refuser de donner un avis consultative," in: Georges Abi-Saab, *The international legal system in quest of equity and universality: liber amicorum* (The Hague: Kluwer Law International, 2002), pp. 609-627.

107. Larson, A., "The Facts, the Law, and the Connally Amendment," *Duke Law Joumal* 74119 (1961).

108. Laudy, M., *Nicaragua ante la Corte Internacional de Justicia de La Haya* (México, D.F., Siglo Veintiuno Editores, 1988).

109. Lauterpacht, Sir Hersch, *The Development of International Law by the International Court* (Cambridge: Grotius Publications, 1960) (reprinted in 1982).

110. Lavalle R., "Nationality as a Factor in the Election of Members of the International Court of Justice with Particular Reference to Occasional Elections", 29 *Revue belge de droit international*625-632 (1996).

111. Lawson, R. C., "The Problem of the Compulsory Jurisdiction of the World Court," 46 *American Journal of International Law* 21938 (1952).

112. Leonhard, A. T., "Regional Particularism: The Views of the Latin American Judges on the International Court of Justice," 22 *University of Miami Law Review* 67485 (1968).

113. Lillich, Richard B. & G. Edward White, "The Deliberative Process of the International Court of Justice: A Preliminary Critique and Some Possible Reforms," 70 *American Journal of International Law* 2840 (1976).

114. Martin, P.M., "L'affaire de la compétence en matière de pêcheries', 78 *Revue générale de droit international public* 435-458 (1974).

115. Mathy, D., "Un juge ad hoc en procedure consultative

devant la Cour internationale de Justice," 12 *Revue Belge de Droit International* 52854 (1976).

116. Maus, B., *Les réserves dans les déclarations d'acceptation de la juridiction obligatoire de la Cour internationale de justice* (Genève: Librairie E. Droz, 1959).

117. Mavungu, M.-d. -. N., *Le règlement judiciaire des différends interétatiques en Afrique* (Fribourg, Suisse: Editions universitaires, 1992).

118. Max-Planck-Institut für Ausländisches Öffentliches Recht und Völkerrecht, *Judicial Settlement of International Disputes: International Court of Justice, Other Courts and Tribunals, Arbitration and Conciliation: an International Symposium* (Berlin; Heidelberg; New York: Springer, 1974).

119. Mbaye, Keba, "L'interet pour agir devant la Cour internationale de Justice," 209 *Recueil des Cours de l'Academie de Droit International de La Haye* 223346 (1988H).

120. Nafziger, James A. R., "Political dispute resolution by the World Court, with reference to United States courts," 26(5) *Denver Journal of International Law and Policy* 775-86 (Winter 1998).

121. Nash, M.L., "A century of arbitration: the International Court of Justice," 274(1600) *Contemporary Review* 242-6 (May 1999).

122. Nanda, V. P. & D. Krieger, *Nuclear Weapons and the World Court* (Ardsley, N.Y., Transnational, 1998).

123. Orihuela Calatayud, Esperanza. "Espana y la jurisdiccion obligatoria del Tribunal Internacional de Justicia," 41 REDI 69105 (1989).

124. Owen, H. J. "Compulsory Jurisdiction in the International Court of Justice," 3 Georgia Law Review 70426 (1969).

125. Obozuwa, A.U., "The Icelandic Fisheries Cases," 1 *Nigerian Annual of International Law* 101-123 (1976).

126. Oda, S. et al., *Liber Amicorum Judge Shigeru Oda* (The Hague; New York: Kluwer Law International, 2000).

127. Oduntan, G., *The Law and Practice of the International Court of Justice (1945-1996): A Critique of the Contentious and Advisory jurisdictions* (Enugu, Nigeria: Fourth Dimension Pub, 1999).

128. Oellers-Frahm, Karin, "Die Verfahrensordnung des Internationalen Gerichtshofs vom 14. April 1978," 18 *Archiv des Vo lkerrechts* 309320 (1978/80).

129. Perez, A.F., "The passive virtues and the World Court: pro-dialogic abstention by the International Court of Justice," 18 *Michigan Journal of International Law* 399-444 (Spring 1997).

130. Pinto, Roger, "La sentence Ambatielos," 84 *Journal du Droit International* 540614 (1957).

131. Pirotte, O., "La notion d'equite dans la jurisprudence recente de la Cour internationale de justice," 77 *Revue Generale de Droit International Public* 92135 (1973).

132. Preuss, Lawrence, "The International Court of Justice, the Senate, and Matters of Domestic Jurisdiction," 40 *American Journal of International Law* 72036 (1946).

133. Prott, L., "The Future of the International Court of Justice," 33 *Yearbook of World Affairs* 284 (1979).

134. Rennie, I., "Philosophical Influences at the International Court of Justice as Demonstrated in the Lockerbie Case," 32 *The Cambrian Law Review* 65-87 (2001).

135. Richardson, H.J.I., "The execution of Angel Breard by the United States: violating an order of the International Court of Justice," 12(1) *Temple International and Comparative Law Journal*121-31 (Spring 1998).

136. Ritter, J.-P., "L'affaire des essais nucléaires et la notion de jugement déclaratoire," 21 *Annuaire français de droit international*, 278-293 (1975).

137. Roben, Volker, "Le precedent dans la jurisprudence de la Cour internationale," 32 *German Yearbook of International Law* 382407 (1990).

138. Robert, E., "L'affaire relative au projet Gabcíkovo-Nagymaros: Un nouveau conflit en matiere d'environnement devant la Cour internationale de Justice?," 47(5) *Studia Diplomatica* 17-52 (1994).

139. Robol, Richard T., "Jurisdiction. Limits of Consent. The Aegean Sea Continental Shelf Case," 18 *Harvard International Law Journal* 64975 (1977).

140. Roche, A. G., *The Minquiers and Ecrehos case; an analysis of the decision of the International Court of Justice* (Genève: Droz, 1959).

141. Rogoff, Martin A., "International Politics and the Rule of Law: The United States and the International Court of Justice," 7 *Boston University International Law Journal* 26799 (1989).

142. Scheffer, David J., "NonJudicial State Remedies and the Jurisdiction of the International Court of Justice," 27 *Stanford Journal of International Law* 83154 (1990).

143. Schlochauer, HansJurgen, "International Court of Justice," in Bernhardt (ed.), *Encyclopedia of Public International Law* 1 (1981), pp.7292.

144. Schmid, K., *Die rechtsprechung des Ständigen internationalen gerichtshofs in rechtssätzen dargestellt* (Stuttgart: F. Enke, 1932).

145. Schmitz, E., Zur auslegung des artikels 305 des Versailler vertrages (Berlin-Schöneberg: Brandenbrugischen buchdruckerei, 1925).

146. Schreuer, C., *Decisions of international institutions before domestic courts* (New York: Oceana Publications, 1981).

147. Schwarzenberger, Georg, "The Judicial Corps of the International Court of Justice," 36 *Yearbook of World Affairs* 23167 (1982).

148. Tomka, P., "The First Site Visit of the International Court of Justice in Fulfillment of its Judicial Function," 92 *American Journal of International Law* 133-140 (1998).

149. Toope, Stephen J., "Pragmatic Compromise or Mere Transaction? The Use of Chamber Procedure in International Adjudication," 31 *Virginia Journal of International Law* 5397 (1990).

150. ToraldoSerra, N. M., *Le misure pravvisorie intemazionali. ricerca storicogiuridica* (Rome: Bulzoni, 1973).

151. Treves, Tullio, "Conflicts Between the International Tribunal for the Law of the Sea and the International

Court of Justice," 31 *N.Y.U. Journal of International Law & Politics* 809 (1999).

152. U.S. Senate Republican Policy Committee, *The International Court of Justice: shall we withdraw the Connally reservation?* (Washington: 1960).

153. United Nations Office of Public Information, *The International Court of Justice* (New York: United Nations, 1969).

154. United States. Congress. House. Committee on Foreign Affairs. Subcommittee on Human Rights and International Organizations. (1981), *Calling for the establishment of a special committee on advisory opinions from the International Court of Justice: hearing before the Subcommittee on Human Rights and International Organizations of the Committee on Foreign Affairs, House of Representatives, Ninety-seventh Congress*, first session, September 24, 1981 (Washington, U.S. G.P.O., 1981).

155. Verhoosel, G., 6 "Gabcíkovo-Nagymaros: The Evidentiary Regime on Environmental Degradation and the World Court," *European Environmental Law Review* 247-253 (1997).

156. Verzijl, J. H. W., *The jurisprudence of the world court: a case by case commentary* (Leiden: A.W. Sijthoff, 1965).

157. Visscher, Charles d., *De l'équité dans le règlement arbitral ou judiciane des litiges de droit international public* (Paris: Pedone, 1972).

158. Wehberg, Hans & H. W. Goldschmidt, *Der Intemationale Gerichtshof. Entstehungsgeschichte, Analyse, Dokumentation* (Berlin: Berlin Verlag, Arno Spitz, 1973).

159. Wehmeyer, D. A., *An attainable international court system* (Washington, World Peace Through Law Center, 1964).

160. Weinberger, S., "The Wimbledon Paradox and the World Court: confronting inevitable conflicts between conventional and customary international law," 10 *Emory International Law Review*397-440 (Spring 1996).

161. Yarnold, Barbara M., *International fugitives: a new role for the International Court of Justice* (New York, Praeger, 1991).

162. Yee, S., et. al., "Forum prorogatum and the advisory proceedings of the International Court," 95(2) *American Journal of International Law* 381-6 (April 2001).

163. Young, D. A., "Contributions to International Law and World Order by the World Court's Adjudication of the Icelandic Fisheries Controversy," 1 *Boston College International and Comparative Law Journal* 175-196 (1977).

164. Ziccardi Capaldo, Giuliana, *Répertoire de la jurisprudence de la cour internationale de justice (1974-1992)* (Dordrecht; Boston: M. Nijhoff Publishers; Norwell, MA, U.S.A.: Sold and distributed in the U.S.A. and Canada by Kluwer Academic Publishers, 1995).

165. Zimmermann, Andreas, "Ad Hoc Chambers of the International Court of Justice," 8 *Dickinson Journal of International Law* 132 (1989).

166. Zoller, E., "La première constitution d'une chambre spéciale par la Cour internationale de Justice: Observations sur l'Ordonnance du 20 janvier 1982," 86 *Revue générale de droit international public* 305-324 (1982).

167. Zubel, E. "The Lockerbie {Libyan Arab Jamahiriya v. United Kingdom, {1998} I.C.J. Rep. 9; Libyan Arab Jamahiriya v. United States, {1998} I.C.J. Rep. 115} controversy: tension between the International Court of Justice and the Security Council," 5(1) *Annual Survey of International and Comparative Law* 259-85 (Spring 1999).

CHAPTER 2

PROCEDURAL JUSTICE POST-9/11: THE EFFECTS OF PROCEDURALLY UNFAIR TREATMENT OF DETAINEES ON PERCEPTIONS OF GLOBAL LEGITIMACY

David Welsh

INTRODUCTION

The Global War on Terror[1] has been ideologically framed as a struggle between the principles of freedom and democracy on the one hand and tyranny and extremism on the other.[2] Although this war has arguably led to a short-term disruption of terrorist threats such as al-Qaeda, it has also damaged America's image both at home and abroad.[3] Throughout the world, there is a growing consensus that America has "a lack of credibility as a fair and just world leader." [4] The perceived legitimacy of the United States in the War on Terror is critical because terrorism is not a conventional threat that can surrender or can be defeated in the traditional sense. Instead, this battle can only be won through legitimizing the rule of law and undermining the use of terror as a means of political influence.[5]

Although a variety of political, economic, and security policies have negatively impacted the perceived legitimacy of the United States, one of the most damaging has been the detention, treatment, and trial (or in many cases the lack thereof) of suspected terrorists. While many scholars have raised constitutional questions about the legality of U.S. detention procedures,[6] this article offers a psychological perspective of legitimacy in the context of detention.

I begin with a discussion of the psychology of terrorism. Next, I argue that the U.S. response to terrorism has been largely perceived as excessive, which has undermined global perceptions of U.S. legitimacy. I address this issue by drawing on a well-established body of social psychology research that proposes "a causal chain in which procedural fairness leads to perceived legitimacy, which leads to the acceptance of policies." [7] In other words, the fairness of the procedures through which individuals are detained and tried will significantly affect the perceived legitimacy of U.S. conduct in the War on Terror. In contrast to current detention policies, which have largely been implemented in an ad hoc manner, I suggest that procedural fairness can be increased through the establishment of a domestic terror court specifically designed to try detainees. Finally, I balance fairness with the competing values of effectiveness and efficiency to provide a framework through which U.S. legitimacy in the War on Terror can be enhanced.

THE PSYCHOLOGY OF TERRORISM

Terrorism can be defined as "politically motivated violence, perpetrated by individuals, groups, or state-sponsored agents, intended to instill feelings of terror and helplessness in a population in order to influence decision making and to change behavior." [8] Contrary to common belief, terrorism cannot be explained by economic deprivation, lack of education, or increased psychopathology.[9] Instead, "terrorism can best be understood through a focus on the psychological interpretation of material conditions and the options seen to be avail-able to overcome perceived injustices, particularly those in the procedures through which decisions are made." [10] In the context of radical Islamist terrorism, the United States is viewed as a threat to Islamic identity and culture in a world that is becoming increasingly secularized and modernized.[11]

Though the root structural, motivational, and triggering causes of terrorism are multifaceted and nuanced, scholars generally agree that acts of terrorism can be traced back to "perceived intolerable injustice." [12] Fathali M. Moghaddam

Citation: David Welsh, Procedural Justice Post-9/11: The Effects of Procedurally Unfair Treatment of Detainees on Perceptions of Global Legitimacy, http://scholars.unh.edu/cgi/viewcontent.cgi?article=1153&context=unh_lr

conceptualizes the psychological process leading to terrorism as a journey up a narrowing staircase that culminates in a terrorist act.[13] On the ground floor exists a large group of individuals who are experiencing injustice and relative deprivation.[14] Consequently, a few of these individuals begin to climb the staircase in search of solutions.[15] If these individuals are unable to address their needs through legitimate means, they will experience anger and frustration that they will seek to displace against those perceived to be responsible.[16] As individuals climb higher, they be-gin to see terrorism as a legitimate strategy reflecting their only means to address injustice.[17] Ultimately, individuals become fully engaged in an "us versus them" mindset that justifies acts of violence against civilians to further a cause.[18] In the same way that soldiers depersonalize the enemy, terrorists are instructed to overcome the inhibitory mechanisms that would normally prevent violence against innocent civilians.[19]

This psychological model for understanding terrorism is critical in responding to individuals at different points on the hypothetical staircase. The use of criminal law as a response to terrorism has been widely criticized for addressing individuals only on the top step who have already committed a terrorist act.[20] In response, the preventive military detention model originally implemented by the Bush Administration has cast a wide net over thousands of individuals alleged to have any sort of terrorist connection.[21] Nevertheless, as former Secretary of Defense Donald Rumsfeld noted, terrorist organizations are "churning out new terrorists faster than the United States can kill or capture them." [22] Paradoxically, some research suggests that U.S. detention policies have actually served to legitimize, rather than deter, extremists.[23] In the next section, I suggest that the United States has alienated an essential group: the millions of individuals near the bottom of the staircase who are weighing the legitimacy of terrorist organizations on the one hand against the legitimacy of U.S. policies in the War on Terror on the other hand.

THE CURRENT U.S. DETENTION REGIME: WHEN EXCESS CREATES INJUSTICE

History has demonstrated that in times of crisis, nation-states frequently err by allowing national security to trump individual liberties.[24] In such situations, political leaders rush to modify or discard the normal rules of law.[25] As Justice Brennan noted:

> After each perceived security crisis ended, the United States has remorsefully realized that the abrogation of civil liberties was unnecessary. But it has proven unable to prevent itself from repeating the error when the next crisis came along.[26]

Consequently, when the current legal framework appears insufficient, the stage is set for impromptu, crisis-based decision-making. Inevitably, a sort of ad hoc balancing is substituted in place of for-mal rules of law leading to excess in the forms of "judgments based on suspicion and not hard evidence" and the jettisoning of "checks on unilateral decision making." [27] The internment of over 100,000 Japanese Americans without an evidentiary basis during World War II is one of the most notorious examples of governmental overreach in a period of crisis.[28] However, the later congressional acknowledgement that these "actions were taken without adequate security rea-sons" and instead were primarily based on "racial prejudice, wartime hysteria, and a failure of political leadership" reflects the current sentiment of millions of Muslims towards U.S. detention policies.[29]

Today, many individuals throughout the world question whether the United States has engaged in excess in response to the attacks of 9/11. A 2004 poll suggests that many people in France (57%), Germany (49%), and Britain (33%) felt that the United States over-reacted in response to terrorism.[30] Among Middle Eastern countries, as many as three-fourths of individuals stated that the United States overreacted in the War on Terror.[31] Additionally, approximately two-thirds of citizens in France, Germany, Turkey, and Pakistan questioned the sincerity of the United States in the War on Terror.[32] Within the United States, nationwide confidence in the White House dropped 40% between 2002 and 2004 while confidence in Congress fell by 25% during this period.[33] Although this worldwide drop in legitimacy is the result of multiple factors beyond the scope of this paper, such as the U.S. decision to invade Iraq, detention remains a controversial topic that continues to negatively affect global perceptions of the United States.

Although this paper focuses specifically on the detention of suspected terrorists at the Guantanamo Bay Detention Camp (Guantanamo Bay),[34] this facility is but one of many detention centers holding suspected terrorists on behalf of the United States.[35] Today, approximately 250 prisoners (out of approximately 800) remain at this U.S.-run military base in Cuba that is outside U.S. legal jurisdic-tion.[36] However, it is critical to note that these 250 individuals represent a mere 1% of "approximately 25,000 detainees worldwide held directly or indirectly by or on behalf of the United States." [37] Prisoners have alleged torture, sexual degradation, religious persecution,[38] and many other specific forms of mistreatment while being detained.[39] In many detention facilities including Guantanamo Bay, Abu Ghraib, and Bagram, these allegations are substantiated by significant evidence and have gained worldwide attention.[40]

While some graphic and shocking cases of abuse have been brought to light,[41] a more typical example is the prosecution of six-teen-year-old Mohamed Jawad by Lt. Col. Darrel Vandeveld at Guantanamo Bay.[42] At first, the case against Jawad looked straightforward, as he had confessed to throwing a grenade that injured two U.S. soldiers and a translator in December 2002.[43] How-ever, a deeper investigation "uncovered a confession obtained through torture, two suicide attempts by the accused, abusive inter-rogations, the withholding of exculpatory evidence from the defense," and other procedural problems. [44] Vandeveld discovered that the military had obtained confessions from two other individuals for the same offense; he ultimately left his post after attempts to provide "basic fair trial rights" failed. [45]

In February 2006, the United Nations Working Group on Arbitrary Detention spoke out against international law and human rights violations at Guantanamo Bay, stating that the facility should be closed "without further delay." [46] This report paralleled earlier criticism from Amnesty International that Guantanamo Bay violates minimum standards for the treatment of individuals.[47] In response, the United States has argued that detainees are not prisoners of war but are rather "unlawful combatants" who are not entitled to the protections of the Geneva Convention because they do not act in accordance with the accepted rules of war.[48] Yet, regardless of the debatable legal merit of this argument, legitimacy is an "elusive quality" grounded in worldwide opinion that will not let the United States off the hook on a mere technicality when moral duties and international customs have been violated.[49] In the next section, I discuss the importance of legitimacy and the ways in which it has been under-mined by U.S. conduct in the War on Terror. By understanding what drives global perceptions of U.S. legitimacy, current detention policies and their ramifications can be more accurately assessed and restructured.

LEGITIMACY: THE CRITICAL MISSING ELEMENT IN THE WAR ON TERROR

In the context of the War on Terror, legitimacy is the critical missing element under the current U.S. detention regime. Legitimacy can be defined as "a psychological property of an authority, institution, or social arrangement that leads those connected to it to believe that it is appropriate, proper, and just." [50] As far back as Plato and Aristotle, philosophers have recognized that influencing others merely through coercion and power is costly and inefficient.[51] To-day, empirical evidence suggests that legitimacy, rather than deterrence, is primarily what causes individuals to obey the law.[52] Thus, while legal authorities may possess the immediate power to stop illegal action, long-term compliance requires that the general public perceives the law to be legitimate.[53] Terrorism is primarily an ideological war that cannot be won by technology that is more sophisticated or increased military force.[54] While nations combating terror-ism must continue to address immediate threats by detaining suspected terrorists, they must also consider the prevention of future threats by analyzing how their policies are perceived by individuals throughout the world. Ultimately, in the War on Terror, "the bene-fits to be derived from maximizing legitimacy are too important to neglect." [55]

Over time, perceptions of legitimacy create a "reservoir of sup-port" for an institution that goes beyond mere self -interest.[56] In the context of government:

> Legitimacy is [an] endorphin of the democratic body politic; it is the substance that oils the machinery of democracy, reducing the friction that inevitably arises when people are not able to get everything they want from politics. Legitimacy is loyalty; it is a reservoir of goodwill that allows the institutions of government to go against what people may want at the moment without suffering debilitating consequences.[57]

The widespread acceptance of highly controversial decisions by the U.S. Supreme Court illustrates the power of institutional legiti-macy.[58] The Court itself noted that it "cannot buy support for its decisions by spending money and, except to a minor degree, it cannot independently coerce obedience to its decrees." [59] "The Court's power lies, rather, in its legitimacy . . . ." [60] For example, by emphasizing "equal treatment," "honesty and neutrality," "gathering information before decision making," and "making principled, or rule based, decisions instead of political decisions," the Court maintained legitimacy through the controversial abortion case *Planned Parent-hood of Southeastern Pennsylvania v. Casey* in 1992.[61] Thus, al-though approximately half of Americans oppose abortion,[62] the vast majority of these individuals give deference to the Court's ruling on this issue.[63]

In the post-World War II era, the United States built up a world-wide reservoir of support based upon four pillars: "its commitment to international law, its acceptance of consensual decision-making, its reputation for moderation, and its identification with the preservation of peace." [64] Although some U.S. policies between 1950 and 2001 did not align with these pillars, on a whole the United States legitimized itself as a world superpower during this period.[65] In the 1980s, President Ronald Reagan spoke of America as a "shining city on a hill," suggesting that it was a model for the nations of the world to look to.[66] While the United States received a virtually unprecedented outpouring of support from the international community following 9/11, a nation's reservoir of support will quickly evaporate when its government overreacts. Across the globe, individuals have expressed a growing dissatisfaction with U.S. conduct in the War on Terror, and by 2006, even western allies of the United States lobbied for the immediate closure of Guantanamo Bay, calling it "an embarrassment." [67] Former Secretary of State Colin Powell proclaimed that "Guantanamo has become a major, major problem . . . in the way the world perceives America and if it were up to me I would close Guantanamo not tomorrow but this afternoon . . . ." [68] Similarly, President Obama noted in his campaign that "Guantanamo has be-come a recruiting tool for our enemies." [69]

Current U.S. detention policies erode each of the four pillars on which the United States established global legitimacy. In fact, critics have argued that the "United States has assumed man y of the very features of the 'rogue nations' against which it has rhetorically—and sometimes literally—done battle over the years." [70] While legitimacy cannot be regained overnight, the recent election of President Barack Obama presents a critical opportunity for a re-articulation of U.S. detention policies. Although President Obama issued an executive order calling for the closure of Guantanamo Bay only two days after being sworn into office,[71] significant controversy remains about the kind of alternate detention system that will replace it.[72] In contrast to the current model, which has largely rendered inefficient decisions based on ad hoc policies, I argue for the establishment of a domestic terror court (DTC) created specifically to deal with the unique procedural issues created by a growing number of suspected terrorists.

THE IMPORTANCE OF PROCEDURAL JUSTICE

In the context of detentions, "the fairness of the procedures" through which the United States exercises authority is the key element driving both national and international perceptions of U.S. legitimacy, and legitimacy ultimately determines the extent to which individuals comply with U.S. policies.[73] Robust empirical evidence has "repeatedly documented a pattern of correlation s consistent with a causal chain in which procedural fairness leads to perceived legitimacy, which leads to the acceptance of policies." [74] Research also suggests that procedural justice creates a "willing ness to empower legal authorities to resolve issues of public controversy." [75] An analysis of how procedural justice has been applied in legal and institutional settings provides a framework for addressing the specific legitimacy problems associated with Guantanamo Bay and how fair process can be effectively incorporated into a DTC model.

Thirty-five years ago, the formal study of procedural justice was born when researchers discovered that individuals " care deeply about the fairness of the process that is used to resolve their encounter or dispute, separate and apart from their interest in achieving a favorable outcome." [76] This research indicates that individuals with control over the process (e.g., telling their side of the story, presenting evidence, and controlling the order and timing of presentation) view the process itself as fair.[77] This outcome, known as the fair process effect, "is one of the most replicated findings in the [procedural] justice literature." [78] A meta-analysis of 120 empirical justice studies covering a twenty-five year period revealed that procedural justice is highly correlated with outcome satisfaction (.48), institutional commitment (.57), trust (.61), and evaluation of authority (.64).[79] These findings indicate the degree of significance that procedural justice has on individuals.

In the legal setting, an exploration of procedural justice in felony cases revealed that defendants' evaluations of the judicial system did not depend exclusively on the favorability of sentencing.[80] Even when verdicts involved incarceration and serious sanctions, litigant evaluations went beyond distributive outcomes to analyze their perceptions of the procedural fairness of the legal system.[81] Additionally, while judges handling minor cases believed that litigants would ignore procedural issues when granted favorable outcomes, litigants' concerns over process led to unanticipated hostilities when procedural shortcuts were used by the court to resolve cases.[82] Thus, while outcomes cannot be entirely disregarded, the fairness of the process used to reach a given outcome is critical to perceptions of legitimacy.

Recent research highlights two reasons why procedural justice may be particularly important in the context of detentions. First, judgments of procedural fairness are particularly important to individuals experiencing uncertainty.[83] Detainees lack the procedural certainties guaranteed in a regular criminal proceeding in that they frequently do not know how long they will be held, why they are being held, what evidence exists against them, and what degree of punishment they may face.[84] Second, the greater the unfavorable-ness of the outcome and the larger the potential harm, the more individuals care about fair process.[85] These findings are reflected in U.S. criminal law provisions requiring certain elements of procedural due process when serious sanctions are involved.[86]

It is also critical to extend procedural justice judgments beyond the individual detainee to the perspective of a worldwide audience. While it is easy to overlook how an alleged terrorist feels about the degree of procedural fairness he or she is receiving, the perceptions of governments, human rights organizations, political groups (including terrorist organizations), and millions of individuals (particularly those who closely identify with that individual's race, religion, or nationality) cannot be ignored. Individuals become upset when they observe unfairness, and such observations motivate them to help victims of this unfairness.[87] Thus, it would be a mistake to think that procedural injustice against a single individual will affect the perceptions of that individual alone.[88] Additionally, efforts to hide procedural injustices, such as the abuse of detainees by U.S. soldiers,[89] have only backfired by creating sympathy for the types of individuals that the United States seeks to dehumanize.[90] In the next section, I identify six rules of procedural justice, evaluate the current detention regime based on these rules, and make recommendations about how these rules could be implemented in a DTC model.

APPLYING PROCEDURAL JUSTICE TO U.S. DETENTION POLICIES

While an extensive theoretical review of procedural justice is beyond the scope of this paper, I use six rules of procedural justice as defined in *Beyond Fairness: A Theory of Allocation Prefe-rences*,[91] in analyzing procedural justice under the current detention regime. These rules are as follows: (1) the consistency rule— allocation procedures should be consistent across persons and over time; (2) the bias suppression rule—personal self interest in the allocation process should be prevented; (3) the accuracy rule—decisions must be based on accurate information; (4) the correct ability rule—opportunities must exist to enable decisions to be modified; (5) the representativeness rule—the allocation process must represent the concerns of all recipients; and (6) the ethicality rule—allocations must be based on prevailing moral and ethical standards.[92]

An examination of each of these procedural rules reveals a variety of ways in which the procedural justice accorded detainees can be enhanced. Given the growing nature of terrorism as a persistent global threat, additional strategic consideration must be given to how these rules will be applied to a more permanent judicial process for detainees. The DTC model that I propose is a hybrid court incorporating many of the procedural safeguards of the U.S. criminal justice system into a model specifically designed to meet the unique challenges posed in trying alleged terrorists.[93] While other scholars have already laid out the legal framework of the DTC model,[94] I consider the degree to which this model incorporates the six rules of procedural justice. Ultimately, the DTC model provides a concrete framework of fair process, while also maximizing effectiveness and efficiency to a greater extent than either the current U.S. detention regime or competing detention models.

Consistency

The rule of consistency requires that all parties have the same rights and that individuals receive equal treatment.[95] Consistency over time is also important, and, thus, procedural changes must be made carefully in a way that puts individuals on notice.[96] Consequently, two defendants prosecuted with identical evidence should ultimately receive the same outcome regardless of any differing, but irrelevant, personal characteristics or the timing of the crime.[97] However, the terrorist attacks of 9/11 shocked the world and instantly changed U.S. policies on terrorism.[98] While significant steps to increase national security were certainly warranted, a rapid discard of traditional rules of law undermined the principle of consistency.

For example, the "Post-9/11 Immigrant Roundup" in the United States of over 1,200 Arab and Muslim immigrants marked a dramatic legal change fueled by perceived necessity.[99] In this instance, Attorney General John Ashcroft "substituted a vague standard for a clear rule in order to justify holding [these immigrants] without charges for extended periods of time." [100] Under U.S. criminal law, these individuals would have been charged within twenty-four hours, while the more expansive Patriot Act allows for a seven-day detention based on reasonable grounds in the belief that an immigrant is engaged in terrorist activities.[101] However, new regulations permit-ted many of these individuals to be held for months.[102] Nevertheless, two years later, an analysis of the roundup by the Michigan Pol-icy Institute revealed that "[w]e haven't learned anything about pre-empting terrorism in America, but we have intimidated, antagonized and alienated many (minority) communities . . . ." [103]

Similarly, the United States sidestepped international laws relating to the detention of prisoners of war by labeling suspected terrorists as "unlawful enemy combatants." [104] "Until 2001, this term appeared nowhere in U.S. criminal law, international law, or the law of war," however, it has subsequently been vaguely construed and applied to hold individuals indefinitely without charges.[105] An additional consistency problem is that this ambiguous definition would cover Osama bin Laden, as well as "a 'little old lady in Switzerland who writes checks to what she thinks is a charity that helps orphans in Afghanistan but really is a front to finance al-Qaeda activities,'[and] a person who teaches English to the son of an al-Qaeda member." [106]

The principle of equal rights suggests that individuals suspected of terrorism should be treated in the same manner whether they are U.S. citizens or citizens of another nation.[107] In *Boumediene v.Bush*,[108] the U.S. Supreme Court challenged two previously accepted distinctions that undermine the principle of consistency.[109] "The first is the distinction between the constitutional rights of American and alien prisoners; the second is the distinction between the rights of those we imprison on American soil and those we imprison everywhere else in the world." [110] As a result, the idea that there is "no moral justification for discriminating against foreigners" in detention procedures is gaining momentum.[111] However, to some extent this principle has been overshadowed by separate agreements regarding the treatment of individuals from certain nations.[112] For example, the Attorney General has promised the British government that its citizens will not face the death penalty.[113] While special treatment may induce the cooperation of an ally, it does so with an associated cost imposed on the citizens of other nations. In contrast, efforts by the U.S. Supreme Court to grant habeas corpus rights to all detainees regardless of citizenship or place of capture enhance perceptions of consistency [114]

To further improve perceptions of U.S. consistency, I suggest:

(1) that traditional rules of law may need to be modified, but cannot be abruptly discarded in periods of crisis; (2) a general uniformity among military commissions must exist as required by the U.S. Supreme Court; and (3) detainees of different nations, ethnicities, and religions must be given equal treatment and equal rights. The DTC model addresses each of these three concerns.

First, the DTC model sets a clear standard of consistency in contrast to current ad hoc policies that have fluctuated in the political winds of this crisis and have been vaguely applied. The DTC model provides clear definitions and specific criteria for determining who is a threat based on information that is "(1) reliable; (2) viable; (3) valid; and (4) corroborated." [115] When individuals are not on notice about how they will be treated, they respond negatively when the law appears to implicate their conduct without adequate warning.[116] Outside observers such as human rights groups and citizens of other nations will similarly be dissatisfied by a system that generates un-predictable results.

Second, the DTC model provides a system of uniformity as required by the U.S. Supreme Court. In *Hamdan v. Rumsfeld*,[117] the Court proclaimed the need for a uniform system of courts-martial and military commission procedures.[118] As a result, procedural rules must be consistent with the Uniform Code of Military Justice, and rules must be the same between military commissions and courts-martial "insofar as practicable." [119] The DTC model proposes uniformity in terms of sentencing as well as procedure. Like the U.S. criminal justice system, the DTC model utilizes maximum and minimum sentencing terms.[120] Additionally, the DTC model rejects the death penalty in all cases rather than providing exceptions to the citizens of certain nations.[121]

Third, the DTC model provides the same treatment for citizens and non-citizens. A 2006 poll suggests that even Americans generally do not feel that their fellow citizens deserve preferential treat-ment.[122] Sixty-three percent of respondents indicated that the detention policies should be the same for citizens and non-citizens, while 33% felt that policies should be different.[123] When granting U.S. citizens additional rights that are not applied to individuals of other nations, a tradeoff is clearly being made. One of the fears surrounding U.S. treatment of foreign detainees is that other nations will reciprocate by treating U.S. prisoners with disrespect.[124] The application of standard rights and procedures to similarly situated individuals under the DTC model comports with universal conceptions of fair-ness and also enhances the next procedural justice factor: bias suppression.

Bias Suppression

The prevention of favoritism, prejudice, and external bias is a critical aspect of procedural justice.[125] Two types of biases are: (1) "a vested interest in the outcome" and (2) "[reliance] on prior views rather than evidence." [126] To illustrate, a judge conducting the trial of a close family member has a strong personal interest in the trial's outcome. Similarly, a jury member who believes all criminal defendants are probably guilty will likely render a biased decision that is not based on evidence.[127] Perhaps what is most critical to the bias-suppression analysis in the context of terrorism is the extent to which the deck is stacked against the detainee from the beginning. Under U.S. criminal law, a defendant can present his or her case to a jury of peers, remove biased individuals from the jury pool, examine all the evidence presented by the prosecutor, object to certain forms of pre-judicial evidence such as hearsay, cross examine witnesses, and re-quire that the charges be proved beyond a reasonable doubt.[128] In a detainee's trial, none of these procedural safeguards exist, and, thus, an important concern arises as to how impartiality can be maintained.[129]

At the start of this analysis, a government must ask itself whether it is willing to let an individual go if the evidence required for a conviction is not present. For example, one of the questions surrounding the famous Nuremberg trials of Nazi leaders following World War II was the extent to which the international tribunal was driven by victor's justice. [130] While many argued for "show trials" or proceedings that were "not too judicial," [131] others, such as Justice Robert Jackson, believed that procedural fairness was essential to ultimate victory (in contrast to the punitive Treaty of Versailles at the end of World War I).[132] Ultimately, the tribunal rendered a wide range of verdicts from death sentences to acquittals.[133] However, questions yet remain as to whether Justice Jackson's ideal of fairness was obtained or whether bias nevertheless crept into the system.[134] Regardless, the Nuremberg trials illustrate that bias suppression demands neutral justice that is not driven by unbridled retribution, political power, or crisis-based fear.

Under the current detention regime, there appears to be little in the way of procedural guarantees to prevent the U.S. government from using indefinite detentions to subvert justice. In the event that a detainee is put on trial, the evidence is evaluated and a decision is reached as to whether that individual will be held or released. However, when no such trial takes place, the detainee can be held without an evaluation of the charges or evidence. Such procedures incentivize bias against those detainees whom the United States speculates are "really bad" but lacks the evidence to convict. Similarly, during precarious periods there is a subtle motivation to keep all the alleged "bad guys" off the streets for long enough to turn the tide of the war effort. Perhaps there is also the cynical viewpoint that even innocent detainees have now mingled with actual terrorists, endured significant mistreatment, and, thus, now pose a threat to the United States.

One of the biggest challenges that the United States faces in the War on Terror is to effectively fight terrorism without simultaneously stereotyping millions of individuals associated with particular religions, nationalities, or ethnic groups. President Obama addressed this issue by declaring that "[t]he United States is not, and never will be, at war with Islam." [135] He also noted that America's "partnership with the Muslim world is critical in rolling back a fringe ideology that people of all faiths reject." [136] These broad policy statements set the right tone for the minimization of bias in detention trials. Yet, more specific procedural guarantees are needed as a check on the potential bias of a military system driven by effectiveness rather than justice.

A positive step in removing bias from detentions is increased process transparency. For example, the Department of Defense has implemented a media-visit program at Guantanamo Bay allowing members of the media to tour the facilities.[137] More recently, the Department of Defense has even gone so far as to create a "Virtual Tour" of the Guantanamo Bay facilities. [138] Instead of seeing dark images of coercion chambers that one might imagine in a secretive detention facility, viewers are greeted with images of basketball courts, libraries, and medical facilities.[139] This voluntary act was no doubt "prompted by a desire to avoid an adverse imp act on societal perceptions of Guantanamo Bay's organizational legitimacy." [140] While some evidence relating to detainees is classified and should not be made available to the public, general information about procedures, living conditions, and the detainees themselves helps turn conceptions of Guantanamo Bay from a concentration camp into a more standard prison facility.

Another way to remove bias from a system is to introduce checks and balances to govern the process as proposed by the DTC model. Here, all three branches are involved in the judicial process as the President is given the authority to nominate DTC judges while the Senate retains the power to confirm them. While current U.S. detention procedures were originally enacted by the executive branch with little congressional or judicial oversight, clear rules for each branch of government are laid out by the DTC model.[141] For example, the executive branch is responsible for setting the criteria for a formal vetting process used by judges to determine who should be de-tained.[142] Transparency combined with this system of checks and balances helps to prevent one branch of government from having too much of a vested interest in a particular outcome and allows the appointment of qualified judges to make unbiased judgments based on evidence and not prejudice. By minimizing bias, a major roadblock to reaching accurate decisions is cleared.

Accuracy

Accuracy requires that decisions be made using correct information. For example, the U.S. criminal justice system prevents individuals from being convicted on mere speculation. Instead, a formal process in which evidence is introduced and testimony is recorded ensures that an informed decision will ultimately be reached. How-ever, obtaining accurate information about hundreds of individuals captured all over the globe presents an overwhelming obstacle to traditional rules of evidence. In contrast, the specialization of the DTC model makes it well suited to handle classified evidence, confrontation clause requirements, and other unique evidentiary problems faced in detainee trials.

Currently, evidentiary issues remain a significant problem, as even the somewhat lax standards of U.S. military tribunals have proved difficult to meet.[143] To date, hundreds of Guantanamo Bay detainees have been released without charges.[144] In fact, one of the challenges delaying President Obama's plan to shut down Guantanamo Bay within one year of taking office is the lack of comprehensive files on detainees.[145] The Obama Administration recently declared that it plans to charge approximately fifty of the roughly 250 remaining detainees and set the other 200 free.[146] On the one hand, this broad net is subjecting about four "innocent" individuals to pro-longed detention for every individual that will be tried. On the other hand, at least some degree of accuracy is eventually being reached in which a large number of individuals are being set free by the U.S. government.

To address the evidentiary problems involved in prosecuting detainees, the DTC model requires that the judge will wear two hats: one as the court and the other as defense counsel. The information and the source must be held to be: (1) reliable; (2) viable; (3) valid; and (4) corroborated. If the intelligence meets the four-part test, then and only then is it admissible and available for use against the defendant at trial. However, a defendant's conviction may not be based solely on confidential intelligence information.[147]

Thus, while the DTC model necessarily allows admission of certain evidence that would not be admitted in a traditional criminal court, it does so only when this evidence meets specific assurances of accuracy in the eyes of a judge who is cognizant of the defendant's interests. Yet, since accuracy is never guaranteed, correctability is the next important element of procedural justice.

Correctability

Correctability requires the availability of procedures to correct unfair or inaccurate decisions.[148] The idea of multiple layers of appeal is fundamental to U.S. criminal law.[149] However, the application of this right to detainees has led to a lengthy foray between the President, Congress, and the U.S. Supreme Court that only recently appears to have been resolved. The constitutional concept of habeas corpus requires that a court inquire into the legitimacy of a detainee's custody and brings up an important correctability issue as to whether only a final outcome (as opposed to the detention itself) can be appealed. If a detainee must wait to be charged and tried, a fundamental correctability problem exists when he or she is held for a significant period of time without legal recourse.

A brief overview of the habeas corpus battle begins with a Presidential Military Order issued on November 13, 2001 by President Bush, asserting that unlawful "enemy combatants" ma y be held indefinitely without charges or a court hearing.[150] However, in the 2004 case *Hamdi v. Rumsfeld*, the U.S. Supreme Court declared that defendants who are U.S. citizens have a right to habeas corpus protec-tions.[151] This led Congress to enact the Detainee Treatment Act of 2005[152] and the Military Commissions Act of 2006,[153] which again stripped the habeas corpus rights from detainees and asserted that they had no right of appeal.[154] In 2008, the U.S. Supreme Court fired back in *Boumediene v. Bush*, holding the Detainee Treatment Act unconstitutional and declaring that detainees have a right to seek a writ of habeas corpus in U.S. Federal Court.[155] On January 21, 2009, President Obama affirmed this right of appeal in an executive order.[156]

In *Boumediene*, the Court overturned the notion "that the Constitution as a whole offers substantially less protection against American tyranny to foreigners than it does to America's own citizens." [157] As a result, detainees can now appeal not only the final verdict they receive but also the government's right to hold them.[158] The seven-year debate described above is itself an important illustration of the principle of correctability, as each branch of government worked to overturn the decision of another branch until an appropriate solution was finally reached by all three branches.

Under the DTC model, detainee appeals are filed directly to the U.S. Court of Appeals.[159] The DTC model also mirrors certain procedures implemented by Israel and the United Kingdom in which the classified information holding a detainee is subject to periodic review.[160] This policy ensures that correctability cannot be side-stepped by indefinite detention. Thus, the justification for an individual's detention must be continually evaluated and his or her procedural rights cannot be indefinitely waived.

Representativeness

Representativeness means "that the concerns of those affected should be represented in all phases of the allocation process." [161] In this context, I suggest that representativeness involves the extent to which the individual detainee's concerns and interests are represented. Procedures that provide legal representation to detainees are one example of how this principle has been applied. This element is critical in the Global War on Terror in which broad government concerns about terrorism readily overshadow the interests of the individual.

I suggest that detainee representativeness occurs both internally (by citizens of the United States) and externally (by citizens of other nations). However, there is an important legitimacy distinction be-tween these two sources of representation. Only when a government internally limits its own self-interest to look out for the interests of the individual can representativeness enhance legitimacy. Thus, while an attorney (internal) who vigorously defends the rights of a detainee probably enhances global perceptions of U.S. legitimacy, a report by Amnesty International (external) arguing for detainee rights is likely to reduce perceptions of U.S. legitimacy. Although non-governmental organizations, foreign governments, and citizens of other nations are all concerned about detainees' interests, only an internally manifested concern by U.S. citizens and political leaders can enhance perceptions of legitimacy. While America's longstanding commitment to individual rights and liberties has been shaken by 9/11,[162] it appears that these values are beginning to reemerge.

The DTC model upholds the principle of representativeness by requiring a "degree of government self-restraint." [163] If an individual is held, the purpose of the detention is to indict and prepare for trial, as opposed to an indefinite substitute for justice. By granting detainees certain rights, and by requiring judges to look out for these rights, the principle of representativeness is upheld and the individual is not overlooked in the midst of a global conflict.

Ethicality

Ethicality means "the degree to which the decision- making process accords with general standards of fairness and morality." [164] Thus, conduct such as bribery, spying, and deception are all widely recognized as violating general standards of fairness.[165] However, ethicality is the most difficult rule to define in the context of terrorism because there is an inherent tension between individual standards of morality, the laws of nations, and international laws and customs. Crisis exacerbates these tensions, as moral and legal standards often appear to be at odds with effectiveness and necessity. The use of torture and other coercive measures against detainees provides a vivid illustration of this conflict that will be discussed later in more detail. However, the use of torture is but one example of a failure to take the "moral high ground" in the War on Terror.[166] When the United States acts unilaterally or declines to follow the laws governing international conflict, it loses the moral high ground that ideologically separates legitimate governments from terrorist organizations that ignore the rule of law. Once on the same moral ground as the terrorists, the United States can no longer rely on legitimacy but must focus entirely on coercion and force in a "might makes right" scenario rather than utilizing legitimacy's more effective "right makes might" paradigm of voluntary compliance.

While ethicality invokes moral arguments and may rightly be considered an end in itself, this paper constrains ethicality by primarily analyzing only the extent to which it enhances procedural justice and legitimacy. Ethical treatment of detainees is not merely a moral obligation, but also a strategic choice.[167] Consider Sherman et al.'s observation:

One of the most striking recent findings is the extent to which the police themselves create a risk factor for crime simply by using bad manners. Modest but consistent scientific evidence supports the hypothesis that the less respectful police are towards suspects and citizens generally, the less people will comply with the law.[168]

Similarly, the U.S. military puts itself in harm's way when it fails to follow international rules of war. "Guantanamo has become a liability. The real and perceived injustices occurring there have given our enemies an easy example of our failures and alleged ill intent," stated Homeland Security Committee member Rep. Jane Harman.[169] The graphic beheading of U.S. citizen Nicholas Berg is one of many retaliatory attacks by terrorist groups in response to perceived abuses of their captured associates.[170] Justified or not, terrorist groups often claim that immoral U.S. conduct has legitimized their actions.[171]

One of the most heated debates about the treatment of detainees surrounds the use of torture and other methods of coercion to extract information from detainees. President Obama's decision to ban certain types of torture, such as waterboarding, reflects his belief that the United States lost its "moral bearing" by utilizing such practic-es.[172] Empirical evidence similarly reveals that America lost legitimacy through the torture of alleged terrorists. A 2006 poll of more than 27,000 individuals in twenty-five different countries indicated that 59% of respondents felt that clear rules against torture should be maintained, while 29% said governments should be allowed to use some degree of torture.[173] Opposition to torture was strongest in Western Europe, Canada, and Australia, with approximately three-quarters of individuals in these regions opposing torture.[174]

In contrast, the United States was more divided, as 58% of citizens opposed torture while 36% indicated that some degree of torture should be allowed.[175] Going back to the earlier discussion about the tendency for governments to overreact during periods of crisis, it is interesting to note that countries that have experienced recent terrorist attacks or political violence are, on average, more willing to allow torture.[176] Even though all twenty-five countries that participated in this survey are parties to the Geneva Convention, which forbids torture under Common Article 3 and the more recent Convention Against Torture, these findings provide evidence that nations are increasingly likely to jettison not only traditional rules of law but also ethical standards when under attack.[177]

Even as the debate over torture begins to wind down (now that the practice has been explicitly outlawed by President Obama), there remains an apprehension about the extent to which the "[p]rocess is the [p]unishment" in the context of detentions. [178] I borrow this phrase from Brenda Sims Blackwell and Clark D. Cunningham, who documented a number of criminal cases in which individuals spent up to twelve days in jail for minor offenses such as jaywalking be-fore their cases could be resolved.[179] However, this concept is magnified in the context of detentions. When an individual is taken from his or her homeland and placed in Guantanamo Bay for an indefinite period, the punishment, independent of ultimate guilt or innocence, has already begun. This is particularly salient because, as mentioned previously within the discussion of accuracy, U.S. detention procedures result in the roundup of a significant number of "innocent" individuals that is well in excess of those whom will ultimately be tried and convicted. Add potential mistreatment, coercion, and depravation, and suddenly the treatment of uncharged detainees looks worse than the lifestyle afforded many convicted criminals. In a legal system that presumes guilt, this outcome might be an acceptable reality. However, it stands in stark contrast to the constitutional notion of innocent until proven guilty.

A consideration of ethicality reveals several ways in which procedural justice can be enhanced by the DTC model. First, the DTC model sets clear ethical limits against "unconstitutional interrogation methods . . . which are illegal, immoral, and do not contribute to 'actionable intelligence.'" [180] Not only is torture prohibited, but evidence obtained through torture is excluded from trial.[181] I address this apparent tradeoff between effectiveness and fairness later in more detail, by arguing that this evidence is not only of questionable reliability but comes at too high a cost to the United States. By set-ting moral boundaries, the United States is in a better position to avoid the sorts of prisoner abuse scandals that have occurred at Abu Ghraib and Guantanamo Bay which have significantly undermined U.S. legitimacy.

Second, a re-articulation of detention policies under the DTC model will limit procedural burdens on detainees to a greater degree. The DTC model requires that detainees be brought before a judge without unnecessary delay.[182] This should occur within seven days unless exigent circumstances arise.[183] Detentions must be independently reviewed at periodic intervals to ensure that the process is progressing either toward trial or release.[184] Fairness and efficiency are maximized by a system adapted specifically to detainees, and holding individuals for years without trial would become the rare exception under this model rather than the norm.

Third, the DTC model is but one aspect of a broader strategic objective designed to retake the moral high ground in the War on Terror. While the United States has frequently asserted its sovereignty in opposition to international law,[185] it would gain much through international cooperation as opposed to unilateral action. While an extensive discussion of the limits of state sovereignty is beyond the scope of this paper, the United States should consider the legitimacy of international laws and customs even in situations where it has the power to go against global norms. By recognizing these universal principles of procedural fairness, the United States gains legitimacy in the War on Terror.

BALANCING FAIRNESS, EFFECTIVENESS, AND EFFICIENCY

Although enhancing procedural justice is critical to U.S. success in the War on Terror, fairness is not an absolute and must be carefully balanced with other strategic objectives including effectiveness and efficiency. Yet, weighing these elements is not inherently a zero-sum game in which one objective can only be maximized at the expense of the others. While some degree of balance is required, a zero-sum mentality is often the result of short-term thinking as op-posed to long-term strategy. In this section, I argue that the DTC model collectively maximizes effectiveness, efficiency, and fairness to a greater extent than either the current U.S. detention regime or competing detention models. I also caution against the misuse of procedural justice and legitimacy to present a front of credibility that is used to manipulate and exploit individuals.

Efficiency

The DTC model represents a method of bringing efficiency and fairness to the detention system. Efficiency suggests that with limited resources, procedural protections cannot be an absolute. Yet, some unfair policies with a guise of efficiency, like a shoot-on-sight policy against suspected terrorists, would actually be incredibly costly when long-term effects on U.S. legitimacy are considered. At the other end of the spectrum, the trial of thousands of suspected terrorists under the U.S. criminal model is also tremendously ineffi-cient.[186] Implementing traditional evidence and jury requirements would be extremely costly and would create significant delays. Critics of Article III courts and international treaty-based terror courts note the impracticability and inefficiency of this system in the con-text of terrorism.[187]

Referring back to the problem of "the process as the punishment," weighing the additional delays and complications required under alternate models such as the traditional criminal justice system eclipses the marginal benefit of any additional rights provided by these models. Under the DTC model, efficiency and fairness work together, as both the detainee and the United States have an interest in expediting the judicial process. Of course, resources could be poured into the criminal system to allow a significantly larger caseload, yet, the proposed DTC model strikes a more suitable balance between efficiency and fairness that does not stretch either of these ideals beyond the point of diminishing returns. Just as judicial statutes allow courts to efficiently provide justice without reinventing the wheel on a case-by-case basis, the DTC framework is an efficient alternative to current ad hoc policies used to try terrorists.

Effectiveness

While short-term effectiveness often appears to be hampered by fair process, procedural justice and legitimacy are the building blocks of long-term effectiveness in the War on Terror. The famous ticking time bomb scenario, in which a terrorist is apprehended after hiding a bomb, is often used as an example justifying torture (procedural injustice) in the name of effectiveness. Choosing not to torture the suspected terrorist appears to compromise effectiveness and potentially sentence thousands of innocent civilians to death. Torture supporters argue that in such a situation the ends justify the means. However, substantial evidence suggests that torture marks the beginning of a slippery slope that ultimately undermines both fairness and effectiveness.[188]

Before analyzing the scenario itself, it is worth noting the improbability of a situation in which the terrorist is apprehended during this short window of time by government agents who understand the plot, but do not yet have enough information to find the bomb.[189] While television dramas frequently show the capture of a terrorist immediately before a massive attack, the reality is that such a situation is highly unlikely.[190] Yet, even in such a scenario, experts question the assumption that torture will be the most effective way to get information from this individual.[191] Professor John Langbein notes that, "[h]istory's most important lesson is that it has not been possible to make coercion compatible with truth." [192] Similarly, empirical evidence suggests that [e]ven if the terrorist begins to talk under torture, interrogators have a hard time figuring out whether he is telling the truth or not. Testing has found that professional interrogators perform within the 45 to 60% range in separating truth from lies—little better than flipping a coin. [193]

Next, this approach is problematic because it casts a wide net that potentially allows the torture of anyone that may have some knowledge of the bomb.[194] "[Y]ou end up going down a slippery slope and sanctioning torture in general," states Professor David Cole.[195] With the lives of thousands of individuals on the line, how far should this individual be tortured? Are any means off limits in such a scenario? What if torturing the alleged terrorist does not pro-duce results, but it is suspected that this individual will talk if the government tortures his six-year-old daughter in front of him? Inevitably, the ticking time bomb scenario leads full circle back to questions about legitimacy and fairness. If the United States is willing to venture down this slippery slope, it will, as the United States Army Field Manual section on torture indicates, "bring discredit upon the U.S. and its armed forces while undermining domestic and international support for the war effort." [196]

While this scenario represents the extreme example, all attempts to circumvent fairness in the name of effectiveness inevitably begin to move down this slippery slope. In a regime without clear rules, effectiveness becomes subsumed in necessity, and in a period of cri-sis, long-term costs are easily overshadowed by perceived short-term gains. It is possible to conceptualize a regime in which bureaucratic procedural red tape ties the hands of the military to a point where effectiveness is undermined. However, this is not the lesson of the last seven years. In contrast, U.S. policymakers are seeking to set rules and limits on a regime that has run largely unregulated and un-checked in the War on Terror.[197] The DTC model maintains effectiveness by recognizing inherent differences between suspected terrorists and domestic criminals. Yet, it also enhances fairness by granting specific procedural rights to detainees. Thus, under the DTC model, if Osama bin Laden was captured today, he would not receive a full Miranda warning or be immediately brought to trial before a jury, as a domestic criminal defendant would be. Yet, he also would not be indefinitely placed in a "black h ole" but would be brought before a judge within seven days. He would be guaranteed certain rights that would allow non-abusive interrogation but not torture. Regardless of whether valuable information is obtained through questioning, to go beyond the rules in this scenario would ultimately undermine both effectiveness and fairness in the long term. The DTC model establishes the correct balance by providing the tools to convict bin Laden without losing sight of his rights as a human being. In the eyes of a global audience, this model of guaranteed rules and rights enhances both legitimacy and long-term effectiveness in the War on Terror.

The Limits of Procedural Justice and Legitimacy

An important limitation of legitimacy is that it "does not address normative issues concerning whether people ought to defer to legal authorities and generally obey the law." [198] Thus, while legitimacy offers a way for the United States to obtain compliance with its policies, legitimacy fails to address whether these policies are inherently good or bad. Under a corrupt regime, legitimacy has the power to manipulate and exploit individuals by overshadowing questionable outcomes under the guise of fair process.[199] While recognizing that legitimacy and procedural justice can combat extremism, protect individual rights, and promote worldwide peace, they can also be misconstrued to achieve less desirable outcomes. Thus, while this paper has focused almost exclusively on process, we must ultimately also consider whether the outcomes derived from a given process align with the values that we want to pursue.

CONCLUSION

The War on Terrorism is an ideological struggle that can only be won through legitimizing the rule of law and undermining extremism. While governments often overreact in periods of crisis by trampling individual rights in the name of national security, govern-mental excess undermines the principle of legitimacy. In the context of terrorism, legitimacy, rather than deterrence, is primarily what shapes compliance with government policies. The DTC model enhances perceptions of legitimacy by providing a procedurally fair process designed specifically to try detainees. By properly balancing fairness, effectiveness, and efficiency, this model provides a workable solution that is better suited to the unique challenges involved in trying suspected terrorists than the vague standards employed by the current U.S. detention regime.

Notes

[1]. The term "War on Terror" became widely used during the presidency of George W. Bush, however this term has proved difficult to define. *See* Guy Raz, *Defining the War on Terrorism*, NPR (Nov. 1, 2006), http://www.npr.org/templates/story/story.php?storyId=6416780. The meaning of the "War on Terror" has evolved during conflicts in Afghanistan and Iraq. *See id.* With no clear beginning or end, and no traditional enemy to defeat, the "War on Terror" is more comparable to the "War on Drugs" or the "War on Poverty" than armed conflicts like World War I or World War II. *Id.*

[2]. Kevin E. Lunday & Harvey Rishikof, *Due Process Is a Strategic Choice: Legitimacy and the Establishment of an Article III National Security Court*, 39 CAL. W. INT' L L.J. 87, 87 (2008).

[3]. *See* STEVEN R. CORMAN ET AL., CONSORTIUM FOR STRATEGIC COMMC'N,

CREDIBILITY IN THE GLOBAL WAR ON TERRORISM: STRATEGIC PRINCIPLES AND

RESEARCH AGENDA 3 (2006), *available at* http://comops.org/article/117.pdf.

[4]. *See id.* at 3–4.

[5]. Lunday & Rishikof, *supra* note 2, at 89–90

[6]. *See, e.g.*, Richard H. Fallon, Jr. & Daniel J. Meltzer, *Habeas Corpus Juris-diction, Substantive Rights, and the War on Terror*, 120 Harv. L. Rev. 2029, 2031 (2007); Tamara Huckert, *The Undetermined Fate of the Guantanamo Bay Detai-nees' Habeas Corpus Petitions*, 9 GONZ. J. INT' L L. 236, 237 (2006); Johan Steyn,

Guantanamo Bay: The Legal Black Hole, 53 INT' L & COMP. L.Q. 1, 1 (2004).

[7]Robert J. MacCoun, *Voice, Control, and Belonging: The Double-Edged Sword of Procedural Fairness*, 1 ANN. REV. L. & SOC. SCI. 171, 180 (2005).

[8]Fathali M. Moghaddam, *The Staircase to Terrorism: A Psychological Explo-ration*, 60 AM. PSYCHOLOGIST 161, 161 (2005).

[9]. *Id*

[10]. *Id.*; *see also* TOM R. TYLER & YUEN J. HUO, TRUST IN THE LAW:

ENCOURAGING PUBLIC COOPERATION WITH THE POLICE AND COURTS 218 (2002).

[11]. *See* Michael Freeman, *Democracy, Al Qaeda, and the Causes of Terrorism:*

A Strategic Analysis of U.S. Policy, 31 STUD. CONFLICT & TERRORISM 40, 41 (2008).

[12]. Laurence Miller, *The Terrorist Mind*, 50 INT' L J. OFFENDER THERAPY & COMP. CRIMINOLOGY 121, 121 (2006); *see also* Andrew Silke, *Fire of Iolaus: The Role of State Countermeasures in Causing Terrorism and What Needs to Be Done*, *in* ROOT CAUSES OF TERRORISM: MYTHS, REALITY, AND WAYS FORWARD 246 (Tore Bjorgo ed., 2005); Freeman, *supra* note 11, at 41; Tim Krieger & Daniel Meierrieks, *What Causes Terrorism?* 4 (Ctr. for Int'l Econs., Working Paper No. 12, 2008).

[13]. Moghaddam, *supra* note 8, at 161.

[14]. *Id.* at 162.

[15]. *Id.*

[16]. *Id.*

[17]. *Id.*

[18]. *Id*

[19]. Moghaddam, *supra* note 8, at 162.

[20]. *See, e.g.*, Lunday & Rishikof, *supra* note 2, at 101–03.

[21]. *See* Jules Lobel, *The Preventive Paradigm and the Perils of Ad Hoc Balanc-ing*, 91 MINN. L. REV. 1407, 1420–21 (2007).

[22]. Dave Moniz & Tom Squitieri, *After Grim Rumsfeld Memo, White House Supports Him*, USA TODAY, Oct. 22, 2003, http://www.usatoday.com/news/wash ington/2003-10-22-defense-memo-usat_x.htm.

[23]. *See* Lunday & Rishikof, *supra* note 2, at 90–93.

[24]. Lobel, *supra* note 21, at 1411–14.

[25]. *Id*

[26]William J. Brennan, Jr., Assoc. J., U.S. Sup. Ct., The Quest to Develop a Jurisprudence of Civil Liberties in Times of Security Crises, Speech at the Law School of Hebrew University, Jerusalem (Dec. 22, 1987), http://www.hofstra.edu/ PDF/law_civil_hafetz_article1.pdf.

[27]Lobel, *supra* note 21, at 1413.

[28]. *See id.* at 1411–12.

[29]. Steyn, *supra* note 6, at 1–2, 8.

[30]. THE PEW RESEARCH CTR. FOR THE PEOPLE &

THE PRESS, A YEAR AFTER IRAQ WAR, MISTRUST OF AMERICA IN EUROPE EVER HIGHER, MUSLIM ANGER PERSISTS 2 (2004), http://people-press.org/reports/pdf/206.pdf.

[31]. *Id.*

[32]. CORMAN ET AL., *supra* note 3, at 3

[33]. *Id.*

[34]. *See generally Guantanamo Bay [GTMO] "GITMO,"* GLOBALSECURITY.ORG, http://www.globalsecurity.org/military/facility/guantan amo-bay.htm (last visited Feb. 17, 2011) (discussing the history of Guantanamo Bay).

[35]. *See, e.g.*, Kal Raustiala, *Is Bagram the New Guantánamo? Habeas Corpus and Maqaleh v. Gates*, ASIL INSIGHTS (June 17, 2009), http://www.asil.org/in sights090618.cfm.

[36]. *See Officials: Taliban's New Top Operations Officer Is Former Guantanamo Bay Detainee*, FOX NEWS (Mar. 10, 2009), http://www.foxnews.com/story/ 0,2933, 508506,00.html.

[37]Amos N. Guiora, *Creating a Domestic Terror Court*, 48 WASHBURN L.J. 617, 625 (2009).

[38]Adam Zagorin, *Exclusive: Charges Sought Against Rumsfeld Over Prison Abuse*, TIME, Nov. 10, 2006, http://www.time.com/time/printout/0,8816, 1557842,00.html.

[39]*See, e.g., Tipton Three Complain of Beatings*, BBC NEWS (Mar. 14, 2004), http://news.bbc.co.uk/2/hi/uk_news/3509750.stm.

[40]*See, e.g.*, SEYMOUR M. HERSH, CHAIN OF COMMAND: THE ROAD FROM 9/11 TO ABU GHRAIB 20 (2004)

[41]. See id. at 39–40.

[42]. Andy Worthington, Former Insider Shatters Credibility of Military Commissions, Describes Brutal Treatment of Teenage Detainee, ALTERNET (July 13, 2009), http://www.alternet.org/rights/141267/former_insider_shatters_credibility_of_military_commissions,_describes_brutal_treatment_of_teenage_detainee.

[43]. Id.

[44]. Id.

[45]. Id.

[46]. Commission on Human Rights: Independent Experts Issue Report on Guan-tanamo Detainees, UN NEWS CENTER (Feb. 16, 2006), http://www.un.org/apps/ news/story.asp?NewsID–17523&Cr=Guant%E1namo&Cr1=Bay.

[47]. AMNESTY INT' L, UNITED STATES OF AMERICA, THE THREAT OF A BAD

EXAMPLE: UNDERMINING INTERNATIONAL STANDARDS AS "W AR ON TERROR"

DETENTIONS CONTINUE 21 (2003), http://www.amnesty.org/en/library/asset/ AMR51/114/2003/en/48a8fe0c-d6a7-11dd-ab95-a13b602c0642/amr51114200 3en.pdf [hereinafter THREAT OF A BAD EXAMPLE]

[48]Pamela M. von Ness, *Guantanamo Bay Detainees: National Security or Civil Liberty*, U.S. ARMY WAR C. 5 (2003), http://www.pegc.us/archive/DoD/docs/ vonness.pdf.

[49]Robert W. Tucker & David C. Hendrickson, *The Sources of American Legitimacy*, 83 FOREIGN AFFS. 18, 18–19 (2004), *available at* http://www.jstor.org/ pss/20034134.

[50]Tom R. Tyler, *Psychological Perspectives on Legitimacy and Legitimation*, 57 ANN. REV. PSYCH. 375, 375 (2006) [hereinafter Tyler, *Psychological Perspectives*].

[51]*Id.* at 376.

[52]TOM R. TYLER, WHY PEOPLE OBEY THE LAW 60 (1990) [hereinafter TYLER, OBEY THE LAW].

[53]. *Id.* at 63

[54]. Moghaddam, *supra* note 8, at 168.

[55]Gregory S. McNeal, *Institutional Legitimacy and Counterterrorism Trials*, 43 U. RICH. L. REV. 967, 967 (2009).

[56]Tyler, *Psychological Perspectives*, *supra* note 50, at 381.

[57]JAMES L. GIBSON, OVERCOMING APARTHEID: CAN TRUTH RECONCILE A

DIVIDED NATION? 289 (2004).

[58]Tom R. Tyler & Gregory Mitchell, *Legitimacy and the Empowerment of Discretionary Legal Authority: The United States Supreme Court and Abortion Rights*, 43 DUKE L.J. 703, 780 (1994).

[59]*Id.* at 714.

[60] *Id*

[61]. 505 U.S. 833 (1992); Tyler & Mitchell, *supra* note 58, at 749.

[62]*Abortion and Birth Control*, POLLING REPORT, http://www.pollingre port.com/abortion.htm (last visited Feb. 17, 2011).

[63]*See id.*

[64]Tucker & Hendrickson, *supra* note 49, at 24.

[65]. *See id.* at 19–23.

[66]. RONALD REAGAN, A SHINING CITY: THE LEGACY OF RONALD REAGAN 178 (D. Erik Felten ed., 1998).

[67]. *France Calls Guantanamo 'An Embarrassment*,*'* EXPATICA (Feb. 20, 2006), http://www.expatica.com/fr/news/local_news/france-calls-guantanamo-an-embarrassment-27768.html.

[68]. *Colin Powell Says Guantanamo Should Be Closed*, REUTERS (June 10, 2007), http://www.reuters.com/article/idUSN1013646920070610

[69]. *Promises to Keep: Candidate Obama vs. President Obama*, FOX NEWS (Nov. 1, 2009), http://www.foxnews.com/politics/2009/10/23/pub-obama-campaign-promises/ [hereinafter *Promises to Keep*].

[70]. Tucker & Hendrickson, *supra* note 49, at 28.

[71]. *See Promises to Keep*, *supra* note 69.

[72]. *See id.*

[73]Tyler, *Psychological Perspectives*, *supra* note 50, at 382.

[74] MacCoun, *supra* note 7, at 180; *see also* Lawrence B. Solum, *Procedural Justice*, 78 S. CAL. L. REV. 181, 183 (2004) (noting that the concept of procedural justice is "deeply entwined with the old and powerful idea that a process that guarantees rights of meaningful participation is an essential prerequisite for the legitimate authority of action-guiding legal norms").

[75]Tyler & Mitchell, *supra* note 58, at 799.

[76]Rebecca Hollander-Blumoff & Tom R. Tyler, *Procedural Justice in Negotiation: Procedural Fairness, Outcome Acceptance, and Integrative Potential*, 33 L. SOC. INQUIRY 473, 477 (2008). *See generally* JOHN THIBAUT & LAURENS WALKER, PROCEDURAL JUSTICE: A PSYCHOLOGICAL ANALYSIS (1975).

[77]. Jason A. Colquitt et al., *Justice at the Millennium: A Meta-Analytic Review of 25 Years of Organizational Justice Research*, 86 J. APPLIED PSYCHOL. 425, 426 (2001).

[78]. *Id.*

[79]. *Id.* at 434–35.

[80]. *See* Jonathan D. Casper et al., *Procedural Justice in Felony Cases*, 22 L. & SOC. REV. 483, 483 (1988)

[81]. *Id.* at 503.

[82]. Tom R. Tyler, *The Role of Perceived Injustice in Defendants' Evaluations of Their Courtroom Experience*, 18 L. & SOC. REV. 51, 69–71 (1984) [hereinafter Tyler, *Perceived Injustice*].

[83]E. Allan Lind & Kees van den Bos, *When Fairness Works: Toward a Gener-al Theory of Uncertainty Management*, 24 RES. IN ORGANIZATIONAL BEHAV. 181, 184 (2002).

[84]*See Some Guantanamo Bay Detainees May Be Held Indefinitely*, VOANEWS

(July 10, 2009), http://www.voanews.com/english/news/a-13-2009-07-10-voa6-68789562.html.

[85]JOEL BROCKNER, A CONTEMPORARY LOOK AT ORGANIZATIONAL JUSTICE: MULTIPLYING INSULT TIMES INJURY 75 (2010).

[86]. RHONDA WASSERMAN, PROCEDURAL DUE PROCESS: A REFERENCE GUIDE TO THE UNITED STATES CONSTITUTION 99–100 (2004)

[87]. BROCKNER, *supra* note 85, at 33.

[88]. *Id.* at 33–35.

[89]HERSH, *supra* note 40, at 19–20.

[90]*See* LARRY J. SIEGEL, INTRODUCTION TO CRIMINAL JUSTICE 179–80 (12th ed. 2010).

[91]Gerald S. Leventhal et al., *Beyond Fairness: A Theory of Allocation Preferences*, *in* JUSTICE AND SOCIAL INTERACTION 167 (Gerold Mikula ed., 1980).

[92] *Id.* at 195–96; T YLER, OBEY THE LAW, *supra* note 52, at 118

[93]. *See* Guiora, *supra* note 37, at 619.

[94]. *See id.*

[95]Leventhal et al., *supra* note 91, at 195.

[96]*See* TYLER, OBEY THE LAW, *supra* note 52, at 118–19.

[97]*See id.*

[98] Lobel, *supra* note 21, at 1419–420

[99]. *See* Jim Lobe, *Post-9/11 Immigrant Roundup Backfired—Report* , INTER PRESS SERVICE (June 26, 2003), http://ipsnews.net/interna.asp?idnews=19000.

[100]. Lobel, *supra* note 21, at 1419–420.

[101]. *Id.* at 1420.

[102]. *Id.*

[103]Lobe, *supra* note 99.

[104]Lobel, *supra* note 21, at 1420.

[105]*Id.* at 1420–22.

[106]*Id.* at 1421.

[107]. *See* OFFICE OF THE UNITED NATIONS HIGH COMMISSIONER FOR HUMAN RIGHTS, THE RIGHTS OF NON-CITIZENS, at 7–13, U.N. Sales No. E.07.XIV (2006), *available at* http://www.ohchr.org/Documents/Publications/noncitizensen. pdf.

[108]553 U.S. 723 (2008).

[109]*See id.* at 739.

[110]Ronald Dworkin, *Why It Was a Great Victory*, 55 N.Y. REV. BOOKS, No. 13, Aug. 14, 2008, at 2.

[111]*See id.*

[112]*See* Steyn, *supra* note 6, at 9.

[113]*Id.*

[114]*See generally* Boumediene v. Bush, 553 U.S. 723 (2008)

[115]Guiora, *supra* note 37, at 631.

[116]*See generally* Tyler, *Perceived Injustice*, *supra* note 82.

[117]548 U.S. 557 (2006).

[118]McNeal, *supra* note 55, at 999.

[119]*Id.* at 972–73, 999.

[120]Guiora, *supra* note 37, at 631–32.

[121]*Id.* at 632.

[122]*Americans Support Full Due-Process Rights for Terrorism Suspects*, WORLD PUBLIC OPINION (July 17, 2006), http://www.worldpublicopinion.org/pipa/articles/ home_page/228.php?nid=&id=&pnt=228&lb=hmpg1.

[123] *Id*

[124]. *See* SUE MAHAN & PAMALA L. GRISET, TERRORISM IN PERSPECTIVE 324 (2nd ed. 2008).

[125]. *See* TYLER, OBEY THE LAW, *supra* note 52, at 119.

[126]. *See id.*

[127]. *See id.*

[128]. *See generally* PAUL BERGMAN & SARA J. BERMAN, THE CRIMINAL LAW HANDBOOK: KNOW YOUR RIGHTS, SURVIVE THE SYSTEM (Richard Stim ed., 11th ed. 2009).

[129]. *See* Harold Hongju Koh, *The Case Against Military Commissions*, 96 AM. J. INT' L L. 337, 341 (2002)

[130]Steyn, *supra* note 6, at 9–10.

[131]*Id.* at 9.

[132]*See* BRADLEY F. SMITH, REACHING JUDGMENT AT NUREMBERG 300 (1977).

[133]*Id.* at 151.

[134] *See* Amy Ross, *The Body Counts: Civilian Casualties and the Crisis of Hu-man Rights*, *in* HUMAN RIGHTS IN CRISIS 39 (Alice Bullard ed. 2008)

[135]. Mark Tran, *US Is Not at War with Islam, Says Barack Obama*, GUARDIAN (Apr. 6, 2009), http://www.guardian.co.uk/world/2009/apr/06/barack-obama-turkey-armenia.

[136]. *Id.*

[137]McNeal, *supra* note 55, at 975–76.

[138]*Virtual Tour—Camp Five*, JOINT TASK FORCE GUANTANAMO, http://www.jtfgtmo.southcom.mil/virtualvisit/camp_5.html (last visited Feb. 17, 2011).

[139]*Id.*

[140]. McNeal, *supra* note 55 at 977

[141]. *See id.* at 992–93.

[142]. Guiora, *supra* note 37, at 619.

[143]. *See, e.g.*, Christopher Flavelle, *You Can Check Out Anytime You Like, But You Can Never Leave: At Least 17 Detainees Have Been Ordered Released from Guantanamo But are Stuck There*, SLATE (Oct. 12, 2009), http://www.slate.com/id/2232000/.

[144]. *See generally USA: Detainees Continue to Bear the Costs of Delay and Lack of Remedy*, AMNESTY INT' L (Apr. 9, 2009), http://www.amnestyusa.org/docu ment.php?id=ENGAMR510502009&lang=e

[145]. *Id.*

[146]Peter Baker, *Obama to Use Current Law to Support Detentions*, N.Y. TIMES, Sept. 23, 2009, at A23.

[147] Guiora, *supra* note 37, at 631

[148]. *See* TYLER, OBEY THE LAW, *supra* note 52, at 119.

[149]. *See, e.g.*, SUP. CT. R. 10

[150]. *See* Dworkin, *supra* note 110, at 2.

[151]. *See id.*

[152]. Pub. L. No. 109-148, § 1005, 119 Stat. 2739, 2742 (2005).

[153]. Pub. L. No. 109-366, § 7, 120 Stat. 2600, 2636 (2006) (amended 2009).

[154]. *See* Dworkin, *supra* note 110, at 2.

[155]. *See id.*

[156]Mark Mazzetti & William Glaberson, *Obama Issues Directive to Shut Down Guantánamo*, N.Y. TIMES, Jan. 21, 2009, at A1.

[157]Dworkin, *supra* note 110, at 2.

[158]. *Id*

[159]. *See* Guiora, *supra* note 37, at 632.

[160]. *See id.* at 619.

[161]. *See* TYLER, OBEY THE LAW, *supra* note 52, at 118

[162]. THREAT OF A BAD EXAMPLE, *supra* note 47, at 1.

[163]. Lunday & Rishikof, *supra* note 2, at 101.

[164]. *See* TYLER, OBEY THE LAW, *supra* note 52, at 119.

[165]. *See id.*

[166]. Gerard P. Fogarty, *Guantanamo Bay—Undermining the Global War on Terror*, U.S. ARMY WAR C. 10 (2005), http://www.dtic.mil/cgi-bin/GetTRDoc?Location=U2&doc=GetTRDoc.pdf&AD=ADA434467

[167]. *See generally* Lunday & Rishikof, *supra* note 2, at 87.

[168]LAWRENCE W. SHERMAN ET AL., NAT' L INST. OF JUSTICE, PREVENTING CRIME: WHAT WORKS, WHAT DOESN'T, WHAT'S PROMISING, at ch. 8 (1997), *available at* http://www.ncjrs.gov/works/wholedoc.htm.

[169]Michael Roston, *Congress Members Sponsor Bill to Shutter Guantanamo Bay*, RAW STORY (May 8, 2007), http://rawstory.com/news/2007/Congress_ mem-bers_sponsor_bill_to_shutter_0508.html.

[170]John O'Sullivan, *Left Eye's View: Seeing Through the Abu Ghraib Cover-age*, NAT' L REV. ONLINE (May 18, 2004), http://www.nationalreview.com/ jos/jos2004 05181427.asp.

[171] *See id*

[172]. David Gardner, *U.S. Lost Its Moral Bearing Over Torture, Says Obama— and Warns Bush Officials Could Be Charged*, MAILONLINE (April 21, 2009), http://www.dailymail.co.uk/news/worldnews/article-1172239/U-S-lost-moral-bearings-torture-says-Obama--warns-Bush-officials-charged.html.

[173]. Press Release, BBC World Service, World Citizens Reject Torture, Global Poll Reveals 1 (2006), http://www.globescan.com/news_archives/bbctorture06.

[174]. *See id.* at 3.

[175]. *Id.* at 1.

[176]. *Id.* at 2.

[177]. *Id.* at 2 (noting that India has signed, but not ratified, the Convention Against Torture)

[178]. *See* Brenda Sims Blackwell & Clark D. Cunningham, *Taking the Punishment Out of the Process: From Substantive Criminal Justice Through Procedural Jus-tice to Restorative Justice*, 67 L. & CONTEMP. PROBS. 59, 60 (2004).

[179]. *Id.* at 59–60.

[180]. Guiora, *supra* note 37, at 628.

[181]. *Id*

[182]. *Id.* at 627.

[183]. *Id.* at 626–27.

[184]. *See id.* at 619.

[185]. *See, e.g.*, Letta Tayler, *U.S. at Odds over World Tribunal*, NEWSDAY 1–6 (Oct. 17, 2004), http://www.amicc.org/docs/Newsday%2010-17-04.pdf

[186]. *See, e.g.*, Guiora, *supra* note 37, at 620.

[187]. *See, e.g.*, *id*

[188]Amos N. Guiora, *Military Commissions and National Security Courts After Guantanamo*, 103 NW. U. L. REV. COLLOQUY 199, 201 (2008).

[189]*See* Alfred W. McCoy, *The Myth of the Ticking Time Bomb*, PROGRESSIVE (Oct. 2006), http://www.progressive.org/mag_mccoy1006.

[190]*Id.*

[191]*Id.*

[192] *Id*

[193]. *Id.*

[194]. *Id.*

[195]. McCoy, *supra* note 189.

[196]. *Id.*

[197]. David Abraham, *The Bush Regime from Elections to Detentions: A Moral Economy of Carl Schmitt and Human Rights*, 62 U. MIAMI L. REV. 249, 267 (2008)

[198]Tom R. Tyler, *Procedural Justice, Legitimacy, and the Effective Rule of Law*, CRIME & JUST. 283, 285 (2003).

[199] *See* MacCoun, *supra* note 7, at 189–90

REFERENCES

1. Adaman, F., Carkoglu, A., & Senatalar, B. (2005). Toplumun Kamu Yönetimine ve Kamu Hizmetlerine ve Reforma Bakışı. Istanbul: TESEV Yayinlari.
2. Adaman, F., Carkoglu, A., & Senatalar, B. (2009). Hanehalki Gozunden Kamu Hizmetleri ve Yolsuzluk (Vol. 43). Ankara: TEPAV.
3. Adana Genel Degerlendirme. (n.d.). Retrieved October 12, 2013, from http://www.adanabld.gov.tr/genel-degerlendirme-sayfa.html.
4. Aytac, O. (2005, May 1), Halkın Polise Bakışı: Güveniyorum ama Rüşvetçi ve Kaba. Retrieved October 5, 2013, from http://www.memurlar.net/haber/20671/
5. Bal, I., & Laciner, S. (2008). The Ideological and Historical Roots of the Kurdist Movements in Turkey. Nationalism and Ethnic Politics. 10(3), 473–504.
6. Balci, H. (2012). An Analysis of Human Rights Violations of The Turkish Security Forces During the European Union Harmonization Process of Turkey. (Ph.D.). Rutgers The State University of New Jersey - Newark, United States - New Jersey.
7. Beetham, D. (1991). The Legitimation of Power. Palgrave Macmillan.
8. Berry, W. (1993). Understanding Regression Assumptions. Newbury Park, USA: Sage Publications. Cao, L., & Burton, V. S. (2006). Spanning the continents: assessing the Turkish public confidence in the police. Policing: An International Journal of Police Strategies & Management, 29(3), 451–463.
9. Cao, L., & Zhao, J. S. (2005). Confidence in the police in Latin America. Journal of Criminal Justice, 33(5), 403–412.
10. Carr, P. J., Napolitano, L., & Keating, J. (2007). We Never Call the Cops and Here Is Why: A Qualitative Examination of Legal Cynicism in Three Philadelphia Neighborhoods. Criminology, 45(2), 445–480.
11. Cerrah, I., Cevik, H. H., Goksu, T., & Balcioglu, E. (2009). Ethical Conduct in Law Enforcement: A study of routine corruption in traffic services of major cities in Turkey. Ankara: Council of Ethics for the Public Service
12. Davis, R. C., Mateu-Gelabert, P., & Miller, J. (2005). Can Effective Policing Also Be Respectful? Two Examples in the South Bronx. Police Quarterly, 8(2), 229–247.
13. Demaris, A. (1992). Logit Modeling: Practical Applications. Beverly Hills, CA: Sage Publications.
14. Dix, M. C., & Layzell, A. D. (1983). Road Users and the Police. London: Croom Helm.
15. Dönmezer, S. (1979). Trafikte Polis-Halk İliskileri. İstanbul Üniversitesi Hukuk Fakültesi Mecmuası, 45(1-4), 571–583.
16. Durmaz, H. (2007, August). Officer attitudes toward organizational change in the Turkish National Police. University of North Texas. Retrieved from http://digital.library.unt.edu/ark:/67531/metadc3977/
17. Ehliyet sorması değil hoyratlığı rencide etti. (2013) Retrieved November 11, 2013, from http://www.ntvmsnbc.com/id/25441109/
18. Elphiston, W. G. (1946). The Kurdish Question. International Affairs, 22 (1), 91-103.
19. Engel, R. S. (2005). Citizens' Perceptions of Distributive and Procedural Injustice During Traffic Stops with Police. Journal of Research in Crime and Delinquency, 42(4), 445–481.
20. Farrington, D. P. (1983). Randomized Experiments on Crime and Justice. Crime and Justice, 4, 257–308.
21. Farrington, D. P. (1997). Evaluating a community crime prevention program. Evaluation, 3(2), 157-173
22. Farrington, D. P., & Welsh, B. C. (2005). Randomized experiments in criminology: What have we learned in the last two decades? Journal of Experimental Criminology, 1(1), 9–38.
23. Gau, J. M., & Brunson, R. K. (2010). Procedural Justice and Order Maintenance Policing: A Study of Inner- City Young Men's Perceptions of Police Legitimacy. Justice Quarterly, 27(2), 255–279.
24. Greene, J. A. (1999). Zero Tolerance: A Case Study of Police Policies and Practices in New York City. Crime & Delinquency, 45(2), 171–187.
25. Holgado-Tello, F.P., Chacon-Moscoso, S., Barbero-Garcia, I, & Vila-Abad, E. (2010). Polychoric versus Pearson Correlations in Exploratory and Confirmatory Factor Analysis of Ordinal Variables. Quality & Quantity; International Journal of Methodology, 1, 153-166.
26. Hough, M., Jackson, J., Bradford, B., Myhill, A., & Quinton, P. (2010). Procedural Justice, Trust, and Institutional Legitimacy. Policing, 4(3), 203–210.
27. Ingram J. (2007). The Effect of Neighborhood Characteristics on Traffic Citation Practices of the Police. Police Quarterly. 10(4). 371-393.
28. Kabukcu, Gokhan. (2006). Active Citizenship and Community Policing in Turkey. Middle East Technical University (METU), Ankara.
29. Karakus, O., McGarrell, E. F., & Basibuyuk, O. (2011). Public satisfaction with law enforcement in Turkey. Policing: An International Journal of Police Strategies & Management, 34(2), 304–325.
30. Lipsey, M. W. (1989). Design Sensitivity: Statistical Power for Experimental Research (1st ed.). Thousand Oaks, CA: SAGE Publications, Inc.
31. Long, J. (John) S. (1997). Regression Models for Categorical and Limited Dependent Variables (1st ed.). USA: SAGE Publications, Inc.
32. Mutlu, K. (2000). Problems of nepotism and favouritism in the police organization in Turkey. Policing: An International Journal of Police Strategies & Management, 23(3), 381–389.
33. Neild, R. (2007). USAID Program Brief: Anticorruption and Police Integrity (Security Sector Reform Program) (p. 26). Vermont: USAID. Retrieved from http://pdf.usaid.gov/pdf_docs/PNADN948.pdf
34. Ortiz C.W., Hendricks N.J. & Sugie N.F. (2007). Policing Terrorism: The Response of Local Police Agencies to Homeland Security Concerns, Criminal Justice Studies: A Critical Journal of Crime, Law and Society, 20(2), 91-109.

35. Ozbaran, Y. (2010). The Relationship between Turkish Traffic Enforcement Officers' Job Satisfaction and Officers' Perception of Their Leaders' Leadership Styles. University of Texas at Dallas, Dallas.

36. Petrosino, A. J., Boruch, R. F., Farrington, D. P., Sherman, L. W. & Weisburd, D. (2003). Toward evidence-based criminology and criminal justice: Systematic reviews, the Campbell Collaboration, and the Crime and Justice Group. International Journal of Comparative Criminology, 3, 42-61.

37. Petrosino, A., Kiff, P., & Lavenberg, J. (2006). Research Note: Randomized field experiments published in the British Journal of Criminology, 1960–2004. Journal of Experimental Criminology, 2(1), 99–111.

38. Radelet, L. A., & Carter, D. L. (1998). The Police and the Community (6 Sub.). Prentice Hall.

39. Raudenbush, S. W., Martinez, A., & Spybrook, J. (2007). Strategies for Improving Precision in Group-Randomized Experiments. Educational Evaluation and Policy Analysis, 29(1), 5–29.

40. Sunshine, J., & Tyler, T. R. (2003). The Role of Procedural Justice and Legitimacy in Shaping Public Support for Policing. Law & Society Review, 37(3), 513–548.

41. Sweet, S.A. & Grace-Martin, K. (2008). Data Analysis with SPSS, Boston, MA: Pearson.

42. Taylor, B., Koper, C. S., & Woods, D. J. (2011). A randomized controlled trial of different policing strategies at hot spots of violent crime. Journal of Experimental Criminology, 7(2), 149–181.

43. Teymur, S. & Smith C.J. (2008). The PKK: A Decades-Old Brutal Marxist-Leninist Separatist Terrorist Organization. Washington: TISD.

44. Unal, M. C. (2009). Turkish Responses to Violence by the Kurdistan Workers' Party (PKK): Policy Choices and Policy Effects. University of Maryland, Baltimore County.

45. Walker, J. T. and L. (1975). Procedural Justice: A Psychological Analysis. Lawrence Erlbaum Associates, Inc.

46. Warren, P. Y. (2011). Perceptions of Police Disrespect During Vehicle Stops: A RaceBased Analysis. Crime & Delinquency, 57(3), 356–376.

47. Weisburd, D. (2005). Hot Spots Policing Experiments and Criminal Justice Research: Lessons from the Field. Annals of the American Academy of Political and Social Science, 599, 220–245.

48. Yalcinkaya A. (2012) Polis Halk İlişkilerini Olumlu Yönde Katalizleyecek Unsurlar ve İzlenmesi Gereken Yol. Polis Akademisi: Ankara. Retrieved from http://perweb.firat.edu.tr/personel/yayinlar/fua_35/35_65788.doc

49. Yılmaz, A., & Demirci, M. K. (2004). Polis-Halk İlişkilerini Vatandaşların Değerlendirmeleri zerine Bir Araştırma. Dumlupınar Üniversitesi Sosyal Bilimler Dergisi, 11, 83–100.

CHAPTER 3

INTERNATIONAL COURTS IN ATYPICAL POLITICAL ENVIRONMENTS: THE INTERPLAY OF PROSECUTORIAL STRATEGY, EVIDENCE, AND COURT AUTHORITY IN INTERNATIONAL CRIMINAL LAW

Ron Levi, John Hagan and Sara Dezalay

INTRODUCTION

The reemergence of a professional field of international criminal law at the end of the twentieth and beginning of the twenty-first century—including prominent institutions such as the International Criminal Tribunal for Rwanda, the International Criminal Tribunal for the former Yugoslavia (ICTY), and the permanent International Criminal Court (ICC)—has reshaped how atrocities are handled at the international level. For the first time since International Military Tribunals (IMTs) at Nuremberg and in the Far East, a legal and normative logic of individual criminal accountability reemerged to respond to massive human rights violations.[1] This framework revived the legacy of Nuremberg and Tokyo, which established modern legal claims of international judicial and court authority. With legal authority delegated to ad hoc international tribunals by the UN Security Council, and with the ICC acquiring legal or de jure authority through treaty obligations or through the UN Security Council, over the past three decades we have witnessed the expansion of an institutional and professional field of "normative legalism" that, outside of the European Court of Human Rights, enjoyed no authority—legal or otherwise during the Cold War.[2]

Given the coercive nature of international criminal courts, and the challenges they present to state sovereignty and sovereign immunity, we identify the geopolitical context as crucial to delineating the scope of authority that these courts enjoy.[3] Indeed, the importance of geopolitical context is evident in the very lead-up to the creation of this field of international criminal law, because even achieving de jure authority has been contentious.[4] And even such courts' de facto authority that resulted in sovereign legal accountability for such crimes was developed in national settings for many years during the Cold War before gaining significant political support on the international stage.[5]

The creation of the International Criminal Tribunals for Rwanda and the former Yugoslavia, along with other specialized ad hoc courts and tribunals from the 1990s forward, built on these approaches to emphasize human rights enforcement through personal responsibility and punishment.[6] By the time the Rome Statute, which created the ICC, was adopted in 1998, the authority of international criminal law had expanded and deepened through the landmark practices of these earlier ad hoc tribunals and the political momentum that supported their work. When one examines the narrow legal authority of these post–World War II and post–Cold War Tribunals—the growth in their legal mandate, the number of courts, the doctrinal expansion of the approach to prosecuting war crimes from the 1990s forward, and the creation of a permanent ICC in their wake—it is tempting to develop a teleological account of the expansion in de jure (and de facto) authority in the field of international criminal law.[7] Yet a teleological account tends to downplay both fine-grained questions that an analysis of de facto authority requires, and also the capacity to gauge the authority of specific courts rather than of the wider field. This article instead analyzes two broad elements: First, the *contextual factors* that shape the authority of international courts, in particular the constituencies they can mobilize, the geopolitical context in which they operate, and their relations with national fields of power; and second,

Citation: Ron Levi, John Hagan and Sara Dezalay, International Courts in Atypical Political Environments: The Interplay of Prosecutorial Strategy, Evidence, and Court Authority in International Criminal Law, http://scholarship.law.duke.edu/cgi/viewcontent.cgi?article=4775&context=lcp

connected to these, the *international legal practices* that these courts and their actors develop.[8] It is this *dual* approach to understanding authority—the articulation between practices and contextual factors, with court practices continuously adapting to external contexts—that we operationalize through the study of international criminal courts.[9]

International criminal courts uniquely draw together these two indicators of authority, with external contextual factors deeply connected to the internal legal practices that these courts go on to develop. This is because international criminal courts operate in what criminal justice scholars identify as "atypical political environments," or highly contentious environments in which surrounding political conditions lead to a departure from routinized criminal justice, so that courts must develop organizational models to cope with, mobilize, and at times deflect, the political landscape in which they operate.[10]

In international criminal courts, such atypical political environments are the norm rather than the exception. For instance, during ongoing conflicts or when dealing with uncooperative states, international criminal courts face unique constraints on their authority—including both the absence of police or arrest authority and limitations on searches and seizure opportunities—requiring prosecutors to develop new evidentiary approaches.[11] Similarly, national governments, their leaders, and their allies often contest the very idea of international criminal prosecutions, so that with every move to build authority these courts can find themselves losing, rather than gaining, adherents and potential legal cases.[12] So, in atypical environments, some of the usual strategies courts could develop to gain wider authority are often unavailable.

Precisely because of these contextual features, we turn to prosecutorial strategies as a salient practice for assessing the authority of international criminal courts. Prosecutorial practices are not the only factor relevant to an international criminal court's authority; but, in these environments, it is the decision to investigate, to prosecute, and to adduce evidence that is the most noticed and dramatic feature of their work, and that is central to their capacity to garner, retain, and expand its audiences and support. This article thus focuses on prosecutorial practices rather than the increases in case volume or the changes in enforcement mechanisms that other international courts use to build constituencies. These strategies work to enhance the authority of international criminal courts in the face of built-in challenges by aligning or deflecting geopolitical factors and constituencies. In other words, prosecutorial practices link the internal bureaucratic organization of these courts to their geopolitical contexts, and the authority of international criminal justice is augmented or constrained through choices that prosecutors develop and through the constituencies to which the prosecutors are oriented in employing these practices.[13]

INTERNATIONAL COURT AUTHORITY IN ATYPICAL POLITICAL ENVIRONMENTS: PROSECUTORIAL STRATEGY AND EVIDENCE

This article thus emphasizes links between prosecutorial strategy, legal evidence, and methods of case development that are crucial for constructing the authority of international criminal courts. Indeed, once one looks beyond the "high politics"[14] question of jurisdiction—which, in the case of these courts, is what implicates their capacity to operate and gain custody over situations and individuals—one quickly recognizes that the question of evidence, its production, and its use in court represent the sort of *practices* that Alter, Helfer, and Madsen identify as international "legal practices" through which officials build authority.[15]

Whereas in many courts international legal practices are linked to how international judges build authority, in the case of international criminal courts the key location for these practices lies upstream in the process, in the office of the prosecutor. Economic and human rights courts are often dependent on the facts and arguments adduced by external litigants; however, in international criminal prosecutions, the in-house indictment and the presentation of evidence produce alliances with external constituencies, and the authority that international criminal justice garners is augmented or constrained by the scope of the network these courts can build. Similarly, indictments and the presentation of evidence are central for building court authority rather than pursuing other international alternatives. Indeed, gaining any toehold is a challenge because salient actors are more likely to snub the prosecutor's indictment or to comply with evidentiary demands than to rebuff a final judgment (prominently seen in the snubbing of the ICC by Sudanese President Al-Bashir).[16] Finally, given that international criminal prosecutions are time-and-space bound, these environments might risk producing, at least domestically, one-shotters rather than repeat players.[17] It is thus a challenge to build relationships of trust with civil society organizations, lawyers, diplomats, or other constituencies that would normally allow for growth in narrow and intermediate authority over time.[18]

In other words, in these atypical political environments, court authority turns on the capacity of prosecutors, rather than judges, to collect and garner evidence of atrocities to be translated into the criminal process. They must organize their evidence and strategy in "loosely coupled" or "tightly coupled" ways with external actors, such as victims or experts.[19] In contrast to economic cases, establishing this evidence is the concern of institutional insiders— prosecutors—and thus these operational "low politics" of evidence collection and presentation are a salient policy concern. For example, a recent article in *The New York Times* focused on the challenges faced by "an extraordinary witness" of the ICTY.[20] Reflecting on her case, an ICTY staff member noted: "Without witnesses, without key insiders, there are basically no trials."[21] And just a few months earlier, a piece in *The Guardian*, noted the challenges of working with witnesses for the International Criminal Tribunal for Rwanda experiencing posttraumatic stress disorder, including "huge amounts of testimony and paperwork [that] were generated," and a prosecutor's comment that "[l]ots of money got spent feeling our way forward. It costs a lot to fly in witnesses from around the world."[22]

This article thus links these organizational practices of evidence collection with the geopolitical context in which these courts operate.[23] At Nuremberg, a political decision was reached to focus the prosecution on a small number of Nazi figures, with particular attention paid to the documenting of atrocities by the prosecution rather than on developing a doctrinal base of judicial decisions. This aligned the prosecution with a U.S.-based legal constituency and helped deflect the critique of a Tribunal merely furthering victor's justice—a claim that bedeviled the "united nations" leading the prosecution at Nuremberg.[24] The ICTY emerged in a context of political and professional alignments, particularly with the growth of the human rights community, to expand a framework for legal accountability in times of conflict.[25] This contributed to the opportunity to produce significant jurisprudence, based largely on the prosecutorial framing of these crimes rather than the reasoning of the final judgments.[26] Despite the financial, moral, and political support of Western governments, civil society organizations, domestic political constituencies seeking economic benefits for reconstruction, and the international human rights community rallying behind the extension of human rights into the complexities of war and conflict, ICTY prosecutors still needed to gain narrow and intermediate authority by enrolling compliance partners with which to do their work.[27] They thus responded to this authority deficit in strategic fashion over time by leveraging the extensive authority they enjoyed to secure defendants and evidence that would expand the Tribunal's caseload, to ascertain the collaboration of media partners to build constituencies, and to later develop a strategy to coordinate with national court prosecutions in Bosnia and Herzegovina.

Compare the ICTY to the treaty-based ICC, which was negotiated during the momentum that grew around the ICTY and the project of international legalism. But despite this momentum, the ICC became operational in the post-9/11 climate, a disjuncture that affected its capacity to deliver on original hopes.[28] Attempts to grow its caseload volume generated resistance to its jurisdiction and the withdrawal of voluntary state parties. Indeed, the authority of the ICC is at stake in the potential withdrawal of African Union states from the ICC, with the African Union expressing concern over the "politicization and the misuse of indictments against African leaders by the ICC,"[29] and a continued call to "speak with one voice" regarding these prosecutions.[30] It is perhaps not surprising that its first prosecutor has insisted that the measure of the Court's success should not be its judgments, but a combination of deterrence and local legal accountability that could drive the Court's caseload to zero. The ICC's early prosecutions to date have thus targeted a small number of high profile cases. In these three courts, once one looks beyond the "high politics"[31] of the field's relationship to peacemaking and diplomacy, court authority relies to a significant degree on, and is reflected in, prosecutors' practices. Prosecutors choose their evidentiary strategies based on the geopolitical context at hand and work to enhance court authority by identifying evidentiary strategies that align the prosecutors with important external constituencies. By analogizing to atypical domestic trials, we identify that the success or failure to build international legal authority in these settings is conditioned by the different political, legal, and organizational arrangements in which international courts operate.[32] Turning to three main cases—Nuremberg, the ICTY, and the ICC— this article examines how these prosecutors build authority differently across geopolitical contexts.

THE INTERNATIONAL MILITARY TRIBUNAL AT NUREMBERG

In his opening statement to the Nuremberg trials in 1945, the Chief Prosecutor for the United States, Justice Robert Jackson, stressed the importance of documentary proof in the prosecution.[33] "We will give you undeniable proofs of incredible events," he said, referring among other items to "hundreds of tons of official German documents," the "captured orders and captured reports" that provide evidence of atrocities, and the violence and criminal enterprise that "we will prove from their own documents."[34] This attention to documents became the leitmotif of the prosecution, and with it a reflection on the machinery of Nazi Germany itself: "There is no count in the Indictment that cannot be proved by books and records," Jackson indicated, emphasizing that "[t]he Germans were meticulous record keepers."[35] And indeed this was Jackson's position for months leading up to the prosecution, in which he stressed the record of the IMT and its need to be perceived as authoritative.[36] In one of his best-known statements at the International Conference leading to the trials, Jackson insisted, "We must establish incredible events by credible evidence," stating that the trial would be "a drab case" based on documentary evidence of Nazi crimes, but that the documents would render it unchallengeable.[37]

The document-based tone of Nuremberg permeated the courtroom. As observed in *The New Yorker*, the trials were frightfully dull—so much so that the lawyers and staff "want[ed] to leave Nuremberg as urgently as a dental patient enduring the drill wants to get up and leave the chair."[38] Similarly, Joseph Kessel wrote that the Nuremberg trial's emphasis on documents did not allow for any "breath of life," with the most animated discussions focusing on the numbering of files and exhibits.[39]

Legal and historical analysts of the Nuremberg tribunal have understood the decision to rely on documentary evidence as driven by the sheer availability of documents of Nazi crimes and atrocities. Yet the extent of the Nuremberg Court's authority at that time demonstrates that the documentary reliance was also a prosecutorial practice tied to both the geopolitical context and the specific support that the prosecution enjoyed with external constituencies. The authority the Nuremberg prosecution strove to develop thereby relied on preexisting U.S.-based legal practices, so as to build extensive authority among a U.S.-based community of lawyers, and to help overcome some of the broader skepticism over the trials.

In their analysis of how international courts expand their authority over time, Alter, Helfer, and Madsen emphasize that recently established courts draw upon preexisting international legal practices from other domains, whereas older international courts are often forced to invent new practices in their area.[40] This article suggests that in the case of the IMT at Nuremberg, building a constituency at home (and a professional constituency that would support the prosecution from within the Tribunal as well) was achieved by drawing on preexisting national legal practices from other domains—in this case prominent antitrust cases in the United States. At an early stage in this field's development, this strategy positioned the tribunal well with respect to the powerful constituency of legal elites in the United States with whom it was in dialogue, and for many of the institutional insiders at Nuremberg represented the professional community to which they belonged.

To understand the prosecutorial strategy of the IMT one must contend with the overwhelming early suspicion—both in the United States and the United Kingdom, and certainly in the former Soviet Union—surrounding the idea of criminal prosecution of Nazi leaders, regarded by many as risky and viewed by some elites and the public as an overly soft response. This was instantiated in the view of Roosevelt's Secretary of the Treasury Henry Morgenthau, who derided the strategy as "kindness and Christianity"[41] rather than a strategy to deindustrialize Germany and to "attack[] the German mind" itself.[42] The IMT's comparative lack of early authority was reflected in the views of elite government lawyers such as Joseph O'Connell, who regarded the Tribunal as a fundamentally "unlegalistic approach" that applies domestic approaches "to a world situation which has nothing in common with it."[43] It was similarly reflected in the early views of President Roosevelt, who sought to emphasize the collective responsibility of the German people, rather than merely that of "a few Nazi leaders."[44] Second, among other segments there was criticism over the tribunal's perceived legitimacy, with the trials often derided as "victor's justice," and the criminal counts enumerated in the Charter of the IMT characterized as ex post facto charges that undercut legal and political legitimacy.[45] Even Judith Shklar, who produced the classic defense of the liberalism of Nuremberg, concluded that "little can be said on behalf of the legality of the Trial,"[46] with some leading legal figures of the time expressing concern over this very point.[47] And third, the prosecution was internally embattled: each of the Allies were pursuing different goals, and each articulated the rationale for the prosecution differently depending on the degree to which they regarded themselves as victims of the Nazi regime.[48]

A strategy of identifying a small number of Nazi leaders for prosecution at trial won out over competing views that emphasized summary executions of leaders or a broad collective punishment of Germans.[49] The documentary approach undergirding this newly adopted strategy was based on a U.S. legal strategy developed for domestic purposes in the antitrust litigation of the New Deal. This was combined with the decision to prosecute leading Nazi figures not for the atrocities of the Holocaust, but for the crime of aggressive war—a crime which turned on a reading of international legal obligations deriving from the Kellogg–Briand Pact of the interwar years.[50] While the prosecution would include war crimes and a newly created "crime against humanity," even these charges were cabined—by the prosecutors and the Tribunal's judges—to atrocities that could be tied to aggressive war.[51]

Jackson's prosecutorial strategy was deeply rooted and mirrored in the experience of his leadership team. This, in turn, was mirrored in the personnel who were drawn to the Court. Most of the prosecutorial team had no international legal capital, and its members were often young and comparatively inexperienced. Indeed, the *jurisconsultes* of the UN War Crimes Commission, who might have brought international expertise to the case, were reluctant to join the Nuremberg prosecution.[52] Yet if junior staff filled the prosecutorial ranks, the most senior of the U.S. lawyers at Nuremberg were those who had been instrumental in U.S. antitrust cases. Robert Jackson played a leading role in such cases throughout the 1930s,[53] and he was joined at Nuremberg by other prominent New Deal veterans of antitrust litigation: William Donovan of the OSS; John Amen of the U.S. Attorney General's Office, who was New York's "leading 'crime buster'" and son-in-law of President Cleveland;[54] and Henry Stimson, the Secretary of War and the leading proponent in the Roosevelt Administration for holding war crimes trials. These lawyers had all invested in antitrust litigation strategies for criminal prosecutions domestically, whether dealing with corporations such as the Sugar Trust or with gangsters in New York.[55] The Sugar Trust prosecution notably built a "joint criminal enterprise" approach that was the foundation for the Nuremberg trials.[56] The strategy displayed positions in the Nazi leadership regime and an analysis of the Nazi organizational structure—with documentary records providing the material needed to establish the IMT's authority over the case.[57]

Taking this shared domestic legal experience to the international stage—and to a tribunal that was considered to be without precedent—was a prosecutorial strategy designed to resonate with the existing practices of a powerful legal expert constituency within the United States. Indeed, the leading U.S. government designer and champion of the trial-based approach at Nuremberg, Henry Stimson took the view that this prosecutorial practice would resolve the "difficult question" of the Nuremberg trials.[58] Relying on documents and adopting an antitrust-type format, Stimson followed a prosecution strategy "in a way which is at the same time consistent with our traditional judicial principles and also will be effective in dispensing adequate punishment and also will leave a permanent record in the shape of the evidence collected of the evils against which we have fought this war."[59] In other words, Stimson not only agreed with Jackson's documentary-based prosecutorial strategy, but he identified it as a way to square the circle of ongoing, potential authority challenges the Tribunal was facing.

Veteran New Deal lawyers were convinced that such a format would resonate with a community of adherents in the United States, while also providing an opportunity for the IMT to build an authoritative narrative about the war. The Assistant Secretary of War and Wall Street Lawyer John McCloy went so far as to enthusiastically assure Secretary of Treasury Henry Morgenthau that "[a]fter Justice Jackson puts the Gestapo on the stand and has indicted them like the American Sugar Company or whatever it was, then he says 'By God, you're guilty.'"[60] This emphasis was perhaps seen otherwise by Sidney Kaplan, a member of the prosecutorial team at Nuremberg, who wrote the day before the trial began, "[T]he prosecution is utterly, completely, hopelessly, unprepared. Jackson will deliver a sensational opening statement— and from that point on we're in the soup."[61] As historian Gary Bass concludes, Nuremberg was mainly U.S.-created and led, with the allies following suit.[62] Procedures would reflect the work of keeping agreement across countries, such as the lengthy indictment that would recite details in a manner uncommon for a U.S. prosecution.[63] Beyond the national legal constituency from which Jackson and many leaders on the team emerged, the IMT prosecution also sought to build authority for the Nuremberg trials by looking to the future and the anticipated legacy of the trial. Jackson sought to do so by building an external constituency for the Tribunal by emphasizing the historical momentum it could spur. In so doing, Jackson privileged documentary evidence and actively sought to limit testimony as much as possible.[64] As he wrote to Stimson, Jackson perceived this evidentiary basis as "the sounder foundation for the case, particularly when the record is examined by the historian."[65]

For this strategy to succeed, Jackson required documentation. Europe was in a ravaged state, and there were an enormous number of documents to locate.[66] Jackson reached out to gain the cooperation of the secretive Office of Strategic Services (OSS), the predecessor organization of the Central Intelligence Agency, and its Director General William Joseph Donovan. Donovan and the OSS had been keeping files on potential Nazi war criminals for years and had a collection of intelligence materials from OSS secret agents who operated within the Nazi hierarchy and resistance networks.[67] The OSS had a long-standing presentation branch that specialized in presenting complex matters by bringing together charts, film, or photography.[68] The OSS also had personnel fluent in German and with deep knowledge of German society.[69]

Yet the OSS would also critique this document-based strategy. Leading officials in the OSS, including Donovan, maintained that Jackson should rely on witness testimony to draw in the mainstream media and depict atrocities.[70] This article ventures that this difference in trial strategy was not only tactical, but was also about the very goals of the Tribunal itself, its capacity to attract adherents, and the audience to which Donovan himself was oriented. For Donovan, Nuremberg "was a lawsuit plus something else."[71] In contrast to building authority with historians or for posterity, Donovan was most sensitive to the short-term political impact of the trial in Germany and its opportunity to set a foundation for de-Nazification policies.[72] Therefore, while proponents of documentary evidence focused on enhancing the Tribunal's legal authority, Donovan was interested in the trial's immediate political effects on post-war Germany.

Jackson's strategies for achieving authority for the Tribunal led him to reject most of Donovan's suggestions regarding witness testimony. Jackson was reticent to include testimony from victims or from defendants: victims could be subject to attacks on their credibility, and defendants testifying could give the impression that a plea bargain had taken place.[73] Witness testimony was regarded as an "unnecessary cumulation of evidence," and importantly for the Court's capacity to build its authority through its prosecutorial practices, witnesses would—in Jackson's view—run the risk of demonstrating "a strong bias against the Hitler regime."[74] He even rejected the views of some on his team who suggested that the case gain "added authority" by having atrocities presented by "a group of high churchmen" who could speak to Nazi atrocities in favor of a strategy that would control the evidence in a measured and systematic way.[75] Although he relented a little with time,[76] Jackson stated that the prosecution would "put on no witnesses we could reasonably avoid."[77]

The evidentiary approach of the IMT at Nuremberg demonstrates the close connection between legal practices and geopolitical context that is critical to international court authority. This was a highly atypical political environment: the Allies had occupied Germany, the Nazi regime had extensively documented its crimes, and the leading defendants were captured and in the dock. The Tribunal itself, in this environment, was perceived as exceptional and the object of widespread skepticism among European and American constituencies. The decision to rely nearly exclusively on documentary evidence, and to resist witness testimony—at the expense of not only media attention, but also immediate political outcomes in post-war Germany, the chance to build such media as a platform for victims of Nazi Germany to speak out, and even a potentially reduced emphasis on some atrocities[78]—can partly be explained as an effort to build authority for the Tribunal and the legalistic approach it pursued.

Nuremburg's prosecutorial practices shed light on an important and potentially generalizable lesson for the study of international court authority. Nuremberg was a new, time-limited court for which narrow and intermediate authority was not an issue, due to the occupation of Germany by the Allies and the availability of incriminating documents. Yet building extensive authority was another matter. With the United States occupying a dominant position among the Allies in the post-war period, the Tribunal's prosecution sought to produce this extensive authority by relying on a well-known and highly regarded domestic legal strategy, as Stimson noted, to resolve the "difficult question" of the Nuremberg trials.[79] Antitrust lawyers with close ties to the state came to dominate at the Tribunal with this move. Thus, Jackson's documentary strategy appears to have bolstered the IMT's authority within the community of elite U.S. lawyers whose work on antitrust cases defined their practices with a prosecutorial approach that built in this extensive authority and that deflected potential resistance from the start.

THE INTERNATIONAL CRIMINAL TRIBUNAL FOR THE FORMER YUGOSLAVIA

The Cold War soon made it politically unfeasible to develop international legal or political responses to war crimes, a geopolitical conjuncture that led to waning professional momentum for international war crimes prosecutions in both Europe and the United States.[80] With the end of the Cold War, however, two influential institutions emerged. The South African Truth and Reconciliation Commission was established in 1995 to investigate human rights abuses that occurred under the apartheid regime, and underwritten by an argument that overtly positioned itself in distinction to that of Nuremberg and of trials.[81] Established in 1992 by the UN Security Council, the ICTY was the first international war crimes tribunal in the post–Cold War era. This turn to law was partly fuelled by political expediency, and as Samantha Power notes, it "seemed a low-cost, low-risk way for Western states to signal that despite their opposition to military intervention, they were not indifferent to Bosnia's suffering."[82]

Basic legal authority (or jurisdiction) was explicitly delegated to the ICTY by Security Council Resolution. Indeed, there was significant appetite and support for a legal framework to respond to atrocities committed in war. This included political support from powerful states and in particular the Clinton Administration, which provided the ICTY with resources, expertise, and political support.[83] This was further supplemented by the expansion of an internationalized field of human rights[84] and the growing influence of human rights organizations that had gained in technical proficiency, professional savvy, and political autonomy over the 1980s. This growing influence included extending to the law of armed conflict—as well as the media savvy of human rights and feminist organizations to raise awareness of the atrocities being committed.[85] Emerging in the early 1990s, the ICTY found itself in a context with a political and professional appetite for articulating the link between human rights and armed conflict.

Yet even with this Security Council delegation, and buoyed by significant political, professional, and social movement support that translated to extensive authority for its work, the ICTY initially found itself in a precarious position respecting its intermediate authority, namely its capacity to attract *compliance partners*.[86] The Court even felt constraints on its narrow authority; it had no indictees to prosecute or tools to do its work. The ICTY's position as a "virtual tribunal" defined the strategies that its prosecutors could develop. Though states are formally required to cooperate with its investigations, as a practical matter, the access of Tribunal prosecutors to documentary evidence, their ability to effect arrests, or to interview witnesses remained dependent on states' willingness to extend such cooperation.[87] As the First President of the ICTY Antonio Cassese emphasized, the Tribunal is "like an armless and legless giant which needs artificial limbs to act and move. These limbs are the State authorities . . . . If state authorities fail to carry out their responsibilities, the giant is paralyzed, no matter how determined its efforts."[88]

In other words, in contrast to the IMT, where prosecutors had the needed intermediate authority thanks to the readily available documentary evidence— and focused on building extensive authority—the prosecutorial strategy at the ICTY needed to build intermediate authority among compliance partners and thereby collect and develop the evidence required for prosecution. The Tribunal was supported in doing so by the broad authority it could draw upon politically and professionally, and from among civil society groups. In what follows, this article demonstrates how the first three Chief Prosecutors of the ICTY were central to developing this authority by turning to political and military partners to obtain detainees, to increase its funding base, to develop new investigatory powers, and to introduce legal practices in the Balkans that allowed the continued development of prosecutable cases. Each Chief Prosecutor did so by building on his or her social and professional background and resources and sought to change the context in which the ICTY's authority was weakest.

The first Chief Prosecutor to enter into this operational context was Justice Richard Goldstone. A South African judge who had just finished as chair of the Commission of Inquiry Regarding the Prevention of Public Violence and Intimidation, Goldstone came to the ICTY with a strong understanding of law and diplomacy, seeing his position as a "big-picture diplomatic role" rather than "hands-on prosecution work,"[89] and endorsing a public role through interviews and travel designed to promote the ICTY's image.[90] This allowed him to enroll compliance partners by integrating prosecutorial strategy with efforts to induce cooperation by external constituencies.

Aware that without indictments he risked UN budget cuts, and conscious of judicial frustration with the Tribunal's empty prison, Goldstone opportunistically relied on the national German police arrest of Duško Tadić to deliver the Court's first, if relatively low-level, detainee. Despite uncertainty as to whether Tadić had been in a leadership position in planning crimes, Goldstone took the position that building compliance was most important.[91]

Indeed, when faced the next year with a continued lack of compliance from the United Kingdom, the United States, and NATO in arresting indictees, Goldstone proceeded—despite the legalistic reservations of prosecutorial staff—with in abstentia hearings to pressure international authorities to apprehend two high-profile indictees, a process that drove Radovan Karadzic out of elected office.[92]

Similarly, when Dražen Erdemović was taken into custody in Belgrade, Goldstone made a public demand that he appear before the Tribunal. This demand combined with American political pressure, leading to Erdemović's transfer to the ICTY within several weeks. Goldstone also drew on diplomatic networks to expand the Tribunal's authority to collect evidence of atrocities, obtaining Central Intelligence Agency aerial imagery to identify mass graves sites, and negotiating with Assistant Secretary of State Richard Holbrooke for Slobodan Milošević to allow State Department visits to the area around Srebrenica. These compliance gains opened the door for the Tribunal's exhumation work. Indeed, once some victims' bodies were exhumed, the Tribunal further claimed search and seizure powers under the Dayton Accords to collect evidence about the massacre from Bosnian Serb military headquarters.[93]

Yet without individuals in custody, it was difficult for the ICTY to enjoy the narrow authority it needed for prosecutions. Goldstone was astute at reconciling this by building the ICTY's intermediate authority through political networks that drew on the Tribunal's existing well of extensive authority. With a limited set of legal tools at his disposal—and despite legal reservations over the legitimacy of some tactics—Goldstone expanded the Tribunal's authority by opportunistically enrolling networks of national and international authorities, with the ICTY gaining influence over politics and diplomacy.[94] In the process, Goldstone obtained a sustained annual budget along with compliance partners outside of the Tribunal. He indicated that "I think I spent more of my time on diplomacy and pushing and talking and screaming and shouting for the Tribunal than on the simply prosecutorial work."[95]

The second Chief Prosecutor, Louise Arbour, pursued a similar path in building the Tribunal's intermediate authority through compliance partners— focusing more on the ICTY's coercive criminal law mandate to increase the ICTY's caseload of indictees by working with external enforcement agencies, gaining state cooperation with the Tribunal, and garnering media interest in the Tribunal's work. Arbour brought training in criminal law that opened avenues for drawing in new compliance partners; perhaps presaging this approach, she began her tenure by distancing the Tribunal from the human rights organizations that had mobilized to create the Tribunal, to instead building a constituency of criminal lawyers and investigators.[96] If the Tribunal already enjoyed the sort of extensive authority that civil society would offer, the prosecution needed to instead focus on gaining custody over defendants and cooperation from recalcitrant states. The first President of the ICTY, Antonio Cassese, noted that the main problem of the Court's authority lay in this practical level: indicating that this war crimes tribunal "purports to exercise international criminal jurisdiction," Cassese stressed that the problem of state sovereignty remains "when it comes to the day-to-day operations of the Tribunal," and that when states do not cooperate with the ICTY "[it] is like lava burning away the foundations of the institution."[97]

Given the Tribunal's lack of police powers, Arbour's first prosecutorial innovation was to open new opportunities for partnership and authority with militaries and intelligence agencies by pursuing "sealed" indictments to detach her prosecutorial strategy from political constraints and resistance of local authorities. This allowed high-profile arrests to be executed by U.S. and UN authorities, the British-led Stabilization Force, and later, arrests effected by Dutch, American, and French-led troops that had previously been shamed by their lack of compliance. In this way, the prosecutor was able to overcome the political stonewalling and hesitation that threatened the Tribunal's relevance. Indeed, when Arbour later indicted Milošević at the end of her tenure, she similarly did so with the benefit of secrecy, which allowed her to work with intelligence agencies across five countries and outside public diplomacy, and to obtain the largest handover to an outside agency in the history of British intelligence.[98] Following this innovation, Arbour's prosecutorial team then defended the approach of third-party arrests by NATO and other forces, an approach that was later backed by the Appeals Chamber in advancing the obligation of third parties to conduct arrests and transfer indictees to the Hague and also in shielding these arrests from claims of illegality. Arbour similarly took the position that despite the conventional internationalist emphasis on state sovereignty, some form of subpoena power must reside in the Tribunal. In response, precisely because it otherwise had no enforcement agents of its own, the Appeals Chamber fashioned a new tool of a "binding order" for the Tribunal.[99]

Arbour's second approach in increasing intermediate authority was to gain greater state cooperation from Balkan states, relying on the extensive political authority of the ICTY with Western nations to induce cooperation as a condition of financial assistance. This compelled national leaders to hand over evidence and indictees to the Tribunal: Croatia thus transferred indictees in conjunction with its acceptance into the Council of Europe and its receipt of monetary aid, and Serbia later did so in transferring Milošević and Karadžić to The Hague following the proffer of U.S. financial incentives.

Finally, in addition to her efforts with militaries, intelligence agencies, and NATO forces, Arbour's third prosecutorial innovation was to gain some control over the public messaging and media image of the Court. She did so by cultivating partners and networks with the media to generate public support for the ICTY and its on-site, real-time, and highly emotive investigations. The extensive media coverage of prosecutor-led exhumations was crucial in capturing the attention of the world and the attention of UN budget officials, who had the capacity to increase their monetary support for the ICTY's investigatory work. Indeed, as widespread media coverage of the Milošević indictment and a prosecutorial showdown at the Macedonian border made clear, media coverage of the Tribunal and its developed ability to capture the attention of the world became one of the key successes of the ICTY.[100]

As Arbour reflected, "I think about Nuremberg *every* day! The images constantly come to mind."[101] In this, Arbour expressed her envy of the Nuremberg prosecutors, where the Court had its defendants in custody, along with every document necessary. It is precisely to fill this gap in authority that the first two ICTY prosecutors engaged with a wider range of compliance partners. This was successful: over the first five years, the ICTY benefited from a consistent rate of arrested individuals transferred to The Hague, a tripling of the annual budget, an increase in voluntary contributions from states that tracked the number of successful arrests, and increased morale among the Tribunal staff sent on missions in the field to conduct investigatory work.[102] In some sense, as the Tribunal achieved greater intermediate authority, it came to enjoy greater extensive authority as well.

The third Chief Prosecutor, Carla del Ponte, inherited an organization with a ninety-million-dollar budget, multiple trials underway, and a high level of staff morale. New state and military cooperation was prompting more arrests, and more indictees arrived at the Tribunal every month. The challenge for del Ponte was to secure convictions while also managing political pressure to end investigations and complete ICTY trials swiftly.

Given this context, del Ponte's efforts to increase the ICTY's authority were no longer as focused on support by militaries and states—other than ensuring the transfer of Milošević to the Hague through a U.S. donor pledge—but on building the Tribunal's legal authority in its prosecutions. To do so, del Ponte focused on the successful prosecution of complex criminal cases, building on her previous work in her capacity as Swiss Attorney General, during which she investigated bankers, politicians, and organized crime members. She is known for claiming to have "never served anyone or anything but the law."[103] In the ICTY she thus went on to develop "monumental" cases, such as that identifying rape as a crime against humanity[104] and the successful prosecution of genocide charges stemming from the Srebrenica massacre—legal successes that del Ponte echoed by reorganizing the Office of the Prosecutor to give lawyers greater control over investigations and to emphasize courtroom successes over new investigations or arrests.[105] When Milošević was indicted for genocide, del Ponte drew on her experience with Swiss prosecutions of complex financial crimes and asserted that "instead of pulling and pushing to get detainees, our work has moved more fully into the courtrooms, which is where it belongs."[106]

Here, del Ponte's prosecutorial strategy echoed the new legal and geopolitical context in which the Court found itself: under political pressure from the United States to wrap up the Tribunal's efforts rather than issue new arrests that would prolong the ICTY's prosecutions. Yet this too necessitated new compliance partners to build the ICTY's authority in a changing geopolitical context, a shifting context that was absent for the shorter-lived Nuremberg trials. With powerful states fatigued over these prosecutions, and with concern in the United States over the potential reach of international criminal law, the ICTY's "completion strategy" resonated with del Ponte's decision to increase the number of trials and to decrease the number of new investigations. Prosecutions were thus limited to "the most senior leaders suspected of being most responsible for crimes within the jurisdiction of the Tribunal" and lower-level cases were transferred to "competent national jurisdictions."[107]

The ICTY then began the transfer of a significant number of cases to domestic courts. These courts became the newest compliance partners for the Tribunal, with transfers legally overseen by the ICTY's Rule 11*bis* to refer indictments to another court.[108] Although political constraints have made this less successful outside of Bosnia and Herzegovina, there have been beneficial effects for extending the ICTY's authority through the War Crimes Section in the State Court of Bosnia and Herzegovina: the transfer of ICTY personnel, the active influence of ICTY prosecutorial know-how, capacity development, assistance with human rights expertise, the use in the War Crimes Section of evidence from ICTY proceedings, lessons learned from the ICTY regarding the need for transparency in case selection, and a reliance on ICTY jurisprudence and sentencing practices as persuasive authority.[109] By expanding the community of actors drawing on ICTY precedents reinforcing the field as a whole, the expansion of ICTY authority has had the effect of establishing greater intermediate and extensive authority for the Tribunal.

Compared to the IMT, the ICTY provides a case study of an international court that—though enjoying formal delegation from the UN Security Council and extensive authority politically—required prosecutorial strategies to build its narrow and intermediate authority by mobilizing external compliance partners. Whereas the prosecutorial team at Nuremberg had the evidence it needed, the first three ICTY Chief Prosecutors instead needed to build alliances across potential compliance partners—diplomats, police forces, and militaries—to secure state cooperation and to cope with a changing geopolitical context toward domestic courts in Bosnia and Herzegovina. They could do so precisely by leveraging the extensive authority among powerful states that the Court already enjoyed. The needed compliance partners reflected the political context in which each of the first three Chief Prosecutors found themselves, and the social backgrounds they could bring to the ICTY to influence the context itself. Thus, these prosecutors successfully solidified the ICTY's narrow and intermediate authority while gaining ever greater extensive authority for the Tribunal and the field as a whole.

THE INTERNATIONAL CRIMINAL COURT

The latest chapter in international criminal justice is being written at the ICC, which faces a precarious political and legal position. Its creation was negotiated at the height of the international human rights community's commitment to international prosecution, but it began its operations in a post-9/11 environment. It is further embattled by resistance among powerful states as well as African Union countries threatening to withdraw from the Court as a backlash to its investigations against sitting heads of state. ICC prosecutors thus find themselves in a unique position regarding Court authority.[110] Perhaps more so than the ICTY, the ICC enjoys extensive authority among the growing professional community in international criminal law. Yet because the ICC deals with ongoing contentious situations—involving states in which multiple actors are engaged with diverse political options to manage conflicts—and because the Prosecutor can investigate all offenses on the territory once a situation is opened, the Court is continually in a weak position. It enjoys *less* narrow authority and *less* intermediate authority than the ICTY. In addition, whereas it enjoys deep extensive authority among international legal experts, this is uneven given the resistance to the Court by powerful states, growing resistance in states where the Prosecutor is likely to pursue situations, and vociferous academic debate over the basic goals and utility of the Court.

In some ways, the ICC finds itself only obliquely as the inheritor of a past trajectory of international criminal law[111] and the wider field of global justice. Compared to the IMT at Nuremberg, the ICC enjoys a professionalized base of legal scholarship and practitioners on which to draw, but it is faced with persistent challenges to its narrow and intermediate authority: states threatening withdrawal from the Court, a range of powerful states that have not joined the Court, and Security Council referrals that risk not succeeding in contentious situations.

For most of the past decade the ICC has been known by association with its first Chief Prosecutor, Luis Moreno Ocampo. Ocampo had headed Transparency International for Latin America, directed a law firm focusing on corruption, criminal law, and human rights, and prosecuted the generals in the post-transition Trial of the Juntas in Argentina. Like his predecessors at the ICTY, Ocampo stated he found the ICC challenging because as Chief Prosecutor he had to pursue war criminals without the benefits of police and arrest powers. "I am a stateless prosecutor," Ocampo lamented. "I have 100 states under my jurisdiction and zero policemen."[112] Indeed, the ICC's budget, though the same as that of the ICTY, is spread across investigations in different countries and situations rather than focused on one geographic region, partly because the ICC is designed to both defer to and encourage domestic investigations and trials.[113] Yet Ocampo also faced a dilemma in his mandate. With the ICC limited by its statute to cases in which countries were unwilling or unable to conduct their own investigations, and is additionally limited, absent a Security Council referral, to countries that joined as state parties, the ICC's docket quickly became focused on African conflicts. This led to deep charges of politicization.[114]

At one level, the resulting crisis of authority lies in the mandate of the Court, because the situations and often real-time crimes that the ICC is seized with are deeply enmeshed within ongoing diplomatic, political, and economic struggles. Its authority is further affected by the fact that the Court must be sufficiently nimble to work with existing cases as well as those that are referred to it by the Security Council. As Alex Whiting, who earlier served in the ICTY and then as both Investigation and Prosecution Coordinator with the ICC notes, in the ICC "each investigation is largely shaped by the constraints and opportunities peculiar to the situation at hand."[115] Yet this article suggests that despite the differences presented by each situation, ICC prosecutors have also adopted strategies designed to reflect the Court's possible sources of authority. The focus of the Office of the Prosecutor has thus been on distancing itself from any charges of politicization by changing the way in which evidence is gathered and presented.

For the ICC Prosecutor, the need to deflect charges of politicization— which, by contrast, were less prevalent in the geopolitical context of the ICTY due to the breadth of political support for the Tribunal—has led to a strategy focused on legal analysis and procedure decoupled from investigations. This is partly explained by the budgetary constraints of the Court, including the cost of witness testimony, the risks of testimony being undermined or withdrawn,[116] and the bureaucratic structure of the Prosecutor's office.[117] It is also the case that the ongoing context of conflict makes it a challenge for the ICC Prosecutor to gauge the strength of eventual testimony in Court.[118] This is further underwritten by security concerns present on the ground during ongoing conflicts,[119] so that the capacity for the Prosecutor to investigate depends on support from interested parties.

Echoing Justice Jackson's strategy at Nuremberg, Ocampo observed that "[o]ur goal is to go even further," in particular, to prosecute "a case with no witnesses, no victims."[120] And indeed the ICC has gone on to invest heavily in the formal legal "in-house" development of its cases, pursuing a strategy relying on social science and documentary methods—even if to-date witnesses remain the core of the prosecutions.[121] And given that the ICC's strongest base of authority lies in the professional and academic legal community, it is not surprising that the Office of the Prosecutor has sought to play to this strength by investing in "pure law"[122] and by seeking to distance investigatory partners so as to control the collection of witness testimony and avoid charges of politicization. Thus a continued strategy to resonate with and shore up support among the Prosecutor's most significant professional constituencies is apparent.

In the ICC, this prosecutorial strategy has been implemented in two main ways. First, at a bureaucratic level, the ICC Prosecutor reorganized the Office of the Prosecutor around a more purely legal orientation.[123] Likely as an outgrowth of the legal professionalization of the field of international criminal law, the staff of the Office came with a legal and specialized training in international criminal law. By 2009, prosecutions were largely overseen from within the Office of the Prosecutor in The Hague and by a staff with a legal background or experience in human rights organizations, rather than a training in police investigation focused, by contrast, more on chain of custody and avoidance of hearsay in the collection of victim statements. The ICC Prosecutor saw himself as developing a strategy involving cases against top figures and as centering on the narrower legal issue of establishing the responsibility for command authority over crimes rather than proving the occurrence of the crimes themselves. As others have pointed out, this decision to avoid on-the-ground field investigations from within the Office of the Prosecutor has been fundamentally strategic on the part of the Prosecutor, and it "seems to have been a point of pride for the Office."[124] The Court's limited authority is also reflected by pressures on its budget, and its hesitation to request additional budgetary resources from the Assembly of States Parties.[125] Conducting investigations has, as one journalist suggests, become "but the poor cousin of the international politics of the [ICC]."[126]

The result of this strategy is that the Prosecutor has relied heavily on developing evidence for the prosecutions by relying on external NGOs already working in the politically charged contexts of the ICC's investigations. In the place of ICC-led investigators, the Court came to rely heavily on NGOs already pre-positioned in Africa when conducting their investigations. This has been harshly criticized by the ICC judges, who in the Court's first prosecution expressed concern with "the use by the prosecution of local intermediaries in the DRC," and indicated that the prosecution "should not have delegated its investigative responsibilities to intermediaries."[127] In the same vein, the Court in *Lubanga* quoted William Pace, the founding convener of the Coalition for the International Criminal Court, stating that "human rights and humanitarian organizations are lousy criminal investigators."[128] It therefore focused the greatest bulk of its decision on these questions of investigation and evidence, and it stressed the gap between "the information provided by human rights groups . . . eager to call international attention to crises and "forensic evidence that can be used by a prosecutor."[129] This prosecutorial strategy was again criticized in the case against former Côte d'Ivoire President Laurent Gbagbo, with the Court expressing its concern over hearsay received from NGO reports.[130]

The second major approach of the Prosecution to emphasize "pure law" is evident in its case development strategy, which focuses on selecting a small number of cases that can have legal impact quickly, rather than undergoing a lengthy process of pursuing all potential leads. This is partly explained, again, by the lack of investigatory staffing. It was also a response to the Prosecutor's desire to move swiftly, in the face of political pressure and an empty docket until the arrest of its first indictee in 2006. Bernard Lavigne, who led an early investigatory team in *Lubanga* and was called to testify on the question of evidence, noted what he referred to as the "pressure [of] public opinion internationally,"[131] which would have included, at the time, fierce U.S. resistance to the Court's operations.

Lawyers representing victims have thus taken the Prosecutor to task for only prosecuting Lubanga for the crime of enrolling children as soldiers, rather than for crimes related to children's treatment and sexual exploitation. This is tied to the lack of prosecutorial attention that is placed within the Office of the Prosecutor on investigations, including the small teams that are deployed and the comparatively short time frame of which they can avail themselves.[132] Yet here too the emphasis has been on producing the ICC's authority by drawing on a limited number of compelling legal cases to launch the Court. As one former investigator said,

> We knew that during killings, rapes happened [but] the idea was that the first ICC trial could not fail. To organize a good trial, the prosecutor selected child soldiers as the only charge against Lubanga and [decided] to drop the others . . . against the will of many investigators.[133]

Throughout the Court's work, then, the focus of the ICC Prosecutor has been on narrowing the scope of investigations, selecting a small number of incidents, and developing cases likely to draw public attention to leading figures rather than prosecuting atrocities more broadly. As a senior ICC prosecutor stated in an interview:

> We have always followed a policy where we do not want to have ICTY type of investigations where we charge basically the history of the Balkans in one case so that is an attempt to write history in criminal proceedings . . . . So what we do is we focus our investigations on a very limited number of crimes, we also focus our investigations on those persons whom we believe bear the greatest responsibility . . . . We are also very selective in how many witnesses we bring.[134]

The prosecutorial strategy of the ICC is not only different, then, from the ICTY—it is most akin to that of Justice Jackson at Nuremberg. The desire to bring a comparatively small number of cases, to highlight leadership figures rather than to prosecute a full scope of atrocities, and to avoid broad witness testimony echoes the evidentiary and prosecutorial strategy of Nuremberg. Although occurring in fundamentally different geopolitical contexts—the IMT at Nuremberg enjoyed access to all documents and defendants and was supported with narrow and intermediate authority, whereas the ICC is in the reverse situation of enjoying extensive authority among a community of practice but has neither narrow nor intermediate authority at its disposal—the two courts have reacted to their authority constraints in fundamentally similar ways at the level of prosecutorial strategy.

CONCLUSION

In many international courts, authority turns on judicial decisions. Yet in the context of international criminal courts, prosecutorial strategy is often at the core of the building or waning of authority. This is partly because of the power of prosecutors to make headlines with indictments, and it is partly because of the highly contentious and atypical political environments in which these courts operate. If these political environments are atypical, this article's survey of the prosecutorial strategy developed by these courts suggests that in building their authority, prosecutors are acutely aware of the authority they enjoy and thus seek to speak to the constituencies they need—while avoiding others—through their prosecutorial practices.

This article provides insight into the varying forms of de facto authority that international criminal courts enjoy, and in light of which prosecutors develop practices that reflect and seek to adapt to the external contexts in which they operate. Further, this article demonstrates that the IMT at Nuremberg, which enjoyed narrow and intermediate authority—with full access to documents and evidence, but also with skepticism in some quarters over its legalistic mandate— sits in stark contrast to the ICTY and the ICC, and their needs for evidence, defendants, and state cooperation.

Different prosecutorial practices thus emerge. Justice Jackson at Nuremberg, by having all available evidence at his disposal, spoke mainly to a professional community in the specific domestic context of the United States rather than draw in the media or others through victim testimony. This article suggests that this internal and external contestation, the unevenness of authority of the IMT at Nuremberg, and the geopolitical centrality of the United States in the post–World War II moment, underwrote the prosecutorial motivation to rely on an evidentiary strategy highlighting documents throughout the trial. ICTY prosecutors, by contrast, drew on the extensive authority they enjoyed to build a range of compliance partners for the Tribunal—at first focusing on building investigatory and media networks for the prosecutors, and then seeking out compliance partners in domestic courts as the Tribunal's extensive authority was in danger of waning. And in the ICC, whose authority is mainly limited to the community of international law practitioners and NGOs directly supporting the ICC and seeking to deflect charges of politicization, the prosecutorial strategy has aimed at distancing itself from investigation and the murky contexts of ongoing conflicts, instead limiting its reach to a narrow set of legal issues and cases.

In the context of international criminal courts, the analysis of authority and prosecutorial practice is tied to the question of how to speak authoritatively about atrocity. In contrast to teleological accounts of international criminal law that presume this authority grows with time, this article suggests that the narrow and intermediate aspects of international criminal court authority have waned over time. In light of this, prosecutors have scrambled to build the authority they need. As a result, the ICTY had sufficient extensive authority from which the Tribunal could draw by tightly coupling its links with compliance partners to overcome weaker narrow and intermediate authority. Yet in the ICC, the risks of being identified as politicized, combined with the mandate constraints in which the Court operates, has led the Office of the Prosecutor to distance itself from compliance partners, a loose coupling that has led to skepticism from judges and victims alike. Perhaps mirroring these courts' loss of authority externally, the result has been that, though prosecutors have matched their strategies to the available forms of authority they could marshal, the field of international criminal law has—if anything—lost more authority than it has gained.

Notes

See generally JOHN HAGAN, JUSTICE IN THE BALKANS: PROSECUTING WAR CRIMES IN THE HAGUE TRIBUNAL (2003); KATHRYN SIKKINK, THE JUSTICE CASCADE: HOW HUMAN RIGHTS PROSECUTIONS ARE CHANGING WORLD POLITICS (2011); Ron Levi & John Hagan, Penser les «crimes de guerre», 173 ACTES DE LA RECHERCHE EN SCIENCES SOCIALES 6–27 (2008).

See generally GARY JONATHAN BASS, STAY THE HAND OF VENGEANCE: THE POLITICS OF WAR CRIMES TRIBUNALS (2000).

See Mikael Rask Madsen, Explaining the Power of International Courts in Their Contexts: From Legitimacy to Legitimization, in COURTS, SOCIAL CHANGE, AND JUDICIAL INDEPENDENCE 23, 23–24 (Adriana Silvia Dreyzin de Klor et al. eds., 2012).

See SIKKINK, supra note 1, at 5.

Id.

See generally John Hagan & Ron Levi, International Police, in THE NEW POLICE SCIENCE: THE POLICE POWER IN DOMESTIC AND INTERNATIONAL GOVERNANCE 207 (Markus D. Dubber & Mariana Valverde eds., 2006); Jane Jenson & Ron Levi, Narratives and Regimes of Social and Human Rights: The Jack Pines of the Neoliberal Era, in SOCIAL RESILIENCE IN THE NEOLIBERAL ERA 69 (Peter A. Hall & Michèle Lamont eds., 2013); Yves Dezalay & Bryant Garth, From the Cold War to Kosovo: The Rise and Renewal of the Field of International Human Rights, 2 ANN. REV. L. & SOC. SCI. 231 (2006).

See SIKKINK, supra note 1, at 14–18; Levi & Hagan, supra note 1, at 6–10.

See generally Karen J. Alter, Laurence R. Helfer & Mikael Rask Madsen, How Context Shapes the Authority of International Courts, 79 LAW & CONTEMP. PROBS., no. 1, 2016, at 17, 32; Jens Meierhenrich, The Practice Of International Law: A Theoretical Analysis, 76 LAW & CONTEMP. PROBS., nos. 3 & 4, 2014, at 1.

See, e.g., DAVID BOSCO, ROUGH JUSTICE: THE INTERNATIONAL CRIMINAL COURT IN A WORLD OF POWER POLITICS 57 (2014); Heather Schoenfeld, Ron Levi & John Hagan, Crises extrêmes et institutionnalisation du droit pénal international, 36 CRITIQUE INTERNATIONALE 37 (2007).

See generally John Hagan, Why Is There So Little Criminal Justice Theory? Neglected Macroand Micro-Level Links Between Organization and Power, 26 J. RES. CRIME & DELINQ. 116, 117 (1989).

See Ron Levi & Heather Schoenfeld, Médiation et droit pénal international, 174 ACTES DE LA RECHERCHE EN SCIENCES SOCIALES 4, 6–9 (2008).

See, e.g., ERIC A. POSNER, THE TWILIGHT OF HUMAN RIGHTS LAW (2014).

Due to space constraints, this article does not systematically address the constituencies to which international prosecutors speak beyond that which is drawn out through an analysis of prosecutorial practices themselves.

NIILO KAUPPI, DEMOCRACY, SOCIAL RESOURCES AND POLITICAL POWER IN THE EUROPEAN UNION (2005).

See Alter, Helfer & Madsen, supra note 8, at 5.

See ADAM BRANCH, DISPLACING HUMAN RIGHTS: WAR AND INTERVENTION IN NORTHERN UGANDA 179 (2011).

See Marc Galanter, Why the "Haves" Come Out Ahead: Speculations on the Limits of Legal Change, 9 LAW & SOC'Y REV. 95, 97–114 (1974).

See Alter, Helfer & Madsen, supra note 8, at 4.

See Hagan, supra note 10, at 117–20.

Marlise Simons, Witness in War Crimes Court Tallies Cost of a Decade in Hiding: Testifying Against Slobodan Milosevic at Tribunal for Former Yugoslavia, N.Y. TIMES, Aug. 16, 2014, at A5.

Id.

Owen Bowcott, Rwanda Genocide: The Fight to Bring the Perpetrators to Justice, THE GUARDIAN (Apr. 2, 2014), http://www.theguardian.com/world/2014/apr/02/rwanda-genocide-fightjustice.

See Alter, Helfer & Madsen, supra note 8, at 26–27; Hagan, supra note 10, at 130.

See MARTHA MINOW, BETWEEN VENGEANCE AND FORGIVENESS: FACING HISTORY AFTER GENOCIDE AND MASS VIOLENCE 27 (1998).

See generally HAGAN, supra note 1.

See Kelly Askin, Analysis: Foca's Monumental Jurisprudence, Tribunal Update 226 (June 18– 23, 2001), https://listserv.buffalo.edu/cgi-bin/wa?A2=JUSTWATCH-L;c4188521.0106.

See, e.g., YVES DEZALAY & BRYANT G. GARTH, DEALING IN VIRTUE: INTERNATIONAL COMMERCIAL ARBITRATION AND THE CONSTRUCTION OF A TRANSNATIONAL LEGAL ORDER (1996).

BOSCO, supra note 9, at 72–76.

Extraordinary Session of the Assembly of the African Union, Addis Ababa, Ethiopia, AFRICAN UNION 1 (Oct. 12, 2013), http://www.iccnow.org/documents/Ext_Assembly_AU_Dec_Decl_ 12Oct2013 .pdf.

Press Release, African Union Assembly, 22nd Ordinary Session of the African Union Assembly Concludes: A Summary of Key Decisions (Jan. 31, 2014), http://summits.au.int/en/ 22ndsummit/events/22nd-ordinary-session-african-union-assembly-concludes-summary-key-decisions-0.

KAUPPI, supra note 14, at passim.

See generally Hagan, supra note 10.

See Robert H. Jackson, Opening Statement Before the International Military Tribunal (Nov. 21, 1945), http://www.roberthjackson.org/the-man/speeches-articles/speeches/speeches-by-robert-hjackson/opening-statement-before-the-international-military-tribunal/.

Id.

Id. This lies in contrast to the later Tokyo trial that relied substantially on affidavits from prisoners of war. See TIM MAGA, JUDGMENT AT TOKYO: THE JAPANESE WAR CRIMES TRIALS 57–58 (2001).

See DONALD BLOXHAM, GENOCIDE ON TRIAL: WAR CRIMES TRIALS AND THE FORMATION OF HOLOCAUST HISTORY AND MEMORY 60–69 (2001); CHRISTIAN DELAGE, CAUGHT ON CAMERA: FILM IN THE COURTROOM FROM THE NUREMBERG TRIALS TO THE TRIALS OF THE KHMER ROUGE 63–82 (2013); LAWRENCE DOUGLAS, THE MEMORY OF JUDGMENT: MAKING LAW AND HISTORY IN THE TRIALS OF THE HOLOCAUST 41–53, 114 (2001); TELFORD TAYLOR, THE ANATOMY OF THE NUREMBERG TRIALS: A PERSONAL MEMOIR 43–55 (1993); Patricia M. Wald, Running the Trial of the Century: The Nuremberg Legacy, 27 CARDOZO L. REV. 4, 1559–98 (2006).

Stephen Breyer, Crimes Against Humanity: Nuremberg 1946, 71 N.Y.U. L. REV. 1161, 1162 (1996).

Rebecca West, A Reporter at Large: Extraordinary Exile, THE NEW YORKER, Sept. 7, 1946, at 34, 35.

JOSEPH KESSEL, JUGEMENTS DERNIERS: LES PROCES PETAIN, NUREMBERG ET EICHMAN (2007).

See Alter, Helfer & Madsen, supra note 8, at 26.

BASS, supra note 2, at 162.

Id. at 152.

Id. at 179.

Id. at 154.

See MINOW, supra note 24, at 27; cf. Susanne Karstedt, The Nuremberg Tribunal and German Society: International Justice and Local Judgment in Post-Conflict Reconstruction, in THE LEGACY OF NUREMBERG: CIVILISING INFLUENCE OR INSTITUTIONALISED VENGEANCE? 13 (David A. Blumenthal & Timothy L.H. McCormack eds., 2008) (discussing the influence of the Nuremberg Trials in Germany).

JUDITH N. SHKLAR, LEGALISM: LAW, MORALS, AND POLITICAL TRIALS 168 (1964).

See, e.g., Max Radin, Justice at Nuremberg, 24 FOREIGN AFF. 369 (1946).

See BASS, supra note 2, at 147.

Id.

See MICHAEL R. MARRUS, THE NUREMBURG WAR CRIMES TRIAL, 1945–46: A DOCUMENTARY HISTORY 229–30 (1997).

See DOUGLAS, supra note 36, at 48–53.

See Guillaume Mouralis, Lawyers versus Jurisconsults: Sociography of the Main Nuremberg Trial, in JUSTICE IN WARTIME AND REVOLUTIONS: EUROPE, 1795–1950, at 315–326, 317 (Margo de Koster et al. eds., 2012).

See Richard Overy, The Nuremberg Trials: International Law in the Making, in FROM NUREMBERG TO THE HAGUE: THE FUTURE OF INTERNATIONAL CRIMINAL JUSTICE 1, 6 (Philippe Sands ed., 2003); William Kolasky, Robert H. Jackson: How a "Country Lawyer" Converted Franklin Roosevelt into a Trustbuster, 27 ANTITRUST 85 (2013).

See SANDRA QUINN-MUSGROVE & SANFORD KANTER, AMERICA'S ROYALTY: ALL THE PRESIDENTS' CHILDREN 134–35 (1995); ANN TUSA & JOHN TUSA, THE NUREMBERG TRIAL 70 (1986).

See BASS, supra note 2, at 148, 171; QUINN-MUSGROVE & KANTER, supra note 54, at 134–35; KIRSTEN SELLARS, 'CRIMES AGAINST PEACE' AND INTERNATIONAL LAW (2013); Kim Christian Priemel, "A Story of Betrayal": Conceptualizing Variants of Capitalism in the Nuremberg War Crimes Trials, 1 J. MOD. HIST. 85, 69–108 (2013).

See Jens David Ohlin, Group Think: The Law of Conspiracy and Collective Reason, 98 J. CRIM. LAW & CRIMINOLOGY 147, 169–72 (2007).

See BLOXHAM, supra note 36, at 60–62; MARRUS, supra note 50, at 40–43.

BASS, supra note 2, at 171–72.

Id.

Id. at 171.

John Q. Barrett, The Nuremberg Roles of Justice Robert H. Jackson, 6 WASH. U. GLOBAL STUD. L. REV. 511, 512–13 (2007).

See BASS, supra note 2, at 150, 182, 196; see also Robert H. Jackson, Some Problems in Developing an International Legal System, 22 TEMP. L. Q. 147, 154 (1948) [hereinafter Some Problems].

See Some Problems, supra note 62, at 151.

See DOUGLAS, supra note 36, at 16–17.

BLOXHAM, supra note 36, at 61.

See generally Telford Taylor, The Nuremberg War Crimes Trials: An Appraisal, 23 PROC. ACAD. POL. SCI. 19 (1949).

See MICHAEL SALTER, NAZI WAR CRIMES: US INTELLIGENCE AND SELECTIVE PROSECUTION AT NUREMBERG 346–51 (2007).

See generally Dan Kiley, Architect of Palace of Justice Renovations, in WITNESSES TO NUREMBERG: AN ORAL HISTORY OF AMERICAN PARTICIPANTS AT THE WAR CRIMES TRIALS 15 (Bruce M. Stave, Michele Palmer & Leslie Frank eds., 1998).

See Mouralis, supra note 52.

See BLOXHAM, supra note 36, at 60–61; JOSEPH E. PERSICO, NUREMBERG: INFAMY ON TRIAL 26 (1995).

See TAYLOR, supra note 36, at 185.

See id. at 183–85; SALTER, supra note 67, at 320.

See TAYLOR, supra note 36, at 184.

BLOXHAM, supra note 36, at 61.

Id. at 67.

SALTER, supra note 67, at 409–10.

BLOXHAM, supra note 36, at 202.

BASS, supra note 2, at 171–72.

Id.

See Levi & Hagan, supra note 1, at 6–10.

See generally Stéphane Leman-Langlois, Constructing a Common Language: The Function of Nuremberg in the Problematization of Postapartheid Justice, 27 LAW & SOC. INQUIRY 79 (2002).

SAMANTHA POWER, A PROBLEM FROM HELL: AMERICA AND THE AGE OF GENOCIDE 484 (2002).

See HAGAN, supra note 1, at 60–92; John Hagan & Ron Levi, Crimes of War and the Force of Law, 83 SOC. FORCES 1499, 1510–14 (2005).

See generally Dezalay & Garth, supra note 6.

See HAGAN, supra note 1, at 33–59; Levi & Hagan, supra note 1, at 13–15.

See Alter, Helfer & Madsen, supra note 8, at 10 (quoting KAREN J. ALTER, THE NEW TERRAIN OF INTERNATIONAL LAW: COURTS, POLITICS, RIGHTS 8–10 (2014)); Andrei Marmor, An Institutional Conception of Authority, 39 PHIL. & PUB. AFF. 238 (2011).

See generally Victor Peskin & Mieczyslaw P. Boduszynski, International Justice and Domestic Politics: Post-Tudjman Croatia and the International Criminal Tribunal for the Former Yugoslavia, 55 EUROPE–ASIA STUD. 1117 (2003).

Jelena Pejic, The Tribunal and the ICC: Do Precedents Matter?, 60 ALB. L. REV. 841, 853 (1997).

HAGAN, supra note 1, at 63.

Hagan & Levi, supra note 83, at 1510–14.

Michael P. Scharf, The Prosecutor v. Dusko Tadic: An Appraisal of the First International War Crimes Trial Since Nuremberg, 60 ALB. L. REV. 861, 876–77 (1997).

Hagan & Levi, supra note 83, at 1513–14.

See Schoenfeld, Levi & Hagan, supra note 9, at 16.

See RICHARD HOLBROOKE, TO END A WAR (1999); GEOFFREY ROBERTSON, CRIMES AGAINST HUMANITY: THE STRUGGLE FOR GLOBAL JUSTICE (1999); Hagan & Levi, supra note 85.

Hagan & Levi, supra note 83, at 1514.

See John Hagan, Ron Levi & Gabrielle Ferrales, Swaying the Hand of Justice: The Internal and External Dynamics of Regime Change at the International Criminal Tribunal for the Former Yugoslavia, 31 LAW & SOC. INQUIRY 585, 593–94 (2006).

Antonio Cassese, On the Current Trends Towards Criminal Prosecution and Punishment of Breaches of International Humanitarian Law, 9 EUR. J. INT'L L. 2, 11–12 (1998).

John Hagan & Ron Levi, Social Skill, the Milosevic Indictment, and the Rebirth of International Criminal Justice, 1 EUR. J. CRIMINOLOGY 445, 462 (2004) [hereinafter Social Skill].

Levi & Schoenfeld, supra note 9, at 31–34.

See Social Skill, supra note 98, at 459–61.

ERNA PARIS, LONG SHADOWS: TRUTH, LIES AND HISTORY 415 (2001).

See HAGAN, supra note 1, at 5.

CARLA DEL PONTE & CHUCK SUDETIC, MADAME PROSECUTOR: CONFRONTATIONS WITH HUMANITY'S WORST CRIMINALS AND THE CULTURE OF IMPUNITY (2009); Ed Vulliamy, Avenging Angel, THE GUARDIAN (Mar. 4, 2001), http://www.theguardian.com/world/2001/mar/04/warcrimes .comment.

See Askin, supra note 26.

Hagan, Levi & Ferrales, supra note 96, at 604.

Marlise Simons, Court on Crimes in Former Yugoslavia Hits Its Stride, N.Y. TIMES (May 15, 2005), http://www.nytimes.com/2005/05/15/international/europe/15hague.html.

S.C. Res. 1503 (Aug. 28, 2003).

See Yuval Shany, How Can International Criminal Courts Have a Greater Impact on National Criminal Proceedings? Lessons from the First Two Decades of International Criminal Justice in Operation, 46 ISR. L. REV. 431, 438 (2013).

See id. at 443–44; Yaël Ronen, The Impact of the ICTY on Atrocity-Related Prosecutions in the Courts of Bosnia and Herzegovina, 3 PENN ST. J. L. & INT'L AFF. 113, 147–56 (2014).

See generally Leslie Vinjamuri, The International Criminal Court and the Paradox of Authority, 79 LAW & CONTEMP. PROBS., no. 1, 2016 (discussing the extent to which international politics have shaped the extent of the ICC's authority among state actors).

Cf. Alter, Helfer & Madsen, supra note 8 (discussing how courts rely on past cases in their field).

Elizabeth Rubin, If Not Peace, Then Justice, N.Y. TIMES (Apr. 2, 2006), http://www.nytimes .com/2006/04/02/magazine/02darfur.html?pagewanted=print.

See Alex Whiting, Dynamic Investigative Practice at the International Criminal Court, 76 LAW & CONTEMP. PROBS., nos. 3 & 4, 2013, at 163, 175–76.

See COURTING CONFLICT? JUSTICE, PEACE AND THE ICC IN AFRICA (Nicholas Waddell & Phil Clark eds., 2008); Branch, supra note 15, at 179; Mahmood Mamdani, The Politics of Naming: Genocide, Civil War, Insurgency, 29 LONDON REV. BOOKS, no. 5, Mar. 8, 2007, at 5, http://www.lrb.co .uk/v29/n05/mahmood-mamdani/the-politics-of-naming-genocide-civil-war-insurgency

Whiting, supra note 113, at 163.

See Thomas Escritt, War Crimes Court Frustrated by Reliance on Witnesses, REUTERS (Sept. 20, 2013), http://www.reuters.com/article/2013/09/20/us-kenya-icc-investigations-idUSBRE98J0HY 20130920.

Philipp Ambach & Klaus U. Rackwitz, A Model of International Judicial Administration? The Evolution of Managerial Practices at the International Criminal Court, 76 LAW & CONTEMP. PROBS., nos. 3 & 4, 2013, at 119.

Whiting, supra note 113, at 185.

See WAR CRIMES RESEARCH OFFICE, INVESTIGATIVE MANAGEMENT, STRATEGIES, AND TECHNIQUES OF THE INTERNATIONAL CRIMINAL COURT'S OFFICE OF THE PROSECUTOR 55–60 (Oct. 2012) [hereinafter INVESTIGATIVE MANAGEMENT], http://www.wcl.american.edu/warcrimes/icc/ documents/ICCReport16.pdf.

College's Center on Law and Globalization Hosts Hague Colloquium Addressing Sexual Violence and Genocide, UNIV. OF ILL. COLL. OF LAW (June 22, 2009), http://www.law.illinois.edu/ news/article/1061.

See Whiting, supra note 113, at 181.

Yves Dezalay, From Mediation to Pure Law: Practice and Scholarly Representation within the Legal Sphere, 14 INT'L J. SOC. L. 89, 89 (1986).

Whiting, supra note 113, at 173–88.

INVESTIGATIVE MANAGEMENT, supra note 119, at 32.

See id.

Stéphanie Maupas, CPI: enquêteurs passifs et sans moyens pour procédures bâclées, LE MONDE (June 8, 2013), http://www.lemonde.fr/europe/article/2013/07/02/cpi-enqueteurs-passifs-et-sansmoyens-pour-procedures-baclees_3440543_3214.html ("L'enquête est le parent pauvre de la politique pénale de la Cour.").

Prosecutor v. Thomas Lubanga Dyilo, ICC-01/04-01/06-2843, Summary of the Judgment, ¶ 17 (Mar. 14, 2012).

Prosecutor v. Thomas Lubanga Dyilo, ICC-01/04-01/06-2842, Judgment, ¶ 130 (Mar. 14, 2012).

Id.

See Prosecutor v. Laurent Gbagbo, ICC-02/11-01/11-432, Decision Adjourning the Hearing on the Confirmation of Charges Pursuant to Article 61(7)(c)(i) of the Rome Statute (June 3, 2013); see also Blake Evans-Pritchard & Simon Jennings, ICC to Unveil New Investigation Strategy, REPORTING KENYA (Oct. 22, 2013), http://reportingkenya.net/reports/icc-to-unveil-new-investigation-strategy/.

Prosecutor v. Thomas Lubanga Dyilo, ICC-01/04-01/06, Deposition of Bernard Lavigne, 21 (2010).

See INVESTIGATIVE MANAGEMENT, supra note 119, at 48.

Katy Glassborow, ICC Investigative Strategy Under Fire, INST. FOR WAR & PEACE REPORTING (Oct. 27, 2008), https://iwpr.net/global-voices/icc-investigative-strategy-under-fire.

Anonymous interview conducted by author.

CHAPTER 4

DEFINING THE CRIME OF ENFORCED DISAPPEARANCE IN CONFORMITY WITH INTERNATIONAL CRIMINAL LAW: A NEW FRONTIER FOR BANGLADESH

MD. Raisul Islam Sourav

INTRODUCTION

Occurrences of abductions, kidnaps, enforced disappearances, and killings have in-creased dramatically in Bangladesh in the last few years. Among these, the case of seven murders allegedly perpetrated by high officials of the Rapid Action Battalion (RAB)[1] at *Narayanganj*[2] in 2014 has created most reaction among civil society such as lawyers, rights activist etc. in Bangladesh. Civil engagement exposed the cruelty and inhumanity of the incident and spread awareness about the gravity of these offences.

Most cases are unresolved to this day and very few abductees have been rescued successfully by law enforcement. However, in most of cases the victim's family members, relatives and friends targeted their allegations towards law enforcement agencies. Specific allegation have been made that individuals wearing civilian dress, but introducing them-selves as members of the RAB, Detective Branch (DB) or of other law enforcement agencies are arresting and forcefully taking the victim with them. The detained person then typically vanishes from custody with none aware of their fate and whereabouts. Corpses were found in very few cases. When confronted with such allegations, law enforcement agencies deny any involvement. To date have few offenders been brought to justice. Such incidents are not properly investigated, and no visible action has been undertaken to prevent their reoccurrence.

It is however clear that the state has a responsibility to prevent such crimes and ensure the punishment of those responsible, failing which a culture of impunity will be allowed to bloom. The object of this paper is to scrutinise and analyse the socio-legal aspects of forced disappearances and to suggest a way towards the ratification of the UN Convention for the Protection of All Persons from Enforced Disappearance ('the Convention'). This would in turn improve the ability of the state to prevent the occurrence of such crime and to combat impunity.

This paper will present and contrast the definition of enforced disappearance in respectively national and international criminal law. The following section will assess the role of the Committee on Enforced Disappearance (CED), which is established by the Convention to monitor and evaluate the overall situation of forced disappearance in the state parties. This paper will also examine the impacts of enforced disappearances on the individual and on society as a whole. It will also be shown that the current situation amounts to a continuous violation of national and international customary law and that continued enforced disappearances constitute international crimes and crimes against humanity. Finally, some recommendations will be put forward to bring about an end to the situation.

THE EMERGENCE AND DEFINITION OF EN-FORCED DISAPPEARANCE IN IN-TERNATIONAL CRIMINAL LAW

Enforced disappearance is not new to international criminal law. Enforced disappearances persist in many countries, having been a continuing feature of the second half of the twentieth century since they were perpetrated on a mass scale in Nazi-

Citation: MD. Raisul Islam Sourav, Defining the Crime of Enforced Disappearance in Conformity with International Criminal Law: a New Frontier for Bangladesh, http://scholarship.law.duke.edu/cgi/viewcontent.cgi?article=4775&context=lcp

occupied Europe.[3] The crime of enforced disappearance of persons became first known when[4] Adolf Hitler issued the *'Nacht und Nebel Erlass'* (Night and Fog Decree). The decree directed that persons in occupied territories engaging in activities intended to undermine the security of German troops were, upon capture, to be brought to Germany 'by night and fog' for trial by special courts, thus circumventing military procedure and various conventions governing the treatment of prisoners. From the mid-1960s, disappearance as a tool of political repression was employed by security forces in Guatemala. It was from Guatemala that the term *desaparecido* (disappeared one) originated in the 1960s. In the 1970s, disappearances occurred in significant numbers in Argentina, Chile, Philippines and Uganda amongst other places.[5]

In Chile, the systematic practice of 'disappearances' lasted from 1973 to 1977, with about 1,300 missing. That is in addition to the 2,000 people who were killed outright in extra-judicial executions. Forced disappearances were also practice in Argentina on a much larger scale and lasted for four years, from 1976 to 1980.[6]

Enforced disappearance was first recognised as a human rights problem in the 1970s, when human rights lawyers in Chile noted that some of the prisoners they were representing had vanished even though they were ostensibly still held in custody by Chilean security forces.[7]

However, enforced disappearance has emerged as a critical problem at the national and international level. In the last decades, the international community has taken steps to combat enforced disappearances, both at the regional and international level, with the Declaration on the Protection of all Persons from Enforced Disappearance of 1992[8], the Inter-American Convention on Forced Disappearance of Persons of 1994[9], and the Rome Statute of the International Criminal Court of 1998. Following this expansion, the UN General Assembly adopted the International Convention for the Protection of All Persons from Enforced Disappearance in December 2006.[10] The Convention entered into force on 23 December, 2010. To date, 90 states have become signatories, and 30 have ratified the Convention.[11] Among state parties, 12 have recognized the competence of the Committee of Enforced Disappearances (CED) to receive and consider communications both by individuals alleging that their rights under the Convention have been violated as well as communications by states claiming that another state party is not fulfilling its obligations under the Convention. Very few states have so far implemented the Convention into national law. The convention aims at preventing enforced disappearances from taking place, uncovering the truth when they do occur, punishing the perpetrators and providing reparations to the victims and their families.

The Convention gives a definition of the crime of enforced disappearance and sets out which state action is necessary in order to prevent the occurrence of the crime, to allow for an effective investigation, and to lead to the prosecution of those responsible. In accordance with Article 2, an enforced disappearance takes place when a person is arrested, detained or abducted by the state or agents acting for the state, who then deny that the person is being held or conceal their whereabouts, placing them outside the protection of the law. The Convention identifies the following elements in the definition of enforced disappearances:

- There is an arrest, detention, abduction or any other form of deprivation of liberty;
- That conduct is carried out by agents of the state or by persons or groups of per-sons with the authorisation, support or acquiescence of the state;
- The conduct is followed either by a refusal to acknowledge the deprivation of liberty or by the concealment of the fate or whereabouts of the disappeared person;
- The objective result of the conduct is that the disappeared person is placed outside of the protection of the law.

Article 1(2) also provides that exceptional circumstances, such as a state or threat of war, internal political instability or any other public emergency, may not under any circumstances be invoked as a justification for enforced disappearance. Under Article 4 state parties also have an obligation to take necessary measures to ensure that enforced disappearance constitutes an offence under national criminal law.

Moreover, the aforementioned Convention in Article 6(1) also provides liability criteria for the offence of enforced disappearance. Under subparagraph (a), '*any person who commits, orders, solicits or induces the commission of, attempts to commit, is an accomplice to or participates in an enforced disappearance,*' is liable. Subparagraph (b) extends liability to any superior who '*knew, or consciously disregarded information which clearly indicated- that subordinates under his or her effective authority and control were committing or about to commit a crime of enforced disappearance.*'

Enforced disappearance is also a cumulative violation of human rights.[12] This is be-cause it may inflict a wide range of human rights violations, including the violation of:

- The right to life, as the person may be killed or his or her fate may be unknown, cf. Art. 32 of the Bangladeshi Constitution;
- The right to personal security and dignity;
- The right to be free from arbitrary detention, cf. Art. 33 of the Bangladeshi Constitution;
- The right not to be subjected to torture or other cruel, inhuman or degrading treatment or punishment, cf. Art. 35 of the Bangladeshi Constitution;
- The right to humane conditions of detention, cf. Art. 33 of the Bangladeshi Constitution;
- The right to legal personality, cf. Art. 31 of the Bangladeshi Constitution;
- The right to fair trial, cf. Art. 35 of the Bangladeshi Constitution;
- The right to free movement, cf. Art. 36 of the Bangladeshi Constitution;
- The right to family life;

All of the above rights are guaranteed as fundamental rights under the constitution and are either directly or indirectly applicable by Bangladeshi courts.[13]

The Rome Statute of the International Criminal Court particularly classifies forced disappearance as a crime against humanity, see Art. 7(1)(i).

For the crime of enforced disappearance to be committed under Article 7, the following elements must be present:

- One or several persons have been arrested, detained, or abducted.
- This deprivation of liberty was preceded, followed or accompanied by a refusal to acknowledge the deprivation of freedom or to give information on the fate or whereabouts of the victim(s).
- Both 1) and 2) were carried out by, or with the authorization, support or acquiescence of an emanation of the state or a political organisation.
- The perpetrator was aware of 1) and 2).
- The intention was to remove the victim(s) from the protection of the law for a prolonged period of time.
- The conduct was committed as part of a widespread or systematic attack directed against a civilian population.
- The perpetrator knew that the conduct was part of such an attack.

In addition, the Inter-American Convention on the Forced Disappearance of Persons also imposes an obligation on state parties *'not to practice, permit or tolerate the forced disappearance of persons, even in the states of emergency or suspension of individuals guarantees'*, see Article 1(a).

As is shown, international law does not only consider enforced disappearances as a cruel crime and gross violation of human rights, it is also considered as a crime against humanity, where the state itself plays vital role behind the scenes. Any prevention mechanism must therefore be directed towards the state, something which is the purpose of the UN Convention. Combating enforced disappearances thus requires that Bangladesh ratifies the UN convention and adopts national legislation that criminalises enforced dis-appearances.

THE SIGNIFICANCE OF THE INTERNATIONAL CONVENTION FOR THE PROTECTION OF ALL PERSONS FROM ENFORCED DISAPPEARANCE

Unlike other human rights violations, enforced disappearances were not considered specifically by a universal legally binding instrument before the Convention came into force in 2010.[14] Before that only the Rome Statute of the International Criminal Court[15] pro-vided for the prosecution and the award of reparation to victims in cases where enforced disappearance amounted to a crime against humanity.[16]

However, the crime of enforced disappearances was prohibited prior to 2010 by the 1992 UN Declaration on the Protection of all Persons from Enforced Disappearance, the 1996 Inter-American Convention, as well as customary international humanitarian law. However, this previously existing framework exhibited serious gaps and ambiguities, and had proven to be insufficient as a protection mechanism. The Convention, despite its own flaws, corrects some of the existing gaps in the legal framework.

- Firstly, the Convention makes enforced disappearance a crime under international law, which is nonderogable even under exceptional circumstances, such as the state or threat of war, internal political instability or any other public emergency.
- Secondly, the Convention obliges states to criminalise Enforced Disappearances in national law.
- Thirdly, it enshrines the right of victims or their relatives to have access to justice and full and to full and effective reparation.
- Fourthly, the Convention sets up the Committee on Enforced Disappearances – which began its work in November 2011.

Prior to the Convention's entry into force, the only mechanism dealing specifically with enforced disappearances was the UN Working Group on Enforced or Involuntary Disappearances.[17] This Working Group, established by the 1992 Declaration, continues to exist and carries out important work as a rapid response mechanism to request states to start investigations where it is believed that an enforced disappearance has taken place, based on reports of disappearances submitted by relatives of disappeared persons or human rights organisations acting on their behalf.

The Convention, in contrast to the 1992 Declaration or the regional conventions, goes further when defining the term '*victim*'. A '*victim*' under the Convention includes the abducted person as well as any individual who has suffered harm as the direct result of an enforced disappearance. This definition covers both direct and indirect victims and thus includes family members who ignore the whereabouts of their relative and can, therefore, be qualified as torture victims.[18] It establishes, for the first time in a human rights treaty, the explicit *right of each victim to know the truth* regarding the circumstances of the enforced disappearance, the progress and results of the investigation, and the fate of the person who has disappeared.

Moreover, the Convention, contrary to the 1992 Declaration and human rights documents, also lists forms of reparation. The right to obtain reparation covers material and moral damages and, where appropriate, other forms of reparation such as:

- Restitution;
- Rehabilitation;
- Satisfaction, including restoration of dignity and reputation;
- Guarantees of non-*repetition.*[19]

These forms of reparation echo the provisions of General Assembly resolution A/ RES/60/147.[20] This resolution emphasised the need for an *effective remedy* in cases of gross violations of international human rights law and serious violations of international humanitarian law. The resolution affirms the obligation on all states to investigate and, if there is sufficient evidence, the duty to prosecute the person allegedly responsible for the violations, and, if found guilty, the duty to punish the perpetrator. It also outlines obligations on states to cooperate with one another, and to assist international judicial organs competent in the investigation and prosecution of these violations.

States are encouraged to facilitate extradition, to surrender offenders to other states and to appropriate international judicial bodies, to provide judicial assistance, and to cooperate in the pursuit of international justice. This includes assisting and protecting victims and witnesses, consistently with international human rights legal standards and subject to international legal requirements such as those relating to the prohibition of torture.[21]

Among other forms of effective reparation, the resolution includes the possibility of *rehabilitation*, which should include medical and psychological care, as well as legal and social services. It is noteworthy that the Convention also provides for access to rehabil-itation.[22] While other forms of reparation for human rights violations are provided for in all core UN human rights treaties, this form of reparation is a novelty in international human rights treaties and is currently only practiced by the Committee against Torture (CAT), which is responsible for monitoring the prevention of torture and other cruel, inhuman or degrading treatment.

The Committee on Enforced Disappearance (CED) can similarly receive requests for urgent action from relatives of the disappeared, their legal representatives or others, which it can transmit to the state party concerned with a request to clarify the fate and whereabouts of the disappeared person. It also competent to consider individual com-plaints by persons who claim to be the victim of a violation of the Convention, although this competence must be specifically recognised by the states. The Committee is also empowered to perform other functions to monitor the Convention's implementation and state parties' compliance with their obligations.

THE ROLE OF THE COMMITTEE ON ENFORCED DISAPPEARANCE (CED) TO PREVENT FORCED DISAPPEARANCES

The Committee on Enforced Disappearance (CED) is similar in form and function to other UN human rights treaty bodies, such as the Committee against Torture (CAT). The CED is composed of ten experts in the field of human rights, who serve on the Committee in their individual capacity and are expected to exercise their functions independently and impartially. Within two years of ratifying the Convention, state parties are required to submit a report to the Committee describing the measures they have under-taken to implement the Convention. After examining the report, the Committee makes general suggestions and recommendations to the state party as it considers appropriate. Furthermore, the Committee can transmit requests for urgent action sent by or on behalf of the relatives of a disappeared person to state parties requesting that they clarify the fate and whereabouts of the disappeared person. It can also undertake visits if it receives re-liable information indicating that a state party is seriously violating the provisions of the Convention, and may bring situations of widespread or systematic practices of enforced disappearances to the attention of the UN General Assembly.

Moreover, the Committee also has an optional individual complaints system. It can under this system consider complaints submitted by or on behalf of individuals alleging to be victims of a violation of the provisions of the Convention by a state party, provided by the state has declared that it accepts the competence of the Committee to receive such individual communications. The Committee may also receive and consider communications in which one state party claims that another state party is not fulfilling its obligations under the Convention provided that both state parties concerned have agreed to the optional inter-state communications procedure.

EFFECTS OF FORCED DISAPPEARANCES ON SOCIETIES AND INDIVIDUALS

Families are often emotionally unable to find closure and come to terms with the disappearance of their loved ones. Many suffer from severe psychological distress, sometimes resulting in physical illness as well. Children are not immune from such anguish; the disappearance of a parent, sibling or other members of the family often adversely affects their educational performance and social behaviour.[23]

Furthermore, families frequently face substantial economic consequences as a result of an enforced disappearance, particularly when the victim was the principal bread-winner of the family. Even if this was not the case, many families find themselves in a dire economic situation while they search for the victim. These families are then frequently isolated socially and culturally, with little support to fall back on. For example, while widows in certain cultures have a well-established support system within communities, wives of disappeared victims are at times left in a limbo.[24]

It is common for people who have disappeared never to be released, with their fate remaining unknown. But the person cannot simply have vanished. Someone surely knows what has happened to them. Someone is responsible, but all too often the offenders are never brought to justice. Nevertheless, the victim and their family have a right to justice and to receive reparations.[25] They also have a right to know the truth about the circumstances of the enforced disappearance and the fate of the disappeared person, and the right to seek, receive and impart information to this end.

FORCED DISAPPEARANCE UNDER THE CRIMINAL LAWS OF BANGLADESH

Enforced, involuntary or forced disappearance is not a crime or offence under Bangladeshi law. Involuntary disappearance is however a domestic crime when it may considered as a crime against humanity under Article 7(1)(i) of the Rome Statute. Thus, unless the act fits the Rome statute's definition the state has sole jurisdiction to prosecute the perpetrator. However, enforced disappearances have taken place to a large extent since last couple of years in Bangladesh. Nevertheless the provisions pertaining to kidnapping and abduction in the Penal Code of 1860 may be applicable.[26]

According to section 362 of the Penal Code, a person is said to commit the offence of abduction when he by force compels or by any deceitful means induces another person to go from one place to another.

Kidnapping as defined by section 359 classifies two types of offences, namely kidnap-ping from Bangladesh and kidnap-ping from lawful guardianship. Whoever carries any person beyond the borders of Bangladesh without the consent of that person, or of some person legally authorised to consent on their behalf, is said to kidnap that person from Bangladesh. On the other hand, whoever takes or entices any minor or any person of unsound mind, out of the keeping of their lawful guardian is said to kidnap that person from guardianship.

The punishment for kidnapping is up to seven years' imprisonment and a fine. Where the kidnapping is undertaken with the intention to murder however, the prison sentence can be increased to ten years or to life imprisonment, pursuant to section 364.

An analysis of the outlined criminal provisions can be summarised as follows:

- Kidnapping is committed when the victim is a minors under sixteen years of age in case of a male or under eighteen years in case of a female, or a person of unsound mind. The crime of abduction is independent of the age of the victim.
- In the event of a kidnapping, a minor is usually taken away, forcefully or not, without the consent of legal guardian. Force, compulsion or deceit are however basic elements of abduction.
- The consent of the minor is immaterial in cases of kidnapping, whereas in cases of abduction, the absence of consent is of vital importance.
- Kidnapping moves the victim away from the custody of legal guardian and being so it is a substantive offence, as opposed to abduction.

In addition to the above, if a person kidnaps or abducts any child under the age of ten, in order for the child to be murdered or to be subjected to grievous harm, slavery, or to sexual abuse; the penalty is death or life imprisonment or imprisonment for a term of be-tween seven and fourteen years.[27] Additionally, if a person kidnaps or abducts a woman in order for her to be compelled to marry someone against her will, or in order for her to be forced or seduced to have intercourse; the punishment is death, or life imprisonment, or imprisonment between ten and twenty years as well as a fine.[28]

The punishment for murder after an abduction is death or life imprisonment, pursuant to section 302 of the Penal Code. In addition to this, if the kidnapping or abduction is committed with an intention to forcible confinement, the punishment is a prison term of up to seven years and a fine.

VIOLATIONS OF NATIONAL AND INTERNATIONAL LAWS

The frequent allegations of involuntary disappearances betray that the rule of law is failing in Bangladesh. The Republic is under an obligation to safeguard every citizen's right to life and property. It also has the responsibility to protect citizens' fundamental rights as guaranteed by the Constitution.[29] By detaining individuals without due process, the government of Bangladesh grossly violates a number of its citizens' fundamental rights.

The Constitution states that

to enjoy the protection of the law, and to be treated in accordance with law, and only in accordance with law, is the inalienable right of every citizen, wherever he may be, and of every other person for the time being within Bangladesh, and in particular no action detrimental to the life, liberty, body, reputation or property of any person shall be taken except in accordance with law. [30]

The constitution also state that '*no person shall be deprived of life or personal liberty saves in accordance with law.*'[31]

In reality, this most fundamental right is repetitively violated with complete impunity. The government has violated these two articles of the constitution by depriving its citizens of the protection of the law, and of the right to be treated in accordance with the law.[32]

Law enforcement agencies have detained victims without a warrant of arrest issued by a court of law, making such arrest illegal. In such cases law enforcement agencies do not inform the arrestee of the ground(s) for the arrest, neither do they produce the arrestee before the nearest Magistrate Court; and nor is the arrestee offered the chance to consult with a lawyer. All these elements are in clear violation of the Constitution.[33]

The Universal Declaration of Human Rights of 1948 prohibits arbitrary arrests.[34] Each enforced disappearance amounts to a violation of right to be safe from illegal arrest.[35] Bangladesh has also ratified the ICCPR.[36] According to Articles 2 and 6 of the ICCPR, Bangladesh has the obligation to defend the right to life of its people and to ensure prompt and effective reparation where violations occur.

It is also obliged to bring legislation into conformity with the ICCPR. Under Article 14, state parties must ensure a fair and public trial for anyone charged with a criminal offense, and such a trial must take place 'without undue delay.' The covenant also re-quires Bangladesh to protect freedom of expression.[37] Bangladesh is also a state party to the Convention against torture (CAT). Under Article 12, the Bangladeshi government must ensure that any person who alleges he has been subject to torture has the right 'to complain to and to have his case promptly and impartially examined by competent authorities.'

A number of decisions of international human rights bodies have clarified which elements of the phenomenon of enforced disappearances can amount to torture. For example, the European Court of Human Rights in the case of *Bazorkina v. Russia*[38] examined an alleged violation of Article 3 ECHR on the prohibition of torture and other degrading or inhuman treatment. The court emphasised that in such a violation, the actual disappearance was not the central criterion; decisive was rather the authorities' reactions and attitude once the matter had been brought to their attention. The court found in the case that the applicant suffered –and continued to suffer– distress and anguish as a result of the disappearance of her son and her inability to learn of his fate. The manner in which her complaints had been dealt with by the authorities had to be considered to amount to 'inhuman treatment' as prohibited by Article 3[39].

It is noteworthy that CAT has become the source of reference for the UN Convention enforced disappearances. One of the features of CAT is the obligation on states parties under Article 4 to criminalise torture in domestic laws with appropriate penalties, and to eliminate safe havens for perpetrators of torture by establishing various types of jurisdictions, including criminal jurisdictions, in accordance with detailed provisions in Articles 5–9.

The importance of torture as an element of enforced disappearances is that it gives rise to state parties' obligation to criminalise torture. The positive obligations on state parties to prevent, investigate and punish the perpetrators in cases of enforced disappearances and torture are explicitly developed in the jurisprudence of regional human rights courts like the ECtHR and the Inter-American Court on Human Rights. In the case of *Velasquez Rodriguez*,[40] the latter court referred to Article 1(1) of CAT and carried out an analysis of the positive obligations it entails. The first obligation on the state party is 'to respect the rights and freedoms' provided for in the Convention, while a second obligation is to 'ensure' every person subject to its jurisdiction the free and full exercise of these rights. The court stated that the states must prevent, investigate and punish any violation of the rights recognised by the Convention and, if possible, attempt to restore the violated rights and provide compensation as warranted for damages resulting from violation.

Similar statements were made by the European Court of Human Rights in the *Bazorkina v. Russia* case. The Court, like its American counterpart, also stressed the obligation of the authorities to act on their own volition once the matter has come to their attention.

For an investigation ... to be effective it may generally be regarded as necessary for the persons responsible for the investigation to be independent from those implicated in the events. The investigation must also be effective in the sense that it be capable of leading to a determination of whether the force used in such cases is or is not justified and lead to punishment for those who are responsible. This is not an obligation of result, but of means.'[41]

The Court noted that delays in the investigation compromised its effectiveness and had a negative impact on the prospect of discovering the truth.

In the *Edriss El Hassy v. The Libyan Arab Jamahiriya* case, the UN Human Rights Committee concentrated on the obligations on the state party and referred to the importance of states parties establishing appropriate judicial and administrative mechanisms for addressing the alleged violations under domestic law. It referred to its General Comment No. 31, which states that failure by a State Party to investigate allegations of violations could give rise to a separate breach of the Covenant. The Committee concluded that state parties were duty-bound to conduct thorough investigations into alleged violations of human rights, particularly enforced disappearances and acts of torture and also to prosecute, try and punish those held responsible for such violations.

CONCLUSION

The government of Bangladesh is under an obligation to ensure a fair and independent investigation into all cases of disappearance. The government also needs to make clear to its security forces that the state is under an obligation not to torture its citizen under various international instruments. Any criminal offence must be tried through the criminal justice system; the suspect must not be punished by security forces outside the due process of law. In cases of serious human rights violations, the government is under an obligation to take necessary actions to prevent such incidents. Every victim should promptly be produced before a court of law by the concerned law enforcing agency within whose custody he is detained.

The international community should consider the issues of human rights violation and enforced disappearances in diplomatic terms when making any decision about their relation with Bangladesh. Donor agencies should ensure that no person is kidnapped or tortured due to their political identity, and that all persons get equal protection from the law. Bangladesh must be urged to halt the growing phenomenon of enforced disappearances and show its commitment to do so by ratifying the Convention for the Protection of All Persons from Enforced Disappearance without delay, as well as fully implementing it in domestic legislation.

States have committed themselves to ending the practice of enforced disappearance and must take steps to respect, protect and fulfill the rights of individuals not to be subjected to enforced disappearance. Furthermore, states must tackle the issue of impunity and ensure that the perpetrators are brought to justice.

Moreover, to maximise the Convention's preventive effect as well as to offer redress to victims and their families, Bangladesh should also accept the competence of the Committee on Enforced Disappearances to receive complaints from individuals and state par-ties under Articles 31 and 32 of the Convention.

Another measure that can prevent enforced disappearances and in the longer term eliminate the phenomenon, would be to adopt a long-term and comprehensive plan, which would establish effective training programs for law enforcement and other personnel. Civil society actors may also take specific actions to support their recommendations to governments to ratify the Convention. Civil society may participate in drafting and debating national implementing legislation. Civil society members can also provide information in relation to the CED's review of state reports and its other functions un-der the Convention; they may submit urgent requests for action to clarify the fate and whereabouts of a disappeared person, or submit individual communications on behalf of an individual who claims to be a victim of a violation of the Convention. Women and women's organisations should be particularly encouraged to do so to ensure that gender issues are taken into account and that the process of preparing the implementing legislation is inclusive. Another argument for the involvement of women's organisations is that it is most often men who are subject to disappearance, and female family members then spearhead efforts to obtain justice for their loved ones

Notes

A specialised battalion in charge of preventing terrorism and militancy in Bangladesh.

A district of Bangladesh situated near Dhaka.

Henckaerts & Doswald-Beck, Customary International Humanitarian Law (CUP 2005), p. 379.

on December 7, 1941.

Amnesty International, Disappearances: A Workbook (AIUSA 1981), p.2.

Walling, Booth & Waltz (ed.), Human Rights: From Practice to Policy, Proceeding of a research workshop (Gerald R. Fold School of Public Policy, University of Michigan 2010), available at: http://humanrightshistory.umich.edu/files/2012/07/Zalquette1.docx (Last accessed on 18 December 2015).

Ibid.

United Nations, General Assembly resolution 47/133, Declaration on the Protection of all Persons from Forced Disappearance, A/RES/47/133 (18 December 1992), available at http:// undocs.org/A/RES/47/133.

Popularly known as Inter-American Convention.

The text was adopted on 20 December 2006 (A/RES/61/177), and was opened for signature on 6 February, 2007.

The countries that have ratified the Convention to date are: Albania, Argentina, Armenia, Belgium, Bolivia, Brazil, Burkina Faso, Chile, Cuba, Ecuador, France, Gabon, Germany, Honduras, Iraq, Japan, Kazakhstan, Mali, Mexico, Montenegro, Netherlands, Nigeria, Panama, Paraguay, Senegal, Serbia, Spain, Tunisia, Uruguay & Zambia.

Ratner, Abrams & Bischoff, Accountability for Human Rights Atrocities in International Law: Beyond the Nuremberg Legacy, 3rd ed. (OUP 2009), pp. 128-29.

Islam, Constitutional Law of Bangladesh, 2nd ed. (Mullick Brothers 2010).

Cassese, International Criminal Law, 2nd edition (OUP 2003), p. 80.

Came into force in 2002.

Meron, The Humanization of Humanitarian Law (Brill 2000), pp. 94 & 239.

Berman & Clark, State Terrorism: Disappearances, in 13 Rutgers Law Journal (1982), pp. 531 ff.

Bazorkina v. Russia, appl. no. 69481/01, 27.07.2006, and Edriss El Hassy v. The Libyan Arab Jamahiriya, No. CCPR/C/91/D/1422/2005.

Article 24 of the Convention.

United Nations, General Assembly resolution 60/147, Basic Principles and Guidelines on the Right to a Remedy and Reparation for Victims of Gross Violations of International Human Rights Law and Serious Violations of International Humanitarian Law, A/RES/60/147 (16 December 2005), available at http://undocs.org/A/RES/60/147. (Last accessed on 18 December 2015)

Ibid.

The possibility of rehabilitation was initially foreseen in the GA Resolution A/RES/60/147.

Amnesty International, Enforced Disappearances: Questions and Answers, 2011, p. 2. Available at: https://www.amnesty.org/en/documents/ior51/010/2011/zh/ (Last accessed on 18 December 2015)

UN War Crimes Commission, Law Reports of Trials of War Criminals, 1949, Volume I, p. 113.

van Schaack, Crimen sine Lege: Judicial Lawmaking at the Intersection of Law and Morals, in 97 Georgetown Law Journal (2008), pp. 97 & 119.

Huq, Penal Code, 5th ed. (Anupam Gyan Bhander 2010).

Sections 6, 7 & 12 of the Prevention of Oppression against Women and Children Act, 2000 (Bangladesh).

Section 5 of the Prevention of Oppression against Women and Children Act, 2000 (Bangladesh).

Listed in Part III of the Constitution of the People's Republic of Bangladesh.

Art. 31 of the Constitution of the People's Republic of Bangladesh.

Art. 32 of the Constitution of the People's Republic of Bangladesh.

Art. 31 of the Constitution of the People's Republic of Bangladesh.

Art. 33 of the Constitution of the People's Republic of Bangladesh. The said Article states: (1) No person who is arrested shall be detained in custody without being informed, as soon as may be of the grounds for such arrest, nor shall he be denied the right to consult and be defended by a legal practitioner of his choice. (2) Every person who is arrested and detained in custody shall be produced before the nearest magistrate within a period of twenty four hours of such arrest, excluding the time necessary for the journey from the place of arrest to the court of the magistrate, and no such person shall be detained in custody beyond the said period without the authority of a magistrate.

Art. 9 of the Universal Declaration of Human Rights, 1948.

Lauterpacht, The Law of Nations and the Punishment of War Crimes, in 21 British Yearbook of International Law (1944), p. 58.

1. ON 6 SEPTEMBER 2000.

2. ART. 19 OF THE INTERNATIONAL COVENANT ON CIVIL AND POLITICAL RIGHTS (ICCPR), 1966.

3. BAZORKINA V. RUSSIA, APPL. NO. 69481/01, 27.07.2006, PARA. 139.

4. IBID, PARA. 142.

5. VELASQUEZ RODRIGUEZ VS HONDURAS, INTER-AMERICAN COURT OF HUMAN RIGHTS (IACRTHR (SER. C) NO. 4), 29 JULY 1988, AVAILABLE AT: HTTP://WWW.REFWORLD.ORG/DOCID/40279A9E4.HTML (LAST ACCESSED ON 17 DECEMBER 2015).

6. BAZORKINA V. RUSSIA, APPL. NO. 69481/01, 27 JULY 2006, PARA. 118

CHAPTER 5

THE PRINCIPLE OF PROPORTIONALITY IN INTERNATIONAL CRIMINAL LAW

Venus Ghareh Baghi and T. R. Maruthi

Keywords: Proportionality, Grave offence, Circumstance, Consistency, Criteria of proportionality

INTRODUCTION

The principle of proportionality creates balance between the cri me and its punishment for establishing criminal justice, instance of the nature of the homicide is altered from murder to manslaughter because the homicide was com mitted by a person with reduced capacity not fully responsible for his or her action. Proportionality between crime and punishment should be transferable to international law for considering to criminal justice. In particular categories of international crimes should be existed in a hierarchy based on gravity of the crimes.

Some support for such as hierarchy of international crimes is found, including the core offense crimes against humanity, genocide, and war crimes the first is distinct from, each other[1].

But it is not clear, which one more serious than another application of this proposition is found in the opinion of judge McDonald and Vohrah in the international criminal tribunal Yugoslavia appeals chamber judgment in Erdemovic, in the context of determining that the accused of a crime against humanity would result in a more straighten punishment than would a guilty plea to a war crime, the two judges advanced in a hierarchy based on moral gravity[2]. However it should be noted that the concept of lesser crimes has not received universal acceptance.[3]

Citation: Venus Ghareh Baghi and T. R. Maruthi, The Principle of Proportionality in International Criminal Law, http://journals.univ-danubius.ro/index.php/juridica/article/view/1058/885

In order to constituting of proportionality the degrees of punishment is specific, definite and clear (Haveman, Kavran & Nicholls, 2003). It also requires the law to differentiate between the specific maximum punishments to different crimes. Second reason for considering to principal of proportionality is that an individual is entitled to know the nature of the charges against him. Finally, it would mean that the law of penalties should also distinguish between different forms of participation in criminal conducts such as omission, attempt, aiding and abetting, and the applicable penalty should be distinguished not only between types of crimes but also between complete and inchoate crimes. The aim of distinguished and codification of crime and punishment is to make sure that a defendant is sentenced to neither more nor less than what he deserves.

As well as, the sentence accorded to a crime should reflect the serious of the offences. Thus It would clearly be wrong if murder carried a less serious sentence than assault, but there are more complex argument over whether one offence is more or less serious than another. For example, is rap more or less serious than hand cut off? " *It should be notice, proportionate not only to the crime itself but also to those sentence impose for similar offences in similar cases. By doing so, the unequal treatment of similar cases may be avoided*". (Shahram, 2009)[4]

[1] Prosecutor Jean Kambanda in case No. ICTR 97-23-5 trail chamber I, judgment and sentence of 4 sept. 1998 – para no. 3.

[2] Ibidem, para no.4.

[3] Ibidem, para 9b.

[4] Available at: http://works.bepress.com/shahram_dana/1

PROPORTIONALITY IN THE FRENCH AND GERMAN CRIMINAL LAW

In the legal systems proportionality indicated to vary ways. Proportionality in French was determinate by 1810 Penal Code France and new 1994 Code classify offences into three groups:

- *"Contraventions"* : very petty offences punished only by fines (minor road offences, breach of bylaws, minor assaults, noise offences etc.);
- *"Délits"* : offences of greater importance subjected to a sentence of a maximum of 10 years. *Délits* include theft, manslaughter, indecent assault, drug offences, fraud and deception, drunken driving, serious unintentional bodily damages etc.;
- *"Crimes":* offences subjected to custodial sentences from 10 years to a life term (murder, rape, robbery, abduction).

The constitutional basis of German, the sentencing structure can be drawn from the notion of the *Rechtsstaat*, which can be translated with the term "rule of la w." This principle, which is laid down in Article 20 1 *Grundgesetz*[1]encompasses the culpability-principle, under which the punishment must be proportionate to the individual guilt of the offender. Thus, section 46 I of the Criminal Code stats " *the guilt of the perpetrator is the foundation for determining punishment*." The culpability-principle is a specific expression of the proportionality principle, which is also a constitutional requirement of the "rule of law." (Streng, 2007, pp. 153-172)[2]

In the German criminal law, research has shown that the sentence is usually based on four factors: The circumstances of the offense, the damage caused, the defendant's prior convictions, and the defendant's behavior in court. In recent years, the bargaining position of the defendant has become probably the most important factor in the determination of the sentence in more serious cases. (Streng, 2007, pp. 153-172).

PROPORTIONALITY IN INTERNATIONAL SUBSTANTIVE LAW

Unfortunately, the principle of proportionality is not obvious in substantive international law. The penalty provision proposed by the International Law Commission in its draft statute for an international criminal court was nearly the same to the penalty provisions of the ad hoc tribunals (ICTY Article 24 and ICTR Article 23), and relied upon the same general criteria as found in the sentencing provisions of the ICC Statute[3]. Article 77 sets out the ICC's powers regarding the sanction of imprisonment. It gives the court two alternatives: judges must make choice between imprisonment of not more than thirty years[4] and life imprisonment. This structure indicated to the maximum sentence. Under the statutes of the IMT, IMTFE, ICTR and ICTY, a person could be sentenced to forty years or fifty years or any other period of time.

The ICC Statute, however, does not provide precise penalties for specific crimes, despite the wide range of offenses and forms of participation that the court is called upon to judge. Thus, the sentencing scheme in Article 77 applies to all crimes within the ICC jurisdiction.

[1] *German Constitution.*

[2] *Available at: http://www.germanlawjournal.com/pdfs/Vol08No02/PDF_Vol_08_No_02_153- 172_Articles_Streng.pdf*

[3] *See Report of the International Law Commission to the General Assembly on the Work of Its FortySixth Session, U.N. GAOR Supp. (No. 10) at 60, U.N. Doc. A/49/10(1994), reprinted in [1994] 2 Y.B. Int'l L. Comm.'s 287, U.N. Doc. A/CN.4/SER.A/1994/Add.1 (providing that "[i]n imposing sentence, the Trial Chamber should take into account such factors as the gravity of the crime and the individual circumstances of the convicted person.").*

[4] *Proposals on the maximum years for a specific term of imprisonment ranged from twenty to forty.*

By the way, determining a sentence within structure, judges must take into account two factors: "gravity of the crime" and "the individual circumstances of the convicted person" [1]. "Gravity of the crime" appears as the key criterion in two places in the Statute of Rome. Under Article 77(1) (b), "gravity of the crime" is relied on to determine the appropriateness of life imprisonment. At least, the "gravity of the crime" must be highest in order to justify life imprisonment. So Life imprisonment should only be imposed "when justified by the extreme gravity of the crime and the individual circumstances of the convicted person." Both criteria must be met before an individual can be sentenced to life presentment. As result, proportionality in tribunal's statute is unspecific and The Trial Chambers keep broad sentencing discretion. Although the Tribunals' Statutes exclude the death penalty as allowable sanction,[2] but the range of potential terms of imprisonment is in remarkable manner, wide. The Rules of Procedure and Evidence provide that "a convicted person may be sentenced to imprisonment for a term up to and including the remainder of the convicted person's life." [3] In theory, then, sentences can range from one day to life imprisonment for any crime over which the Tribunals have jurisdiction. The ICTY and the ICTR statues contain sentencing provisions providing that the penalty imposed by the trial chamber shall be limited to imprisonment.[4]

[1] *ICC Statute art. 78 (1).*

[2] *ICTR Statute, art. 23 (1); ICTY Statute, art. 24 (1). See also (Morris & Scharf, 1995).*

[3] *ICTY RPE, R. 101(A), U.N. Doc. IT/32/Rev/39 (Sept. 22, 2006); see also Int'l Crim. Tribunal for Rwanda Rules of Procedure & Evidence, Rule 101(A) (Nov. 10, 2006) [hereinafter ICTR RPE].*

[4] *The Security Council found it conflicting with human rights.*

The 1993 draft statute allowed for right of appeal against sentences where there was obvious disproportion between the crime and the sentence. The Tribunals' Rules of Procedure and Evidence has been given additional directives on sentencing

In the Rule 101 of the ICTY for governing penalties states:

- A convicted person may be sentenced to imprisonment for a term up to and including the remainder of his life.
- In determining the sentence, the Trial Chamber shall take into account the factors mentioned in Article 24, paragraph 2 of the Statute, as well as such factors as: (i) any aggravating circumstances; (ii) any mitigating circumstances including the substantial cooperation with the Prosecutor by the convicted person before or after conviction; (iii) the general practice regarding

prison sentences in the courts of the former Yugoslavia; (iv) the extent to which any penalty imposed by a court of any State on the convicted person for the same act has already been served, as referred to in Article 10(3) of the Statute.

- Credit shall be given to the convicted person for the period, if any, during which the convicted person was detained in custody pending his surrender to the Tribunal or pending trial or appeal.

CRITERIA OF PROPORTIONALITY

Criteria of proportionality depended on aim of criminal law as well as therefore whether punishment is meant to deter offenders, the higher sentence should be imposed for those crimes that are more a threat to the international community.

In according to article 10 (3) of international convention on civil and political rights states that the penitentiary system shall comprise treatment of prisoners the essential aim of which be their reformation and social retribution. Also in the trail chamber Arusha, noted that retribution and deterrence are the main principle in sentencing for international criminal law.[1] The international criminal law recognized principle of punishment –deterrence and retribution that are originally derived from criminal law and criminal tribunal have conformed these objectives as well as [2]

Grave Offence

The gravity of the offence deserved special attention; the gravity of the offense includes two elements, the magnitude of the harm caused by the offender and the offender's capability with respect to that harm. These elements caution different interpretation in criminal tribunal. For solving this difficult, the grave offfence should be codified and fit punishment or constituting a judicial institution with authoring making law for making uniform between difference sentence. [3]

[1] *Prosecuter V. Stevan Todorvic, case No IT _95-9 /I-S, Sentencing Judgment 31 July 2001.*

[2] *Prosecutor V. Tadic, supra note 75, para. 61.*

[3] *However, international tribunals regarding the concept of gravity of the offence and the issue of the comparative seriousness of crimes. First of all on the IMI judgment exist the legal distinction between different crimes and the law relating to war crimes and crimes against humanity. The study of the grave offence may be approach from two angles, one may be termed gravity in personam, subjective gravity or gravity in concreto. In this connection, the ICTY chamber in the Aleksovski case, has noted that the gravity of on offence is the result of circumstance of the case and degree of the accused participation in the crime.*

However, in order to obtain a uniform approach in the imposition of penalties in different cases, The evaluation of the gravity of the offence should be completed by a more general analyses placing a grave offence into a wider form, where it's gravity can be assessed in relation to that of other offence Like that In the common law countries of the concept of gravity of the offence is widely adopted and is used often under the label seriousness of the offence. As the benchmark for offence scale prepared by interpreters or sentencing commission, so international law is close with this approach. In some countries belong to the civil law tradition such as the criminal code in order to help judges to assess the appropriate penalties.

Grave Offence in the Tribunal Jurisprudence

The idea that there is a hierarchy of crimes in international humanity law has been the subject of debate since the ICTY hand down its first sentence Drazen Erdemovic was the first defendant to be sentenced by either tribunal. He pleaded guilty to murder as a crime against humanity and was sentenced to ten years in prison but the appeal chamber argued that, since a crime against humanity is a more serious charge than a war crime and thus carried a heavier penalty, Erdemovic would not have pleaded guilty to a crime against humanity and he understood the difference between the two offence. Judge express disagreement on this point. Consequently, Erdemovic pleaded guilty to murder as a violation of the laws or customs of war and the trail chamber resented him to five years in prison and the second defendant ICTY was declared that crimes against humanity should attract a higher sentence than war crimes.

But there is confront about hierarchy between crimes in tribunal jurisprudence because of an ICTY trail chamber convicted a third defendant 'Anto Furundzija, of one count of rape and one count of torture, both as violations of the laws or customs of war.[1] The trial chamber sentenced Furundzija to ten years imprisonment. He appealed against his sentence that it was overly harsh. The appeals chamber rejected his appeal and affirmed its decision that there is no inherent difference in gravity between a crime against humanity and a war crime again, one judge dissented on this point. Subsequent ICTY trial chambers have followed the holding of the appeals chamber and have rejected the hierarchy of crimes. [2]

By contrast, the ICTR has frequently referred to genocide as the crime of crimes it has also stated that war crimes are considered a lesser crimes than genocide or crimes against humanity[3].

[1] *Prosecutor Jean Kambanda case No. ICTR 97-23-5 trail chamber I, judgment and sentence of 4 sept. 1998 – para no 3.*

[2] *Ibidem para no 4.*

[3] *Ibidem para 9b.*

According to the trial chamber, there were no doubts that violations of article 3 common to the 1949 Geneva conventions were less serious offence than genocide or crimes against humanity at the same time, the trial chamber observed that it was more difficult to rank genocide and crimes against humanity in items of their respective gravity. Furthermore, until recently, there was no clear jurisprudence relating to lesser included offenses in International Criminal Law.

Victim Interest

The recent call for more respect for the victim's interests, rights, and perspective within the criminal justice system is sympathetic to the victims. There really is a consensus that crime victims should occupy an important role in the administration of criminal law, and then we are faced with an amazing inconsistency between this view and the absence of the victim in traditional penal theory. (Coughlin, 1998)[1]

Joel Fienberg suggests focusing on the victim's loss of opportunity or range of choices. Professor Shworth state: the retributive theory is based on the concept of proportionality. That punishment system shall be guided by such a theory.

Circumstances

The element of circumstance has grave place to determine fair practice of the ICTY and ICTR. Thus the means employed to execute the crime the degree of participation of the convicted person, the degree of intent, time and location and age, education, social and economic condition of the convicted person, but some criteria of the above are uncertain in tribunal statutes.

Gravity Circumstance. The circumstance factors developed by the ICTY and ICTR in the jurisprudence include scale of the crime, the length of time during which it continued, the age, number and suffering of the victim, the nature of perpetrators involvement, premeditation and discriminatory intent, abuse of power and position as a superior.[2] Criminal participation, in determining a sentence ICTY and ICTR have mentioned in three most direct forms of participation, planning, ordering, instigating as possible aggravating circumstance in the case of a highly placed accused[3].

[1] Unpublished manuscript, on file with the Buffalo Criminal Law Review.

[2] Cetebictic judgment para 1268 and Jelsic judgment, para 132.

[3] Kambanda judgment, para. 44.

Mitigating Circumstance. The only mitigating circumstance expressed in the ICTY and ICTR RPE is substantial cooperation with the prosecution before or after conviction. Extent of a guilty plea should be a mitigating factor and expression of remorse, voluntary surrender, assistance to detainer s or victims and personal circumstance such as good character age comportment in detention and family circumstance and poor health the role of the accused may have an impact on the penalty.

DIFFICULTIES OF THE PROPORTIONALITY

Legal System

Historical events indicate that legal system deem appropriate to these convention into their domestic legislation and enforce international crime in accordance with their domestic law also they have challenge for determining of penalties some country favor of abolishes of death penalty, several countries also expressed their reservation about sentence of life imprisonment, which they said were also a form of cruel, inhuman and degrading punishment and some Islamic country argue imposing death penalty so the legal system no uniform in the capital sentence.

Therefore some international criminal tribunal have included in their charter or statute a provision of penalties, through never in specific terms enough to satisfy a positivist legal interpretation of the requirement *nullapoena sine lege.*[1] Then the respective charter and statute of the international criminal tribunal delegate to the judge to determination of penalties as well as the sentencing.[2] And the statute of Rome also do not refer to any limitation on penalties and complimentary in the ICC have been admitted to state for determining punishment.

Nature of International Crimes

The complex nature of international criminal cases, sentences often must respond to multiple crimes committed over an extended time and involving numerous victims. In the vast majority of cases, the Trial Chambers have dealt with this complexity by imposing a single, global sentence encompassing all the convictions rather than sentencing the defendant separately for each individual crime.[3]

The principle of uniformity and proportionality, widely accepted for sentencing in domestic jurisdictions (Frase, 2001, pp. 259-261), is arguably even more compelling in the international criminal law context. International criminal tribunals operate in an ethnically charged context, often trying defendants from all sides of a conflict.[4] Unlike most domestic trials, international criminal trials attract global attention and speak to multiple audiences: not only the victims, victors and defeated.

[1] Statute of ICTY art. 24.

[2] See prosecutor V. Ruggiu, case No ICTR-97-32-I. judgment and sentence (june 2000).

[3] See, e.g., Prosecutor V. Blagojevich & Jokic, Case No. IT-02-60-T, Judgment, X. Disposition (Jan 17, 2005) (sentencing Blagojevich to a single sentence of eighteen years for complicity to commit genocide, the crimes against humanity of murder, persecution, and inhumane acts, and the war crime of murder).

[4] See Office of the High Representative BiH Media Roundup (July 4, 2006), http://www.ohr.int/ohrdept/presso/bh-media-rep/round-ups/default.asp?content_id_37592 (last visited Jan. 14, 2008) (summarizing the strong reactions in Serb and Bosnian Serb media to the ICTY's twoyear sentence for Bosnian Muslim defendant Naser Oric, calling the sentence "shameful" and accusing the ICTY of employing double standards based on ethnicity).

CONSISTENCY IN PROPORTIONALITY

The Trial Chambers, then, have remarkably wide discretion to fix the sentence for each individual. The Ad Hoc Tribunals embrace this discretion repeatedly emphasizing the central importance of individualized sentences.[1] At the same time, the Appeals Chamber has acknowledged that the Tribunals' legitimacy depends on consistency in punishment: " *Public confidence in the integrity of the administration of criminal justice (whether international or domestic) is a matter of abiding importance to the survival of the institutions which are responsible for that administration. One of the fundamental elements in any rational and fair system of criminal justice is consistency in punishment. This is an important reflection of the notion of equal justice. The experience of many domestic jurisdictions over the years has been that such public confidence may be eroded if these institutions give an appearance of injustice by permitting substantial inconsistencies in the punishment of different offenders, where the circumstances of the different offences and of the offenders being punished are sufficiently similar that the punishments imposed would, in justice, be expected to be also generally similar.*[2]"

The ICTY Trial Chamber separately convicted two high-ranking Bosnian Croat officials, Generals Tihomir Blaskic and Dario Kordic, for crimes in the Lasva Valley region of Bosnia (Shahram, 2004, p. 321). Both convictions covered "substantially similar conduct," [3] including the crimes against humanity of persecution, murder and inhumane acts.[4] Despite the similarities in the cases, the Trial Chambers sentenced Blaskic to forty-five years, but Kordic to only twenty-five years.[5]

[1] See, e.g., Prosecutor v. Babic, Case No. IT-03-72-A, Judgment on Sentencing Appeal, ¶7 (July 18, 2005) ("Trial Chambers are vested with broad discretion

in determining an appropriate sentence, due to their obligation to individualise the penalties to fit the circumstances of the accused and the gravity of the crime.").

[2] *Prosecutor v. Delalic, Mucic, Delic & Landzo (Celebici II), Case No. IT-96-21-A, Judgment, ¶ 756 (Feb. 20, 2001); see also Prosecutor v. Jelisic, Case No. IT-95-10-A, Judgment, ¶ 96 (July 5, 2001) ("The Appeals Chamber agrees that a sentence should not be capricious or excessive, and that, in principle, it may be thought to be capricious or excessive if it is out of reasonable proportion with a line of sentences passed in similar circumstances for the same offences. Where there is such disparity, the Appeals Chamber may infer that there was disregard of the standard criteria by which sentence should be assessed, as prescribed by the Statute and set out in the Rules."); Allison Marston Danner, Constructing a Hierarchy of Crimes in International Criminal Law Sentencing, 87 VA. L. REV. 415, 440–42 (2001) (noting the Appeals Chamber's recognition in the Celebici II case of the importance of consistent sentencing practices).*

[3] *Prosecutor v. Kordic & Cerkez, Case No. IT-95-14/2-A, Judgment, ¶ 1058 (Dec. 17, 2004).*

[4] *Ibidem at XI disposition.*

[5] *Ibidem.*

Role of Appeals Chamber

The role of appeal camber for uniform sentences is common in domestic jurisdiction but the Ad Hoc Tribunals are not like domestic systems. By their very nature, they must blend different legal systems The first time the appeal Chamber had to consider whether to exercise review over sentencing, it based its affirmative decision in part on appellate review of sentences in several domestic systems;

The question then arises whether the Appeals Chamber should review the sentence. Appellate review of sentencing is available in the major legal systems but it is usually exercised sparingly. For example, the New South Wales Court of Criminal Appeal in Australia has stated that "an appellate court will only interfere if it is demonstrated that the sentencing judge fell into material error of fact or law. Such error may appear in the reasons given by the sentencing judge, or the sentence itself may be manifestly excessive or inadequate, and thus disclose error." In civil legal systems such as Germany and Italy the relevant Criminal Codes set out what factors a judge must take into consideration in imposing a sentence. The appellate courts may interfere with the discretion of the lower court if its considerations went outside these factors or if it breached a prescribed minimum or maximum limit on sentence. So, for making uniform sentence in international criminal law, should be constituted judicial institution for law making that it create obligation for lower court.

Constitutionality of Proportionality

Constitutionality proportionality is means that not only the individual crimes are laid down in the Criminal Code, but also the general principles concerning sentencing are contained there in proportionality same as most domestic law must be codification for consistency in sentence so same domestic criminal cod should be set up precise e and detail range of sentencing option and each offence should be companied by the applicable penalty, including references to maximum and minim term. So codification would make limitation for determining the appropriate sentence, by the judge that provide difference sentence for same case.

But none of the international conventions that formed the bases of the crimes within the Tribunals' jurisdictions, however, include sentencing provisions, and customary law does not set down specific penalties for violations of international humanitarian law.

In England and Wales in recent decades the sentencing process has been reformed with the aim of reducing disparities, promoting consistency, and reassuring the public about the purpose of sentencing. In England and Wales as common law the general sentencing framework is determined by the maximum sentences set out in statutes, a few mandatory sentences (such as life imprisonment for murder), and statutory criteria such as those related to the use of custody. A major influence on judges in the Crown Court are the decisions made by the Court of Appeal and particularly the Court of Appeal Sentencing Guideline Cases.

In the German, the relationship between the legislature and the persons who are responsible for sentencing in practice— the public prosecutor and the trial courts— is structured by provisions on sentencing. The basis is constituted by the authorized sentences on which the penal codes have individual indications for each offense.

THE ROLE OF JUDGE IN DETERMINING OF PROPORTIONALITY

However Article 23 of statute of Rome, limits the form and imposing of the punishment to those penalties were enumerated in the Statute, it cannot be said that it likewise limits the factors, especially aggravating circumstances, that judges may rely on to increase the severity of a sentence. ICC imposes limitation imprisonment up to 30 years for accused.

Its effectiveness to limit judicial discretion to the factors enumerated in the Rome Statute or the ICC RPE is weakened by open-ended language in other articles and rules. For example, Article 78 instructs judges to "take into account such factors as the *gravity of the crime and the individual circumstances* of the convicted person." [1]

As well as article 145 RPE, contains a non-exhaustive list of aggravating factors.[2] Thus, in determining a sentence, judges may take into account "other circumstances" not found in the Statute or ICC RPE. [3] Prior to the adoption of Rule 145, the potential scope of Article 23 was a matter of interpretation for the judges. The threshold issue would have been whether the language "in accordance with this Statute" requires that the factors impacting the sentence be enumerated in the Statute or the RPE, or whether it is permissible for the Statute or ICC RPE to allow consideration of factors not enumerated.

Even in the civil law still significant room for judge for determining sentence, for instance It should be pointed out that the French criminal system still relies on the investigation system with an instructing judge (*"le juge d'instruction"*) whenever a major crime is committed (murder, for example).

All cases of crimes and major *"délits"* are brought by the public prosecutor's office to the instructing judge prior to the court hearings. Seven percent of all criminal cases are processed by instructing judges.[4]

The new penal code of 1994 reiterates the principle of "strict interpretation. More power is also given to the judge in correctional mater. The incorporation of the individualization of the penalty [5]is concept as it gives much more discretionary powers to the judge.

[1] *ICC Statute,, art. 78(1)*

[2] *International Criminal Court Rules of Procedure and Evidence, ICC-ASP/1/3, Rule145(2)(b)(vi).*

[3] *Ibidem.*

[4] *Ibidem.*

[5] *Code de Procedure Criminelle.*

Gives the judge the possibility to choose among the existing pre-defined penalties, which one is the most appropriate and efficient. Hoverer extenuating circumstances increase the discretionary power of judges but extenuating circumstance are taken out of the law[1].

In the German, Statutory penalty ranges tend to be fairly broad, thus allowing significant room f or judicial sentencing discretion. But Mandatory sentencing guidelines would contradict this self-conception of the judges and under sec. 6 of the International Criminal Law Code also points to the necessity to open up a leeway for the judges in determining the punishment.

CONCLUSION

There is no consensus about grave crime in ICL as above mention the ICTY's rejection of the hierarchy of crimes has serious implications for the fairness of sentencing standards in international criminal law the ICTY and the ICTR have taken different position on the question and the radical difference between the sentencing methodologies used by the two tribunals lessons the coherency of international justice and provide conflicting precedent for the ICC. The provision deals with international criminal law no specific penalties and how they is to be determined as well as they don't identify criteria for aggravating and mitigating factor. So grave offence as criteria of proportionality Providing that differentiate interpretation in criminal tribunal for avoiding as possible as it should be codified grave criminal law and fit punishment or should be constituent a judicial institution authoring making law for making uniform between difference sentence.

REFERENCES

1. Haveman, Roelof (2003). The Principle of Legality *in Supernational Criminal Law: a System sui generis* 39, 40.
2. Shahram, Dana (2009). Beyond Retroactivity to Realizing Justice: A Theory on the Principle of Legality in International, Criminal Law Sentencing in *The Journal of Criminal Law & Criminology*, vol. 99, no. 4.
3. Streng, Franz (2007). Sentencing in Germany: Basic Questions and New Developments, *German Law Journal*, Vol. 08, no. 02, pp. 153-172.
4. Coughlin, Anne M. (Sept. 11, 1998). *Guilty Victims* (unpublished manuscript, on file with the Buffalo Criminal Law Review).
5. Frase, Richard S. (2001). Comparative Perspectives on Sentencing Policy and Research in *Sentencing And Sanctions in Western Countries.* (Michael Tonry & Richard Frase, edits). Oxford Univ. Press.
6. Shahram, Dana (2004). Revisiting the Blaskic Sentence: Some Reflections on the Sentencing Jurisprudence of the ICTY in *International Criminal Law Review*, vol. 4, no. 3, pp. 321-348.

CHAPTER 6

THE MILITARY PERPETRATOR: A NARRATIVE ANALYSIS OF SENTENCING JUDGMENTS ON SEXUAL VIOLENCE OFFENDERS AT THE INTERNATIONAL CRIMINAL TRIBUNAL FOR THE FORMER YUGOSLAVIA

Inger Skjelsbæk

Keywords: Perpetrator, Sexual violence, Military identity, ICTY, Bosnia and Herzegovina

In her essays on the International War Crimes Tribunal for the former Yugoslavia (ICTY) the esteemed fictional and journalistic writer Slavenka Drakulić asks "can we in fact understand war criminals? More importantly, should we even try?" (Drakulić, 2004, p. 1987). Through observations in the court and elaborations in her essays on the theme she concludes that "As frightening as this idea is [that 'ordinary' men become perpetrators of evil so quickly], it is precisely the reason we should learn more about extraordinary situations and ordinary people's reactions to them" (p. 191).

How, then, can it be helpful to understand mass sexual atrocities through individual court cases against the (far too) few who are brought to justice? There are several studies of the legal discussions pertaining to sexual violence crimes in armed conflicts (de Brouwer, Ku, Römkens, & van den Herik, 2013; Fineman & Zinsstag, 2013; Henry, 2011; Houge, 2008), but few, if any, studies of these court cases are written from a social science perspective, and even fewer from a narrative psychological perspective. Yet, psychological assessment in both a popular as well as clinical sense is omnipresent in the legal proceedings. Through the legal dialogue in the international court room, and assessment of the criminal actions, a picture of the accused emerges based on a bifocal view of the person and the crimes, and discussions of normality and abnormality linked to the person and the situation underpin the court transcripts. My aim is to better understand how narratives of the perpetration of sexual violence crimes situate the notion of normal and abnormal behavior and to discuss what this might entail for our understanding of the sexual violence military perpetrator.

The basis for this analysis is sexual violence perpetrators brought to justice in the International Criminal Tribunal for the former Yugoslavia (ICTY). This article presents a narrative analysis of the sentencing judgments against nine individuals in the ICTY against principal sexual violence perpetrators and asks what the cases against them tell us about military perpetrators of sexual violence crimes. Ultimately, the article explores the extent to which sexual violence in war is seen as normal military behavior or not, in the eyes of the court.

SETTING THE STAGE FOR A NARRATIVE PSYCHOLOGICAL ANALYSIS OF ICTY SENTENCING JUDGMENTS

While the Nuremberg and Tokyo trials did prosecute major war criminals after World War II, crimes of sexual violence were not prosecuted, nor were they documented to any significant extent. This lack of engagement with crimes of sexual violence in war seems puzzling. Both de Brouwer (2005) and Henry (2011) have argued that there was ample legislative leverage within the law at both tribunals to prosecute crimes of sexual violence, yet the courts failed to do so. There are many possible

Citation: Inger Skjelsbæk, The Military Perpetrator: A Narrative Analysis of Sentencing Judgments on Sexual Violence Offenders at the International Criminal Tribunal for the Former Yugoslavia (ICTY), doi:10.5964/jspp.v3i1.273

reasons for this: lack of evidence,[i] lack of legal will, or lack of female lawyers and judges. These reasons may all apply, but another possible explanation for why these types of crimes were not prosecuted may be found in Neitzel and Welzer's (2012, p. 13) extraordinary analysis of conversations between German soldiers, which reveal that acts of extreme brutality such as rape, killings and bombings were commonplace elements within the daily conversations of these soldiers. Acts of rape and sexual violence were the modus operandi in war and were accordingly seen as not worth paying particular attention to: such activities were nothing special and the trials were set up to prosecute extraordinary crimes, not "normal" ones. Accordingly, stories of sexual violence failed to become part of the collective memory of World War II through these trials, even if these actions were an integral part of a behavioral repertoire of German, Axis and Allied soldiers alike (Lily, 2007).

Attitudes against sexual criminal behavior in war have since changed dramatically, accompanied by significant changes in how legal institutions, policymakers and scholars seek to understand how victims, communities and perpetrators are affected by these types of crimes (Skjelsbæk, 2012), and not least seek to bring perpetrators to justice. Both supranational and national criminal prosecutions of crimes of sexual violence are now taking place in several courts around the world, though it was the ICTY that was the first to systematically prosecute crimes of sexual violence committed during armed conflict. The central principle of the ICTY trials is the same as that of the proceedings in Nuremberg and Tokyo: to hold individuals, as opposed to states, responsible for crimes committed in times of war. However, with the ICTY's added focus on crimes of sexual violence, understandings of what crimes individuals may be held accountable for has changed. Work that has been carried out since the establishment of the ICTY has altered the perceptions of crimes of sexual violence in ways that were unimaginable some decades ago.[ii]

The ICTY was established in 1993, while the Bosnian War was still raging, as an attempt to ensure that major perpetrators of all crimes committed during the wars in the former Yugoslavia would be held responsible for their actions. The many years of dedicated work that followed have resulted in a wealth of documents in the form of indictments, court transcripts and judgments. With respect to crimes of sexual violence, these documents provide unique insight into the complexity of such offences: the types of victims affected the perpetrators, and the legal implications of the actions themselves. Since its establishment, the court has indicted 161 individuals, and has concluded court hearings in the case of 141 of these.[iii] Since the start of the Tribunal's activities, 78 individuals – or 48% of the 161 accused – have had charges of sexual violence included in their indictments. The work of the ICTY will come to an end when all of the above cases have completed proper trial procedures. After that point, further cases will be prosecuted in national courts in Bosnia and Herzegovina. This process began in 2003, when a completion strategy for the termination of the ICTY was finalized. No new indictments were formulated after that time. As of mid-2011, 13 of the ICTY cases have been referred to national jurisdiction in Bosnia. These cases primarily involved individuals of lower rank.

As part of its work, the ICTY has needed to define and conceptualize various issues: What constitutes a war or an armed conflict? What constitutes a crime and of which kind? Which responsibilities did the accused have and what was his/her involvement in the criminal acts? All of these considerations come together in the Tribunal's judgments (which include both trial and appeal decisions), which therefore comprise the most comprehensive texts available for gaining insights into the reasoning, in theatre, of the Tribunal within the parameters in which it operates. Of the various types of crimes with which the court has had to deal, crimes of sexual violence appear to have been among the most difficult to address. This is primarily because of challenges related to the question of how to establish that sexual violence formed part of a pattern of violence (Aranburu, 2010, p. 609);[iv] how to ensure that victim witnesses dare testify and have a language with which to discuss the crimes they have experienced;[v] the lack of sufficient numbers of trained court staff and professionals (Bergsmo & Skre, 2012, p. 3); and general inexperience with the prosecution of such crimes within an international legal framework.

STATUS OF RESEARCH ON SEXUAL VIOLENCE PERPETRATORS

There is an emerging literature on perpetrators of sexual violence crimes in war (Baaz & Stern, 2013; Cohen, Hoover Green, & Wood, 2013; Leiby, 2009; Nordås, 2013). While the early scholarly literature on sexual violence in war was primarily focused on the impact this particular violence has on its victims (Skjelsbæk, 2001), there is a now a shift in the empirical focus in the direction of the perpetrator. This shift can be seen as a response to a general lack of empirical knowledge on perpetrators, increased attention by the United Nations Security Council on how to prosecute and prevent perpetrators, and lack of conceptualization of the sexual violence perpetrator as opposed to other crimes committed by soldiers in war time. So far, the literature on perpetrators draws on a set of quantitative and qualitative studies which have different conceptual aims.

One example of the quantitative approach can be found in Cohen et al. (2013), who list a set of misconceptions regarding sexual violence in war, a sub-set of which relate to sexual violence perpetrators. These misconceptions include the notion that the perpetrators are always men; that sexual violence is more common among rebel groups than state militaries; that given an opportunity, men will rape; and that sexual violence is always perpetrated by combatants. The ways in which these claimed misconceptions are addressed is by discussing definitional and measurement challenges which need to be "more systematically addressed if we are to continue our progress toward a full understanding of wartime sexual violence" (Cohen et al., 2013, p. 11).

The authors make an important point in showing that there is a great degree of variation in the perpetration of sexual violence: that not all perpetrators are men, that state actors are no less involved in these crimes than other military groups, that not all men will rape if the opportunity arises and that not all perpetrators in armed conflicts are combatants. Their scholarly aim, however, appears to be to come to a "full understanding" of sexual violence crimes, which would entail closing identified research gaps such as exploring "how and why groups do not use sexual violence [...], which types of formal and informal armed group institutions promote sexual violence as a practice; the conditions under which commanders (at lower as well as high levels) adopt rape as a strategy; and why many commanders believe the cost of prohibiting sexual violence is high" (Cohen et al., 2013, p. 13). A full understanding is a laudable goal, but as the authors state in their conclusion, "direct on the ground engagement and service provision rightly take precedence" (p. 13), suggesting that this as a goal is, perhaps, unattainable.

Another way of generating knowledge about sexual violence perpetrators, therefore, can be as Baaz and Stern (2009, 2013) have done; by extensive field work and qualitative interviews on the ground, in their case in the DRC. Based on a discourse analysis of interviews with 193 people in 43 group interviews, Baaz and Stern (2009) were able to detect discourses of different forms of rape: lust rapes (which were seen as more "normal", i.e. not linked to the conflict pattern) and evil rapes (which happened in conjunction with other forms of war violence in the armed conflict). Their aim was not to reach a full understanding of the phenomenon of sexual violence perpetration, but rather to illuminate how "perpetrators, themselves, understand their violent crimes" (Baaz & Stern, 2009, p. 496) and "how the soldier's testimonies must be seen as a product of the particular context of the DRC – a warscape which has its local particularities, but which must also be seen as a reflection of the warscapes in diverse contexts which are crafted out of the increasingly globalized context of militarization and attendant notions of 'normal' heterosexual masculinity" (p. 515). Leiby (2009) provides yet another approach by combining methods and comparing cases: sexual violence in Guatemala and Peru. The basis for her work is a quantitative coding of the published reports from the truth and reconciliation commissions in both countries, supplemented by field work. Her focus is on the state as perpetrator, and more specifically on how the "state either explicitly encouraged, condoned, or at the very least had knowledge of the crimes being committed" (Leiby, 2009, p. 456). In concluding her work she asks whether there are differences "in rebel groups – such as their size, their proximity to civilian populations, their resource base or their politico-military strategy – that make some more likely to commit these kinds of human rights abuses? Do these factors in turn make the state more likely to use sexual violence?" (p. 466) As both of the latter studies show, their findings are local, but their aims are global in that they situate their findings within different conceptual aims for understanding sexual violence perpetration; in Baaz and Stern's (2009) case by linking their findings to globalized understandings of militarization and heterosexual masculinity and in Leiby's (2009) case by focusing on the mechanisms which enables sexual violence perpetration and its instrumental gain.

As can be seen from these examples from the emerging literature on sexual violence perpetrators, methods, analyses and scholarly aims vary, but together they bring new empirical insights and debates to the conceptualization of the military sexual violence perpetrator. Following Leiby's (2009) example, however, it is clear that there is an ever growing data material which lends itself to substantive new analyses of the sexual violence perpetrator in armed conflicts: truth commissions as well as indictments, court transcripts and judgments from various criminal courts provide a wealth of material which can, and should, be analyzed. Leiby (2009) has done exactly this by a quantitative coding of the transcripts from the truth commissions, which was important in order to get an overview of "the type of sexual violence and the context under which it occurred" (Leiby, 2009, p. 453), in order to be able to answer her research question about state involvement. However, it can be argued that official texts from truth commissions and criminal courts also can be subject to a different kind of analysis, more along the lines of Baaz and Stern (2009): by asking qualitative questions about how the narratives of sexual violence perpetrators in armed conflicts situate their actions, behavior and ultimately identities in such texts. In doing so, we gain insight not only into the ways in which they are situated through testimonies but also how the reactions from the court/truth commission/other are to them.

While much of the social science research on sexual violence perpetrators in armed conflict has been dominated by political science and international relations scholars, it is clear that the field of psychology has something unique to offer in order to further this field of knowledge. The conceptualization of the individual in a socio-political context is at the core of social and political psychological scholarship, and a narrative gaze at how non-psychological scholars use psychological language in their assessments of sexual violence perpetrators in armed conflicts helps us better understand how these perpetrators can be placed along a normal to abnormal behavioral continuum.

STATUS OF RESEARCH ON PERPETRATORS OF INTERNATIONAL CRIMES

There is also an established and rich scholarly literature which analyzes international crimes, mass atrocities and genocidal behavior in armed conflict. This literature stems in large part from holocaust studies which have been supplemented and expanded by the literature on the many armed conflicts in Latin America during the 1970s and 1980s. Within these studies there are different ways of categorizing the perpetrators, such as Hilberg (1992) who discusses perpetrators in relation to victims and bystanders; Baum (2008) who adds to this by suggesting that some see themselves as rescuers; Kelman (1995) who argues that certain perpetrators are simply obedient; and finally Smeulers (2008) who gives perhaps the most comprehensive overview and typology. Conceptually, Smeulers (2008, p. 241) argues, a distinction can be drawn between the organizers, the specialists, the executors, the criminal mastermind, the fanatic, the criminal sadist, the profiteer, the careerist, the devoted warrior, followers and conformists, the compromised perpetrator and, finally, the professional. All of these play different roles in a perpetrator scheme. What unites most of the leading scholars in this field is an overall analysis along an axis of normal versus abnormal behavior. Waller (2007), a leading expert on genocide behavior, sums this distinction up by stating that the:

> [...] social construction of cruelty—buttressed by professional socialization, group identification, and binding factors of the group—envelops perpetrators in a social context that encourages and rewards extraordinary evil. It reminds us that the normal reaction to an abnormal situation is abnormal behavior; indeed, normal behavior would be an

abnormal reaction to an abnormal situation. We must borrow the perspective of the perpetrators and view their evil not as the work of "lunatics" but as actions with a clear and justified purpose—so defined by a context of cruelty. (p. 271)

Smeulers (2008), again, adds to this understanding by arguing that "within a malignant governmental system, military organizations or police units, it is those who do not break the rules but those who abide by the rules who become perpetrators" (pp. 236–237). Arendt's (1963/2006) infamous elaborations of the Eichmann case fit into this assertion; Eichmann acted and saw himself as a bureaucrat. That he was a bureaucrat of genocide is part of Arendt's conceptualization of the banality of evil; it becomes an everyday practice. How this transformation takes place is what several scholars attempt to understand from a vast array of different data material. Payne (2008), for instance, has gone through confessions of state violence in various court and truth commissions from Argentina, Chile, Brazil and South Africa. These confessions do not, the author points out, disclose the truth but are "merely accounts, explanations and justification for deviant behavior, or personal versions of a past" (p. 2). Crelinsten (1995) also makes this point by stating that "the language of torture is one that replaces the world of cruelty with euphemisms" (p. 39), and through this we can conclude that the truth about the reasoning of the individual perpetrator at the moment of action cannot be uncovered. We can only come close to an understanding by examining narrative construction in hindsight. What this literature has in common is a focus on international crimes and torture, but not on sexual violence crimes exclusively. My aim, therefore, is to attempt to add to this literature by examining the narratives on sexual crimes (and the criminals), in the context of mass atrocities.

THE NARRATIVE METHODOLOGICAL APPROACH

The narrative turn in psychology has opened up for a vast array of analyses which focus on the content and form of how life histories form social constructions of selves. Sarbin (1986) has argued that "in giving accounts of ourselves or of others, we are guided by narrative plots [...] whether for formal biographies or autobiographies, for psychotherapy, for self-disclosure, or for entertainment, we do much more than catalog a series of events. Rather, we render the events into a story" (p. 23). The ways in which narrative data are gathered and analyzed varies and the approach taken in this study is somewhat different from what is most often recognized as narrative research in psychology; studies where the researcher and the research subject create a storied account of people and events through transactional methodology. In this study, the stories are told without the interaction of the researcher with the research subjects. The data analyzed should therefore be considered as secondary data. The researcher has undertaken a thematic analysis of the elements of the court cases which pertain to sexual violence offenders in war, and has attempted to untangle how the themes raised in relation to the sexual violence offender create a narrative account which situates the perpetrator along a normal to abnormal continuum. The narratives analyzed are organized by themes, or thematic clusters, which have, in turn, been related to a narrative plot structure.

The international criminal proceedings in this study lend themselves exceptionally well to this thematic narrative approach because the proceeding can, and ought to be, seen as narrative constructions of people and events for legal purposes. [vi] In the ICTY's assessments of individuals and their crimes, the court is obliged to consider the "appropriate punishment in relation to the individual as well as the crime".[vii] The process of sentencing, thereby, does more than simply punish perpetrators: it also involves an assessment of the individuals concerned – or, narratives of the individuals concerned – in relation to the law. Skilbrei (2010) argues that the application of law is an inscription of norms when she says that "[t]he law is not only the result of cultural norms; it is also a political and formal process whereby public concern and international obligations are translated into law" (p. 42). The ICTY is the manifestation of a normative shift by the international community to end the impunity surrounding crimes of sexual violence in armed conflict, in other words to give these criminal acts a different meaning. Further, while the rationale behind criminal law sanctions includes such aims as just punishment, deterrence, incapacitation of the dangerous and rehabilitation, the ICTY Trial Chamber accepts that the "modern philosophy of penology [is] that the punishment should fit the offender and not merely the crime".[viii] In the Trial Chamber's judgments, such concerns are discussed at great length, especially in the sentencing section of the judgments, where aggravating and mitigating circumstances are spelled out.

According to Ricoeur, "every narrative combines two dimensions in various proportions, one chronological and one non-chronological. The first may be called the episodic dimension, which characterizes the story made out of events. The second is the configurational dimension, according to which the plot construes significant wholes out of scattered events" (cited in White, 1987, p. 51). The narratives to be presented have been coded according to the following story line, or chronological order (see Table 1): beginning (accounts of pre-war life and personalities), middle part (accounts of war rapes), and end (accounts of post-conflict life).

Table 1 Overview of Narrative Chronological Coding

Coding Format	Coding Themes
Beginning	Accounts of pre-war life and personalities. Descriptions of how the perpetrators were seen to be (as family members, civil citizens, and military actors) before the sexual violence crimes took place.
Middle	Accounts of war rapes. These are the factual discussions in the court transcripts: where the events took place, who the victims were, the physical settings of the crimes, and the involvement of the perpetrators.
End	Accounts of post-conflict life. These are stories about how the perpetrators were taken to the ICTY, their collaboration with the court and their behavior in the detention setting.

Having organized statements and descriptions along these narrative dimensions, three different plot structures emerged – namely, that of being a normal person responding adequately to a situation that is seen as normal; being an abnormal person who is responding to what is seen as an abnormal (or extreme) situation; and finally being a normal person responding inadequately to what is seen as an abnormal (or extreme) situation. The ways in which these plots come out depend on how the various voices in the courtroom position the perpetrator within their stories. Furthermore, as Murray (2003, p. 116) argues, narrative accounts are not told in a vacuum, but are shaped and encouraged by specific contexts. In other words, there is a layer outside the story – that is, the sociopolitical context in which it is told – which influences what, how and why elements within the story are seen as important and relevant. In a court room the legal as well as normative framework clearly shapes the way in which the narratives emerge.

Twenty-eight individuals have been convicted of crimes of sexual violence in the ICTY, but only nine have been convicted as principal perpetrators. For the purpose of the narrative analysis it was the sentencing judgments of principal perpetrators who were the most informative to study. The reason for this choice was pragmatic; it was in these judgments that acts of sexual violence were discussed at the greatest length and where the richest material about these crimes and the perpetrators could be found.[ix] After this selection had been made, the sentencing judgments were carefully analyzed by means of coding the descriptions of the sexual violence crimes within a narrative structure as described above. This non-chronological coding devoted special attention to episodic elements such as the ways in which the settings in which sexual violence occurred was described (see Table 2). In this process it was primarily the voices of the victims, perpetrators and others who were called as witnesses that were coded. The coding was done by looking at how the violence was carried out: by types of detention facilities, in connection with other kinds of war violence or in a "recreational" setting, and the political categorization of the victims (e.g., prisoners or not). It was primarily the victim witness accounts that served as the basis for this part of the analysis. Further, the role of the perpetrator was essential to map out and in this effort it was primarily the discussions between the defense council, the prosecutor and to some extent the perpetrators' themselves whose voices were coded according to: if the crimes were carried out by one or several perpetrators, comments made by the perpetrators to victims/others at the moment of the criminal action, role of perpetrator in the military setting, and how the crimes were carried out. Finally, the assessment of the judges was coded according to the ways in which aggravating and mitigating circumstances were discussed (explicitly or indirectly) in each case. Aggravating circumstances considered by the court included: the role of the accused, whether the victims were particularly young, the duration of the crimes, whether more than one victim was involved, whether more than one perpetrator was involved, the vulnerability of the victims, and whether there had been widespread and systematic persecution that involved sexual violence in inhumane conditions.[x] Mitigating circumstances that were discussed were: providing a guilty plea, expressing remorse, voluntary surrender, and cooperation with the Office of the Prosecutor.

Table 2 Overview of Narrative Non-Chronological Coding

Coding Themes	Primary Voices Coded
Settings of crimes	Primarily victim witness accounts (but also some perpetrators)
Role of the perpetrator	Defense council, prosecutor and perpetrator
Sentencing	Judges discussions

Through the different chronological as well as episodic coding of statements, the elements of the three different narrative plot structures emerged. By presenting multiple voices from the court room within a narrative format the following analyses should be read as motifs (and not typologies of perpetrators) for violence that coexist and which perpetrators, their defense councils, judges and prosecutors draw on selectively and discuss in the context of the court proceedings. Through these conceptualizations of motifs a psychological conceptualization of the perpetrators comes to light which in turn helps us better understand dominant discourses around sexual violence perpetration.

MILITARY PERPETRATORS OF SEXUAL VIOLENCE CRIMES

The nine convicted principal perpetrators examined below were found guilty of crimes of sexual violence against 32 identified women and 5 identified men (see Table 3). In addition, one of the individuals was convicted of raping and sexually assaulting an unidentified number of women and girls in a classroom in Foča. For these and other crimes, the perpetrators received prison sentences ranging from 5 years (Milan Simić) to 28 years (Dragoljub Kunarac). Three of the men in the group pleaded guilty to crimes of sexual violence (Miroslav Bralo, Milan Simić and Dragan Zelenović).

Table 3 Overview of Principal Perpetrators of Crimes of Sexual Violence

Name of the Accused	Case information	Acts of sexual violence
Miroslav Bralo	http://www.icty.org/cases/party/671/4	He brutally raped and tortured a Bosnian Muslim woman, Witness "A", and imprisoned her for approximately two months to be further violated at the whim of her captors.
Hazim Delić	http://www.icty.org/cases/party/676/4	He violently raped two female detainees during interrogations inside the Čelebići prison camp. One of the rapes was conducted in the presence of other guards.
Radomir Kovač	http://www.icty.org/cases/party/713/4	He raped two victims along with other soldiers. He raped another two victims along with other soldiers during a period in which they were kept in his apartment. He assisted other soldiers in the rape of three victims.
Drgaoljub Kunarac	http://www.icty.org/cases/party/712/4	He raped three victims at his headquarters in Foča. He and two other soldiers raped and threatened to kill a witness and also threatened to kill her son. He also aided and abetted the gang-rape of four victims by several of his soldiers.
Esad Landžo	http://www.icty.org/cases/party/677/4	He placed a burning fuse cord against the genitals of a male detainee.
Mlado Radić	http://www.icty.org/cases/party/677/4	He raped one detainee and attempted to rape another. He participated in sexual intimidation, harassment and assaults against three other detainees in Omarska.
Milan Simić	http://www.icty.org/cases/party/751/4	Together with other men, he personally beat four detainees at the Bosanski Šamac primary school. He also kicked the men in their genitals and, during the beatings, fired gunshots over their heads. One victim was forced to pull down his pants, and one of the men threatened to cut off the victim's penis.
Zoran Vuković	http://www.icty.org/cases/party/714/4	Along with another soldier, he took a victim from the Partizan Sports Hall, Foča, to a nearby apartment and raped her, knowing that she was only 15 years old.
Dragan Zelenović	http://www.icty.org/cases/party/794/4	He raped, participated in the gang-rape of, and tortured a number of the women and girls held in classrooms at Foča High School, which was used as a short-term detention facility. He and three other men gang-raped one woman held at the Partizan Sports Hall, a detention facility in Foča. He and two other perpetrators raped four female detainees from the premises known as Karaman's house.

This group contains two particularly historic judgments in relation to the criminal prosecution of crimes of sexual violence. The first comprises the judgments against Hazim Delić and Esad Landžo, who were prosecuted together in what is referred to as the Mucić et al. case, where rape was recognized as torture, a grave breach of the Geneva Conventions, and a violation of the laws and customs of war. In addition, the case against Kovač, known as the Kunarac et al. case, was the first case in which sexual enslavement was classified as a crime against humanity.

Beyond the legal categorizations, which psychological conceptualization underpins the legal discussions of the individual perpetrators in the sentencing judgments? In what follows, I will argue that at least three different military perpetrator narratives can be detected in the sentencing judgments, which lend themselves to different conceptualizations of the military perpetrator.

NARRATIVES OF CHIVALRY – NORMAL REACTIONS TO NORMAL SITUATIONS?

The notions of chivalry and militaristic identities are strongly interlinked (Young, 2007) and the masculine protector can be seen as the archetypical soldier (Elshtain, 1987; Enloe, 1989). But can a chivalrous narrative be evoked vis-à-vis sexual violence perpetrators? Can sexual activities in a forceful setting be considered as something other than crimes and involuntary acts for the victims? Or, is this conceptualization part of a military normality?

Role of the Perpetrators: Protectors

Consider the following passage from the Kunarac et al. case before this conceptualization is discussed further. It is Kunarac himself whose voice is heard:

[T]hen she started beseeching me that I do not ask her. Then she was sitting next to me. She fell on me. She put her head on my chest and begged me not to ask her anything. This gesture on her part did surprise me. I tried to pacify her, to convince her that there was no reason for her to be frightened, that nothing would happen to her, that she would be protected. At that point, she started kissing me and begging me not to ask her a thing. At that moment, I was totally confused. I absolutely did not understand what she was doing. I tried to refuse this behavior of hers and to tell her again that I had to find out who these men were, because I do not want my name to be mentioned in such contexts. I don't want this journalist[xi] to write such articles that I had nothing to do with. Then she started kissing me on the mouth, on the body. She started unbuttoning me. I remained totally confused. After this, even when I wanted to say something, she would either put her hand on my mouth or she would start kissing me on the mouth. She did not allow me to say anything. After that, I accepted this behavior of hers and we had full sexual vaginal intercourse, although I did nothing to give her a reason or pretext for this. And I did not refuse her in any way; I accepted her behavior.

JUDGE MUMBA: Is it your position, accused, that DB seduced you?

At any rate, at that point in time when this was happening, not a single moment did I give any reason – I did not give her a pretext for having sexual intercourse. I didn't say I wanted it at that moment; I had sexual intercourse with her against my will. I mean, without having a desire for sex. I will explain this later. She did this quite consciously for other reasons that I was not aware of at that moment.

Q. I shall remind you, Mr. Kunarac, of the following: During her statement, during her testimony, this witness, Witness DB, said that she was not sure that there would have been sexual intercourse if she had not taken an active role. What can you say as far as this claim is concerned?

I assert that had she not started doing all of this, I would have not – I would not have done a thing. I did not have any ideas about doing anything to her or sexually abusing her. I said that this behavior of hers really took me by surprise. I cannot say that I was raped. She did not use any kind of force, but she did everything. The way she acted was that she did not give me any manoeuvring space. As a man, I accepted her behavior and I did not refuse her as a woman. I did have sexual intercourse with her. (Kunarac et al. transcript, 6 July 2000, pp. 4541–4542)

Bearing in mind that Kunarac has been given the most severe (crimes against humanity) and longest (28 years) sentence for sexual violence crimes to date, reading this passage is chilling. He admits having had sexual intercourse with the victim, but does in no way see himself as a perpetrator.

Similar arguments and reasoning can be found elsewhere in the sentencing judgment, which encompassed two other co-accused. Kovač was one of them and in his case attempts were made to argue that one of the women Kovač was convicted of raping (FWS-87[xii], aged 15) had claimed to have been in love with Kovač. This particular witness, together with another young victim of multiple rapes (Witness A.S., aged 19, who had not been raped by Kovač), had been kept locked up in an apartment in Foča for at least two months, where they were both raped on multiple occasions and subjected to other forms of degrading sexual treatment, such as being forced to dance naked in front of groups of men. After their time in the apartment, they were sent to Montenegro in exchange for money. Kovač's defence lawyers claimed that FWS-87 had in fact been in love with him and that they had had a relationship, thereby portraying this as a voluntary relationship in which the girl(s) were protected, presumably against other potential perpetrators, by Kovač. Further, the transfer to Montenegro was presented as an attempt to further protect the two girls and get them out of Bosnia. The defence lawyers called several witnesses who claimed that there must have existed a relationship between Kovač and FWS-87 because the latter had sent Kovač "a letter with a heart drawn on it" (Kunarac et al. sentencing judgment, 22 February 2001, para. 142, p. 62), because she was seen as being in a "good mood" at a party (Kunarac et al. sentencing judgment, 22 February 2001, para. 148, p. 64), and because "she was allegedly dancing" at a café on the night of Orthodox New Year's Eve, 13 January 1993 (Kunarac et al. sentencing judgment, 22 February 2001, para. 149, p. 64). All these observations relate to the alleged actions of FWS-87 as these were perceived and presented by the witnesses for the defence, and are based on assumptions on observed and alleged behavior by this young girl.[xiii]

Similarly, Vuković, who was also convicted at the same trial of raping a girl the same age as his own daughter (FWS-50, aged 16 at the time), is said to have told the victim that "she was lucky in that she was the same age as his daughter, otherwise he would have done much worse things to her and that she was lucky about this conscience" (Kunarac et al. sentencing judgment, 22 February 2001, para. 814, p. 255). In other words, he is portrayed as cautious, or "protective", by being less violent than he could have been. The defence argued further that his acts had been committed out of "sexual urge, not out of hatred" (Kunarac et al. sentencing judgment, 22 February 2001, para. 816, p. 256), thereby suggesting that the acts were disconnected from the war, somewhat in contrast to the perpetrator's own accounts of various forms of protection in the war situation.

Returning now to Kunarac – who was the de facto commander of the other two accused men (Kovač and Vuković) in the case – claimed to have been seduced by victim DB (who was 19 years old when the relevant events took place), and that he had sex against his will, or to be nice and "not refuse her as a woman" (as stated in the quote above). Listening to DB, however, a very different story is told. After she had been first raped by several soldiers, DB was told by one of them that Dragoljub Kunarac was their commander, just minutes before the following events took place:

After these events [the preceding rapes], "Gaga" told her to have a shower because his commander was coming, and he threatened to kill her if she did not satisfy the commander's desires. He repeated this when the accused Dragoljub Kunarac walked in. D.B. took off the trousers of the accused, kissed him all over the body, and then had vaginal intercourse with the accused. D.B. said she felt terribly humiliated because she had to take an active part in the events, which she did out of fear because of "Gaga's" threats earlier on; she had the impression that the accused knew that she was not acting of her own free will, but admitted after a question by Defence counsel that she was not sure if there would have been intercourse, had it not been for her taking some kind of initiative. After some time, "Gaga" returned to the room and asked the accused whether he was satisfied, addressing him as "commander", to which the latter did not reply. (Kunarac et al. sentencing judgment, 22 February 2001, para. 219, p. 84)

SETTING OF THE CRIMES: YOUNG VICTIMS IN CAPTIVITY

The common denominator in the chivalrous narratives of the sexual violence crimes is the fact that the perpetrator was at least twice the age of the victim. Kunarac, who received the longest custodial sentence of the group (28 years), was found guilty of acts of rape against one girl who was 15½ years old, two who were 19 years old, one who was 16, and one who was 17½. In Kovač's case (sentenced to 20 years), the girls were 20 and 12 years old. In the case of Vuković (sentenced to 12 years), one of the victims was only 15½ years old and this was also the case in the Zelenović case (sentenced to 15 years). In blatant contrast to the sentence by the Trial Chamber, which found that these sexual relationships were abusive and involved the enslavement and terrorizing of the victims, the defence counsel attempted to construct an image that portrays the convicted perpetrators as lovers and the girls as temptresses who seek protection and comfort.

The fact that such a large group of the victims had been so young enabled the defence counsel of the accused men to construct a series of argument that there were purely sexual intentions behind the perpetrators acts, and that they were not discriminatory acts against Muslim women by Serb perpetrators. As Vuković's defense counsel argued, he did not have hatred, only lust. Kunarac took pleasure in being the first to have forced sex with a girl who stated that she was a virgin, and claimed to have felt almost pressured to have sex with a young girl who allegedly seduced him.

In the discussions of the factors relevant for sentencing for the various crimes, the young ages of the victims were commented upon in the following ways: "this further increases the gravity of the crimes committed against her" (Zelenović sentencing judgment, 4 April 2007, para. 39, p. 13); "offences were committed against a particularly vulnerable and defenseless girl" (Kunarac et al. sentencing judgment, 22 February 2001, para. 879, p. 279); "the youthful age [...] and very young age are aggravating circumstances [...] against particularly vulnerable and defenseless girls and a woman" (Kunarac et al. sentencing judgment, 22 February 2001, para. 874, p. 278); and "the youthful age of certain of the victims of the offences [...] is considered an aggravating factor" (Kunarac et al. sentencing judgment, 22 February 2001, para. 864, p. 276).

In three of the four formulations regarding how the age of the victims was seen as an aggravating circumstance, the judgment also made specific mention of the fact that these were young girls. As young girls these victims were both children and adolescents and had come to a stage in their lives when they would be maturing both emotionally and physically. Witness FWS-191, who was 17 years old when the relevant events occurred, "told him she was a virgin and Dragoljub Kunarac said that he would then be the first" (Kunarac et al. sentencing judgment, 22 February 2001, para. 259, p. 95). At this crucial time, they were molested by multiple men, twice their age and over extended periods of time, under terrifying conditions. What this has done to the victims was not discussed at any length in the judgments, but from other studies we know that fears of being unattractive and unmarriageable and feelings of shame caused by such events can often be overwhelming (Skjelsbæk, 2012).

SENTENCING DISCUSSIONS: CHALLENGING CONCEPTUALIZATION OF NORMALITY

What do these acts mean for the perpetrators? Why would these men resort to violence against such young female victims and simultaneously see these as chivalrous acts? What actually motivated them to commit these acts at the time we will probably never know, but the ICTY's legal proceedings require that a rationalization of the events be presented to the court. The attempt by the defence counsel to portray the perpetrators as heroic or romantic/sexually driven men, was strongly dismissed by the judges. In Kunarac's case, the court commented that "the accused Dragoljub Kunarac used his bravery in combat to gain the respect of his men and he maintained it by providing them with women" (Kunarac et al. sentencing judgment, 22 February 2001, para. 585, p. 207). In relation to the situation with the girl who had been a virgin when she was raped by Kunarac, the court commented that "he rejoiced at the idea of being her 'first', thereby degrading her more" (Kunarac et al. sentencing judgment, 22 February, para. 724, p. 236). In relation to the alleged love affair between Kovač and FWS-87, the court commented: "The relationship between FWS-87 and Kovač was not one of love as the defence suggested, but rather one of cruel opportunism on Kovač's of constant abuses and domination over a girl who, at the relevant time, was only about 15 years old (Kunarac et al. sentencing judgment, 22 February 2001, para. 762, p. 245). At one point during their imprisonment in Kovač's apartment, the young girls were forced to dance naked on a table while Kovač watched them from the sofa, pointing weapons at them. The court made the following comments on that incident: "The accused Radmir Kovač certainly knew that having to stand naked on a table, while the accused watched them, was a painful and humiliating experience for the three women involved, even more so because of their young age. The Trial Chamber is satisfied that Kovač must have been aware of that fact but he nevertheless ordered them to gratify him by dancing naked for him" (Kunarac et al. sentencing judgment, 22 February 2001, para. 773, pp. 246–247). In the case of Zelenović, the court commented that "an important factor is the physical and mental trauma suffered by the victims, even long after the commission of the crime", and this comment was immediately followed by an account of the victims' ages: "In 1992, FWS-75 and FWS-87 were 25 and 15 years old, respectively" (Zelenović sentencing judgment, 4 April 2007, para. 40, p. 13).

As this discussion shows, acts of sexual violence, particularly against young girls, by military men in times of war will not enhance their masculinity in the eyes of the court, rather the contrary. Yet, sexual violence against young girls by men in uniform does lend itself to an attempted conceptualization of chivalrous behavior by the defence counsel. The soldiers had sex with the girls as a response to alleged infatuation (Kovač) and seduction (Kunarac) in addition to claiming that the involuntary sexual behavior was not so bad because it could have been worse (Zelenović), presumably by others. Sexual behavior is conceptualized as a masculine issue along the line of the "boys-will-be-boys argument"; the acts were seen as an expression of sexual lust which needed an outlet, in other words as normal male behavior. The response by the court suggests, however, that this viewpoint of the military perpetrator is strongly challenged.

NARRATIVES OF OPPORTUNISM – ABNORMAL REACTION TO ABNORMAL (OR EXTREME) SITUATIONS?

If we see the chivalrous narrative as one which situates the perpetrator as a soldier who is driven by a protection rationale and normal sexual desires, then the narratives of opportunism can be said to do the opposite. War provides opportunities to commit sexual violence crimes with impunity, but not all soldiers will take advantage of this situation. What, then, of those who do? How can perpetrators of sexual violence crimes be understood when these acts of crime happen in clearly coercive settings where the perpetrator is the prison guard? A closer look at what the court labelled "opportunistic perpetrators" reveals a second conceptualization of the military perpetrator, one in which sexual violence sets the perpetrator apart from fellow-soldiers in a non-chivalrous way. The cases discussed in this section relate to crimes of sexual violence committed by soldiers who worked in a range of different detention facilities. The sexual violence perpetrators in this group were all found guilty of having committed sexual crimes against women who were imprisoned and who were subjected to criminal sexual violation on multiple occasions in these detention facilities.

Setting of the Crimes: Prison Inmates in Detention Facilities

We can start with Milorad Radić, who worked as prison guard shift leader at the Omarska concentration camp. In this camp a relatively small number of detainees, approximately 36 according to the ICTY, were women. The oldest of these were in their 60s, and only one of them was particularly young (Radić sentencing judgment, 2 November 2001, para. 98, p. 31), but they were all considered to be threats to the Serb regime (Radić sentencing judgment, 2 November 2001, para. 19, p. 7). In their testimonies, several of the women told of multiple rapes that were committed against them in a somewhat orderly fashion, where they would be taken out of the rooms where the women were being held to a different location, where they would be raped by several men, before typically being sent back to the rooms where the women were being kept. Under these circumstances, in addition to the direct traumas caused by individual acts of sexual violence, the women at the camp were continually traumatized by each other's experiences, as they would never know who would be next in line. This, the court commented, created a constant atmosphere of fear and terror for all. Ultimately, Milorad Radić was sentenced to 20 years' imprisonment for acts that included crimes of sexual violence at the Omarsaka camp in central Bosnia. In its assessment of the charges and evidence regarding Radić's involvement in crimes committed at the camp, the court stated:

> The Trial Chamber heard compelling evidence that Radić was personally involved in the sexual harassment, humiliation, and violation of women in Omarska camp. He would call particular women out from their place of detention and when these women returned, it was apparent to the other women that something terrible had happened to them. Typically, they did not speak to or look at the other women. (Radić sentencing judgment, 2 November 2001, para. 546, p. 153)

Radić was found guilty of having abused Witness F by telling her that "he could help her if she agreed to sleep with him and that she would get out of the room where she was held one night when he was on duty. He then touched her 'female parts' of her body" (Radić sentencing judgment, 2 November 2001, para. 547, p. 153). According to a witness (Sifeta S.), he also grabbed another female inmate while she was clearing a table and told her, "It's better for me to rape you than somebody else did" (Radić sentencing judgment, 2 November 2001, para. 547, p. 153). Yet another victim, Witness J, was threatened with rape, though Radić did not succeed in carrying out this threat fully (Radić sentencing judgment, 2 November 2001, para. 548, p. 154), while Witnesses K, AT and A all testified that Radić had sexually assaulted them in various ways. On Radić's role on crimes committed at the camp, the court commented the following:

> The Trial Chamber has found that Radić played a substantial role in the functioning of Omarska camp as a guard shift leader. He remained at the camp for its entire duration never missing a single shift, guards on his shift were notoriously brutal and he played a role in orchestrating the abuses, and he personally committed crimes of sexual violence against female detainees. Radić is thus a co-perpetrator of the joint criminal enterprise. (Radić sentencing judgment, 2 November 2001, para. 575, p. 161)

In the outline of the court's assessment of the crimes, the judges do not conceal their outrage at the crimes with which they had been presented. In mapping out the factors relevant for Radić's sentencing, the court stated that he had "grossly abused his position of power in the camp by forcing and coercing the women into sexual activity for his own pathetic gain (Radić sentencing judgment, 2 November 2001, para. 740, p. 202), adding that "by all indications Radić relished and actively encouraged criminal activity in the camp. He appeared to regard abuses as entertainment" (Radić sentencing judgment, 2 November 2001, para. 741, pp. 202–203). This was all made possible because the victims were in detention and Radić could do as he pleased. In other words, the opportunity to commit acts of sexual violence with seemingly total impunity presented itself, and Radić seems to have thrived on the possibility, more so than others.

Role of the Perpetrator: Terrorizing and Unpredictable Behavior

Similar personality traits (sadistic and abusive) were also described in the discussion of the sentencing factors pertaining to Hazim Delić. Delić was found guilty of raping two women in the Čelebići prison camp that had been set up close to the town of Konjic in southwestern Bosnia, where Serb prisoners were held by Croat (and Bosnian) defence council HVO[xiv] soldiers. Hazim Delić was the deputy commander at the camp from May to November 1992, and was alleged to have also been in charge during the last month before the camp was closed down in December 1992. Women held at the camp (the number of whom is not stated in the sentencing judgment) were housed in a separate building, but were taken to a separate room where they were held together for interrogation. One of the victim witnesses, Mrs Grozdana Ćećez, said that she had been raped by Hazim Delić and four other men, in the presence of two more. Both before and after these events, she was asked about the whereabouts of her husband. Other witnesses reported that Hazim Delić would boast about this incident and of having raped at least 18 women, claiming that "it was his intention to rape more in the future" (Delić sentencing judgment, 16 November 1998, para. 928, p. 325). Mrs Ćećez testified that Hazim Delić had told her, while she was being raped, that she was in the camp because of her husband (who was thought to be hiding in the vicinity of Konjic) and that she would not have been there if he had been around (Delić sentencing judgment, 16 November 1998, para. 929, p. 325). The other victim, Ms Antić, was raped on three occasions by Hazim Delić. Another witness, Witness P, stated that Hazim Delić had said that he was keeping Ms Antić for himself and that she was a virgin (Delić sentencing judgment, 16 November 1998, para. 948, p. 331). The story of Ms Antić is also mapped out in the judgment, where it is made clear that she was not married, was 44 years old at the time of the crimes, and was living with her mother when she was arrested in her village and taken to the Čelebići camp, where the following events took place:

Upon her arrival at the Čelebići prison-camp, she was immediately interrogated together with another woman, by Hazim Delić, Zdravko Mucić and another person. In answer to a question by Mr. Mucić, she stated that she was not married, at which point Mr. Mucić said to Mr. Delić, "[t]his is just the right type for you". (Delić sentencing judgment, 16 November 1998, para. 955, p. 333)

The judgment then proceeds to detailed descriptions of rapes that were violent, intimidating and physically damaging for the victims. In its summary of how it viewed Hazim Delić's behavior, the court wrote:

The rapes were committed inside the Čelebići prison-camp and on each occasion Hazim Delić was in uniform, armed and viciously threatening towards Ms. Antić. The purpose of these rapes was to intimidate, coerce and punish Ms. Antić. Further, at least with respect to the first rape, Delić's purpose was to obtain information from Ms. Antić, as it was committed in the context of interrogation. In addition, the violence suffered by Ms. Antić in the form of rape, was inflicted upon her by Delić because she is a woman. As discussed above, this represents a form of discrimination which constitutes a prohibited purpose for the offence of torture. Finally, there can be no question that these rapes caused severe mental and physical pain and suffering to Ms. Antić. The effects of the rapes that she suffered at the hands of Hazim Delić, including the extreme pain of anal penetration and subsequent bleeding, the severe psychological distress evidenced by the victim while being raped under circumstance where Mr. Delić was armed and threatening her life, and the general depression of the victim, evidenced by her constant crying, the feeling that she was going crazy and the fact that she was treated with tranquilizers, demonstrate most emphatically the severe pain and suffering that she endured. (Delić sentencing judgment, 16 November 1998, paras 963–964, p. 335)

Hazim Delić was found guilty of torture for the multiple rapes of Ms Antić. In the court's discussion of factors relevant for sentencing, a number of issues pertaining to Hazim Delić's personality were raised and the following formulation was used: "Hazim Delić [is] guilty of committing a series of violent crimes upon detainees who were at his mercy in the Čelebići prison camp" (Delić sentencing judgment, 16 November 1998, para. 1253, p. 429). In other words, the prisoners were not only extremely vulnerable owing to the fact of their incarceration, but had also been subject to Delić's whims and impulses, as the prosecution had pointed out. In its closing statements, the prosecution pointed out that "he participated in monstrous crimes [...] he brutally raped a number of the women in the prison camp and then boasted about it [...] he took sadistic pleasure in the infliction of pain [...] he would laugh in response to pleas for mercy from the victim" (Delić sentencing judgment, 16 November 1998, para. 1254, p. 429). Further, the prosecution submitted that the Trial Chamber should regard, as an aggravating factor, that the suffering of the victims took place within the context of the conditions of their imprisonment (Delić sentencing judgment, 16 November 1998, para. 1256, p. 429). The defence, on the other hand, argued that Delić had had no prior trouble with the law, had been charged with no criminal offences before this time, and had no training prior to his assignment to the prison camp (Delić sentencing judgment, 16 November 1998, para. 1257, p. 429). The court, however, found few mitigating circumstances for Hazim Delić. Rather, and in relation to the rapes in particular, the Trial Chamber pointed out that:

Hazim Delić is guilty of torture by way of the deplorable rapes of two women detainees in the Čelebići prison-camp. He subjected Grozdana Ćećez not only to the inherent suffering involved in rape, but exacerbated her humiliation and degradation by raping her in the presence of his colleagues. The effects of this crime are readily apparent from the testimony of the victim when she said "... he trampled on my pride and I will never be able to be the woman that I was." Before the first rape of Milojka Antić, Hazim Delić threatened her and told her that, if she did not do whatever he asked, she would be sent to another prison-camp or shot. He then forced her to take her clothes off at gunpoint, ignored her pleas for mercy and cursed and threatened her while raping her. The following day he compounded her fear and suffering by stating " ... [w]hy are you crying? This will not be your last time". This rape was followed by two others, one of which involved painful and physically damaging anal penetration. These were committed by Hazim Delić when he was armed, in total disregard of his victim's pleas for mercy. Ms. Antić testified as to the effect these crimes had on her, including feelings of misery, constant crying and the feeling that she had gone crazy. In a victim impact statement submitted by the Prosecution for the purposes of sentencing, she stated, "[t]he wounds that I carry from the rapes in Čelebići will never go away". (Delić sentencing judgment, 16 November 1998, paras 1262–1263, p. 431)

The Trial Chamber further commented on the way in which Hazim Delić was said to have behaved in the prison facility, and concluded that both the crimes (and their underlying motivations) were some of the most serious offences a perpetrator can commit. Further, the Trial Chamber commented that the "manner in which these crimes were committed are indicative of a sadistic individual who, at times, displayed total disregard for the sanctity of human life and dignity (Delić sentencing judgment, 16 November 1998, para. 1268, p. 433). The next paragraph stated:

As well as having a general sadistic motivation, Hazim Delić was driven by feelings of revenge against the people of Serb ethnicity. Before raping Ms. Antić, he stated that "the Chetniks were guilty for everything that was going on. He [Delić] started to curse my Chetnic mother. (Delić sentencing judgment, 16 November 1998, para. 1269, p. 433)

Finally, Esad Landžo was also found guilty of crimes of sexual violence in the same judgment as that in which Hazim Delić was convicted and sentenced. Landžo, however, had not had a leadership role in the camp, nor did he commit acts of sexual violence against female detainees, but rather performed acts of sexual torture against male detainees by forcing two brothers to fellate each other and by tying a burning fuse-cord to the genitals of Vukasin Mrkajic. Landžo, a prison guard, had been a young man when the war started, only 19 years old, and the defence asserted that this should be taken into account as a mitigating circumstance – a view that received support from the prosecution. The defence further argued that he was only an ordinary soldier, with no higher responsibilities, and that he had simply committed acts he had been ordered to carry out (Landžo sentencing judgment, 16 November 1998, para. 1281, p. 438). The Trial Chamber rejected these claims, however, and interpreted the facts as indicating that the accused "took some perverse pleasure in the infliction of great pain and humiliation" (Landžo sentencing judgment, 16 November 1998, para. 1281, p. 438). Nevertheless, the Trial Chamber agreed with both parties that both Landžo's age at the time of the offences and his family background, which was described as being poor, should be seen as mitigating circumstances, since they contributed to his "immune and fragile personality at the time" of the relevant events (Landžo sentencing judgment, 16 November 1998, para. 1283, p. 438). Furthermore, Landžo had received no military training or instructions as to how to conduct himself in relation to detainees, in conjunction with the overwhelmingly harsh environment because of the war. Yet, the offences for which he was found guilty were of such a nature that he was seen by the prosecution as constituting a continuing danger to society owing to personality problems ascribed to post-traumatic stress disorder. The Trial Chamber acknowledged that Esad Landžo has personality issues that would be taken into account in sentencing, and Landžo was sentenced to 15 years in prison.

Sentencing Discussion: Abnormal Personality Traits

What sets these three sexual violence perpetrators apart from the three perpetrators in the past category is that they exercised a different power and control. All victims were held in different detention facilities and the perpetrator all had different levels of superior responsibilities in these facilities. In addition, they had different levels of professional training; Radić was a former policeman and served a shift guard in the camp; Delić had military background from the JNA (Jugoslavenska Narodna Armija, Yugoslav National Army) army but had worked as a locksmith in a wood working plant up until the war (in the camp he was the deputy commander); and Landžo had no formal education nor military training and was Delić's subordinate as a prison guard. This context is different from the alleged homes in which the sexual violence victims in the former category were placed. The fact that Radić and Delić had a formal background which should have trained them to understand what to do and not in a prison setting is seen as particularly aggravating. In addition, their position of authority meant that their behavior set an example to others. In the case of Radić the court asserted that he "had substantial authority over guards on his shift in the camp and that he used his power to prevent crimes selectively" (Radić sentencing judgment, 2 November 2001, para. 526, p. 148).

Further, while the perpetrators in the former category were conceptualized as committing acts of sexual violence to boost their military status, the court is much more focused on sadistic aspects of the crimes committed by the perpetrators in the present category. The use of words like pathetic pleasure, revenge, sadistic motivation, whims and impulses, etc. suggest that the court views the perpetrators as having low self-control and that the possibility to commit acts of sexual violence was something they sought out, because the opportunity was there. In addition, it is underscored that these perpetrators were particularly violent and their shifts when they were on guard stood out due to this. The fact that these men stood out in the setting they were in is further underscored by their respective defense lawyers who attempt to build a case narrative in which it is the perpetrators' deviant personalities which are in focus, and where attempts were made to view their deviant personalities as mitigating circumstances.

NARRATIVES OF REMORSE – NORMAL RESPONSE TO AN ABNORMAL (OR EXTREME) SITUATION?

A final narrative format which emerged in the sentencing judgments were those where remorse was expressed and a guilty plea was submitted. In these judgments it is the expression of guilt itself which is at the core and where the perpetrator himself agrees, by and large, to the factual basis and gives an assessment of his own behavior. In other words, these are the judgments where the perpetrators' voices are the most pronounced. How then do the perpetrators, in their own words, situate themselves as soldiers vis-à-vis these crimes?

Role of the Perpetrator: Following Orders and Feeling Shame

The final group of perpetrators of sexual violence consisted of three men who entered guilty pleas and expressed deep remorse for their actions: Miroslav Bralo, Milan Simić and Dragan Zelenović, who were sentenced to 20, 5 and 15 years imprisonment, respectively. Miroslav Bralo admitted guilt on all counts against him, including the rape and imprisonment of Witness A, whom he violated over a period of approximately two months. In his guilty plea, he expressed deep discomfort with the person he was at the time of the war and the actions and behaviors he admitted having carried out:

These were acts which I always knew to be wrong, which anyone would know to be wrong, and for which there really can be no excuse at all. I know I acted badly, and compounded this later by my words. Our wrongs were so terrible – I include others here – that we clung to them, and tried to justify them. I tried to be proud of my actions and to think they were the actions of a successful soldier. Today I am ashamed of my conduct and ashamed how I behaved. No, these were not the actions of the soldier I once wanted to be. I was present when women and children were gunned down in front of me, and at that moment the good soldier in me was gone, silent. (Bralo, guilty plea, 19 July 2005)

Unlike the other perpetrators in this sample, who had violated multiple women, Bralo had committed acts of sexual violence against a single woman, Witness A, over an extended period of time. In his guilty plea, he did not address the claims of sexual violence directly – a pattern that can be seen in all of the guilty pleas entered by the 28 people convicted of crimes of sexual violence by the ICTY. However, he clearly addressed his failed status as soldier. His behavior, according to his own statement, had been at odds with what that of a soldier should be. The two other perpetrators in the sample who entered guilty pleas talked about neither their rape charges nor their soldier identities, but addressed their personal struggles with what they had done. Milan Simić, for example, stated that:

I have done that, but in addition to my sincere regret and remorse and personal apology that I extended to them, I was still haunted by guilt and it continues so until this day. (Simić, guilty plea, 15 May 2002)

In entering a plea of guilty, Simić admitted his responsibility for having orchestrated acts of sexual torture against male victims in the following manner:

Safet Hadžialijagić was forced to pull down his pants, and one of the men accompanying Milan Simić brandished a knife and threatened to cut off Safet Hadžialijagić's penis; the other assailants were challenging and exhorting the man wielding the knife to cut off Safet Hadžialijagić's penis. (Simić sentencing judgment, 17 October 2002, para. 11, p. 5)

The judges agreed with the prosecutor's argument that "[t]he sexual, violent and humiliating nature of the acts are [...] considered in aggravation, as it would certainly have increased the mental suffering and feelings of degradation experienced by the victims" (Simić sentencing judgment, 17 October 2002, para. 63, p. 21). Yet, Simić's guilty plea (even though it was entered late in the proceedings)[xv] and his expression of remorse were considered mitigating factors, and the judges regarded his regrets as sincere since he both had taken the opportunity to publicly extend an apology to all his victims and had apologized personally to two of his victims (Simić sentencing judgment, 17 October 2002, para. 94, p. 30). In sum, the court found that the aggravating circumstances pertaining to Simić's case (for all of the crimes he had committed, both crimes of sexual violence and other forms of torture and killing) included: the circumstances in which the offences were committed, his official position, the vulnerability of the victims, and his discriminatory intent. The mitigating factors that led to a drastic reduction in his sentencing were: his admission of guilt and expression of remorse, his voluntary surrender, and his lack of a prior criminal record, along with his comportment in the Detention Unit and his attitude towards the proceedings (Simić sentencing judgment, 17 October 2002, para. 113, p. 35). For his crimes, Simić received only a five-year prison sentence.

Sentencing Discussions: Assessing Guilt and Remorse

Dragan Zelenović was found guilty of committing, of aiding and abetting, and of co-perpetrating multiple rapes at various times and at different locations in Foča over an extended period of time in 1992. On 17 January 2007, he pleaded guilty to seven counts of rape and torture.[xvi] In his plea statement, he focused on the religious dimensions of his regrets:

Guided by Biblical teachings that the truth is not to be feared because that is the only thing that will help all, I have confessed as to my guilt, and I am prepared to bear all the consequences of that. I know that not a single form of punishment can erase the sufferings sustained by my victims. However, faith teaches us that admission of having committed injustice to someone is the best way of helping them. [...] I feel sorry for all the victims who were victimized by anything that I did, and that is why I express from this forum my deepest remorse and regret. I am a human being with virtues and vices, and I didn't know how to deal with these vices when I should have. [...] I will courageously take any sentence meted out, and I hope that God will give me strength to go through all of this and that I go back to my family. (Zelenović, guilty plea, 17 January 2007)

In the court's discussion of the particular aggravating and mitigating factors of this case, the judges commented that "rape is an inherently humiliating offence, and humiliation is generally taken into account when assessing the gravity of the crime" (Zelenović sentencing judgment, 4 April 2007, para. 36, p. 12). In addition, it was stated in the sentencing judgment that it was essential to take into account the vulnerability of the victims when assessing the gravity of a crime (Zelenović sentencing judgment, 4 April 2007, para. 39, p. 13), along with the physical and mental trauma suffered by the victims even long after the commission of the crime (Zelenović sentencing judgment, 4 April 2007, para. 40, p. 13). These elements would suggest a long sentence for Zelenović. However, as was pointed out in the sentencing judgment, entering a guilty plea was also given considerable weight, "since the admission of guilt may show honesty and readiness to take responsibility, it may help establishing the truth and contribute to reconciliation, and [...] because of the guilty plea victims are relieved from giving evidence in court and thereby re-living their trauma" (Zelenović sentencing judgment, 4 April 2007, para. 45, pp. 14–15). It is interesting to note that the prosecution pointed out that the guilty plea entered by Zelenović was "the first time in the history of the Tribunal that a perpetrator admits to and confirms what happened to the female non-Serb population in Foča in 1992 [...] not only does [this contribute to] the establishment of the truth, but also to the reconciliation in the area" (Zelenović sentencing judgment, 4 April 2007, para. 48, pp. 14–15). In the summary of how the court viewed the mitigating circumstances, the following considerations were spelled out: "his family situation,[xvii] together with his health condition,[xviii] the fact that he had no prior convictions and his good behavior while in the United Nations Detention Unit. Taken together, these factors were assigned some, albeit limited, weight in mitigation (Zelenović sentencing judgment, 4 April 2007, para. 55, pp. 14–15). Zelenović was sentenced to 15 years' imprisonment.

Setting of the Crimes: Aberrant Personality During War

In all three of these cases, the fact that the accused entered a plea of guilty was given considerable weight by the court, and the sentences the accused men received for grave offences were substantially lighter than those in the other cases examined. The central element in the evaluation of the court was not just the fact that a plea of guilty had been entered, but also its timing, its wording and whether it was seen as being sincere and a true expression of remorse. The way in which this admission of guilt was formulated in the guilty pleas varied, but the central tenet was that the perpetrators distanced themselves from the persons they were at the time when the admitted crimes took place. Bralo saw himself as a damaged soldier; Simić saw himself as a person tormented by guilt (i.e., that he committed acts he knew to be wrong); and Zelenović described himself as a failed human being who did not deal appropriately with his own virtues and vices, for which he was prepared to pay the appropriate cost both in a legal and in a religious sense. All three cases contain descriptions of altered identities: the soldier, the person of conscience and the humane person. These insights and admissions were given considerable punitive leverage by the court, even though the crimes the accused men admitted to having committed were arguably among the gravest instances of humanitarian violation in the war.

THE NORMAL-ABNORMAL CONTINUUM

The three different perpetrator narratives in the court conceptualize the intersectionality between militarism and masculinity along a normal to abnormal continuum. On the one extreme is the narrative of the sexual violence perpetrator as a chivalrous militarized individual. We are presented with the defense lawyers' claim that the perpetrator(s) commit(s) acts of sexual violence out of lust and not hatred, that they could have been more violent (but refrained to be), that they are seduced (by very young girls) and that there is a love relationship between perpetrator and victim. All of these events are further set within the framework of a protectionist aim, and the sexual violence behavior is construed as part of normalized military behavior. These constructions were strongly contested by the judges and the prosecutors. At the other extreme is the narrative of opportunistic military perpetrators who commit acts of sexual violence because they have authority and access to defenseless women and because they display sadistic pleasure in inflicting humiliating pain. In these cases acts of sexual violence serve to set the perpetrators apart from other military individuals; they are seen as deviant and abnormal individuals. These narratives are mutually reinforced by the judges, defense lawyers and prosecutors, albeit with different legal concerns in mind. In addition to these opposite extremes, there are the remorseful perpetrators who plead guilty and express regret, shame and guilt. At the core of their guilty plea statements are what they portray as failed soldiers. The acts for which they plead guilty are in contrast to how a good soldier should behave. Sexual violence, then, does not simply set these individuals apart from other soldiers, but becomes a different expression of a failed military identity altogether. What sets the remorseful narratives apart from the two others is that they refer to an aberrant, or temporarily abnormal, behavior which the perpetrator sees and recognizes in hindsight. The judges' assessment of the perpetrator focuses on the validity of this temporality: is the perpetrator really sincere in his expression of remorse and thereby distancing himself from who he was during the war?

How then do these narratives add to the understanding of perpetrators of mass atrocities in armed conflicts? What do these narratives represent? It is clear that that the notions of the chivalrous, opportunistic and remorseful perpetrators to a large extent overlap with the categorizations by Smeulers (2008) and others. In different ways these narratives suggest criminal masterminds, fanatics, the criminal sadists, the profiteers, and devoted warriors, which Smeulers discusses in her overview. Yet, sexual violence crimes involve the notion of sexual pleasure in addition to the infliction of pain; a way of thinking which opens up for a conceptualization whereby the crimes can be narrated in a different way than as torture and mass atrocities. One could therefore question if these crimes come across as more normal to the perpetrators than other kinds of crimes: the victims are not seen as dehumanized in the context of the armed conflict, but as gendered object of masculine lust, which is what the chivalrous narratives would suggest is in a way a normal behavior. At the other extreme, sexual violence crimes set perpetrators apart from other perpetrators in the same setting as the opportunistic narrative would suggest, situating the perpetrators as abnormal individuals. Finally, the narrative of remorse is perhaps most in compliance with the more established conceptualization of perpetrators of mass atrocities: a new identity (the soldier) takes precedence over other identities and primes the individual for behaviors and reasoning that seem aberrant for the civilian in the aftermath.

CONCLUSION

The focus of this article is the presentation and analysis of how sexual violence crimes are discussed in theatre in an international criminal court. By contributing to this social science analysis with a narrative psychological reading it has been possible to focus on how the court assesses the identities and responsibilities of individual sexual violence perpetrators. To reiterate: the court has assessed the individual and the crime. The analysis presented here has tried to map out how the court has assessed the societal and cultural dimensions (in addition to the law) which underpin the conceptualization of nine principal sexual violence perpetrators.

Having presented the three conceptualizations above, one could argue that acts of sexual violence place the perpetrators on a continuum where it is the notion of the militarized individual which is cast in different lights depending on how the discussions in the court unfold. These findings do not suggest a linear instrumental use of sexual violence on a group level as was Cohen et al.'s (2013) approach, but takes the acts themselves as the starting point and asks how they reflect back on the perpetrator and how the perpetrator is situated as a militarized individual through these acts. What we find by doing this is that sexual violence in war has at least two opposing consequences for the perpetrators: it can enhance a militarized masculinity, but it can also do the opposite.

In a discussion of the role of perpetrators in war, Hutchings (2008) asks whether war provides an arena for hegemonic masculinities to be played out or whether it could be that the so-called new wars force us to focus on the "formal, relational properties of masculinity as a concept" (p. 390)? Perhaps the discussions of the three perpetrators in this category constitute a good illustration of Kaldor's (1999) discussions of the so-called new-wars, as Hutchings sees them. She argues that Kaldor diagnoses the "masculinity of the new warrior as pathological, something that takes a recognizable form of human behavior to new and extreme limits and that needs to be countered by responsible and autonomous action on the part of the cosmopolitan law enforcer" (Hutchings, 2008, p. 399). The nature of wars has changed and the display of hegemonic (and militarized) masculinity is seen as pathological, and the response is not a privileged status but potential international criminal prosecution. These insights suggest that the ICTY represents a strong conceptual shift from the laissez-faire attitude expressed in the memoirs of General Patton that "unquestionably there shall be some raping" (quoted in Brownmiller, 1975, p. 31), to harsh moral condemnation of this allegedly normal state of affairs.

Notes

However, both de Brouwer (2005) and Henry (2011) argue that there was evidence, but that it was ignored and overlooked.

In addition, a set of United Nations Council Resolutions (one adopted in June 2008 (UNSCR 1820), one in September 2009 (UNSCR 1888), one in December 2010 (UNSCR 1960), and one in June 2013 (UNSCR 2106)) have formulated how sexual violence in war is perceived by the international community at large. They all focus on the protection of women and vulnerable groups against sexual violence – based on the central argument that lack of protection perpetuates vulnerability, which in turn may be detrimental to international peace and security. This is the essence of the conceptual shift that has taken place regarding crimes of sexual violence.

Update from www.icty.org, 20 January 2015.

Xabier Agirre Aranburu (2010, p. 609), former senior analyst at the Office of the Prosecutor of the ICTY, writes of his experiences: "A pattern of crime is the aggregate of multiple incidents that share common features related to the victims, the perpetrators and the modus operandi. Pattern evidence and analysis have been used successfully, mainly in the investigations of large-scale killings, destruction and displacement; the use for sexual violence charges has been remarkably more limited."

This was a core theme of a presentation entitled "Rape as a War Crime: How To Investigate and Prosecute?" by Patricia Viseur Sellers, Legal Advisor for Gender Related Crimes and Acting Senior Trial Attorney at the ICTY, at a conference held in Oslo on 8 May 2007, entitled "The Impact of Armed Conflict on Women", which was organized by the Peace Research Institute Oslo (PRIO) and the Norwegian Red Cross.

Despite their differences, there are certain narrative elements that characterize all of the sentencing judgments in the ICTY Trial Chamber: a list of the charges against the accused, the evidence presented to the court, a discussion of the applicable law, the findings of the Trial Chamber, and, finally, a discussion of the factors considered relevant for sentencing. In cases where a guilty plea has been entered by the accused, this plea is given considerable weight in the sentencing judgment.

See Commentary to Article 46 'Sentencing', Draft Statute for an International Criminal Court, Report of the International Law Commission on the work of its forty-sixth session, UN Doc A/51/10 (1994), p. 123 (Article 46, Commentary, para. 1).

Prosecutor v Tadć, supra note 75, para. 61

Miller (2004), Zimbardo (2008) and Baum (2008) argue for a distinction between evil actions and evil inactions. This distinction proved very useful, because it permitted me to distinguish between those who had perpetrated acts of sexual violence with their own bodies or with tools/weapons they held and used directly on other persons and those who had not. The "inactive" perpetrators were by no means passive, but they were not as directly involved in the crimes of sexual violence for which they were held responsible as those who actually committed such acts. It turned out, however, that the "inaction category" needed to be further subdivided, as the cases classified under this heading comprised a wide variety of inactions. There was a subgroup to which the label "evil inaction" did not seem to fit, because the individuals concerned had given direct orders to others to commit acts of sexual abuse, rather than committing such acts themselves. These individuals seemed to fall somewhere between being personally active and being inactive. It therefore seemed useful to distinguish this group further into those who had instigated sexual violence by ordering or being physically present and those who had known about such events but had not intervened to prevent them. In sum, the case material gave 15 people who had been found guilty of crimes of sexual violence on the basis of their inactions, and 4 who were held responsible because they had issued direct orders, but who had not themselves directly committed acts of sexual violence. All of the sentencing judgments for these cases were read through as background material, but do not form part of the material analyzed in this article.

This list is taken from the details of the Kunarac, Kovačand Vuković trial provided in de Brouwer (2005, pp. 363–364).

Elsewhere Kunarac argued that he had been approached by a journalist who was writing a story in which it was claimed that Kunarac had raped young women in Foča, and that he wanted to find out who had given the journalist this information. The passage is his explanation to the court about what the journalist allegedly had misunderstood.

'FWS' stands for 'Foča Witness Statement'.

None of the defence witnesses had actually talked to the witness herself or seen the alleged letter. In a discussion about law, memory and justice in relation to rape crimes in war, Henry (2011, p. 86) quotes from an Institute for War and Peace Reporting (2000) interview with the woman in question, in which she explained that she had gone out with Kovač because he wanted her to go and she denied having been in love with him, saying "I was not in love, nor did I look like I was his girlfriend. I think that all the people who saw us in the café knew who I was and why I was with him."

In Croatian, Hrvatsko vijeće obrane

Simić first pleaded not guilty to all charges against him, despite his voluntary surrender to the court on 14 February 1998. After the fourth amended indictment, however, he pleaded guilty to two counts of torture as crimes against humanity on 15 May 2002.

Dragan Zelenović pleaded guilty to aiding and abetting the rape against FWS-75 and committing rape against FWS-

87 (which was defined as torture and rape as crimes against humanity). In addition, he pleaded guilty to co-perpetration of rape in relation to FWS-87 and two unidentified women, and to committing rape three times against FWS-75 and three times against FWS-87. (Zelenović sentencing judgment, 4 April 2007, para. 13, p. 4).

Zelenović had a wife and a son who was 13 years old at the time of the sentencing judgment.

Zelenović's medical conditions include diabetes mellitus type 2, and he is disabled with 80% established disability.

ACKNOWLEDGMENTS

In addition to the generous funders of this research mentioned above, I wish to thank the Human Rights Center at University of California, Berkeley who let me spend two summers as a Visiting Fellow working my way through the judgments analyzed in this article; Kim Thuy Seelinger, Eric Stover and Alexa Koeing deserve special mention and thanks. Important insights which have informed this work have also come through fantastic cooperation with Kathleen Kuehnast at United States Institute of Peace (USIP), Chantal de Jonge Oudraat (SIPRI, North America) and Kim Thuy Seelinger (HRC, UC Berkeley) on the Missing Peace Symposium 2013 http://www.usip.org/events/the-missing-peace-symposium-2013 which focused on the policy and research front on sexual violence crimes in war. Most importantly, however, my colleagues at the Peace Research Institute (PRIO) have been a constant source of support and encouragement when working with this dark and troublesome research theme; Torunn L. Tryggestad, Kristian Berg Harpviken, Henrik Syse and Helga Hernes, thank you for your critical reading and comments, talks, insights and laughter. Finally, I wish to thank the JSPP anonymous reviewers for sincere, critical and above all very useful comments.

REFERENCES

1. Aranburu, X. A. (2010). Sexual violence beyond reasonable doubt: Using pattern evidence and analysis for international cases. Leiden Journal of International Law, 23, 609-627. doi:10.1017/S0922156510000245
2. Arendt, H. (2006). Eichmann in Jerusalem: A report on the banality of evil. New York, NY: Penguin Books. (Original work published 1963)
3. Baaz, M. E., & Stern, M. (2009). Why do soldiers rape? Masculinity, violence, and sexuality in the armed forces in the Congo (DRC). International Studies Quarterly, 53(2), 2495-518. doi:10.1111/j.1468-2478.2009.00543.x
4. Baaz, M. E., & Stern, M. (2013). Sexual violence as a weapon of war? Perceptions, prescriptions, problems in the Congo and beyond. London, United Kingdom: Zed Books.
5. Baum, S. K. (2008). The psychology of genocide: Perpetrators, bystanders, and rescuers. New York, NY: Cambridge University Press.
6. Bergsmo, M., & Skre, A. B. (2012). Towards a more comprehensive understanding and effective proving of international sex crimes. In M. Bergsmo, A. B. Skre, & E. J. Wood (Eds.), Understanding and proving international sex crimes (pp. 1-10). Beijing, China: Torkel Opsahl Academic EPublisher.
7. Brownmiller, S. (1975). Against our will: Men, women and rape. New York, NY: Simon and Schuster.
8. Cohen, D. K., Hoover Green, A., & Wood, E. J. (2013). Wartime sexual violence: Misconceptions, implications, and ways forward (Special Report 323). Retrieved from United States Institute of Peace (USIP) website: http://www.usip.org/publications/wartime-sexual-violence-misconceptions-implications-and-ways-forward
9. Crelinsten, R. D. (1995). In their own words: The world of the torturer. In R. D. Crelinsten & A. P. Schmid (Eds.), The politics of pain: Torturers and their masters (pp. 35-65). Boulder, CO: Westview Press.
10. de Brouwer, A. M. (2005). Supranational criminal prosecution of sexual violence: The ICC and the practice of the ICTY and the ICTR. Antwerp, Belgium: Intersentia.
11. de Brouwer, A. M., Ku, C., Römkens, R., & van den Herik, L. (Eds.). (2013). Sexual violence as an international crime: Interdisciplinary approaches. Antwerp, Belgium: Intersentia.
12. Drakulić, S. (2004). They would never hurt a fly: War criminals on trial in The Hague. New York, NY: Viking Penguin Press.
13. Elshtain, J. B. (1987). Women and war. New York, NY: Basic Books.
14. Enloe, C. (1989). Bananas, beaches & bases: Making feminist sense of international politics. Berkeley, CA: University of California Press.
15. Fineman, M. E., & Zinsstag, E. (Eds.). (2013). Feminist perspectives on transitional justice: From international and criminal to alternative forms of justice. Antwerp, Belgium: Intersentia.
16. Henry, N. (2011). War and rape: Law, memory and justice. London, United Kingdom: Routledge.
17. Hilberg, R. (1992). Perpetrators, victims, bystanders – The Jewish catastrophe 1933-1945. New York, NY: Aaron Asher Books.
18. Houge, A. B. (2008). Wartime rape and sexual violence (Master's thesis). Department of Political Science, University of Oslo, Oslo, Norway.
19. Hutchings, K. (2008). Making sense of masculinity and war. Men and Masculinities, 10, 389-404. doi:10.1177/1097184X07306740
20. Institute for War and Peace Reporting (IWPR). (2000, October). 'Foča rape trial: Prosecution witness recalled to rebut "Girlfriend" claims'. Institute for War and Peace Reporting, Tribunal Update No. 196, 23-30.
21. Kaldor, M. (1999). New and old wars: Organized violence in a global era. Stanford, CA: Stanford University Press.
22. Kelman, H. (1995). The social context of torture: Policy process and authority structure. In R. D. Crelinsten & A. P. Schmid (Eds.), The politics of pain: Torturers and their masters (pp. 19-35). Boulder, CO: Westview Press.
23. Leiby, M. L. (2009). Wartime sexual violence in Guatemala and Peru. International Studies Quarterly, 53, 445-468. doi:10.1111/j.1468-2478.2009.00541.x
24. Lily, R. J. (2007). Taken by force: Rape and American

GI's in Europe during World War II. New York, NY: Palgrave Macmillan.

25. Miller, A. G. (Ed.). (2004). The social psychology of good and evil. New York, NY: The Guilford Press.
26. Murray, M. (2003). Narrative psychology. In J. A. Smith (Ed.), Qualitative psychology: A practical guide to research methods (pp. 111-131). London, United Kingdom: Sage.
27. Neitzel, S., & Welzer, H. (2012). Soldater: Beretninger om krig, drap og død [Soldiers: Stories of war, killings and death] (N. Zandjani, Trans.). Oslo, Norway: Forlaget Press.
28. Nordås, R. (2013). Preventing conflict-related sexual violence (Policy Brief, 2). Retrieved from Peace Research Institute Oslo (PRIO) website: http://file.prio.no/publication_files/prio/Nordas-Preventing-Conflict-related-Sexual-Violence-PRIO-Policy-Brief-02-2013.pdf
29. Payne, L. A. (2008). Unsettling accounts: Neither truth nor reconciliation in confessions of state violence. London, United Kingdom: Duke University Press.
30. Sarbin, T. (Ed.). (1986). Narrative psychology: The storied nature of human conduct. New York, NY: Praeger.
31. Skilbrei, M.-L. (2010). Taking trafficking to court. Women & Criminal Justice, 20, 40-56. doi:10.1080/08974451003641438
32. Skjelsbæk, I. (2001). Sexual violence and war: Mapping out a complex relationship. European Journal of International Relations, 7(2), 2211-237. doi:10.1177/1354066101007002003
33. Skjelsbæk, I. (2012). The political psychology of war rape: Studies from Bosnia and Herzegovina. London, United Kingdom: Routledge.
34. Smeulers, A. (2008). Perpetrators of international crimes: Towards a typology. In A. Smeulers & R. Haverman (Eds.), Supranational criminology: Towards a criminology of international crimes (pp. 233-263). Antwerp, Belgium: Intersentia.
35. Waller, J. (2007). Becoming evil: How ordinary people commit genocide and mass killing. Oxford, United Kingdom: Oxford University Press.
36. White, H. (1987). The content of the form: Narrative discourse and historical representation. Baltimore, MD: Johns Hopkins University Press.
37. Young, I. M. (2007). Global challenges, war, self-determination and responsibility for justice. Cambridge, United Kingdom: Polity Press.
38. Zimbardo, P. (2008). The Lucifer effect: Understanding how good people turn evil. New York, NY: Random House.

CHAPTER 7 OSAMA BIN LADEN AND NUREMBERG PRECEDENT

Martin Paul Eve

There has been much discussion of whether the US should have captured Osama Bin Laden alive and put him on trial, as per the Nuremberg precedent set in the apprehension and subsequent judicial sentencing of Nazi World War II war criminals. I felt it was worth making a slightly more critical evaluation than some of those viewsalready put out there about this.

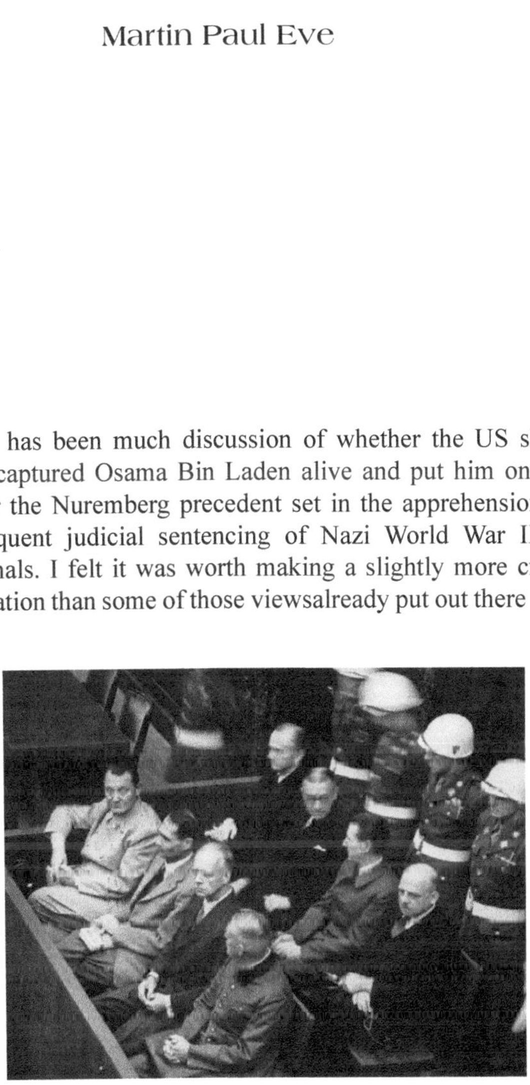

The Nuremberg defendants. Front row, from left to right: Hermann Göring (death; suicide before sentence), Rudolf Heß (life imprisonment), Joachim von Ribbentrop (death), Wilhelm Keitel (death). Second row, from left to right: Karl Dönitz (10 years), Erich Raeder (life; later released), Baldur von Schirach (20 years), Fritz Sauckel (death).

The Nuremberg Trials: All that is Solid Melts into Air

The first thing that must be noted about the Nuremberg trials, as did Judge Charles E. Wyzanski, Jr., is that while I am here going to be extremely critical of the Nuremberg trials, and also of Osama Bin Laden, that does not mean that I think nothing should be done against those who commit genocide, crimes against humanity or other acts that fall so far outside the realm of humanity as to forfeit that very title. These critiques are put forward, instead, to disturb the notion that a trial would have been any different to the decision the US eventually took. These critiques are meant to enlighten those who believe that there is such a notion as a universal system of human rights, or international law, that would make such a trial possible. As Wyzanski puts it:

> Before I come to the discussion of the legal and political questions involved, let me make it clear that nothing I may say about the Nuremberg trial should be construed as a suggestion that the individual Nuremberg defendants or others who have done grievous wrongs should be set at liberty. In my opinion there are valid reasons why several thousand Germans, including many defendants at Nuremberg, should either by death or by imprisonment be permanently removed from civilized society. If prevention, deterrence, retribution, nay even vengeance, are ever adequate motives for punitive action,

Citation: Martin Paul Eve, Osama bin laden and Nuremberg precedent, https://www.martineve.com/2011/05/20/osama-bin-laden-and-nuremberg-precedent/.

then punitive action is justified against a substantial number of Germans. But the question is: Upon what theory may that action properly be taken?

With this out the way, what is the basis of the (now well known) critique of the Nuremberg trials? These hinge, twofold, on ex post facto violation of nullum crimen sine lege and victor's justice (Siegerjustiz). These need to be considered in turn.

Ex-post facto/nullum crimen sine lege

The phrase "nullum crimen sine lege" means that it is impossible for there to be a crime, without a law at the time of the "offense". A judgement that goes against this principle is called "ex post facto", or after the event. This principle is, in the majority of cases, sound. It is not fair to judge someone for a crime that was retroactively made criminal. If I try and convict you for the crime of buying milk, criminalised today, on the basis of the milk you bought yesterday, this is hardly sound legal logic.

But we are not talking about buying milk. *We are talking about the mass murder of millions and waging of aggressive war.* It was argued, by the Nuremberg judges, that in the absence of an international authority that could have written such a criminal statute, an ex post facto ruling was acceptable because it violated the universally regarded norms of any civilized world. This was most clearly expressed in the Justices trial:

The defendants claim protection under the principle nullum crimen sine lege, though they withheld from others the benefit of that rule during the Hitler regime. Obviously the principle in question constitutes no limitation upon the power or right of the Tribunal to punish acts which can properly be held to have been violations of international law when committed. By way of illustration, we observe that C.C. Law 10, Article II, 1 (b), "War Crimes", has by reference incorporated the rules by which war crimes are to be identified. In all such cases it remains only for the Tribunal, after the manner of the common law, to determine the content of those rules under the impact of changing conditions.

Whatever view may be held as to the nature and source of our authority under C.C. Law 10 and under common international law, the ex post facto rule, properly understood, constitutes no legal nor moral barrier to prosecution in this case.

Under written constitutions the ex post facto rule condemns statutes which define as criminal, acts committed before the law was passed, but the ex post facto rule cannot apply in the international field as it does under constitutional mandate in the domestic field. Even in the domestic field the prohibition of the rule does not apply to the decisions of common law courts, though the question at issue be novel. International law is not the product of statute for the simple reason that there is as yet no world authority empowered to enact statutes of universal application. International law is the product of multipartite treaties, conventions, judicial decisions and customs which have received international acceptance or acquiescence. It would be sheer absurdity to suggest that the ex post facto rule, as known to constitutional states, could be applied to a treaty, a custom, or a common law decision of an international tribunal, or to the international acquiescence which follows the event. To have attempted to apply the ex post facto principle to judicial decisions of common international law would have been to strangle that law at birth . . . .

As a principle of justice and fair play, the rule in question will be given full effect. As applied in the field of international law that principle requires proof before conviction that the accused knew or should have known that in matters of international concern he was guilty of participation in a nationally organized system of injustice and persecution shocking to the moral sense of mankind, and that he knew or should have known that he would be subject to punishment if caught. Whether it be considered codification or substantive legislation, no person who knowingly committed the acts made punishable by C.C. Law 10 can assert that he did not know that he would be brought to account for his acts. Notice of intent to punish was repeatedly given by the only means available in international affairs, namely, the solemn warning of the governments of the States at war with Germany.

The question that one accustomed to relativistic thinking immediately asks, however, is: whose norms? Clearly, the "norm" that emerged to enforce this justice was not actually as big a majority as we would like to think. World War II was not an outright thrashing of one small upstart nation by the mass forces of outrage. It was, rather, a near miss for a fork in humanity's history that would have plunged ethics worldwide into a crisis of genocide and racial extermination. This near miss, therefore, is better attributed to victor's justice, rather than a transcendental disgust at the policy's of the Nazis.

Siegerjustiz

The victor's justice of the Nuremberg trials, wherein one set of rules was applied to the losers and another to the victors, is best put by Marianna Torgovnick:

The first and major Nuremberg trial, the International Military Tribunal (IMT), carefully constructed charges against the defendants to avoid the possibility that using atomic bombs against civilians could be construed as war crimes. (Torgovnick, 6)

Another example, probably made more forcefully in the fiction of Kurt Vonnegut's *Slaughterhouse-Five*, is the fire-bombing of Dresden. Arguments have been made that these events, which undoubtedly indiscriminately targeted civilians and should, therefore, be regarded as war crimes (despite the odious far-right's appropriation of this reasoning, it remains valid), shortened the war and prevented loss of life. But whose loss of life? Loss of Allied life. Again, the Allies did not start World War II. Neither, however, did the thousands upon thousands of civilians killed in these events. Regardless of what one wishes to believe regarding these events, the Axis powers were prosecuted, convicted and sentenced -- in many cases, to death -- for waging total war. The Allies who committed the same acts of total war were commended for preventing loss of life.

In retrospect, I believe that if these acts would have prevented the Holocaust, they could have been justified for that reason. It should probably be remembered, however, that the Allies were not fighting to stop the Holocaust. They were fighting for their freedom. The Holocaust was played down at the time and it was only afterwards the horrors of Auschwitz as the metonym for the Shoah entered the public consciousness. If you think that the atomic bombings and Dresden fire-bombings were conducted to save the victims of the extermination camps, you are sadly mistaken (particularly as the atomic bombings occurred after the surrender of Germany!)

So what am I saying?

What I'm trying to say is that the Nuremberg trials, with their logic of ex post facto judgements, is a relativistic phenomenon that relied upon justice of the victors. I cannot say that I do not think it was the right thing to do. The Nazi war crimes were the most severe of any atrocities ever committed by humankind. There is no question that they must have been held to account for their crimes and my unerring belief that the death penalty should never be used is tested to the utmost when these actions are considered. However, those who believe that the Nuremberg trials were a rock-solid pillar, a precedent, that can be hauled out and applied to anybody who commits atrocities are wrong. Nuremberg, even if it came to a just conclusion, did not achieve it by just means.

The situation with Osama Bin Laden is, therefore, different.

Firstly, if you want to use the Nuremberg precedent, which part of Nuremberg are you referring to? If it's a specific charge, which is it? Crimes against humanity? Check the definition given by the Rome Statue of the International Criminal Court:

These crimes are particularly odious offences in that they constitute a serious attack on human dignity or grave humiliation or a degradation of one or more human beings; they are not isolated or sporadic events, but are part either of a government policy (although the perpetrators need not identify themselves with this policy) or of a wide practice of atrocities tolerated or condoned by a government or a de facto authority. (RSICC/C, Vol. 1, 360)

Osama Bin Laden may have wanted to be a government, or de facto authority, but was he? The wording here relates to a world pre-decentralized terrorist entities. It is formulated for a world of States, where only territorial actors can count. Demonstrating that Bin Laden was a de factor authority would be crucial in bringing a charge to light of crimes against humanity as it currently stands.

Indeed, all of the current precedents set by Nuremberg are defined in relation to States and their political leaders. This does not seem appropriate to Bin Laden.

No, instead, it seems, what people actually want when they say that Bin Laden should have been tried, as per Nuremberg, is the ability to retrospectively invent laws, based on a notion of universal human values, and to impose the death penalty. *This means that, at the end of the day, the outcome is no different to an assassination.*

So what do I think should have been done instead?

I believe that, fundamentally, a lot of Western values are, in principle, extremely good. I do not believe that murdering civilians is an appropriate tactic to achieve your point of view. I believe that Bin Laden should be morally damned for the campaign he fought, the slaughter of thousands of people who did not deserve what they got.

I do not believe the death penalty to be a valid punishment in any circumstance, however. Life imprisonment would have sufficed, which means that I do not believe the United States should have killed Bin Laden in their raid.

I believe that redefined notions of crimes against humanity, that can be applied to individuals, should be established as an international criminal statute. These should be put into place and used in further cases of international atrocities. I am sure this is being thought of by more knowledgeable minds of jurisprudence than my own. Bin Laden, should, therefore have been brought to trial, with similar ex post facto conditions as at Nuremberg, in consultation with the international community; possibly at The Hague. Without the international consensus, it would purely have been a desire for victor's justice, with retrospective laws.

Finally, I believe that there is some, vague semblance of truth that rests on our complicity in creating the world that created Bin Laden. In the Hegelian ethics that pervades this thinking (can we do any good, or merely avoid doing bad?), none of us is truly innocent. Every action I take in my life for my own benefit is probably to the detriment of someone else. If you want to make the Nuremberg analogy, consider the statements made by Philip Potter in the light of the Barbie trial:

In reality, Barbie and his like are the products of your [French] history. Hitler, Barbie, Eichmann, and company represent the end of the Aufklärung (century of Enlightenment) which produced four things: the Industrial Revolution, which subordinated man to the machine; the founding of the United States on a declaration of independence where liberty and equality were applied to all men -- except for blacks and Indians; the French Revolution of 1789 where liberty, brotherhood, and equality were indeed claimed by the bourgeoisie; and imperialism based on racism (Woodrow).

Consider that Bin Laden and his ilk could well have been the product of a similar culture of worldwide inequality. Does this excuse murder? No, nothing does. Understanding this, though, may help us to come to terms with the logic of terrorism for, as Gus Martin puts it:

This presumption suggests that terrorism is a priori [...] irrational behaviour and that only deranged individuals [...] would select terrorist violence as a strategy. Most experts agree that this blanket presumption is incorrect [...] their behaviour is neither insane nor necessarily irrational (Martin, 48).

In this consideration of how economic injustice contributes towards a worldwide climate in which terrorism is fostered and thrives, we find a true parallel with Nuremberg; we are offered an opportunity for reflection. Furthermore, there is another, final parallel. In the reflection that is Guantanamo Bay, we see a direct manifestation of a justice system that presumes guilt and introduces ex post facto laws. The only difference is, this time there cannot even be a show trial.

REFERENCES

1. RSICC/C, Vol. 1, cited by Guy Horton, Dying Alive - A Legal Assessment of Human Rights Violations in Burma April 2005, co-Funded by The Netherlands Ministry for Development Co-Operation. Section “12.52 Crimes against humanity”, p. 201.
2. Gus Martin, Essentials of Terrorism: Concepts and Controversies (Los Angeles: Sage, 2008).
3. Marianna Torgovnick, The War Complex: World War II in Our Time (Chicago: University of Chicago Press, 2005).
4. Excerpt from U.S.A. v. ALSTOETTER ET AL. http://law2.umkc.edu/faculty/projects/ftrials/nuremberg/alstoetter.htm [accessed 2011-05-15]
5. Alain Woodrow, «Le Pasteur Potter: ‹Il sommeille en chacun de nous,› « Le Monde 11 February, 1983, cited at http://www.jewishvirtuallibrary.org/jsource/Holocaust/barbietrial.html#5
6. Judge Charles E. Wyzanski, Jr., The Atlantic Monthly, April, 1946; «Nuremberg--A Fair Trial? Dangerous Precedent,» Volume 177, No. 4 (p.66-70). http://www.mtholyoke.edu/acad/intrel/nuremb.htm [accessed 2011-05-15].

CHAPTER 8

THE INTERNATIONAL CRIMINAL COURT: ITS SUCCESS AND LIMITATIONS FOR PURSUING INTERNATIONAL JUSTICE

Mohammad Rabiul Islam

Keywords: International Criminal Court (ICC), ICTR, ICTY, Criminal justice

INTRODUCTION

The International Criminal Court (ICC) is the last great international institution of the twentieth century [1]. In July17, 1998, 120 states voted to adopt the Rome statute of the ICC at the headquarters of the FAO (Food and Agriculture Organization of the United Nations) in Rome [2]. The elaborate and complex negotiated instrument, a framework for an international criminal justice system, represented the highest point of a process that began in the wake of the Nuremberg Judgement, when the first time United Nations considered the establishment of an international criminal jurisdiction [3]. Less than four years later - far sooner than even the most hopeful observers had imagined the statute had obtained the essential sixty ratifications for its entry come into the force, on July 1, 2002 [2]. The ICC was officially opened in The Hague on March 11, 2003 in a special ceremony attended by the Queen of Netherlands and Secretary General of the UN Kofi Ann an [4]. While the Nuremberg and Tokyo Tribunals were established by the occupying and victories powers, the ICTY (International Criminal Tribunal for the Former Yugoslavia) and the ICTR (International Criminal Tribunal for Rwanda) are the first truly international criminal courts [5]. The setup of an International Criminal Court has twofold purpose. In one hand, the court would thereby preserve a common belief in the importance of implementing the legal order by punishing those guilty of serious breaches of intention and humanitarian law, which itself, would be an important goal to attain. Erstwhile, the court may be expected to have a strong preventive impact on those who plan to commit a criminal act [6]. In future, the ICC resolve more increasingly be capable of show, by way of powerful judgements resulting from fair and efficient trials, that it sets legal and moral standards that will contribute to the expansion of International Justice [4]. The ICC is based on a treaty, joined by 123 countries. The mechanism of Art.21 (3), which is more precise than that of the ICTs, could encourage them to give greater weight to international human rights instruments [7].

International Criminal Law

International law as an nearly shadowlike form that, having an important effect in the 6th and 17th centuries, than hovers above the future world [8]. International criminal law is a comparatively new and early branch of public international law. Nowadays, it is consist of a body of laws that includes statutes, customary international law, and, to a slighter extent, case law [9]. International criminal law is the law that governs international crimes. It may be said that this discipline of law is where the penal aspects of international law, including that body of law protected victims of armed conflict known as international humanitarian law, and the international aspects of national criminal law [10]. International law originated like a product of the customs along with practices of states, but it all derived from certain basic national principles, and

Citation: Islam MR (2016) The International Criminal Court: Its Success and Limitations for Pursuing International Justice. J Civil Legal Sci 5: 180. doi:10.4172/2169-0170.1000180

these in time became a separate source of international law known as "general principles" [11]. A key concern of the ICC, as it will operate in the Hague, will be how to ensure that it is speaking to local needs as well as broader concerns for justice [12]. ICC combines the universalism of global criminal justice which bases the gravity of international crimes on their attack on universal values, with the relativism of national concepts, which encourage taking into account certain criteria, in a differentiated fashion [13].

Rome Statute of the International Criminal Court

The ICC statute is that is to say core document of International Criminal law today. It lay down the legal bases of the essence International Criminal Court and develops of new brands of procedure. The ICC statute was also a most important step self-assured for substantive international criminal law [14]. Intended for all its imperfections, the statute of the ICC, implemented on July 17 1998 by the Rome Diplomatic Conference, was a major breakthrough in the effective enervated of international criminal law [15]. The statute of the state parties, determined to these ends and on behalf of present with upcoming generations, to institute an independent permanent International Criminal Court in relationship with the United Nations system, by jurisdiction over the most ruthless crimes of concern to the entire international community [1]. The Court has jurisdiction in accordance with this statute with respect to the following crimes:

- The Crime of Genocide
- Crime against humanity
- War Crimes
- The Crime of aggression [11]

The Nuremberg and Tokyo Trials

It was precisely such scenarios that lead to the successful establishment, in that way immediate post–war period, of the Nuremberg and Tokyo Tribunals. These tribunals were a response to the overwhelming horrors of the Nazi genocide in Europe and the Japanese wartime occupation of large parts of the many South – East Asian nations [15]. In its judgement of 1446, the International Military Tribunal at Nuremberg assumed that Art.6(a) of the London Charter is declaratory of modern international law, which regards war of aggression as a gave crime [16]. The framers of Nuremberg were confronted with a new offence, the bureaucratic crime, and a novel political menace, the criminal state [17]. Although according to long tradition, international law had permitted to try member of the aristocracy forces of an enemy state committing war crimes during the 19th and the 20th centuries no actual cases occurred where the political leadership of a defeated country had been put on trial [18]. The reception of the historic trial by the German legal community, and its legacy, that is its evolution into modern international criminal justice, should be understood as the result of a highly complex mixture of moral, political and legal considerations [19]. The Nuremberg and Tokyo Tribunals drew heavily on the 1929 Geneva prisoner of war convention and the Fourth Hague Convention of 1907 as establishing the substantive law to be applied - that is, as customary law, and as norms of both state responsibility and individual criminal liability [5].

The Nuremberg Charter

The subsequent acts, or several of them, are crimes coming within the jurisdiction of the tribunal for which there shall be individual liability: (a) Crime against peace, (b) War Crimes (c) Crimes against humanity [20]. In a world raven by lawless violence, it demonstrated that people need not stand by helplessly and witness atrocities without bringing the perpetrators to justice. Nuremberg began our halting efforts to impose the rule of law worldwide [21].

The Tokyo Charter

Like the Nuremberg charter, the Tokyo Charter, which was actually issued on 26 April 1946, included the newly articulated crimes against peace and humanity (Art.5). As defined in the Tokyo Charter the crimes against peace and humanity target high level orchestrates of war [22]. The Tokyo Tribunal relied heavily on the Pact of Paris of 1928 for the legal basis for the crime against peace. In addition, the Nuremberg and Tokyo tribunals represented a first effort by the international community to create a judicial mechanism for addressing the atrocities that can be committed during war [23]. These trials are the first major precedents of our time. Much less weight is generally accorded to the decision of the International Military Tribunal for the Far East than to Nuremberg for a variety of reasons, including the perception that the Tokyo proceedings were substantially unfair to many of the defendants. Indeed, its example is primarily relevant in considering what a credible international criminal justice system ought not to look like [1].

The International Criminal Tribunal for the former Yugoslavia On Feb.22, 1993 the Security Council of the UN adopted a resolution envisaging the creation of an ICTY (International Criminal Tribunal for the Former Yugoslavia) shortly afterwards, on May 25, 1993, the tribunal was established by Security Council Resolution 827 [24]. Whatever the practical achievements of the ICTY may prove to be, the UN Security Council has recognized the first truly international criminal for the prosecution of persons responsible for serious violations of international humanitarian law [25]. " The Tribunal" means the International Tribunal for the Prosecution of persons Responsible for serious violation of International humanitarian law committed in the territory of the Former Yugoslavia since 1991, established by the SC (Security Council) pursuant to its resolutions 808(1993) and 827(1993) [26]. The establishment of the ICTY under Chapter VII was a measure not concerning the use of force and, thus, fell squarely within the influence of Art. 41 of the 1945 UN Charter, even though the fact that the indicative list of measures envisaged in that article make reference to judicial bodies. Its relation to the Security Council is that of a subsidiary organ under Art.29 of the UN Charter [27]. The Tribunal was established, and which are comprehensive in Article 2 to 5 ('grave breaches' of the Geneva Conventions, genocide and crimes against humanity ,violations of the laws or customs of war,) are of relatively recent origin going back to the immediate aftermath of the Second World war [28]. The UN War Crimes Commission shares the view the conflicts in

Yugoslavia be international along with thus the intention of all the laws of war, including, of course, the rules governing war crimes, are applicable [25]. According to the UN Secretary General report on the ICTY Statute, crimes against humanity were primary acknowledged in the Nuremberg Charter and in the trials of war criminal following World War II [29]. The ICTY Statute, in Art.5 defines "crimes against humanity" subject to the Jurisdiction of the Tribunal as certain crimes "committed in armed conflict, wherever charter of Internal or International [5]." The definition of 'crimes against humanity' in Art.6(c) of the Charter of the IMT (International Military Tribunal) exception that such crimes not to linked near the war or to the commission of other crimes [30].

Pursuant to Art.13 of the ICC statute, there are three modes of triggering the ICC'S jurisdiction: (a) recommendation of a situation to the prosecutor by a state party; (b) referral of a situation to the prosecutor by the Security Council of the UN acting under chapter VII of the UN Charter; (c) initiation of an investigation by the prosecutor his own initiative [10]. The relationship of the Tribunal to national jurisdiction, as enunciated in Art.9 and 10 provides insight regarding to possible intent of the Security Council. Art. 9 of the statute clearly establishes concurrent jurisdiction between national courts and the Tribunal, while Art.10 gives the Tribunal qualified primacy [31].

Subsequently, customary international law, Art.5 of the ICTY Statute (1993) defined the crimes against humanity , when crimes committed in armed conflict internationally or internally directed against any civilian population: "(a) murder; (b) extermination ;(c) enslavement;(d) deportation;(f) torture; (g) rape; (h)persecutions on political, racial and religious grounds; (i) other inhumane Acts" [28]. Since the Appeals Chamber decision referred to the Tadic Case assessment on protection motion for interlocutory appeal on jurisdiction (Oct 2, 1995), proof that the armed conflict in question in international in character has been treated as a jurisdictional must for the applicability of Art.2 [32]. The question in dispute was whereas the accused might be held criminally liable for breaches of international humanitarian law allegedly committed in an internal armed conflict; in other words, whether he might be held responsible for war crimes perpetrated in a civil war [33]. Wilfully causing great suffering or serious injury, a grave breach of the Geneva Conventions, is punishable under Art.2(c) of the statute. Cruel treatment, a violation of the laws or customs of war is punishable under Art.3 of the statute and is recognised by Art.3(1)(a) of the Geneva Conventions [34].

Art.2(3) of the statute contains a list of punishable crimes, including 'genocide' and 'complicity in genocide'.Art.2(2), which prescribes the dolus specials, does not say that it pertains to 'genocide' with the other crimes listed in Art.2(3) including 'complicity of genocide'. Nor does Art.2(3) which contains the list of crimes, say so [35]. In terms of the ICTY'S establishment, the international court should be build up to attempt those responsible for war crimes and crimes against humanity committed in the former Yugoslavia. To prove a charge under Art.5 of the ICTY statute (on crime against humanity), the prosecution has to prove not only that crimes took place, but also that those crimes were committed as part of a 'widespread or systematic' attack [36]. The ICTY case has often stressed that Art.3 of its statute constitutes a broad section which is intended to cover all serious violations of international humanitarian law not falling under other specific provisions ,e.g. Art.2 (grave breaches) [37]. Much of the prosecution case in ICTY trials in concerned with evidence of the commission of crimes by subordinates of the accused, called 'Crime base' evidence. The prosecution must also lead other to link the accused to the crimes [38].

Art.25(3)(d) was problematic because it equated the responsibility of the defendant who intended to further the aim of the criminal enterprise with the defendant who was merely aware of the groups intention to commit the crime [39]. Security Council Res.1503 (2003) was the first comprehensive blueprint for the ICTY completion strategy, emanating from the Security Council rather than ICTY itself [40]. Dominic Raab, says there are two lessons for the ICC: First, the ICC will need to foster a degree of collective responsibility to enable it to operate with greater transparency. Secondly, the ICC status parties will need to take up the mantle of conducting meaningful oversight in relation to matters of general legal policy [40]. Art.5(h) of the ICTY Statute prohibits' persecution on political and religious grounds.' This offence has been used to encapsulate as a crime the ethnic cleansing practices relied upon by certain parties to the conflict in former Yugoslavia territory [41]. Art.19(2) of the ICTY Statute provides that, "upon confirmation of an incident, the judge may, at the request of the prosecutor, issue such as orders and warrants for the arrest, detention, surrender or transfer or persons, and any other orders as may be required for the conduct of the trial [42]." Extensive powers of arrest have been provided expressis verbis in the ICTY'S rules of procedure and evidence, and few objections based ahead the contents of rule 59 bis or other relevant rules vis-à-vis the overall scope of the ICTY'S general framework of delegated competence from UN Security Council Resolution 827 and chapter VII of the UN Charter appear convincing [42]. Art.2(7) of the UN Charter – which provides that the prohibition of UN intervention in matters fundamentally surrounded by states' domestic measures under Chapter VII – paved the way for the evolution of norms applicable to internal conflicts and, eventually for the resolutions by which the security council has authorized forcible interventions in response to internal atrocities [29]. The ICTY Prosecutor's decision not to investigate NATO, for example, which is further discussed in part IV of this article, was widely reported in the media and affected attitudes toward that tribunal [43].

International Criminal Tribunal for Rwanda

The International Criminal Tribunal for Rwanda (ICTR) was set up by UN Security Council Res. 955 of Nov.8, 1994, in response to genocide along with other systematic, widespread, and blatant violations of international humanitarian law which had been committed in Rwanda [10]. For the period of time approximately 800,000 people were killed in the genocide of Rwanda. The methodical massacre of men, women and children that took over the course of about 100 days since April and July 1994 will be remembered as one of the most distasteful measures of the twentieth century [44]. In the first week of the genocide, it is estimated that 10,000 people a day were killed [45]. Contained by two weeks after the genocide started some 250,000 Tutsis were massacred.

As Tutsi refugees in Uganda reported the atrocities, the RPF (The Rwanda Patriotic Front) launched a northern offensive; however, the RPF'S offensive "simply could not match the pace at which the militiamen and soldiers were massacring civilians [46]. The violence in Rwanda was distinctive of many brightly and euphemistically titled "post –conflict" operations that were overseeing transitions from civil war to civil peace [47]. The organizers of the massacres wanted to create a new Rwanda a community of murders, who shared a collective sense of accomplishment or guilt. The new Rwanda's would undergo an initiation rite by killing their neighbour [48]. The ICTR shall have the power to prosecute persons responsible for serious violations of international humanitarian law committed in the territory of Rwanda and Rwandan citizens responsible for such violations committed in the territory of neighbouring states, among Jan 1, 1994 and Dec.31, 1994, in agreement among the provisions of the present statute [49].

Mr. Waly Bacre Ndiyae argued (Rapporteur of the Commission on Human Rights), massacres and superfluity of other serious of human rights violations were pleasing in Rwanda. The targeting of the Tutsi population the term genocide might be applicable [50]. The former Prime Minster of the Interim Government of the Republic of Rwanda, Jean Kambanda, pleaded guilty to the crimes of genocide, conspiracy to commit genocide, direct and public incitement to commit genocide, complicity in genocide and crime against humanity [51]. Art.27(1) primarily addresses the substantive responsibility of state officials for international crimes rather than questions of immunity. The main effect is to set up the official capacity of a person does not relieve him of individual criminal accountability and it eliminates a substantive defence that may be put forward by state officials [52]. After the Second World War, in 1994 Rwanda erupted into one of the major horrendous cases of mass murder the world had witnessed. The killings fell into three broad categories: (a) combatants killings combatants; (b) Hutu citizens and military and paramilitary forces killing Hutu citizens because the victims were either moderates willing to live and work with Tutsi or persons whose land and wealth the murderers wanted to appropriates; and (c) Hutu killing Tutsi because they were Tutsi. Of these, the second and clearly constituted grievous crimes; the third amounted to genocide [48]. The jurisdiction of ICC'S is limited to cases alleging the commission of crimes against humanity, genocide, or war crimes, occurring after 1 July,2002, the date of entry into force of the Statute, as defined in the Rome Statute [43].

The subject matter of the ICTR is formulated differently and covers the crime of genocide (Art.2), crimes against humanity (Art.3) and violations Art.3 common to the Geneva Conventions and of Additional Protocol 11(Art.4). The Crime of genocide is formulated identical towards the one laid down is the ICTY Statute [53]. Every single individual indicted by the ICTR has been stimulated with genocide or else of the other punishable, genocidal acts such as conspiracy to commit genocide (Art.2(3)(b) of the ICTR'S Statute), direct and public incitement to commit genocide (Art.2(3)(c) and complicity in genocide Art.2(3)(e)) [32]. Jean Mukimbiri, described the Rwanda genocide happened in the following ways : (a) definition of the target group; (b) registration of the victims; (c) designation of the victims; (d) restrictions and confiscations of goods; (e) exclusion; (f) systematic isolation; (g) mass extermination [54]. Even though the top officials were detained by the ICTR, immeasurable fatalities cover to live subsequently to neighbours who participated in the killings. Channeling the wish for retribution keen on legal process, constant with the sentence of thousands, bought time until incident enhanced and mitigated the cruelty of castigatory abuses [55]. The Genocide Convention in Art.6 provides that: "persons charged with genocide shall be tried by a competent tribunal of the state in the territory of which the act was committed, or by such international penal tribunal as may have jurisdiction [56]." One year after it was established, the Rwanda tribunal issued its first indictments on December 12, 1995, accusing eight Rwandans of genocide [57]. Art.6(c) of the Nuremberg Charter acknowledged that two categories of crimes against humanity relating to: (a) inhumane acts, and (b) persecution on specified grounds [49]. Art.2.1. of the Rwanda Tribunal Statute confers on the Rwanda Tribunal the authority to accuse persons accountable for the crime of genocide [49]. The definition of the genocide, the prohibited acts that may constitute the crime of genocide when committed with the necessary intent are set forward in Art.2.2.a-e of the Statute of Rwanda Tribunal [49].

Art.6 of the International Criminal Court statute reproduces Art.11 of the Genocide Convention. Statute of the ICC provides separately for those forms of criminal participation which entail individual criminal liability under the statute, including relative to genocide. The organization of the ICC Statute also excludes potential contradictions between genocide provision and the provision providing for individual criminal responsibility, as has been the case with the ad hoc Tribunals where Art.4/2 and Art.7/6 of the ICTY/ICTR status overlap and may contradict each other in part [58]. The Appeals Chamber started that there is denial provision in the statute limiting the criminal accountability under common Art.3 and Protocol 11 to a specified class of persons. No special and a priori relationship to individual party to the conflict or towards public authority in necessary for triggering criminal responsibility under Art.4 of the Statute [37]. The offence of incitement to commit genocide requires two essential conditions under Art.2(3) (c), namely : (1) a public statement; (2) call for direct action [49]. Art.3 of the Rwanda Tribunal Statute confers on the authority to prosecute persons responsible for inhumane acts which constitutes crimes against humanity. The definition of this category of crimes against humanity consists of three essential elements which relate to the prohibited act, namely: (1) the act must be inhumane character, (2) the act ought to be dedicated as a part of a extensive or systematic attack against any civilian population, and (3) the act must be committed on political, national, racial, ethnic, or religious grounds [49]. At least some of the possible factors in the Rwandan genocide imply, the limits on the ICTR'S Jurisdiction are not simply the result of resource constraints. Broader jurisdiction for the ICTR could well have led to inquiries that would have embarrassed either the UN as a whole or particular the Security Council permanent members [59]. Additionally, Genocide is liable where the power of govern elites or eroding. In Rwanda, multiparty politics, fierce intra-ethnic political opposition, the original low–grade civil war with Tutsis, and the Arusha peace agreement compromised Habyarimana's ruling party and his inner circle [60]. In brief, the decisive cause of Rwanda genocide was the increasing imbalance in land, food and people that led to malnutrition, hunger, periodic famine along with fierce competition for land to farm [48]. The criminal responsibility of the superior for the unlawful acts of his subordinates, if he failed to discharge his duty of prevention or suppression (after the fact), is well established in customary and conventional international law (Art.7(3) of ICTR Statute; Art.6(3) of ICTR Statute) [37].

Comparison and Contrast between the ICTY and the ICTR Similarities

- Both are the set up by the UN Security Council exercising its enforcement power under chapter VII of the UN Charter maintain international peace and security.
- Both are the subsidiary organs of the UN Security Council.
- Both are bound to apply rules of international law that are beyond doubt part of customary international law.
- Both have almost identical Rules of Procedure and Evidence.
- Both have the same Prosecutor [10].
- Both the engagement of national and foreign courts has in some way exorcised the spectre of genocide and other massive crimes from our midst [55].

Differences

- The ICTY has jurisdiction over crimes in both international armed conflicts and internal armed conflict. The ICTR has jurisdiction over crimes committed in internal armed conflict only.
- The ICTY has jurisdiction over crimes against humanity only if they are 'committed in an armed conflict'. The ICTR has jurisdiction over crimes against humanity only if they are committed "on national, political, ethnic, racial, or other religious grounds."
- The ICTY has jurisdiction over crimes under the ICTY statute dedicated the territory of the former Yugoslavia since 1991.The ICTR has jurisdiction over crimes under the ICTR Statute committed in Rwanda and Rwandan neighbouring States since January 1, 1994 to December 31, 1994.
- Unlike the ICTY, the ICTR does not have a pool of ad litem judges to help in its work [10]. The fundamental distinction among the ICC along with the ICTY-ICTR model is the primarily consensual starting point for the exercise of ICC jurisdiction [3].

Since the ICTR has no jurisdiction over aggression and does not limit criminal liability to offenses committed in the course of aggressive war, it does not run the same risks. Neither the ICTR nor the ICTY is required to show that the crime against humanity known as persecution, for example, occurred in the course of international armed conflict [59]. Both ICTY and ICTR have remarkably contributed to peace building in post war societies, along with to introducing criminal responsibility into culture of international relations. Both institutions have helped to marginalized nationalist political leaders along with other armed forces related to ethnic war and genocide, to discourage retribution by victim groups, and to transform criminal justice which is an important aspect of the current international agenda [55].

Deciding upon the powers of the Security Council vis-à-vis the ICC was a controversial aspect of the deliberations. It implicated potential conflicts between the Council's mandate to maintain international peace and security, on the other hand, and the prospect that ICC indictments against political or military leaders may complicated power transitions and the conclusion of armistices, on the other hand [3]. One of the criticisms of the ad hoc international criminal tribunals has been their absence and rejection of provisions related to victim participation in the proceedings. With the increased focus on victims by several UN Organs, however, early on, the issue of victimrelated provisions was included in the agenda of drafting the statute for proposed international criminal tribunal [61]. The contradiction inherent in the decision to refer the Darfur situation to the ICC, on one hand, and, on the other hand, to expressly confine the obligation to cooperate with the court to the states party to the status, is however, nothing but one sign of the overall scant coherency of Res.1593 (2005) [62]. It has been argued that Security Council Resolutions 1422, 1487 and 1497 are all unlawful. At the time of its adoption a number of statuses criticized Resolutions 1422 because it provided for 'blanket immunity' rather than immunity on a 'case–by-case' basis. This, it was argued, put the resolution outside the scope of Art.16 of the Rome Statute [63]. Apart from Security Council referral, the ICC had two viable " triggering mechanism", or bases, for exercising jurisdiction: a state's referral of a situation to the prosecutor pursuant to Art.13(a) and 14 of the statute, and the prosecutors initiation of investigations proprio motu pursuant to Art.13(c) and 15 [64].

In recent years, detailed theoretical and practical analyses of the Rome Statute, have made it increasingly clear that the complementarily principle, as the most important principle for the courts functioning, indeed its crucial foundation, amounts to far more than an element in the competence of the court [4]. For both Uganda and the ICC, the case presented an important opportunity. For Uganda, the referral was an attempt to engage an otherwise aloof international community by transforming the prosecution of LRA (The Lord's Résistance Army) leaders into a litmus test for the much celebrated promise of global justice. Art.16 was already controversial at the preparatory committee and at the Rome Conference. In any case, due to the precedence of the charter over other international agreements (Charter Art.103 and 25), UN members are under an obligation to follow the council rather than the court. This does not answer the question, however, of what happens in the event that the Security Council acts ultra-virus, that is, beyond the powers conferred upon it by the charter [65]. In addition to protecting the specific 'minimum guarantees' listed in article 67, the court has residual authority to 'ensure that a trial is fair and expeditious and is conducted with full respect for the rights of accused' (Art.64(2)) [66]. One rationalist counter–argument could be the following - if too much tribute was paid to sovereignty and support by the powerful, the ICC would fail to solve the problem of impunity that it was meant to address. One NGO represent warned that the amendments sought by the US would create 'a loophole the size of the Grand Canyon that any rogue state would drive right through [67].' At least three ways the standards set for the deployment of criminal sanctions are more stringent. They guarantee stronger rights of defence; they impose a higher standard of proof; and they are more insistent on the burden of proof remaining with the body bringing the prosecution [68].

CONCLUSION

A successful International Criminal Court have to need American support and it can simply gained if both the United States and the leadership of the preparatory commission seek an acceptable compromise which would not reduce the power of the court [29]. China should accede to the Rome Statute and make good use of its rights as a state party in order to fulfil the aim of ending impunity, and thus also protect its national interests [69]. The United States maintains its present position of seeking immunity against the ICC jurisdiction, there seems little likelihood of any improvement of its relations towards the ICC. The gap between the concept of international law upheld by the USA and that on which the ICC is based is simply too wide for any common ground to emerge [70]. Art.7 of the statute, on crimes against humanity, and problems that potentially from the scarcity of Muslim judges at the court [71]. Moreover, a great deal, and of greater extent, remains to be done if into justice is to attain determined roots and achieve its potential in the present world order. The early jurisprudence of the ICC will provide one opportunity to begin proposing approaches to the outstanding problems [72]. The coming out of an prolonged humanitarian regime intimidate to wear down the human rights discourse and value system, which was previously and independent perspective that legitimate for normative critique of the global rule of law in prevailing political here [73].

REFERENCES

1. Sadat LN (2002) The International Criminal Court and the Transformation of International Law: Justice for the New Millennium. Transnational Publishers, Inc. New York.
2. Schabas WA (2011) An Introduction to the International Criminal Court. Cambridge University Press.
3. Akhavan P (2003) Review: The International Criminal Court in Context: Mediating the Global and the Local in an age of Accountability. The American Journal of International Law 97: 712-721.
4. Kaul HP (2005) Construction Site for More Justice: The International Criminal Court After Two Years. American Journal of International Law 99: 370-384.
5. Meron T (2006) Reflections on the Prosecution of War Crimes by International Tribunals. American Journal of International Law 100: 551-579.
6. Brooms B (1996) The Establishment of an International Criminal Court. In: Dinstein Y, Tabory M (eds.), War Crimes in International Law. Martinus Nijhoff Publishers, London.
7. Marty MD (2006) Interactions between National and International Criminal Law in the Preliminary Phase of Trial at the ICC. Journal of the International Criminal Justice 4: 2-11.
8. Strawson J (2004) Book Review: Universalizing International Law by Christopher Weeramantry. Melbourne Journal of International Law.
9. http://www.internationalcrimes.com/
10. Kittichaisaree K (2001) International Criminal Law. Oxford University Press.
11. Bassiouni MC (1988) The Statute of the International Criminal Court: A Documentary History, Transnational Publishers, Inc. New York.
12. Sriram CL (2004) Globalising Justice: From Universal Jurisdiction to Mixed Tribunals. Netherlands Human Rights Quarterly.
13. Marty DM (2006) Interactions between National and International Criminal Law in the Preliminary Phase of Trial at the ICC. Journal of International Criminal Justice 4: 2-11.
14. Werle G (2005) Principles of International Criminal Law. Oxford University press.
15. Cassese A (2002) From Nuremberg to Rome: International Military Tribunals to the International Criminal Court. In: Cassese A, Gaeta P, Jones JRWD (eds.), The Rome Stature of the International Criminal Court: A Commentary.
16. Dinstein Y (1996) The Distinctions between War Crimes and Crimes Against Peace. In: Dinsteim Y, Tabory M (eds.), War Crimes in International Law. Martimus Nijhoff Publishers, London.
17. Luban D (2004) The Legacies of Nuremberg. 54: 779-829.
18. Tomsuchat C (2006) The Legacy of Nuremberg, Journal of International Criminal Justice 4: 830-844.
19. Burchard C (2006) The Nuremberg Trial and its impact on Germany. Journal of International Criminal Justice 4: 800-829.
20. Marrus MR (1997) The Nuremberg War Crimes Trial 1945-46: A Documentary History, St. Martins press, New York.
21. Landsman S (2005) Crimes of The Holocaust: The Law Confronts Hard Cases. University of Pennsylvania Press, Philadelphia.
22. Roling BVA, Cassese A (1993) The Tokyo Trial and Beyond: Reflections of a Peacemonger.
23. Kaufman ZD (2007) Designing Criminal Tribunals: Sovereignty and International Concerns in the Protection of Human Rights by Steven D.Roper and Lilian A. Barria. Yale Human Rights and Development Law Journal 10: 209-214.
24. Neussl P (2006) Introductory Note, International Criminal Tribunal for the Former Yugoslavia (ICTY). The Hague, Human Rights Law Journal.
25. Meron T (1994) Editorial Comment, War Crimes in Yugoslavia and the Development of International Law. American Journal of International Law.
26. Morris V, Scharf MP (1995) An Insider's Guide to the International Criminal Tribunal for the Former Yugoslavia. Transnational Publishers, Inc.
27. Bantekas I, Nash S (2003) International Criminal Law. Cavendish Publishing Ltd, London.

28. Campbell K (2004) The Trauma of Justice: Sexual Violence, Crimes Against Humanity and The International Criminal Tribunal for the Former Yugoslavia, Social and Legal Studies 13: 329-350.
29. Meron T (2000) The Humanization of Humanitarian Law. American Journal of International Law 94: 239-278.
30. Naftali OB, Tuval Y (2006) Punishing International Crimes Committed by the Persecuted: The Kapo Trials in Israel (1950s-1960s). Journal of International Criminal Justice.
31. Bassiouni MC, Manikas P (1996) The Law of the International Criminal Tribunal for the Former Yugoslavia. Transnational Publishers, Inc. New York.
32. Jones JRWD (1998) The Practice of the International Criminal Tribunals For the Former Yugoslavia and Rwanda, Transnational Publishers, Inc. New York.
33. Cassese A, Gaeta P, Jones JRWD (2002) The Rome Stature of The International Criminal Court: A Commentary. Oxford University Press.
34. Ackerman JE, Sullivan EO (2002) Practice and Procedure of the International Criminal Tribunal for the Former Yugoslavia: With Selected Materials from the International Criminal Tribunal for Rwanda, Kluwer Law International, London.
35. Eboe-Osuji C (2005) Complicity in Genocide' versus 'Aiding and Abetting Genocide': Construing the Difference in the ICTR and ICTY Status, Journal of International Criminal Justice 3: 56-81.
36. Nice G, Valliere-Roland P (2005) Procedural Innovations in War Crimes took Place Trials. Journal of International Criminal Justice 3: 354-380.
37. Kolb R (2000) The Jurisprudence of the Yugoslavia and Rwanda Criminal Tribunals on Their Jurisdiction and on International Crimes. British Yearbook of International Law 75: 269-335.
38. Robinson PL (2005) Rough Edges in the Alignment of Legal Systems in the Proceedings at the ICTY. Journal of International Criminal Justice 3: 1037-1058.
39. Ohlin JD (2007) The Conceptual Problems with The Doctrine of joint-Criminal enterprise. Journal of International Criminal Justice.
40. Raab D (2005) Evaluating the ICTY and its Completion Strategy: Efforts to achieve Accountability for War Crimes and Their Tribunals. Journal of International Criminal Justice 3: 82-102.
41. Fenrick WJ (2001) The Crime Against Humanity of Persecution in the Jurisprudence of the ICTY. Netherlands Yearbook of International Law.
42. Lamb S (1999), The Powers of Arrest of the International Criminal Tribunal for the former Yugoslavia. British Yearbook of International Law 70: 165-244.
43. Danner AM (2003) Enhancing the Legitimacy and Accountability of Prosecutorial Discretion at the International Criminal Court. American Journal of International Law 97: 510.
44. Carlsson I (2005) The UN Inadequacies. Journal of International Criminal Justice 3: 837-846.
45. Melvern L (2005) The Security Council in the Face of Genocide. Journal of International Criminal Justice 3: 847-860.
46. Roper SD, Barria LA (2006) Designing Criminal Tribunals: Sovereignty and International Concerns in the Protection of Human Rights.
47. Barnett M (2002) Eyewitness to Genocide: The United Nations and Rwanda. Cornell University Press, London.
48. Magnarella PJ (2005) The Background and Causes of the Genocide in Rwanda. Journal of International Criminal Justice 3: 801-822.
49. Morris V, Scharf MP (1998) The International Criminal Tribunal for Rwanda. Transnational Publishers, Inc .New York.
50. http://www.globalpolicy.org/security/issues/rwanda/1999inquiry.pdf
51. Aptel C (1998) International Criminal Tribunal for Rwanda. Yearbook of The United Nations.
52. Akande D (2004) International Law Immunities and The International Criminal Court. American Journal of International Law 98: 407-433.
53. Hebel HV (1992) Aspects of the Statute. In: Lammers JG, Schukking J (eds), Reflections on the International Criminal Court. T.M.C. Asser Press,The Hague.
54. Mukimbiri J (2005) The Seven Stages of the Rwanda Genocide. Journal of International Criminal Justice 3: 823-836.
55. Akhavan P (2004) Beyond Impunity: Can International Criminal Justice Prevent Future Atrocities. American Society of International Law 95: 7-31.
56. Bassiouni MC (1999) Crimes against Humanity in International law. Kluwer Law International, London.
57. Mutua MW (2004) Never Again: Questioning the Yugoslavia and Rwanda Tribunals. Temple International & Comparative Law Journal 11: 167-187.
58. Mettraux G (2005) International Crimes and The ad hoc Tribunals. Oxford University Press.
59. Alvarez JE (2004) Crimes of States/ Crimes of Hate: Lessons from Rwanda. In: Gerry Simpson (ed), War Crimes Law.
60. Straus S (2006) The Order of Genocide: Race, Power, and War in Rwanda. Cornel University Press, London.
61. Aldana-Pindell R (2004) An Emerging Universality of Justificable Victims' Rights in the Criminal Process to Curtail Impunity for State-Sponsored Crimes. Human Rights Quarterly.
62. Condorelli L, Ciampi A (2005) Comments on the Security Council Referral of the situation in Darfur to the ICC. Journal of International Criminal Justice 3: 590-599.
63. Happold M (2006) Darfur, the Security Council and International Criminal Court. International and Comparative Law Quarterly.
64. Akhavan P (2005) The Lord's Ressistance Army Case: Uganda's Submission of the First State Referral to the International Criminal Court. American Journal of International Law 99: 403-421.

65. Paulus AL (2003) Legalistic Groundwork for the International Criminal Court: Commentaries on the Statute of the International Criminal Court. European Journal of International Law.

66. Young SNM (2000) Surrendering the Accused to the International Criminal Court. The British Yearbook of International Law.

67. Fehl C (2004) Explaining the International Criminal Court: A 'Practice Test' for rationalist and Constructive Approaches. European Journal of International Relations 3: 357-394.

68. Guinchard A (2005) Fixing the Boundaries of the concept of Crime: The Challenge for Human Rights. International and Comparative Law Quarterly 54: 719-734.

69. Jianping L, Zhixiang W (2005) China's Attitude towards the ICC. Journal of International Criminal Justice 3: 608-620.

70. Hafner G (2005) An Attempt to Explain the Position of the USA towards the ICC. Journal of International Criminal Justice 3: 323-332.

71. Abtahi H (2005) The Islamic Republic of Iran and the ICC. Journal of International Criminal Justice 3: 635-648.

72. Broomhall B (2003) International Justice and the International Criminal Court: Between Sovereignty and the Rule of Law. Oxford University Press.

73. Teitel RG (2002) Humanity's Law, Rule of Law for the New Global Politics. Cornell International Law Journal 35: 356-380.

CHAPTER 9

CRIMES AGAINST HUMANITY: THE ROLE OF INTERNATIONAL COURTS

Éder Milton Schneider, José Roberto Iglesias, Karen Hallberg, Marcelo Néstor Kuperman

INTRODUCTION

The aftermaths of the two major war conflicts of the 20th century showed the imperative need of official institutions capable of doing justice in a global way, beyond the limits imposed by the borders of the nations. After WW1, the first initiative to judge political leaders accused of war crimes took place in the Paris Peace Conference of 1919. In this conference, the participants discussed about the convenience of establishing an international tribunal that would act when the states were absent or acted irresponsibly. At the end of WW2, two international tribunals were in charge of providing justice for the victims of the atrocities that occurred during the previous years and punished the responsible of those acts. The victorious nations established the International Military Tribunals at Nürenberg, Germany [1] and Tokyo, Japan [2]. Several years later, after serious episodes of state-sponsored crimes, similar tribunals were organized including those set up in Bosnia and Rwanda in the 1990's. Nevertheless all these examples were isolated reactions to particular events. For example, in the case of Bosnia the United Nations created a special tribunal, the International Criminal Tribunal for the Former Yugoslavia [3]. There was a lack of a permanent and internationally recognized tool of justice to punish political leaders responsible of crimes against humanity.

Citation: Schneider ÉM, Iglesias JR, Hallberg K, Kuperman MN (2014) Crimes against Humanity: The Role of International Courts. PLoS ONE 9(6): e99064. doi:10.1371/journal.pone.0099064

A widespread consensus was achieved in Rome in 1998, where 122 countries agreed to create the International Criminal Court (ICC) as a response to the desire for international justice. The ICC was created by the Rome Statute to be a permanent, non-partisan judicial instrument to "promote the rule of law and ensure that the gravest crimes do not go unpunished [4]". The Statute of Rome came into force in 2002 when 60 countries ratified the treaty, and the ICC was settled in The Hague, Netherlands. Its mission is to detect and judge the responsible of genocides, crimes against humanity, war crimes, and the crime of aggression. After the adoption of the Rome Statute, more than half of the countries of the world have ratified it. Since the Court was established, the Prosecutor has launched investigations into crimes committed in Uganda, Democratic Republic of Congo, Darfur (Sudan) and Central African Republic.

The main role of the ICC is to investigate and prosecute genocide, crimes against humanity and war crimes when national authorities are unable or unwilling to do so. Its actions are expected to serve as a catalyst for states to fulfill their responsibilities in investigating and prosecuting those crimes [5]. Being the ICC a fairly new institution, it has yet to show its effects as a crime deterrent [6]. In this manuscript we are not intending to judge its efficacy, instead, we aim to simulate, by means of a simple mathematical model, the role it plays in bringing justice in countries in which the authorities are not able to assume their primary obligations to warrant the citizens the necessary protection against the worst atrocities.

The interdisciplinary study of criminal activities, its economic consequences, the effect and cost of punitive actions and related subjects have been a very active area in recent years, as a natural extension of studies in opinion dynamics and game theory both in regular and complex networks [7]–[13].

Here, in order to study the role of the ICC we simulate an artificial country as a connected society with some degree of hierarchy, and the action of the ICC as a punctuated activity directed to remove evil agents in key positions. In the next section we describe the model for the artificial society and the action of the ICC while in the following sections we present the results and compare the effects of the intervention of the ICC with a possible action by national courts.

MODEL

We present first a model that describesthe expansion of a criminal (or illegal) behavior as a kind of epidemics and, secondly, the corrective effect of the action of an external mechanism, such as the intervention of the International Criminal Court (ICC).

The aim of the model is to mimic a situation in which the ethical inclination of the individuals is the result of a feedback between the individual and its environment at different levels of social organization: the neighborhood, the country and the global dynamics. In turn, the attitude of each individual shapes the macroscopic behavior of the society.

A fundamental component in the study of any structurally organized criminal group is the social network [10], [14], [15]. Crimes under the ICC jurisdiction in particular are committed in the context of a hierarchical structure, and this kind of social network can be studied using complex network models [16]–[18].

The model incorporates social networks, characterized by a particular topology, as a means to represent the interactions between individuals. Each individual is inserted in a social environment socially and politically organized. This organization will be coded into the topology of a complex network, representing the underlying weave of individual connections. By means of this network we want to capture the insertion of each subject in the society. To start with, we will not consider individual connections between subjects belonging to different countries, but this interaction can be included in a subsequent analysis. By assigning different number of connections to each of the nodes of the network -the degree of the node-, the topology determines not only the neighborhood of each individual but can also indicate which type of political organization is present in the country. Consider for example that the country has a strongly democratic organization, so there will be no individuals whose decisions can absolutely outweigh those of others. Topologically, this can be translated into a hierarchical distribution with no peaks at high values. However, even in a democracy the influence of national and regional leaders is strong, the discourse of a president has a very wide network of recipients, probably more that a secretary, a governor, a major or an army general. This influence is stronger in dictatorial regimes where some kind of control of the press is also imposed. So, in different political regimes, the network of influences keeps a hierarchical structure. If one wants to consider the full details, links between individuals can also be directional, shaping the degree of influence of each of the individuals on the others. Thus, individuals are related to each other at the lowest organizational level and with many different degrees of connectivities. In order to take into account the fact that authorities, or mass media owners, or persons placed in high hierarchical positions may transmit their points of view to subordinates or people in lower hierarchical levels, we adopt a scale-free (SF) network [19] as it exhibits a wide distribution of connectivity with highly connected nodes (called "hubs", or high degree nodes) and many nodes with very low connectivity (or low degree), forming a power law distribution of the frequency of the degree, with a connectivity exponent γ. High degree nodes correspond to authorities or persons in power positions, i.e. we assume agents placed in the top of the authority and/or leadership scale will have a large connectivity, either directly or trough other mechanisms like the mass media. In Fig. 1 it is possible to see a schematic representation of the network, which exhibits highly connected nodes (painted black in the figure) linked to many nodes with one or a few connections (painted white). There exist many algorithms to create SF networks: We particularly used the Barabási-Albert (B-A) algorithm [20], in which the network is built from an initial fully connected network of m_0 nodes by adding new nodes sequentially, each new node connecting itself to m of the previous nodes with preferential attachment to the more connected ones. This network, built through growth and preferential attachment will develop into a SF network (with a power law distribution of degree exponent γ) held together by highly connected hubs.

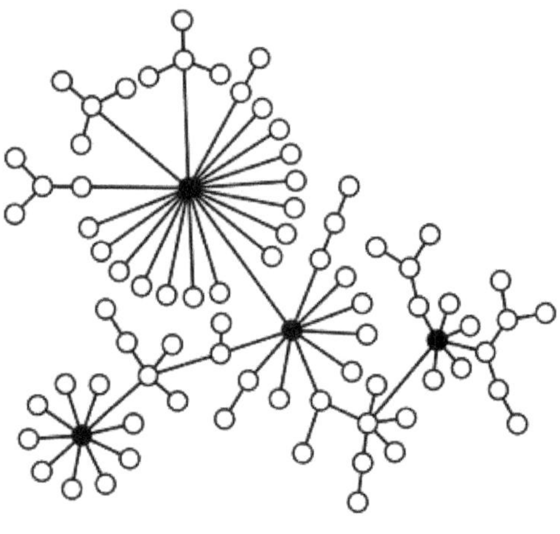

Figure 1. Schematic representation of a scale-free network.

The "hubs", nodes with high degree are painted black, while the low degree nodes are represented in white. Note that many nodes are related to just one hub.

The basis of the model is the individual behavior which, as mentioned earlier, will be affected differently by the state of the components of the system in each of its levels. The behavior of each individual i is schematically represented by a time-dependent scalar $\sigma_i(t)$ which, for simplicity, can adopt two different values, -1 or $+1$, respectively representing evil and good behavior. Real situations are more subtle and less Manichean. Some individuals may adopt an evil behavior because of being afraid of retaliations, some others are concerned with the criminal behavior, but adopt a passive standing. In short, different degrees of moral behavior may be studied, as in Ref. [22], but this is a level of detail that we think would be overstated at this point of the study of the problem. So, restraining ourselves to this two state behavior, during the dynamical evolution of the system, the state of the individuals changes according to the social contacts, that we will reduce to three levels: a) The weight of the own position that will be greater the greater the influence, or connectivity, of the agent, b) The directly connected environment, i.e the influence of the agents connected to the one we are examining, and finally, c) The influence of the full society, measured as the average inclination of the agents. This last term may also represent the effect of external influences, as the international pressure applied to a given country. We remark that the method adopted here is similar to the one used to describe contagion of a disease on a complex network [11], [12]. However in our model the probability of "contagion" of the bad or good behavior will depend on the connectivity of the agent, as will be explained below. In the following we describe briefly the effect of the own state, the one of the neighbors and the average of all states on the dynamics of contagion.

Individual Level

Each individual agent has an inner nature, either because it is pretty sure of its ideas or because it has a high adamancy, and this can prevent it from being influenced by others. textcolorblueAlso, if it is a politician it is compelled to respect certain engagements that helped it to arrive to and to keep its power position. We will consider that the weight of the own opinion is stronger the higher the connectivity, i.e. a more connected (meaning a more powerful) agent will hardly change its attitude. Mathematically we define the weight of the opinion of the j-agent on itself, W_j^1 as proportional to its connectivity k_j:

$$W_j^1 = \sigma_j \frac{k_j}{k_{max}}, \tag{1}$$

where k_{max} is the connectivity of the most connected agent(s). Thus, if a particular agent is the most connected one, its weight will be ± 1, i.e. its own state. For low-connected agents one expects $k_j << k_{max}$, then its own opinion will have a much lesser weight.

Local Influence

Furthermore we define how the state of every agent in the social group is affected by the mood of its neighbors. We will consider as the most important influence the interaction of one agent with the other subjects directly connected to it (nearest neighbors). We define the weight of the neighbors on agent j as W_j^2. At each time step, the individual j checks the state of its neighbors and makes a weighted average of these states to get a value between −1 and 1, calculated as

$$W_j^2(t) = \frac{1}{k_j} \sum_{i \in \Omega} \sigma_i \frac{k_i}{k_{max}}, \tag{2}$$

where k_j is the degree of agent j, k_i is the degree (connectivity) of the i-neighbor, k_{max} is the maximum degree present in the network, and Ω denotes the full neighborhood of a node. Here, we have assumed that the degree of a node, i.e. the size of its neighborhood, is a measure of its social influence. Thus, agents with the highest degree will exert a stronger influence on their neighbors. On the other hand, the influence of the neighbors on agent j is divided by its own connectivity k_j. The higher k_j the lower the weight of the opinion of the neighbors.

Global Level

While the individual level defines a type of local influence, the global level defines the environmental effect in a wider range. This level takes into account the topology of the influences of the whole country to weigh the influence of each of the individuals over the rest, independently of whether they are connected or not. We collect the information already considered at the individual level but use it in a wider sense. We calculated a weighted average of the state of each of the individuals in the country to get $W_j^3(t)$, the weight of the global influence on agent j.

$$W_j^3(t) = \frac{1}{N} \sum_{i \neq j}^{N} \sigma_i \tag{3}$$

where N is the number of individuals in the country. This term is an average of the national opinion, however it is probably the less effective in changing the state of one agent.

We remark that the dynamics of contagion is different from previous studies on the diffusion of a disease in a complex network [12]. The agents are not equivalent in their resistance to adopt a different moral standing: Hubs are almost insensitive to their environment while less connected agents are more susceptible. In societies where crimes against humanity are detected other factors are relevant to the adoption of an immoral attitude. Cultural and historical factors are also relevant. However, as we are more interested here in the ICC action than on the details of how a society could eventually endorse genocides or other crimes against humanity, we skip the details of the corruption process and retain the importance of agents in high hierarchical position and the consequences of their possible eradication.

One can further include an international influence, by taking into account interactions with other countries. Again, we can consider local or global interactions. The bilateral relations between countries can be also represented by a network of communities, analogously to what we have done with individual interactions or individual national levels. We should define a topology for the network of countries and consider that countries are new individuals that interact with each other in the same way agents did in individual and local levels. However, in order to isolate the effect of each of the terms considered, and also to minimize the number of parameters in the model, in this first stage we will consider just a single country and do not include the international contacts.

RESULTS

We consider two stages in the dynamics: a) Contagion effects: This is the change in the state of the individuals of the system as a result of the different influences described above. The contagion may in some cases induce a state of complete polarization in the evil or good state. b) Action of the ICC. The action of the ICC will be sporadic and will be directed to remove from the society an evil hub, i.e. a highly connected agent that exerts an evil influence on the community. We can also say that the contagion effect is internal to the society, while the action of the ICC is external. Hereafter, we are going to discuss both dynamics separately.

Internal Dynamics: Contagion

Let's consider that the three influences described above have different weights, being the first two, the own and local influences, the stronger, and the national one, the weaker. If we increase too much the national influence the network effects are erased and a kind of mean-field solution prevails. For each agent j we calculate a change exponent r_j defined as:

$$r_j = \frac{1}{2}(1-\alpha)(W_j^1 + W_j^2) + \alpha W_j^3 \quad \textbf{(4)}$$

where the parameter α is in the range $0 < \alpha < 1$ and measures the relative weight of the effect of the national level, compared with the individual and local ones. A typical value is $\alpha \sim 0.1$ (bigger values of α will increase the effect of the average opinion and erase the influence of the network; the final state will depend only on which of the attitudes is preponderant at the beginning). It is evident that each of the terms in Eq. 4 may be positive or negative and then r itself maybe positive or negative. One possible dynamical evolution would be to prescribe that if r_j is negative (positive) at a given time step, agent j will remain evil (good) or change to the evil (good) state $\sigma = -1$ $(+1)$. To avoid such a deterministic behavior we introduce a factor of "social" temperature (that is: a non-zero probability of spontaneous changes) in the probability of changing attitude. This temperature takes into account spontaneous and unpredictable changes of attitude, but also the fact that in some situations fractions or the whole population can exhibit a certain alienation, that is, a confusion about what right or wrong is. So, we define a probability p_j that agent j changes to (or remains in) the state $\sigma = 1$ as:

$$p_j = (e^{-r_j/T} + 1)^{-1} \quad \textbf{(5)}$$

where T is the social temperature. One can observe that if $r_j = 0$, $p_j = 0.5$, then agent j can adopt either of the attitudes with equal probability. If $r_j > 0$ $(p_j > 0.5)$ there is a higher probability of changing to the good state, while if $r_j < 0$ $(p_j < 0.5)$ there is a higher probability of changing to the evil state. We have represented in Fig. 2 the probability of change as a function of r for different values of the social temperature. We assume a low value of the national influence, by considering $\alpha = 0.05$. We will keep this value all along the simulations, in order to emphasize network effects over ambiance effects.

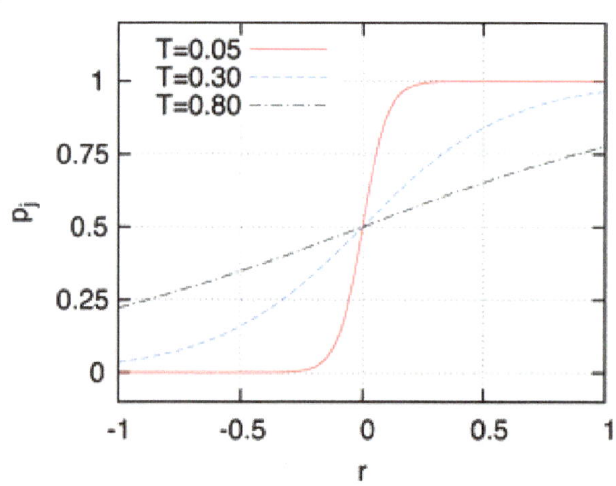

Figure 2. Probability of changing state for different social "temperatures".

Probability of changing state to state $+1$ as a function of r for different values of the "social" temperature, given by Eq. 5. For high temperatures the probability is almost linear in r while for low temperatures it approaches a step function.

Now, in order to study the dynamics of contagion, we assume a network with N agents (in the simulations we will consider $N = 1000$ and 10000 but, unless explicitly stated, we always present the results for $N = 1000$, as they are similar for larger systems). Also, we make the hypothesis that almost the full society is initially in the good state (in average $<\sigma> \approx +1$). However, there will be a very small fraction of evil agents placed in sites with high connectivity that will trigger the contagion. To show this point we have made a simulation of a SF network using the B-A algorithm [20] with $m_0 = 3$ initial nodes, $m = 2$ nodes added each growth step and $N = 1000$ agents at the end (which gives a power law exponent of about $\gamma \approx 2.5$), placing a small percentage of evil agents in the most connected positions. Also, we have performed an average over 100 samples. The deleterious effect of the strategically placed evil agents can be seen in the simulations plotted on Fig. 3, where one can verify that a very small percentage of evil agents (about 0.5%) in key positions (hubs) is enough to drive the full society to an evil behavior $(<\sigma> = -1)$. As the value of $<\sigma>$ determines the behavior of the society (good if $+1$, evil if -1) we will call it the *moral* index.

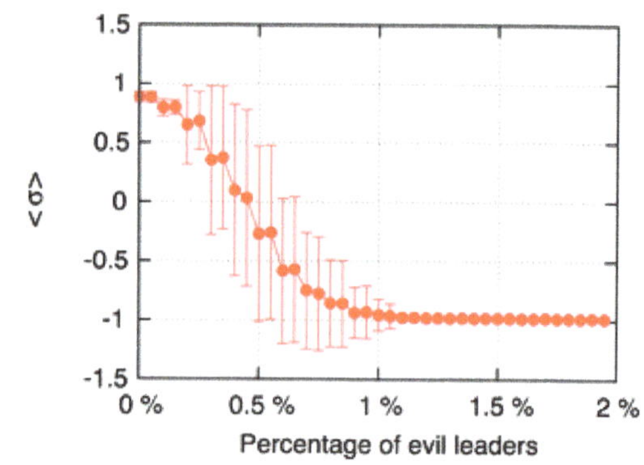

Figure 3. Effect of the initial number of evil leaders.

The figure shows the final state of the society as a function of the initial fraction of evil leaders without ICC intervention. One may see that a small percentage of the population (less than 0.5%) occupying the most connected positions, may transform the full society to the evil state. We have considered 100 samples with $N = 1000$ agents each, solid lines describe the averaged values over all the simulations, and the error bars correspond to the standard deviation. Note that the transition region with high error bars shows that the final state of the different samples may be a completely degraded or non-degraded populations.

So, it is clear that evil agents placed in strategic positions of high hierarchy or authority may induce a despicable behavior of the whole population in a very short lapse of time.

Action of the ICC

We model now the regulatory effect of an international institution acting on individuals, penalizing those whose behavior falls under the guise of "crimes against humanity". In this sense the simulation imitates the objectives of the ICC: Bringing to the Court the highest accountable leaders such as presidents, prime ministers, army commanders or others. In our model, the action of the Court is simulated by removing the highest connected evil leader. Because of the length of the investigations, the action of the court can take place with some delay, and during the delay, the evil behavior spreads and can affect the whole society (contagion effect). The removal of a high-degree node from the lattice may produce undesirable effects and even destroy the unity of the network [21]. Also, if the removed authority is substituted by a new one, the connections of this newcomer maybe very different of the original ones. Consequently, the aftereffects of the demotion of a leader maybe very difficult. In this first approach to the problem we have decided to avoid the complications arose by the re-designing of the network and we have considered that the removed evil leader is just replace by a "good" one. This is a simple approach but we believe it contains the essential of the action of the Court, particularly because, after the contagion, the new leader will be surrounded by lots of evil agents as well in the old or in a new structure of neighborhood.

Thus, the simulations proceed in the following way: We build a SF network with the B-A algorithm ($m=2$, $m_o=3$ and $\gamma \approx 2.5$). The number of agents is initially taken to be $N=1000$ and averages of σ over 1000 samples are studied. The global factor in the calculation of the probability of changing mood is $\alpha=0.05$ and a percentage of 0.05% initial evil leaders is placed in the most connected hubs. Finally, the social temperature is chosen to be $T=0.05$ in order to obtain a society with a well-defined polarization. The Court acts periodically, every Δt contagions steps, replacing the most connected evil agent by a good agent and in between the system evolves with its own contagion dynamics.

The following figures represent different situations: In Fig. 4 we show the evolution of the average behavior of the society. An early intervention of the ICC guarantees a rapid and full recovery. However, this is probably unrealistic, as the detection of violations of human rights is not an easy and rapid task. To simulate a more realistic situation, in Fig. 5 we show the time evolution after the full deterioration of the moral index. It is comforting that even in this case, when the action of the ICC starts from $<\sigma> = -1$, the recovery is complete but, as expected, within a longer recovery time.

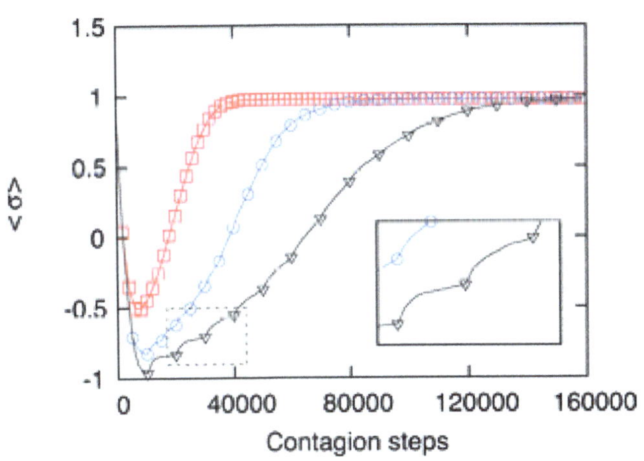

Figure 4. Moral index of the society as a function of time.

The figure shows the evolution of the moral indexs when contagion is combined with the action of the ICC. Three values of the time separation among ICC's interventions are shown: $\Delta t=2000$ (red squares), $\Delta t=5000$ (blue circles) and $\Delta t=10000$ (black triangles). Early intervention (after 2000 time steps) prevents the contagion of the full society and the recovery is relatively rapid. Longer times for interventions (5000 or 10000 time steps) result in a deteriorated society and longer recovery times. In these simulations we use $\alpha=0.05$, $T=0.05$ and an initial fraction of 2.5% evil leaders and we average over 1000 samples. The points along the curves correspond to ICC interventions and are not the only data points drawn, the curves between ICC actions are composed by one data point per step. Looking in greater detail the dotted box it's possible to see a change in the derivative: i.e. a quick increase in the moral index following each intervention of the Court; This rapid but small increase corresponds to the local influence of the new good agent replacing the evil leader removed.

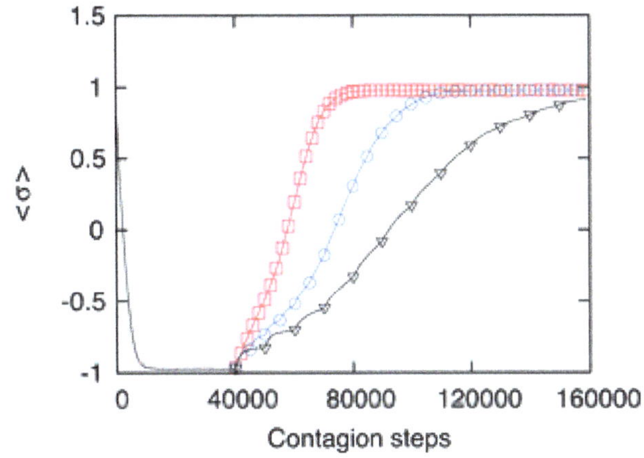

Figure 5. Recovery of the moral index of the society after full deterioration.

If one waits 40000 time steps for the action of the Court, the society is fully degraded when the Court finally acts. However the time to full recovery is not very different from the previous situation. Here the Court acts after 40000 time steps and after that the action is repeated after $\Delta t=2000$ (red squares), 5000 (blue circles) or 10000 (black triangles) time steps. This simulation used $\alpha=0.05$, $T=0.05$ and a percentage of 10% evil leaders; results are averaged over 1000 samples.

Efficiency and Relevance of the ICC

After verifying the effect of the intervention of the ICC some questions may arise concerning the real necessity of this international court. Opponents to this mechanism may argue that national courts are able to do the job if allowed for and that there is no need of an international intervention. To address this issue we will compare the action of the ICC with the possible intervention of national courts in an environment where human rights and basic law principles are violated.

Can National Courts do the Work of the ICC?

It is evident that a national court taking the same measures as the ICC would produce the same effect. However the problem with national courts is that, even when they act within the law, frequently they are not able to process highly ranked officials. Quite often, the law, the practice or the custom is such that highly placed officials cannot be subjected to prosecution, and only intermediate or low level officials can be prosecuted. Thus, in order to compare the effect of the action of national courts, we have repeated the simulations of the previous section but, instead of prosecuting the most connected agent we have selected highly but less connected agents. Thus, we made a simulation similar to the one shown on Fig. 5, with intervention of the national courts every 5000 time steps, but assuming that the national court cannot prosecute the most connected agents. The results are shown in Fig. 6 where it is evident that the recovery of the society is faster and complete when the most connected leaders are subjected to process than when a fraction of the leaders is protected from prosecution. To better illustrate this effect, in Fig. 7 we show the fraction of times the society recovers up to a moral index higher than 0.8 as a function of the number of agents that are screened from prosecution because of national laws or due to corruption. It is evident that the prosecution of the most connected leaders is necessary for a full social recovery. When a fraction of the leaders is protected from prosecution the recovery of the society is only partial and will degrade again when the court interrupts its action. One interesting result is that the absolute number of protected agents necessary to produce a given level of recovery is independent of the size of the society. In Fig. 7 we present results for a society of 1000 and 10000 agents and the curves are very similar, indicating that one needs to prosecute a low number of agents and not a percentage (that would be impossible in a society of millions of people). This is a validation of the model and of the simulation, showing that there is no need to perform simulations with millions of agents. As a matter of fact, even if sometimes a big fraction of the society is concerned with human rights violations, most of the time the blamable agents are authorities or highly placed leaders and their number maybe well estimated in the thousands.

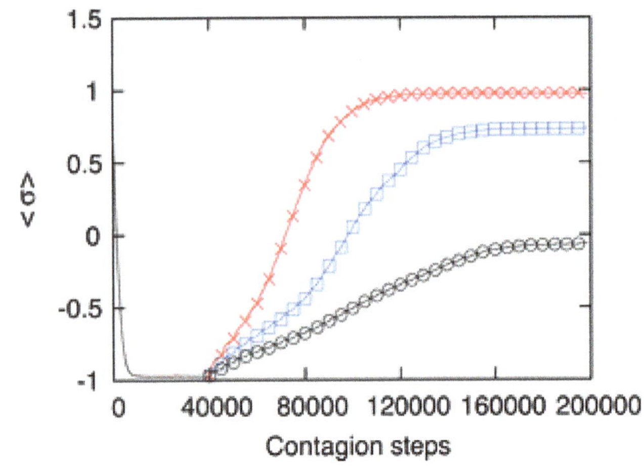

Figure 6. Comparison of the action of the ICC vs. national courts.

The moral index of the society is represented as a function of time, comparing the action of the ICC (red crosses) every $\Delta t = 5000$ times, with the action of national courts protecting the top 0.1% (blue squares) or 0.5% (black circles) evil leaders. This simulation used $\alpha = 0.05$, $T = 0.05$ and a percentage of 10% evil leaders, results are averaged over 1000 executions.

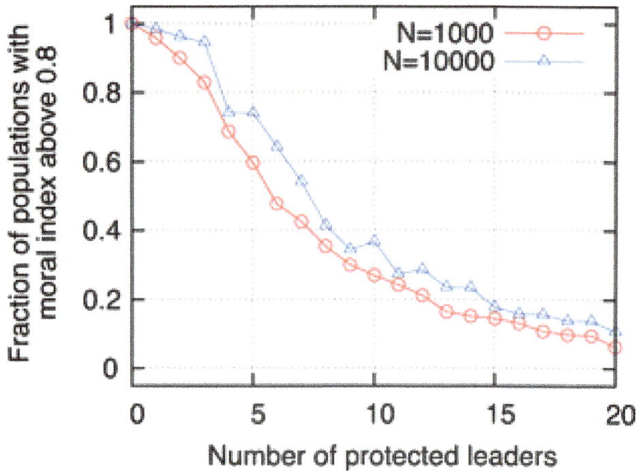

Figure 7. Society recovery as a function of the fraction of "protected" agents.

Fraction of the simulated society that recovered up to a moral index higher than 0.8 as a function of the number of agents "protected" by national rules (or by corruption) from the prosecution of national courts. Red circles correspond to a sample of $N = 1000$agents and blue triangles to a society of 10000 agents. This simulations used $\alpha = 0.05$, $T = 0.05$ and a percentage of 2.5% evil leaders; results are averaged over 100 (red circles) and 30 (blue triangles) executions.

How many times should the ICC intervene?

Once we have shown that the effect of the ICC is different and more efficient than the work of national courts, one could ask how many interventions of the ICC are necessary to induce full recovery of a given society. In the previous sections we have simulated periodic interventions of the ICC. The question is whether it is really necessary to act periodically or if just a finite number of actions are enough to produce the desired effect. To answer this question we show in Fig. 8 the number of times a simulated society arrives to moral index of 0.8 or higher (i.e. 90% or above of the population in the "good" state) as a function of the number of actions of the ICC. It is a very good sign that a small number of interventions, of the order of five, is enough to guarantee recuperation of most of the simulated societies. Probably a more realistic simulation, including the effects of a rebuilding of the network, will reduce even more the minimum number of interventions.

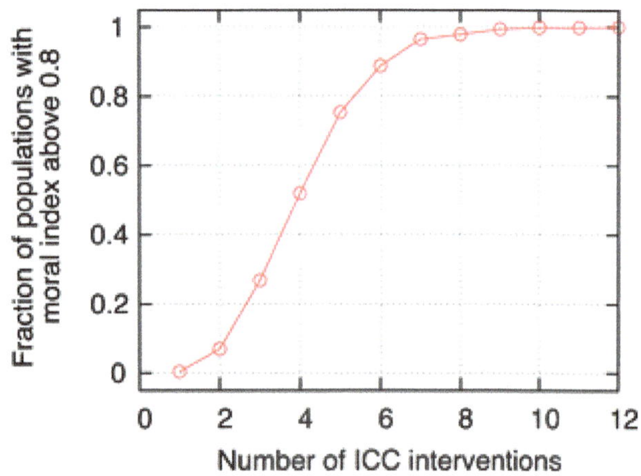

Figure 8. Minimum number of actions of the ICC required.

Fraction of the simulated societies that recovered up to a moral index higher than 0.8 after a number of interventions of the ICC. This simulation used $\alpha = 0.05$, $T = 0.05$ and a percentage of 10% evil leaders, results are averaged over 100 executions. The interval $\Delta t = 5000$ between CPI actions is used but the same result is obtained for other values of Δt, as long as the total amount of steps of each simulation is sufficient for the system to stabilize once the actions have ceased. In this figure a total amount of 1000000 steps is used.

CONCLUSIONS

We have presented here a simple model of a scale free complex network representing the network of influences in a society with a hierarchical structure. The state of each member of this society is represented, in a rather Manichaean way, as good or evil. To start the contagion dynamics we plant a very few bad seeds in key positions, i.e. highly connected hubs. One of the original features of this article is that the probability of contagion strongly depends on the connectivity: Hubs are excellent transmitters of behavior and very resistant to changes induced by their neighbors. On the other hand agents with one or a few connections are very susceptible to contagion. This is at variance with most models of contagion on complex networks, where the most connected agents are more susceptible to infection. Once the society is partially or fully contaminated with the bad behavior we simulate the action of the International Criminal Court, ICC, by removing the most connected bad agent and replacing it by a good one. The fact that this new good agent possesses a great capacity of contagion, implies that a few interventions of the ICC allow for the complete recovery of the society. We have proven also that the action of the ICC is different and much more effective than the one of national courts. The model still needs some improvements. We need to incorporate a more detailed description of the topology of the social network, including dynamical networks as well as different architectures to mimic a wider spectra of political regimes. Also, the influence of neighboring countries should be considered. Thus, in future developments we plan to simulate a dynamic network and, in further stages interaction between different countries, showing particularly that impunity is an incentive to the ethic degradation of countries, just because of imitation. Nevertheless, the present results are very encouraging, as they show that the strategy of attacking the top corrupt figures in a political system is the best suited to diminish the number of crimes against humanity and genocides. It is interesting to note that the fact that the leaders deserve great visibility facilitates the actions of the courts. This is not the case of organized crime, where the leaders are frequently invisible. If in the near future more countries will adhere to the ICC statute, the action of the Court will be even more effective.

ACKNOWLEDGMENTS

We would like to address a particular acknowledgement to ICC former prosecutor Luis Moreno-Ocampo who suggested this work and made a critical reading of the manuscript. We also thank Sebastián Gonçalves, Sérgio Souza, Roberto Silva, Leonardo Brunet, Juan Carlos González-Avella and Carmem Prado for enlightening discussions.

REFERENCES

1. Wikipedia (2013) Nuremberg Trials. Available: http://en.wikipedia.org/wiki/NurembergTrials. Accessed 20 November 2013.
2. Wikipedia (2013) International Military Tribunal for the Far East. Available: http://en.wikipedia.org/wiki/International Military Tribunal for the Far East. Accessed 20 November 2013.
3. Wikipedia (2013) International Criminal Tribunal for the former Yugoslavia. Available: http://en.wikipedia.org/wiki/International Criminal Tribunal for the former Yugoslavia. Accessed 20 November 2013.
4. ICC (2013) The International Criminal CourtWebsite. Available: http://www.icc-cpi.int/. Accessed 20 November 2013.
5. Schabas WA (2007) An Introduction to the International Criminal Court. New York: Cambridge University Press.
6. Mullins CW, Rothe DL (2010) The ability of the international criminal court to deter violations of international criminal law: A theoretical assessment. International Criminal Law Review 10: 771–786. doi: 10.1163/157181210x528414
7. Castellano C, Fortunato S, Loreto V (2009) Statistical physics of social dynamics. Reviews of Modern Physics 81. doi: 10.1103/revmodphys.81.591
8. Dietz T, Ostrom E, Stern PC (2003) The struggle to govern the commons. Science (New York, NY) 302: 1907–1912. doi: 10.1126/science.1091015
9. Dreber A, Rand DG, Fudenberg D, Nowak MA (2008) Winners don't punish. Nature 452: 348–351. doi: 10.1038/nature06723
10. Gambra MB, Frey E (2011) Social dynamics with peer support on heterogeneous networks. The European Physical Journal B 83: 507–518. doi: 10.1140/epjb/e2011-10359-0
11. Pastor-Satorras R, Vespignani A (2001) Epidemic spreading in scale-free networks. Physical review letters 86: 3200. doi: 10.1103/physrevlett.86.3200
12. Kuperman M, Abramson G (2001) Small world effect in an epidemiological model. Physical Review Letters 86: 2909. doi: 10.1103/physrevlett.86.2909
13. Iglesias JR, Semeshenko V, Schneider EM, Gordon MB (2012) Crime and punishment. Does it pay to punish? Physica A: Statistical Mechanics and its Applications 391: 3942–3950. doi: 10.1016/j.physa.2012.03.001
14. Coles N (2001) It's Not What You Know-It's Who You Know That Counts. Analysing Serious Crime Groups as Social Networks. British Journal of Criminology 41: 580–594. doi: 10.1093/bjc/41.4.580
15. Perc M, Donnay K, Helbing D (2013) Understanding recurrent crime as system-immanent collective behavior. PloS one 8: e76063. doi: 10.1371/journal.pone.0076063
16. Boguná M, Pastor-Satorras R, Diaz-Guilera A, Arenas A (2003) Emergence of clustering, correlations, and communities in a social network model. arXiv preprint cond-mat/0309263.

17. Copelli M, Dos Santos RMZ, Martins JSS (2002) Emergence of hierarchy on a network of complementary agents. International Journal of Modern Physics C 13: 783–797. doi: 10.1142/s0129183102003528

18. Laguna MF, Risau Gusman S, Abramson G, Gonçalves S, Iglesias JR (2005) The dynamics of opinion in hierarchical organizations. Physica A: Statistical Mechanics and its Applications 351: 580–592. doi: 10.1016/j.physa.2004.11.064

19. Albert R, Barabási A (2002) Statistical mechanics of complex networks. Reviews of modern physics 74: 47–97. doi: 10.1103/revmodphys.74.47

20. Barabási AL, Albert R (1999) Emergence of scaling in random networks. Science 286: 509–512. doi: 10.1126/science.286.5439.509

21. Albert R, Jeong H, Barabási AL (2000) Error and attack tolerance of complex networks. Nature 406: 378–382. doi: 10.1038/35019019

22. .Dirk Helbing, Attila Szolnoki, Matjaz Perc, Gyorgy Szabó (2010) Evolutionary Establishment of Moral and Double Moral Standards through Spatial Interactions. PLoS Comput Biol 6(4): e1000758 doi:10.1371/journal.pcbi.1000758

CHAPTER 10

UNDERSTANDING THE CONTENT OF CRIMES AGAINST HUMANITY: TRACING ITS HISTORICAL EVOLUTION FROM THE NUREMBERG CHARTER TO THE ROME STATUTE

Brian Dube

Keywords: Crimes against humanity, Political violence, Hostis humani generis.

INTRODUCTION

There is a lot of misconception on the actual meaning of crimes against humanity as a category of crimes under international criminal law. The term has been used to mean different things by different groups of people around the world. The term has been used loosely by politicians to describe and demonise activities of political opponents. This is so for example when activities of revolutionary or nationalist movements result in deaths of people as acts of terrorism and crimes against humanity in the eyes of governments opposed or threatened by the revolutionary activities. Media practitioners use the term to describe various events covered in the media where activities under publication have some elements of cruelty, suffering or intolerance of any kind, whether or not such events are systematic or widespread. The term clearly means something technically different to those studying or practicing International criminal law, in terms of both scope and content. From an international criminal law perspective, a crime against humanity is a category of international crimes punishable under international criminal law. This therefore invites an analysis of the subject and object of the crime, that is to say;

- Who is liable for prosecution?
- As well as against whom the offence or the crime can be committed?

Citation: Brian Dube, Understanding the content of crimes against humanity: Tracing its historical evolution from the Nuremberg Charter to the Rome Statute, DOI: 10.5897/AJPSIR2015.0742.

This position is derived from the general legal framework classifying crimes in relation to either the subject or object as is even the case in domestic law, where there are classifications such as crimes against persons, crimes against property, crimes against morality, crimes against public order, and hence likewise crimes against humanity. This therefore is a demonstration that a crime is defined or elaborated through the pointing of the legally protected values that the law is targeting. From this background, crimes against humanity implies that the legally protected value is "humanity" at large, meaning therefore that this is a crime which is designed to protect humanity as the object of the law and a value that the law is intended to be protected..

THEORETICAL FRAMEWORK

The term 'crimes against humanity' is partly premised on the theory that human beings as political beings live under the permanent threat of politics gone cancerous, and therefore:

- All humans share an interest in suppressing grave acts of destruction of human livelihood, dignity, and value;
- Crimes against humanity are simultaneously offences against humankind and injury to humanness;
- Crimes against humanity are so odious that they make the criminal hostis humani generis (an enemy of all humankind);
- Crimes against humanity are universally odious because they injure something fundamental to being human in a way that municipal legal systems fail to address, and,

- Crimes against humanity represent the worst of threats to the well-being of humans and their survival (David, 2004).

According to David Luban, the theory of crimes against humanity is based on the finding that human beings are political animals who cannot live without politics (David, 2004). He propounds that human beings as political animals live under the permanent threat of politics gone cancerous. All statutory definitions of crimes against humanity have something in common; that is, the element of criminalization of atrocities and severe persecutions inflicted on civilian populations as part of a political plan by a State, semi-state like organization or a political body as will more fully appear in the definition of crimes against humanity in the ICTY Statute, ICTR Statute and ICC Statute. Crimes against humanity therefore refer to organized attacks of great and gravest magnitude which is most barbaric, which is carried out by political entities against those that are under their control or influence, as clearly elaborated in the Sudanese and Kenyan Situations. Therefore the crime carries a great political and legal weight in the international sphere.

Justification of the Research

Since the term crimes against humanity has been frequently used and preferred to define or condemn actions by political players in the contemporary error, it has become imperative to revisit the definition so that there is a clear understanding of the crime. Because politics has many a times involved violence and killing in many instances even outside armed conflict, it is important to study and understand at what level any violent political activity becomes a crime against humanity. It has become clear that there is use of the term as a general definition of condemnation of intolerable political behavior in the eyes of political activists, and political news reporters. For those practicing or studying international criminal law, they must be guided to understand and distinguish the term crimes against humanity from a socio-political perspective and the one referred to in international statutes and understood by judges in the courts dealing with the legal aspects of the crime. Crimes against humanity must therefore be distinguished from street political violence and death struggles.

Political struggles will always be fought as long as human beings exist, but they can be waged without murder, extermination, enslavement, rape, or persecution of civilian populations, and these are the acts that international criminal law aims to punish under the provision for the crimes against humanity. The political actors must be in a position to realise or to be advised that their actions have ceased to be just political activism, but purely criminal, and this is only possible when the common crime under international law, that is, crime against humanity is demystified so that it can be easily understood. This research will seek to unpack the content of the crime referred to as crimes against humanity as well as distinguish it from other international crimes. The origins of the crime will be traced from Nuremberg Trials to the ICC with a view of making a clear assessment. This research will investigate the content and context of the crime as has been understood and developed in the contemporary international criminal justice system by the International Criminal Tribunals and the ICC.

Background

Crimes against humanity have origins from various conflict situations in the 19th and 20th century and the term was first used in the Nuremberg trials. These conflicts were really wide spread and committed on a massive scale, which resulted in a desire to codify rules to regulate the conduct of individuals and groups in both armed and unarmed conflicts as well as defining core crimes that reflected behavior that can never be tolerated in any political conflict at all.

Crimes against humanity therefore refer to all acts or conduct that are atrocious and are committed on a large scale.4 In the foregoing, a crime against humanity can be described as a crime of all crimes, in that the acts which constitute crimes against humanity are crimes on their own, such as rape, enslavement, torture and murder, but will only become crimes against humanity when committed on a larger scale and targeting a civilian population. Any such acts which are discrete and offensive to common humanity or which conflict with laws of humanity are qualified as crimes against humanity.

Lary May , has observed that crimes against humanity is a term that has been widely used in the 20th century without natural boundaries or limits, but to describe the unacceptable acts that are destructive to common human existence. Numerous conflicts that have resulted in serious loss of life, wide displacements, massive sexual violence, abductions and enslavement in many parts of the world, from the World War II, to situations in Somalia, Bosnia, Rwanda, Kosovo, East Timor, Sudanese, DRC, Uganda, Central Africa Republic and Kenya, to mention but a few have made the term crimes against humanity more common, popular and widely used. The global spread of international criminal justice which characterized the formation of international tribunals and courts also contributed much to the popularity of crimes against humanity. The term crimes against humanity has been more commonly used than genocide and as such has become a more useful term for purposes of discussions and descriptions of various conflict situations because it is broader than genocide which is specific.

The origins of crimes against humanity are therefore historical, social, political and legalistic. It is based on the desire by the human community to prevent human excesses during political conflicts. It is a crime that is defined more precisely by its content and not based purely on any statute or convention from a socio-political perspective. The crime has been used as a meaningful and comprehensive tool for intervention in trouble spots, where there is widespread political violence such as the Ivory Coast and Libya, where both the legal and political intervention was done. Crimes against humanity can be regarded historically as a legacy of the Nuremberg trials.

Origins of Crimes against Humanity

At the end of the World War II, it was realized that a lot of crimes had been committed, which were unprecedented but which the world could not afford to ignore. The most significant crimes observed at the end of the devastating war were war crimes, crimes against peace and crimes against humanity as well as persecution (now genocide). In the definition of all these crimes, war or armed conflict was an integral part of the elements of the crime. At that early stage, genocide took a centre stage as the mother of all crimes. This was first explained by Raphael Lamkin and subsequently developed in the Genocide convention. By its definition and the manner and method in which it is committed, genocide is a crude crime, which frightens the entire human existence. However, because it is very difficult to establish the essential elements, particularly the mental element of "intention to destroy in whole or in part", very few convictions have been sustained. In the history of the ICC it has been even difficult to pass the confirmation of charges stage, in a number of cases brought before the Court such as in the Sudanese situation. As a result, the assessment reflects that crimes against humanity can be easily investigated in situations of political violence in both armed and unarmed conflict, as has been done by the ICC in its interventions in the situations in Sudan, Kenya, Ivory Coast, and Libya. Crimes against humanity charges are more preferred than genocide because of the complexity of proving the specific intention to destroy in whole or in part required for genocide charges to be sustained.

Crimes against humanity were first preferred against the Nazi leadership during the Nuremberg trials in 1945 and were defined by the Court as "including but not limited to murder, extermination, enslavement, deportation, imprisonment, torture, rape or other inhuman acts committed against any civilian population, or persecution on political, racial or religious grounds whether or not in violation of the domestic laws of the country were perpetrated". At that point, this offence had not been clearly defined anywhere before and thereafter, no convention has been made to clearly define crimes against humanity. In the Nuremberg trials, crimes against humanity were used interchangeably with war crimes and crimes against peace.

The legacy of the Nuremberg trials was to establish the term crimes against humanity. One of the greatest developments pursuant to this was the gradual erosion of State sovereignty, in particular, relating to crimes against humanity and the assertion of individual rights and responsibilities in the course of justice, as a clear demonstration of the desire to defend individual rights of human beings everywhere, hence confirming the sovereignty of humanity, and crimes against humanity developed into independent and specific crimes apart from war crimes or armed conflict situations.

In its development, crime against humanity relates to a wide range of cruel conducts performed by States or nonState actors in times of war or peace consisting of a wide range of most severe and abominable acts of violence and persecution of victims because of their membership to a particular group rather than their individual characteristics. The offence from the wording implies or suggests an offence that aggrieves not only the victim and their communities, but all human beings, regardless of their community and refers to conduct that cuts deep and violates the core of humanity that we all share and that distinguishes us from other natural beings.

In this scenario, the transgressor becomes a criminal against humanity an enemy and legitimate target of all humankind, a "hostis humani generis", who, in principle, anyone can bring to justice. Crimes against humanity have not been clearly defined in any convention but have been referred to in the statutes of international tribunals and latest in Article 7 of the International Criminal Court Statute, structuring crimes against humanity in terms of context and individual acts which amount to crimes against humanity. It reads thus; "...for the purpose of this Statute, crimes against humanity means any of the following acts, when committed as part of a widespread or systematic attack directed against any civilian population with knowledge of the attack..."

There are distinct elements or requirements that are highlighted in the ICC Statute which are very important in order to determine whether under any particular situation, crimes against humanity has been committed, which are:

- The disjunctive widespread or systematic attack;
- The civilian population as object of attack;
- The distinct element of planning;
- A special mental requirement of the knowledge and,

The existence of individual criminal acts committed within the framework of the attack such as murder, rape, sexual slavery, enforced prostitution, forced pregnancy, enforced sterilization, persecution, enslavement, extermination, enforced disappearances, deportation, apartheid and torture.

It is in this framework that the content of the crime must be considered as a development or evolution from the Nuremberg trials to the International Criminal Court regime and it assists in finding out whether in a particular situation the political activities have become criminal acts forming part of crimes against humanity.

The significant aspect dealt with under Article 7 of the Rome Statute is the widespread or systematic component. It confirms that acts only qualify to be crimes against humanity when they are committed as part of a widespread or systematic attack. This is intended to ensure that only serious violations are the concerns of the international community and as a result, single, isolated or random acts do not qualify as such. This is derived from the case of Prosecutor vs Milutinovic as well as the case of the Prosecutor vs Katanga & Ngudjolo . In these cases, the expression or phrase "widespread" was interpreted to mean or reflect a quantitative assessment of acts in terms of impact. It requires that the act be carried out on a large scale and involving a large number of victims. In these instances the most important component will be the number of victims not the number of acts in as far as the definitional element is concerned. In the Katanga case, a single act was held to be sufficient to constitute crimes against humanity if it is of an extraordinary magnitude. It is the depth of the impact of the act that is evaluated, in terms of the far reaching consequences.

In the case of The Prosecutor vs Al Bashir on the prosecution's application for a warrant of arrest against Omar Hassan Ahmad Al Bashir, the Sudanese President, and the widespread component was interpreted to mean the targeting of the large group in the acts, as sufficient basis to charge a suspect for crimes against humanity. In this case, the attack of the Fur, Masalit and Zaghawa groups because of their ethnicity by groups believed to be under Al Bashir's influence or command was the basis to raise the charges of crimes against humanity. The PreTrial Chamber refused to confirm charges and issue a warrant of arrest for alleged genocide on the grounds that there was no sufficient evidence to establish the special intent to destroy in whole or in part the target groups.

This was despite the fact that the United States of America and various humanitarian agencies had declared that genocide was being committed in Darfur. The Sudanese case makes it clear that, it is easier to prosecute an accused person for crimes against humanity than genocide, as long as there is proof of a greater degree of impact of the cruel acts, because there is no specific intention required. Any political activities which result in the commission of acts constituting crimes against humanity may lead to prosecution regardless of the intentions of the actors as long as such acts were systematic or widespread.

In the case related to the post-election situation in the Republic of Kenya, the ICC Pre-Trial Chamber held that the attacks must not be random occurrences but targeted at a perceived group using a variety of means to identify the group. The Court went on to explain that both requirement of widespread and systematic may exist in one scenario but the existence of either of them is sufficient to establish the offence. The Court held that an act may either be widespread or systematic or may be both widespread and systematic. The systematic element connotes a rather qualitative meaning requiring that the attack be carried out as a result of a methodological plan, whereas widespread refers to the magnitude or extent of the attack.

From the Sudanese and Kenyan case authorities cited above, the widespread element has been read disjunctive or alternative to systematic and as such, an attack can either be widespread or systematic. This definition in Article 7 of the ICC Statute was an adoption of the reading in the case of Prosecutor vs Akayesu which defined widespread as "... a massive, frequent, large scale action, carried out collectively with considerable seriousness and directed against a multiplicity of victims" and systematic "as thoroughly organized and following a regular pattern on the basis of a common policy involving substantial public or private resources...". In a sense, the commission of crimes against humanity involves either the quantitative element of the attack or the methodology of the attack. In some instances, both the qualitative or methodological elements may be available yet in some only one element may be pronounced.

However, in order to clearly understand the provisions of Article 7 (1) of the Rome Statute, it is important to also read it together with Article 7 (2) (a) of the same, which explains ".......a course of conduct involving the multiple commission of acts......, pursuant to or in furtherance of a State or organizational policy to commit such attack......". From reading the provisions of Article 7, it would reflect that widespread is replaced with "...multiple commission of acts.." and systematic is replaced by "..a State or organizational policy...", and in this instance, there is no longer any emphasis of the distinction of the two phrases as alternative modes but they are now interconnected in the sense that the multiple commission of acts must be in furtherance of a policy, and as a result, policy becomes a very important and decisive element of the crime. As in the Kenyan situation , the prosecutor explained a combined elementary view of crimes against humanity, as he sought to establish in the confirmation of charges that there were "........coordinated attacks that were perpetrated by the Mungiki and Pro-Party of National Unity (PNU)....." and that ".......these attacks were not random occurrences but were targeted at perceived Orange Democratic Movement (ODM) supporters......." and also that ".....the attacks affected a large geographical area......".

This version was the same version founded in the post World War II case law and the International Law Commission Draft Codes. Although the case of Prosecutor vs Kunarac30 and Prosecutor vs Visikjevic as well as the case of Prosecutor vs Muvunyi made it clear that it is possible to establish the offence of crimes against humanity by exhibiting the existence of either widespread or systematic attacks, the development of the law as per Article 7(2) makes it clear that it is easier and more desirable to establish both elements. This is meant to show that crimes against humanity intend to deal with some elements of political power as well as organizational planning that facilitate politically motivated criminal activities. As clearly put by Kai Ambos , there is a difference between a systematic attack and a widespread attack. He explains that the former entails a link between the individual perpetrators to the prospective victim and the later connotes the link between the perpetrator and the ultimate policy or organization in terms of acquiescence and knowledge of both the existence of the plan as well as its execution.

The other element dealt with is the civilian object of the attack. In the Nuremberg trials, crimes against humanity are linked to civilians killed in an armed conflict. Article 7(1) of the Rome Statute criminalizes any acts when they are directed against a civilian population. The ICTY recognized this problem when the Court was dealing with the case of Prosecutor vs Kupreslak and it held that "....One fails to see why only civilians and not also combatants should be protected by these rules. (in particular by the rules prohibiting persecution), given these rules maybe held to possess a broader humanitarian scope and purpose than those prohibiting war......". This, it is argued by Kai Ambos, as a reflection, that crime against humanity is not recognized as a crime in its own right, but rather as an extension of war crimes into peace times only. The major difficulty is in the definition of a civilian in peace times since, everyone is a civilian including soldiers because there will be noncombatant. The civilian population requirement in Article 7 (1) of the ICC Statute reflects the unwillingness of the drafters and States to expand the definition of the crime to protect all human beings. This indicates that the protection is not intended for the collective nature of the attack but on the individuals affected. This definition has not been developed since the Nuremberg Charter 1945 which defined crimes against humanity as "murder, extermination, enslavement, deportation and other human acts committed against any civilian population before or during the war".

Article 7 (1) of the ICC Statute also has the knowledge requirement in the definition of crimes against humanity. This implies that the accused person must know the existence of the attack as well as that his/her conduct or acts form part of the broad objective of the attack. This knowledge requirement is an additional element to be distinguished from the mens rea requirement in Article of the ICC Statute. This requirement is designed to link the individual acts of the perpetrator with the general attack. In the case of Prosecutor vs Kordic and Cerkez it was held that an accused person may not be held accountable for crimes against humanity unless he or she was aware that his acts form part of the collective attack on the group. Knowledge includes deliberate taking of risk in the form of constructive knowledge, which implies general knowledge of the existence of the attack or detailed knowledge of its peculiarity and circumstances that may render the perpetrator's conduct to contribute to the crimes of others. This was clearly articulated in the Kenyan situation, where the ICC Pre-Trial Chamber linked the politicians with the militia on the basis that they knew what the militia was doing and condoned the acts and the acts were clearly benefiting the accused politicians. The politicians had general knowledge of the attacks on their opponents by the supporters of their parties.

Article 7 of the Rome Statute has gradually expanded the individual acts and the contextual elements of crimes against humanity. The ICTY Statute included deportations, imprisonment, torture and rape as individual acts of crimes against humanity. The Draft Code went further to include discrimination based on racial, ethnic or religious grounds, forcible transfer, forced disappearances, enforced prostitution and other forms of sexual violence. In Article 7 of the Rome Statute, there is an extension to include sexual crimes such as forced pregnancy, enforced sterilization or any other form of sexual violence of comparable gravity. The Rome Statute reflects a clear progression on what acts constitute the crime as long as it constitutes a destructive and dangerous effect to the victims or the target group in pursuant to the policy. Article 7 (1) (h) has also expanded the scope of the target group to include political and gender based violence. In this instance, crimes against humanity can be referred to as a broader crime than genocide, which only protects or punishes acts of violence intended to "destroy, in whole, or in part, a national, ethnical, racial or religious group".

Article 7 of the Rome Statute, contrary to Article 3 of the ICTR Statute, no longer requires a special discriminatory intent or motive and also removes completely the link between crimes against humanity and armed conflict. The link had long been ruled to be undesirable and unnecessary as indicated in the Tadic case, where it was held "...there is no logical or legal basis for (a war nexus) and it has been abandoned in subsequent state practice with respect to crimes against humanity…" In this regard, there is a clear distinction between international humanitarian law, which was applicable during the Nuremberg trials and international human rights law, applicable in the contemporary. International criminal law is broader and applicable in all times, whereby international humanitarian law applies in situations related to international armed conflicts.

From the foregoing, it is clear that crime against humanity is broader than that the crime of genocide and as such it is the most ideal crime to address the contemporary human rights violations and political excesses. Larry May (Robert, 2002) has put it clear that "….when a state deprives its subject of physical security or substance or is unable or unwilling to protect its subjects from harm to security or subsistence, it loses its right to prevent international bodies from crossing its borders for remedial purposes….". In a sense prosecutions are intended to signify the importance or magnitude of the violations perpetrated against human civilian populations by States or organizations in furtherance of their policies or political agendas. Crimes against humanity incorporate already existing common crimes such as murder, rape, torture and slavery, into international crimes, if their magnitude is so great that they cannot be ignored by the international community. It is only when the governments or domestic legal actors are complacent to act that it becomes imperative to apply international criminal justice mechanisms. In the Kenyan situation as well as the Sudanese situations, crimes against humanity were preferred against the most influential and powerful political players for their involvement in the organization or supporting or conspiracy or abetting gross human rights violations.

There is a higher probability of success in prosecuting crimes against humanity than genocide as reflected in the Sudanese and Kenyan situations because all that is required is to establish that there exists an attack against a civilian population, which is systematic or wide spread. The specific intention of the attack is not looked into when prosecuting crimes against humanity, whereas for purposes of genocide, it is not enough to show that there has been an attack on a civilian population but that the population must be part of the national, ethnic, racial or religious group and the ultimate intentions must be to "destroy in whole or in part". If the prosecutor fails to establish that the group so targeted is within the four specific categories or that the intention is to wipe out in whole or in part, the charges of genocide automatically falls. Under these circumstances crimes against humanity become the ideal crime to tackle political excesses, which may result in serious violation of civilian and vulnerable populations. Political excesses may not be within the intention to destroy in whole or in part, but for other purposes, such as to change voting patterns or to weaken opposition elements.

When dealing with crimes against humanity with particular reference to Article 7 (1) (h) of the Rome Statute, it becomes clear that genocide is one side of crimes against humanity . The acts under genocide general qualify to be crimes against humanity but if the prohibited act is accompanied by specific genocidal intent (dolus specialis), and is committed against a protected group it can now be punished under genocide and as such, genocide can be regarded as the most serious and most aggravated type of crimes against humanity (Schabas, 2004). As a general consideration, acts of genocide also form part of crimes against humanity, which are seriously aggravated by the existence of some specific intention, which would require to be specifically attended to in a special way because of the level of culpability. It is the mass destruction element of the acts that calls for it to be addressed as genocide, since the mens rea becomes higher and more frightening. For genocide, the intention to destroy a large number or all the members of the target group is the most important element, where as for crimes against humanity, the offence is committed when acts affect large group regardless of whether or not the group is homogenous.

Crimes against humanity may be committed against an individual, whereas genocide can only be committed against individuals who belong to a specifically protected group characterized by national, ethnical, racial or religious identity (Short, 2003). As alluded in the Akayesu case, the four protected groups usually share a common feature, that such membership would not be normally and easily challengeable by its members, who belong to it automatically, by birth, in conscience and often irremediable manner, such that the target and the victim is the group itself and not the individual.48 It is very difficult to investigate the existence of the elements referred in the genocide crime and would take longer and require more time to establish than to simply establish that an attack was made against a civilian population in a wide spread or systematic manner. As far as actus reus, mens rea and victim requirements are concerned, there is a higher level of rigidity in prosecuting the crime of genocide than in prosecuting crimes against humanity.

The two crimes are intersecting crimes which only call for some higher level of specialization in order to determine whether it is genocide or crimes against humanity (Cassese, 2003). From the foregoing, it is clear that genocide is restricted to act perpetrated against certain protected groups and furthermore an intention to destroy in whole or in part, which is very difficult to prove, since the perpetrators will not ordinarily document or publish their policies. Clearly as a threshold for intervention to stop atrocities, the definition is a very difficult one to work with. Crimes against humanity on the other hand is broader and arguably more useful for purposes of discussing intervention proposals because it is not legally restrictive (United States institute of peace, 2008). since it requires acts to be committed against any civilian population and does not require any specific intent like genocide. It is much easier to justify an international intervention for the prevention of crimes against humanity than for genocide because all that is required will be to prove that there has been an attack on a civilian population for whatever reason of the attack, as long as the attack is either widespread or systematic. The development of crimes against humanity reflects a continued desire to hold accountable those responsible for serious violations of humanity. It has also arisen to show that even non-state actors can be held to account as subjects of international criminal law, and has greatly strengthened the principle of individual criminal responsibility and accountability under international criminal law.

It is clear that crime against humanity is the most preferred crime than it was in 1945. Because its essential elements have been expanded and broadened, since the Nuremberg Charter, it has become the most preferred crime to charge on human rights violation in times of war and peace and has grown naturally as its original nature permitted. It is arguably the most significantly preferred charge in the contemporary times. Although in its early development, crime against humanity was treated as a component of war crimes, it has developed in the recent changing history and has become an ideal crime of international justice. Its broad elements as articulated in Article 7 of the Rome Statute have made it possible to prefer crimes against humanity instead of genocide to deal with non-armed conflict situations and the Courts have also been quick to confirm charges of crimes against humanity referred to it than genocide, because the charge is less technical and fairly broad.

History shows that the practice of prosecuting for crimes against humanity was very weak since no trials before International Criminal Tribunals were held subsequently to the Nuremberg trials until the early 1990s (Gerhard, 2005). The Yugoslavia and Rwanda Tribunals reaffirmed the customary law character of crimes against humanity and the ICTY Statute, in Article 5 clearly pronounced that the crime must occur in armed conflict and the ICTR Statute in its Article 3 limited the crime to acts committed on "natural, political, ethnic, racial or religious grounds". It is only in the broad definition of the crimes against humanity in Article 7 of the Rome Statute that gives the crimes a wide definition, which makes it a core crime which can play an important role in the international criminal justice system and enable intervention and punishment for international violations. Crime against humanity has gradually developed to become the most significant and frequently preferred crime in the international criminal court history as compared to genocide.

In tracing the history of the development of crimes against humanity, it related to mass crimes committed against a civilian population (Gerhard, 2005) and most of the serious acts which form part of genocide also form part of crimes against humanity. In the Nuremberg trials, all the genocide that was committed against European Jews was viewed and punished as crimes against humanity. Crimes against humanity was first explicitly formulated as a category of crimes in Article 6 of the Nuremberg Charter and since then it has been specifically referred to in dealing with subsequent political violence in different parts of the world (Gerhard, 2005). The preference of crimes against humanity has grown stronger during the International Criminal Court era as the most convenient and usable tool against political violence.

The charge of crimes against humanity is designed to protect specific human interest. The threat to peace, security and wellbeing of the civilian populations of the world in a widespread and systematic form and the general attack and the violation of fundamental human rights is what crimes against humanity stands to address. The label of crimes against humanity is against the organized violence and setting of minimum standards on how political humans can exist and core-exist. Crimes against humanity generally enforce values which transcend the individual and protects the victim's rights to life, health, freedom as well as dignity which are threatened and usually compromised in political violent situations.

CONCLUSION

Crime against humanity is not just a semantically-neutral label but it has an internal structure and a history, which is both legal and political. It is a crime with a contextual relevance to deal with excesses in political activities done by political entities against vulnerable civilians under their control or influence. It is a crime that is designed to contain political excesses by making sure that those who exceed the limits become enemies, not only of their political opponents in their area of influence or control, but become enemies and legitimate targets of all humankind. The crime is broad and less technical than that of genocide and war crimes, as clearly illustrated by precedents in international criminal tribunals and courts.

Crimes against humanity are designed to vindicate human interests which are under constant threat from political excesses. There is a lot in the wording of this crime, which has become very useful in international criminal justice system's quest to end or avert political excesses. This crime represents the limit to where political events in a particular situation are legally reviewed and regarded as ultra vires and punishable under international criminal law.

The historical developments and content of crimes against humanity is purely a legal response to political excesses. It validates the theory by David Luban to the effect that human beings as political animals live under the permanent threat of politics gone cancerous. The crime is designed as a measure on how political excesses which are a concern to the whole human family can be curtailed. The name is neatly chosen to fit both the political as well as the legal scope of international criminal law. Although the label has been casually used in politics and in the media, it has managed to develop into a scientific definition of the political excesses that the international community intents to proscribe. There is no other better term or label that could have been used to define the crime in terms of content and context other than crimes against humanity to define prohibited acts in hot and deep political environments that the civilian human population finds itself under.

REFERENCES

1. Cassese A (2003). International Criminal Law, Oxford university press.
2. Gerhard W (2005). Principles of International Law. T.M.C Asser Press.
3. Robert G (2002). Crimes against humanity, the struggle for Global Justice, 2nd Edition. Penguin Books.
4. Schabas W (2004). An Introduction to International Criminal Court. 2nd edition Cambridge University press.
5. Short JMH (2003). Sexual violence as genocide. The developing law of the international criminal tribunals and the international criminal court, Michigan journal of race and law. Spring.
6. Christian T (2006) The legacy of Nuremberg. Journal for international criminal justice 4 (2006) 830-844. Oxford University Press
7. David L (2004). A Theory of Crimes Against Humanity; Georgetown Law Faculty Publications. 29 Yale J. Intl Law. 85-167
8. Peter TB (2007). QC. Aspects of crimes against humanity and the international criminal court. International centre for criminal law reform and criminal justice policy 1822 East Mall, Vancouver, BC Canada.
9. Kai A (2011). Crimes against humanity and the international criminal court. 1st ed
10. Larry M (2004). Crimes against humanity. A normative account: Cambridge University Press 310
11. Phyllis H (1998). Defining crimes against humanity in the Rome Statute of the international criminal court: Fordham Intl. law J.22(2):5
12. Tom Stenson: Crimes and criminal responsibilities under international law. United States institute of peace, (2008.) Confronting crimes against humanity. A study guide series on peace and conflict Yavuz A The distinction between crimes against humanity and genocide focusing most particularly on the crime of persecution. Judge 0general directorate of EU Ministry of Justice of Turkey.

CHAPTER 11 ENDING RAPE IN WAR: HOW FAR HAVE WE COME?

Lucy Fiske and Rita Shackel

Keywords: Rape in war, Gender justice, Sexual violence

INTRODUCTION

Rape of women has long been an endemic feature of war. For centuries, perpetrators of sexual attacks during conflicts have enjoyed effective impunity. Public narratives of war tend to focus on the victories and defeats of military troops or perhaps on the impacts on a de-gendered civilian population, such as displacement or death as 'collateral damage' (Palmieri et al. 2012, pp. 10-13; Henry 2011, p. 20; Puechguirbal 2012, p. 140). Until very recently, the ways in which conflicts impact on women in particular received very little attention. At least since the International Criminal Tribunals for Rwanda and Yugoslavia, there is a growing awareness and concern in both public consciousness and among legal and political leaders, of the extent and need to address the rape of women in war. The incidence of rape in war is such that Major General Patrick Cammaert, former Commander of the UN Peacekeeping operations in Democratic Republic of Congo (DRC) in 2008, declared that '[i]t is now more dangerous to be a woman than to be a soldier in modern conflict' (Chaikel 2011).

An estimated 25 – 50,000 Bosnian women and girls were raped in the Bosnian war from 1991 – 1995 (Chaikel 2011). In a landmark study of 68 victims of this abuse Loncar et al. (2006, p. 71) reported that of these women, 44 were raped more than once and 21 were raped daily during their captivity. Most of the rapes (96%) were also accompanied by physical torture. Between 250,000 and half a million women and girls were raped during the 1994 genocide in Rwanda; Special Rapporteur on Rwanda Rene Degni-Segui remarked in 1996 that '[r]ape was the rule, and its absence the exception' (UN Special Rapporteur 1996, p.16). In the Nanking Massacre of 1937 during the Second Sino-Japanese War somewhere between 20,000 and 80,000 women and girls were raped (Williams 2014). A 2011 study conducted by scholars at Harvard School of Public Health estimated that 48 rapes took place every hour in the DRC, this translates to 1,152 women raped every day (Peterman et al. 2011, p. 1060).

It is difficult to establish accurate statistics on the incidence of rape in conflict for a range of social and methodological reasons including the widespread under-reporting of rape due in no small part to social stigma attached to the status 'raped woman' and the collapse of social infrastructure which would ordinarily assist in the collation of such information, such as health services, police, courts, and psychosocial services (Palmieri et al. 2012, 13-14). Argument around the accuracy of rape statistics, however, is a diversion which obscures the lived experiences of women and the catastrophic effects that rape has. For example in the Bosnian study by Loncar et al. (2006) noted above, most of the women revealed psychological trauma. The most frequent psychological symptoms were depressiveness, avoidance of thoughts or conversations associated with trauma, and suicidal ideas. None of the women in this study had a psychiatric history before the rape, but at the time of the study, over 76% suffered from depression, 75%

Citation: Lucy Fiske and Rita Shackel, Ending Rape in War: How Far Have We Come, http://dx.doi.org/10.5130/ccs.v6i3.4183.

from social phobia, almost a third from post-traumatic stress disorder and a quarter of the women in the study had sexual dysfunctions. The link between militarisation and rape is clear (Henry 2011), but focusing on the number of rape victims also diverts attention away from the more important questions of '*why* does a rise in militarism bring with it a rise in rape?' And 'how can we stop rape in war?'

This paper briefly maps historical attitudes towards rape in war, outlines some analyses and explanations of why rape in war occurs and finally turns more substantively to recent efforts by the international community to prosecute rape as a war crime and a crime against humanity. Drawing on academic and legal sources as well as our own empirical work in the Great Lakes region of Africa we argue, that while commendable in many ways, contemporary approaches to rape in war risk reinforcing aspects of women's status which contribute to the targeting of women for rape and continue to displace women from the centre to the margins in debates and practices surrounding rape in both war and peace time. We conclude by arguing that criminal prosecutions alone are insufficient and that, if we are to end the rape of women and girls in war (and peace), we need a radical restructuring of gender relations across every sphere of social and political life.

Mainstream and high-level political and juridical concern about rape in war is a very recent phenomenon. Hagay-Frey (2011) identifies three historical phases in international law's approach to rape of women: the 'Era of Silence' (prior to the Geneva Conventions of 1949), the 'Era of Honor' (from 1949 to the mid 1990s) and the 'Third Era' (from the prosecutions of rape in the International Criminal Tribunals of Yugoslavia and Rwanda in the late 1990s). Historically, the rape of women by victorious soldiers has been sanctioned as the 'spoils of war', fairly won in battle. The Bible for example, albeit historically contestable in parts, contains several tracts which sanction raping women as the 'spoils of war.' For example, in Zechariah 14: 1-2 (cited in Turano 2011, 1047) it is stated that:

Behold, a day is coming for the Lord when the spoil taken from you will be divided among you. For I will gather all the nations against Jerusalem to battle, and the city will be captured, the houses plundered, the women ravished…

Numbers 31: 17:18 states:

Now therefore, kill every male among the little ones, and kill every woman who has known man intimately, but all the girls who have not known man intimately, spare for yourselves. (cited in Turano 2011, p. 1047)

Analogous sanctions are found in the Koran. In Koran 3.50 it is stated:

O Prophet! Lo! We have made lawful unto thee the wives unto whom thou hast paid their dowries, and those whom thy right hand possesseth of those whom Allah hath given thee as spoils of war. (cited in Turano 2011, p. 1047)

Attitudes to rape in war have progressed considerably over the last two centuries, moving from sanctioning of rape, through to official prohibition but little enforcement, to a recent trend towards prosecution. In 1863 Abraham Lincoln made rape by Union soldiers an offence punishable by death. Prohibitions against the violation of 'family honour' are found in the Hague Convention (1907) and the Geneva Conventions (1949). Despite these legal prohibitions however, there has been widespread political and popular silence around rape (Palmieri et al. 2012, Puechguirbal 2012, Snyder et al. 2006). The deep-rooted religious and historical sanctioning of rape continues to echo through the ages underpinning a fatalism that tacitly accepts the practice as an unfortunate, but natural and inevitable side effect of war ('boys will be boys').

There is also an argument to be made that to acknowledge rape in war poses a risk to 'higher order' goals and the protection of the nation and polity: exposing the rape of women and girls unsettles nationalist narratives of the soldier as hero, the selfless and innocent defender of the nation and its values (Henry 2011, p. 20). Despite extensive evidence of sexual offences during World War II, there were no prosecutions at Nuremberg, and only peripheral mentions of rape, subsumed under the larger category of 'atrocities' in the International Military Tribunal for the Far East (Hagay-Frey 2011, p. 62). Asia's 'comfort women' are to this day still seeking acknowledgement and justice for their sexual enslavement (Arakawa 2001).

Rape and other forms of sexual violence such as forced marriage, enforced prostitution, sexual humiliation and forced pregnancy committed in war time were first prosecuted in the International Criminal Tribunal for Former Yugoslavia (ICTY) and the International Criminal Tribunal for Rwanda (ICTR), despite the fact that rape was not expressly mentioned in either statute governing these courts (O'Connor 2012). Rape is included in the Rome Statute (2002), establishing the International Criminal Court, as a war crime (Article 8), a crime against humanity (Article 7) and, in certain circumstances, as genocide (Article 6).

Moves by the international community both to legally prohibit *and* prosecute rape in war have been welcomed by many as an important step in confronting the culture of impunity surrounding rape in war and bringing an end to the practice (HRW et al. 2014). Some human and women's rights advocates hope that establishing women as legal subjects in international law will have a positive impact on women's standing in national jurisdictions, bringing consequent gains in women's rights more broadly (Eaton 2003, UN ECOSOC 2003). There are however, questions regarding the efficacy of prosecutions to achieve these goals and a risk that celebrating successful prosecutions on the international stage may deflect attention away from a lack of progress in other areas such as enhancing women's safety in conflict and post-conflict environments and programs aimed at changing unequal power relations between men and women which arguably underpin violence against women.

Why does Rape happen?

The link between militarisation, war and rape of women and girls is irrefutable and well established (Henry 2011, Palmieri 2012, Brownmiller 1975, Hagay-Frey 2011), but it is important to ask the question 'why?' Why is rape so prevalent during many (but not all) conflicts? Why do men rape women in war time? There are many possible reasons advanced for this. First is the power of rape as a weapon of war to dishonour, demoralise and emasculate the enemy, which is well recognised (El-Bushra and Mukarubuga 1995, Meger 2010). Secondly, rape can occur with the intention of genocide, particularly in societies in which national and ethnic identity is patrilineal (Chesterman 1997; Snyder et al. 2006, p. 190). The deliberate impregnation of a community's women by the enemy disrupts the group's ongoing existence as a defined ethnic group. Rape is also sometimes used to terminate existing pregnancies – with the same intent of discontinuing ethnic bloodlines (Snyder et al. 2006). Thirdly, rape provokes terror. The widespread rape of women and the violence that accompanies such attacks affects whole communities acting to destabilize and disempower (Puechguirbal 2012). Fourthly, rape begets food insecurity. This occurs particularly in societies where women are responsible for working the fields, procuring food and water and collecting firewood. By raping women while they are working or collecting wood or water, the food supply for the entire community is disrupted (El-Bushra and Mukarubuga 1995). Moreover, in some sites, magic plays a role, some men have reported beliefs that raping women will cure them of AIDS, make them undefeatable in battle, or that they had been overcome by the devil or spirits and directed to rape (Lent Hirsch and Wolfe 2012). The rape of women may also be seen as a result of amplified gender roles in war time and an extension of pre-existing power relations and inequalities in many societies (Mazurana and Proctor 2013). Susan Brownmiller (1975, pp. 32-33) argues that rape during war is an extension of pre-existing misogyny:

War provides men with the perfect psychologic backdrop to give vent to their contempt for women. ... [War] confirms for men what they long suspect, that women are peripheral, irrelevant to the world that counts, ... war provides men with a tacit license to rape (1975, pp. 32-33).

A detailed discussion of all the varied reasons that may explain the phenomenon of rape in conflict is beyond the scope of this paper. In order however to probe further the question of why rape is used as a war strategy, we focus on the links between women as bearers of honour and on the amplification of particular and idealised gender roles during conflict.

Honour, Nation and Gender

Yuval Davis (1993, p. 627) argues that the 'nation' is an imagined community 'which divides the world between 'us' and 'them'' and which 'is maintained and ideologically reproduced by a whole system of ... symbolic 'border guards'', with gender playing 'an especially significant role.' The territory on which a nation exists and upon which its members are born and depend for survival and for the reproduction of their collective national identity is imagined as feminine; the giver of life who must be defended by her sons1. The territory is feminised and the imagined ideals of the nation, its most sacred attributes are symbolically represented by the women of the nation (Yuval Davis 1993, Saigol 2012). 'Women often come to symbolize the national collectivity, its roots, its spirit, its national project. Moreover, women often symbolize national and collective 'honour'' (Yuval Davis 1993, p. 627). Thus, in most societies, the category 'woman' is invested with powerful labels and symbolism. Women are reified as the mothers of the nation, bearers of ethnic or national identity and bearers of the group's honour. These reified ideals are problematic for women in peacetime, tightly circumscribing what is appropriate conduct for women (the policing of which is diffused as a sometimes sacred obligation amongst all members of society, making a woman's body and behaviour not entirely her own), with serious consequences for those who transgress.

However problematic such collectively held ideals of womanhood and honour may be in peacetime, such tropes tend to be amplified in war with profound implications for women in conflict and post conflict societies. Snyder et al. (2006, p. 188), in exploring possible roots of the systematic rape of women as a feature of the Yugoslav wars in the 1990s, identify a 'rising tide of nationalism' in which 'women became popular symbols who both embodied and marked the boundaries of the homeland in a nationalist discourse that conflated images of mothers with the nation itself'. Examples of images and narratives of women as essentialised symbols of nation and honour deployed to justify and fortify the nation's war effort – either as the worried, but essentially powerless mother/sister/daughter, or as the victim of a barbaric monstrous enemy can be found throughout history. Propaganda posters from World War Two are particularly illustrative of such discourses. Whilst such overt woman-nation-honour images are seldom seen today, similar discourses are nevertheless still easily found. For example, TIME Magazine's cover of the 9 August 2010 edition urging America and her allies to 'stay the course' in Afghanistan reveals the hegemonic tropes of idealised masculinity and femininity put to service in the war effort

These gender roles however are not spontaneously created at the outbreak of fighting, rather they are pre-existing and deeply embedded in patriarchal notions of the family, community and nation. When conflict erupts gender roles become narrowed and amplified. Hegemonic masculinity is aggressive, brave, conquering and powerful; whereas the corresponding femininity is the symbol of purity, the keeper of honour and home, the goodness worth fighting, killing and dying for. That these forms of masculinity and femininity may not be an accurate reflection of actual people matters not, for the hegemony needs simplicity and clarity, a clear demarcation of 'good' and 'evil' for it to mobilise into action (Mazurana and Proctor 2013).

The amplification of women's symbolic power elevates her value as a strategic target in war. And it is this honour, rather than the integrity of the woman as individual, autonomous legal subject which earlier prohibitions against rape in war sought to protect. The Hague Convention and the Geneva Conventions all articulate the prohibitions as a protection of 'family honour'. The commentary accompanying the Geneva Conventions explains that 'women . . . have an absolute right to respect for their honour and their modesty, in short, for their dignity as women' (cited in Chesterman 1997, p. 332), and in so doing, makes a woman's right to the protection of the law contingent upon the highly contextual and problematic notions of 'honour' and 'modesty'. Chesterman (1997, p. 332) argues that framing rape as an injury to honour 'mask(s) the violent nature of the crime' and 'is contingent upon hierarchized gender relations that naturalise the experience of women as victims.'

Susan Brownmiller goes further, arguing that the rape of women in war is a form of communication between men and that the woman herself is incidental, a mere message board in the correspondence:

The body of a raped woman becomes a ceremonial battlefield, a parade ground for the victor's trooping of the colors. The act that is played out upon her is a message passed between men – vivid proof of victory for one and loss and defeat for the other (Brownmiller 1975, p. 38).

Rape in International Criminal Law

As noted above despite international law purporting to have long offered protection to women against rape and offences against their honour, rape was first prosecuted in the ICTY and ICTR. The *Akayesu* decision of the ICTR (handed down in Rwanda in September 1998) was revolutionary in several respects. Apart from being the first conviction for sexual violence against women on the international stage, it found that rape in the Rwandan genocide was used as part of a widespread and systemic attack and constituted genocide and a crime against humanity. It further developed a progressive definition of rape as 'a physical invasion of a sexual nature, committed on a person under circumstances which are coercive.' This definition is crucial as it does not require the victim to demonstrate her/his non-consent, nor does it require that the perpetrator used threats or force, instead understanding the circumstances of conflict to constitute coercion. Finally, Akayesu was not personally accused of committing any rapes himself, but as a commander he was held responsible for rapes committed in and around his *bureau communal* and of sending 'a clear signal of official tolerance for sexual violence, without which these acts would not have taken place.'

The ICTY further developed jurisprudence on rape in war through several other decisions. Importantly it sought to establish more specific elements of the crime of rape and considered the issue of consent, stating that 'the true common denominator which unifies the various systems [of law] ... is the basic principle of penalising violations of sexual autonomy.'

On a more positive note however, it also extended liability of superior officers for the conduct of their soldiers to impose a duty for officers to proactively investigate 'in order to ascertain whether offences were being committed'.

While recent efforts to articulate and prosecute sexual crimes against women is a welcome departure from both euphemising sexual violence as an offence against a woman's honour (as offences are codified in the Geneva Conventions) and the historical reluctance to prosecute, there remain several concerns. We limit discussion here to three key points which by no means represents an exhaustive critique. First we argue that there are ongoing echoes of women as bearers of a group's honour; secondly that there is a legal focus on certain types of sexual violence to the exclusion of other types of sexual violence; thirdly that there is a privileging of criminal justice over physical, emotional, social and economic recovery for the woman.

Echoes of Honor

While women appear before International Criminal Law (ICL) due to violations of their bodies and minds, rather than of her modesty or honor, a woman still does not appear as an autonomous rights bearing subject. As several scholars have persuasively argued, 'sexual violence is not in and of itself an international crime' (Grewal 2010, p. 75). In order to be a crime in international law, sexual violence must occur in specific contexts and circumstances. Chesterman (1997, p. 333) argues that the treatment of sexual violence in international law 'impos(es) a definition that depends not on experience but on the legally validating circumstances in which that experience obtains a context'. He goes on to argue that 'the legal response to rape in war' is based on 'the effacement of the feminine subject, and her selective appropriation into the discourse of war crimes as the bearer of essentialized feminine virtues (protecting men's interests in "their" women)' (Chesterman 1997, p. 332). Kirsten Campbell concurs, noting that International Criminal Law, for all its progressive developments continues to misunderstand the atrocity of rape at a fundamental level by continuing to treat it as significant 'only where it is understood in terms of a crime against a victim's community or nation' (cited in Grewal 2010, p. 76).

Although the terminology of 'honour' has been expunged, women's experiences of sexual violence continue to be interpreted through national, communal and predominantly patriarchal lenses. The effects this has are multiple and profound. Rather than radically de-linking women and honour, modern ICL has potentially reinforced women becoming visible in the high status public sphere of international law through her ethnic or national identity rather than her gender identity, even though it may be her gender that is primarily determinative in terms of her life experiences in both war and peace. ICL has also arguably created a new role for women to play in service of the nation – that of testifying at international tribunals about the victimisation of her national or ethnic group and the criminality and barbarity of the 'other side' (Mertus 2004).

The raped woman witness is of great value during the trial, but if patriarchal constructions of womanhood remain uncritiqued, she returns not as 'national hero', but instead takes up her position as a 'raped woman'; sullied, without honour and of little or no value in future life. Redress Africa, a British based NGO, interviewed several Rwandan women who had testified about sexual violence at gacaca (the domestic special courts set up to respond to the mass violence of the genocide). One woman complained that 'Wherever I went, people mocked and made fun of me. It affected me so much that I became sick and remained bed-ridden for a long time' (Redress 2008, p. 88).

This corresponds with interviews we conducted with women in DRC in April 2014 as part of a research project exploring women's experiences of justice following mass violence8. Many of the women we spoke with recounted trying to hide their rape from husbands and communities for fear of being abandoned and stigmatised, a fear which was sadly realised for many:

> I remember before being raped that my health was very fine and I had sufficient means. After rape, my husband left me. ... I am unable to do anything by myself. Even if he comes, I am unable to satisfy his needs, so I am nothing in the society. (41 year old woman, mother of seven children, 22 April 2014, Rutshuru, DRC)

Focus on certain types of sexual violence

For rape to constitute a war crime, crime against humanity or genocide, the act of rape itself is insufficient, it must be committed in particular circumstances (such as during a genocide, an inter-ethnic war or other circumstance that enables the violence to come under ICL jurisdiction) or in the context of a particular relationship between the woman's and the perpetrator's ethnic or religious identities. The effect of this is that only certain types of rape can be prosecuted – those conducted by, or at the instruction of, a member of the enemy forces committed during a genocide or armed conflict. Women who are raped in circumstances that do not meet the legal definition, such as those raped by members of their own 'side', by peace-keepers or other actors in emergencies, gain no benefit from recent advances in ICL. This is a significant omission. In 2004 the UN launched an investigation into sexual assaults by peace-keepers in DRC, leading to the expulsion of 65 military personnel and 9 civilian staff of MONUC in 2005 (Fleshman 2005). Allegations have been made against UN peace keepers in Cambodia in the early 1990s and again in former Yugoslavia in the mid-1990s. In the early 2000s reports emerged of peace keepers and humanitarian workers seeking sexual favours from women and girls in exchange for food, water and medicine in refugee camps in Sierra Leone, Guinea and Liberia. No charges were laid in any of these cases (Fleshman 2005). In northern Uganda the entire population was forced into IDP camps and a position of dependency on UPDF soldiers and humanitarian agencies for the necessities of life. Here too, stories of 'survival sex'; when women 'consent' to sex with those in positions of power in exchange for food, water, access to firewood, or protection against assaults by others, have been extensively recorded (Okello & Hovil 2007).

Even in cases where the act may meet the elements of the definition, decisions to prosecute and on which charges are made according to a range of considerations. Although law as an institution and legal prosecutions of rape draw upon a narrative of concern for women, women's experiences and desires are often relegated to secondary concerns in prosecutorial decision making (Mertus 2004). Cases are chosen for their strategic value. Which are most likely to secure a conviction? Which will advance jurisprudence on an issue? Which are politically palatable? Which will develop the historical record in the 'right' manner? Political context, for example, was key in the inability of the Special Court for Sierra Leone to prosecute any sexual offences committed by the Civil Defence Forces (CDF), with the Trial Chamber ruling all evidence relating to sexual violence inadmissible.

As one woman told researchers:

> I feel so bad, because they raped me very brutally, and that was the main reason for going to court to testify. As soon as I got there, my lawyer told me that I should not talk about that anymore. And up to now, that still causes me pain. It makes me feel bad. (cited in Grewal 2010, p. 72)

Furthermore, it does not address the heightened levels of sexual and other violence that women experience before and after periods of conflict. Grewal (2010, pp. 75-76) argues that while the highly specific definitions of sexual crimes as international crimes are necessary for the law 'it is based on a fiction: that a clear distinction can be drawn between women's experiences in war and women's lives in peace.'

Privileging of Criminal Justice over Woman-Centered Recovery

The recent enthusiasm for prosecutions of rape in conflict focuses attention and resources on legal responses to rape, rather than on direct efforts to prevent rape or to assist women to recover after the event. Our current qualitative research in DRC anecdotally accords with larger, quantitative studies (e.g. Bartels 2010) that women there are most commonly raped while in their homes at night, while working in the fields during the day or are abducted from either home or the fields and raped in captivity in the forest. With such a predictable pattern of risk identified, it is difficult not to have questions about the criteria for decision making about where protective forces are deployed and which targets attract priority status for protection.

The prosecution of rape in conflict is important and may yet deliver on its intended aim of ending impunity and bringing the practice to an end. However, practices entrenched across centuries, even millennia, will not be eradicated easily and we must approach this as a long term project. We must also approach the task holistically and keep women and their experiences at the centre of thinking and planning.

Courts and tribunals are expensive ventures to run. The ICTR operated with a biennial budget of $269,758,400 for 2006 and 2007. In the same period, the ICTY operated at a cost of $276,474,100. By October 2006 the ICTY had tried 51 cases and the ICTR 22 (Wippman 2006, p. 861). While significant attention and resources are directed to courts and tribunals; health, psychosocial, economic empowerment and community attitude programs are struggling. While juridical approaches to rape may focus on the elements of the event and conclude at the end of the rape, the legacy of rape reverberates throughout a woman's life in multiple ways long after the attack is over.

One of the questions we are currently asking in our research and an interview with women from DRC, Kenya and Uganda is 'what would justice look like for you?' Some women have talked of wanting to see the perpetrators of violence against them and others, prosecuted and jailed, or even killed, but the common responses focus on the need to recover. Women have talked of the need to heal their hearts, provide for their children, recover from the injuries and illnesses sustained during the rape and to establish economic independence.

> We need peace in our areas so that we may come back home and continue our former activities. In addition we need money to help children study or create schools for them. But the most important need is to take care of the victims both after rape and in case the perpetrator is captured. Actually by giving us sewing machines to become dress makers for the family to survive. But we notice the DRC government thinks capturing the perpetrator is sufficient whereas the victim is still suffering. (25 year old woman, mother of three children, 19 April 2014, Minova, DRC)

The conviction of the perpetrator is an important and necessary part of justice, but it is insufficient in itself. A woman-centred approach to justice for rape would look very different. The under-funding of woman-centred services is so chronic that one woman told us she was unable to complete an essential course of post-rape anti-HIV medication as the hospital supply was unable to keep pace with the rate of need: 'When I went there they missed the medicine saying that we are too numerous.' (27 year old woman, six children, 23 April 2014, Bweremana, DRC).

The focus on prosecutions also serves to obscure the catastrophic impact that rape can have on a woman's life.

A woman's emotional pain and loss of a sense of safety in the world, her low social status, poor marriageability, economic precarity, chronic illnesses such as HIV, or injuries such as fistulas or maiming sustained during the attack, her abandonment by her husband or her becoming pregnant and then having a child born of rape are all excluded from the judicial process, yet it is precisely these issues that women in Kenya, DRC and Uganda are raising in interviews.

CONCLUSION

Rape is a scourge with wide-reaching and lasting effects for its victims. It is undoubtedly a practice which needs concerted attention aimed at prevention, prosecution and healing for survivors. Effective actions to end rape in war need to be based in multivariate understandings of the phenomenon, acknowledging the deep historical roots, contemporary power relations and social structures and contextualized critiques of rape's function in specific conflicts. The prosecution of rape in war in some ways marks a radical departure from previous responses, but must also be scrutinised for inadvertent effects such as the potential for reinforcing unhelpful gendered ideals and its approach to rape in war as exceptional, thereby reinforcing a delinking from sexual violence in peace and from other types of violence that women experience. If rape, in both war and peace, is to be effectively addressed we require a radical restructuring of gender relations in society. Women need to be freed from the burden of honour and recognized legally, politically and socially as autonomous rights bearing human beings in their own right. This task requires a more holistic approach engaging prosecutions, health, reparations, long term attitudinal change programs and community development approaches.

REFERENCES

1. Arakawa, M. (2013) 'A New forum for Comfort Women: Fighting Japan in United States Federal Court' 16 Berkeley Journal of Gender, Law & Justice 174.
2. Bartels, S. (2010) Now the World is Without Me. An Investigation of Sexual Violence in Eastern Democratic Republic of Congo. Harvard Humanitarian Initiative and Oxfam International, Boston. Available: http://www.oxfam.org/sites/www.oxfam.org/files/file_attachments/DRC-sexual-violence-2010-04_2.pdf Accessed 20 September 2014
3. Chaikel, D. (2011) 'Does Gender Matter at the International Criminal Court?' The Hague Justice Portal Available: http://www.haguejusticeportal.net/index.php?id=12400 Accessed 16 September 2014
4. Chesterman, S. (1997) 'Never Again... and Again: Law, Order, and the Gender of War Crimes in Bosnia and Beyond' Yale Journal of International Law 22, pp. 299 - 343
5. Eaton, S. (2004) 'Sierra Leone: The Proving Ground for Prosecuting Rape as a War Crime' Georgetown Journal of International Law, 35, pp. 873 – 919
6. El-Bushra, J. and Mukarubuga, C. (1995) 'Women, War and Transition' Gender and Development 3(3) pp. 16 - 22
7. Fleshman, M. (2005) 'Tough UN line on peacekeeper abuses. Action initiated to end sexual misdeeds in peacekeeping missions' Africa Renewal. (April 2005) Available: http://www.un.org/africarenewal/magazine/april-2005/tough-un-line-peacekeeper-abuses Accessed 28 August 2014
8. Grewal, K. (2010) 'Rape in Conflict, Rape in Peace: Questioning the Revolutionary Potential of International Criminal Justice for Women's Human Rights' The Australian Feminist Law Journal 33, pp. 57 - 79
9. Lent Hirsch, M. and Wolfe, L. (2012) 'Conflicts Profile: Democratic Republic of Congo' Women Under Siege Project. Available http://www.womenundersiegeproject.org/conflicts/profile/democratic-republic-of-congo#reasons Accessed 19 September 2014
10. Loncar, M., Medved, V., Jovanovic, N. and Hotujac, L. (2006). 'Psychological Consequences of Rape on Women in 1991-1995 War in Croatia and Bosnia and Herzegovina' 47(1) Croatian Medical Journal 67.
11. Meger, S. (2010) Rape of the Congo: Understanding sexual violence in the conflict in the Democratic Republic of Congo, Journal of Contemporary African Studies, 28:2, pp. 119-135, DOI: 10.1080/02589001003736728
12. Mertus, J. (2004) 'Shouting from the Bottom of the Well. The Impact of International Trials for Wartime Rape on Women's Agency' International Feminist Journal of Politics, 6:1, 110-128
13. Mazurana, D, and Proctor, K, (2013) Gender, Conflict and Peace. An Occasional Paper. World Peace Foundation, Fletcher School, Tufts University, Boston
14. O'Connor, V. (2012) Prosecution of Rape as a War Crime International Network to Promote the Rule of Law (INPROL) July 2012 at http://www.inprol.org/publications/prosecution-of-rape-as-a-war-crime [accessed 16/09/2014]
15. Okello, M C, and Hovil, L, (2007), 'Confronting the Reality of Gender-Based Violence in Northern Uganda', International Journal of Transitional Justice, vol. 1 (3), pp. 433-443.
16. Palmieri, D., Branche, R., Horne, J., Lagrou, P., Virgili, F. and Delpla, I. (2012) 'Writing the History of Rape in Wartime' in Branche, R and Virgili, F. (ed.) Rape in Wartime Palgrave Macmillan, London
17. A Peterman, T Palermo and C Bredenkamp (2011) 'Estimates and Determinants of Sexual Violence Against Women in The Democratic Republic of Congo' American Journal of Public Health, 101(6), pp. 1060 -
18. Redress and African Rights (2008) Survivors and Post-Genocide Justice in Rwanda. Their experiences, perspectives and hopes. Redress and African Rights, London
19. Saigol, R. 'Gendered Conflicts: A Feminist Perspective on Knowledge of Conflict'
20. Snyder, C., Gabbard, W., May, D. and Zulcic, N. (2006) 'The Battleground of Women's Bodies: Mass Rape in Bosnia-Herzegovinia' Affilia vol.21, pp. 184 - 195
21. Turano, L. (2011) 'The Gender Dimension of Transitional Justice Mechanisms' 45 International Law and Politics 1045, 1047.

22. UN Special Rapporteur to the Commission on Human Rights, 'Report on the Situation of Human Rights in Rwanda' (E/CN.4/1996/68) at para 16 Available: http://www1.umn.edu/humanrts/commission/country52/68-rwa.htm Accessed 16 September 2014
23. Williams, K (2014) 'Conflicts Profile: Nanking' Women Under Siege Project. Available http://www.womenundersiegeproject.org/conflicts/profile/nanking
24. Accessed 21 September 2014
25. Wippman, D (2006) 'The costs of international justice' The American Journal of International Law 100(4), pp. 861 - 881
26. Yuval-Davis, N. (1993) Gender and nation, Ethnic and Racial Studies, 16:4, 621-632

CHAPTER 12

THE POLITICS OF UNIVERSALISM. STRATEGIC USES OF HUMAN RIGHTS DISCOURSES IN EARLY MODERNITY

Karen-Margrethe Simonsen

Keywords: Human rights, Politics of universalism, National sovereignty, America, Bartolomé de las Casas, Etienne Balibar, Power, Imperialism

"Is globalization promoting or undermining human rights prospects?" Micheline Ishay poses the question in her book on *The History of Human Rights*.[1] She concludes that globalization does both, blaming the undermining on the unequal economic development and explaining the increasing promotion by referring to the extended communication.[2] Ishay›s way of posing the question seems to think globalization as a complex reality and human rights as an ideal "prospect" that can or cannot be realized within this reality. Her question presupposes a dichotomy between real, factual globalization and ideal, cosmopolitan community. This dichotomy haunts discussions of human rights since human rights are never a fully established reality but seem to hover over us as a utopian hope yet to be fulfilled. Yet, one step in the direction of a critical reflection on the dichotomy is to ask how cosmopolitan ideals function in a concrete global and politicized world.

To focus on the politics of human rights may also help explain why human rights discourses turn up today at the very historical moment of the decline of political ideologies. Human rights are not ideology but they may serve the same utopian goals as political ideologies once served: that of envisioning and hopefully creating a better and more equal world. At the same time, human rights have a surprising function in historical and political culture, that of creating, legitimizing, branding, or even expanding different "local" communities: national, European, American, and so on.

Citation: Karen-Margrethe Simonsen, The politics of universalism. Strategic uses of human rights discourses in early modernity, doi.org/10.3402/jac.v5i0.23157.

Human rights discourses are thus a rewarding area of research when it comes to understanding the way local politics strategically relate to global and potentially universal communities. Human rights discourses are not only embedded within a globalized world, they are a central means of developing local–global dynamics. This can be seen at the very outset of European modernity, just as it can be seen today, when modern "universalists" or "cosmopolitanists" reshape European and global identity on the basis of human rights.[3] The paradoxical situation is that the development of human rights is tightly interwoven with the processes of globalization,— they can hardly be understood outside of this context—, but the content of human rights is supposed to be beyond these historical processes because it is universal. What we need to understand the function of human rights is therefore what Etienne Balibar has called "a politics of universalism."

A "politics of universalism" investigates the political mechanisms within universalism; it asks questions about the relations between subjectivity and power within specific contexts. In a radical reading of human rights, rights can only be true rights if the bearer of rights articulates them. No one can speak on behalf of somebody else. This is also what Balibar calls the "autonomy of politics," and this is one of the reasons why universalism always has to redefine the relationship between the global and the local. "Politics of universalism" is not to be confused with "universalism of politics." A politics of universalism is not about propagating the right politics or the right understanding of politics but about understanding the political function of universalism, or as Balibar describes it: "how politics defines itself when it refers to a *de jure* universality."[4]

This article claims that the public use of human rights discourses is split down the middle: it serves both as a means of widening the cosmopolitan understanding *and* as propagating local interests, or to phrase it differently: both as a critique of power and as an extension of power, and the disclosure of this split helps us understand the inner politics of human rights. However, the ambition is also to understand what kind of institution or discourse or what kind of agency that makes it possible to activate transnational or cosmopolitan arguments. The focus of the article is on the use of human rights discourses in 16th-century Spain, just after the discovery of the new world. In this period, when Spain develops into an empire, and tries to come to terms with her new power within a global world, there is a very visible link between human rights discourses and politics, as well as an interesting mix of national, global, and universalistic arguments concerning human or natural rights.

THE POLITICS OF HUMAN RIGHTS AND THE DISCOVERY OF THE NEW WORLD

As already hinted, the interest of the period of the 16th- and 17th century in the context of globalization is that the relation between the eternal and the worldly is being reconceptualised under the impression of global forces. Spain is in particular an interesting example, not only because of the legalistic culture of the country, but also because the discovery of the new world led to an explicit clash between universalistic, global and national logics. This is discernible in the debate on the humanity of the Indian and in the debates on the right of the Spanish crown to conquer and possess the new land. In Carl Schmitt's words, the question about "who is free" became extremely closely related to the question about "who decides."[5] From the very beginning of renaissance modernity, the question of who counts as a human being with universal rights was thus connected with the discussion of master–slave relations.

The simultaneity of the development of human rights and the imperialistic suppression of the rights of the Indians and the blindness of European intellectuals to this duplicity has often been pointed out. Most recently and convincingly by Susan Buck-Morss, who argues that not only is this a historical truth but also that an awareness of the fact must lead to a remapping of our understanding of the history of humanism—a remapping that is of importance in relation to actual discussions about *humanism*: "Present realities demand such historical remapping as an alternative to the fantasies of clashing civilizations and exclusionary redemptions."[6]

An important step in such a remapping is, according to Buck-Morss, the turn to dialectics: "to turn the tables" and ask: what if the "slave" (in this case, Haiti) is not seen as "a victim of Europe but as an agent in Europe's construction."[7] To make this move means not only to make a critique of the simultaneity of the development of European enlightenment and the development of slavery but also to pose the question of the relationship between humanism (the concept of natural freedom) and slavery (the restricted admission of equality). The question is how to understand this relationship. Is slavery only a sign of a certain regrettable but still historically admissible delay in the extension of freedom to all?—Or is there a more intricate link between freedom and slavery?

I will argue that the master–slave relation is not only an external relation between those who have rights and those who do not (yet) but also an internal relation between positions of power and powerlessness within human rights discourse. The political element is thus both outside and inside human rights. Etienne Balibar has coined the term "equaliberty" for designating what he believes to be the true political moment, which is marked both by freedom and equality. It cannot only be liberty since this does not guarantee access to the political scene. Therefore, he sees the *Declaration of the Rights of Man and the Citizen* (1789) as a decisive statement of politics. The declaration states the principle of autonomy, that is, the fact that no one can be *made* equal by an external force, since "politics is an unfolding of the self-determination of the people" or, Balibar says, referring to Kant, politics is "the people›s own responsibility."[8] However, in order for a group of people to have this responsibility, it has to be recognized as a subject who is the bearer of universal rights without being idealized as universal bearer of rights, or even worse: as a universal victim which would bestow a false pathos on the universal.

Just as in the case of Buck-Morss, dialecticism is the answer to the problem of the excluded and victimized people. However, the problem of understanding the function of human rights and politics is not only on the side of the dominated but also on the side of that who dominates. Balibar›s argument here rests on a displacement of Nietzsche›s argument that democratic politics expresses a "slave morality." Balibar writes:

The most important thing here is not the counter-revolutionary stigmatization of a politics made by and for the masses, nor the correlative idealization of exceptional individuals, but the proposal of an analysis and a genealogy which lay bare the mechanics by which hegemony is constructed and consensus engineered. I shall take the liberty of advancing the following interpretation: domination by an established order does indeed rest, as Marx argued after Hegel, on the ideological universalization of its principles. But, contrary to what Marx believed, the 'dominant ideas' cannot be those of the 'dominant class'. They have to be those of the 'dominated', the ideas which state their theoretical right to recognition and equal capacity. More precisely, the discourse of hegemonic domination has to be one in which it is possible to appeal against a *de facto* discrimination to a *de jure* equality – […].[9]

There are four important points to be made here: first that Balibar's understanding of human rights undermines the self-evidence of "human rights for all"—universalism and in contrast opens up for a discussion of social power-relations between dominated and dominant within human rights discourses. The dominated can only in ambiguous ways become subjective bearers of the universal, and the dominant cannot universalize themselves without contradicting themselves. They are dependent on the dominated for their own position. Equality is thus not only a right or an ideal of the suppressed, but also and necessarily, a strategic ideal of the suppressors.[10] Second, that the mechanics of politics and human rights are historically dynamic, meaning that positions can be changed and transformed. Third, that the idea of incorporating human rights within a general understanding of a "politics of universalism" avoids the eternal debate between universalism and historicism. Universalism cannot be reduced to history, but neither does it float in an ideal sphere by itself. Finally, and most important in my context, the insistence on the double character of "*de facto* discrimination" and "*de jure* equality" of hegemonic domination creates an interdependent relationship between "master" and "slave."

The appeal of any hegemonic power to universalism, thus necessarily implies that it becomes purged with a "slave morality." If this logic is established, all protests can, according to Balibar, "turn into legitimation since, against the injustice of the established order, protest appeals not to something heterogeneous to that order, but to identical principles."[11] Balibar relates his analysis to the period of Enlightenment but claim it to constitute a general principle, even in non-democratic societies.

Now, my question is how that relates to the early period of globalization and to the Spanish empire? In the 16th-century Spain, royal power was absolute and despotic: national sovereignty was established and strengthened from the conquest of Granada and through the following centuries. Spain became the Empire where the sun never sets; Spanish conquerors ruled and behaved in the new land as they wanted to. According to numerous reports the Spanish conquest was extremely violent; thousands of aborigines died or were deprived of their land and property, and turned into slaves. Yet at the same time, the Spanish Kings,—from Ferdinand and Isabella to Charles V and Phillip II—seemed to be extremely preoccupied both with the legal foundation of the conquest, with the justice of it, *and* with the wellbeing of the aborigines.

According to Lewis Hanke, who is still considered to have written one of the most important books on the issue, this royal preoccupation and "care for the aborigines" was not only a symptom of bad conscience or lip-service to mitigate critical voices about the violence of the conquest, but was an earnest interest in moral universalism in the midst of an extremely tense political climate.[12]However, keeping Balibar's dialectics of universalism in mind, one may ask how this "de jure universalism" was used politically in the face of the undeniable evidence of the "de facto" discrimination of the Indians during the conquest. Why should the king be interested in showing interest in human rights?

Let us have a look at one of the most interesting historical examples of a politically motivated trial about universalism.

POLITICS OF HUMAN RIGHTS IN PRACTICE: UNIVERSALISM ON TRIAL

In 1550, Charles V set up an astounding "trial" in Valladolid. The aim of the trial was to establish whether the Spanish conquest and warfare in America was just or unjust. King Charles V (King Charles I in Spain) called for this "trial" after some years where doubt had been raised regarding the legitimacy of the Spanish conquest; and not least the legitimacy of the brutality of the Spanish conquest. Ever since the papal bull *Inter Caetera* from 1493, in which the Spanish born Pope Alexander VI "by the authority of the almighty God" had "given" all islands and mainlands west of The Azores and Cape Verde to the Spanish King, Spain had claimed that she entered upon the conquest "by divine justice."[13] Papal authority bestowed universalistic value on the conquest and the Spanish King took this so seriously that he ordered the words of the pope to be inscribed in the Requirement that by royal decree was to be carried across the ocean by the Spanish conquerors and read to the Indians before the conquest could take place.[14]

Since the very beginning of the Spanish conquest, its legitimacy and its fairness had been debated and critiqued not only by other nations who questioned the Spanish right to all land west of the Azores, but also by ecclesiastics, soldiers, and jurists inside of Spain. However, it was not until 1532 that an important Spanish jurist questioned the authority of the papal bull. This was done by the Dominican monk and jurist Francisco de Vitoria, who is often said to be the founder of modern international law. In his *De Indis De Jure Belli* from 1532, Francisco de Vitoria claimed in a number of titles that "The Pope [was] not civil or temporal lord of the whole world, in the proper sense of civil lordship and power." that "Even if the Supreme Pontiff had secular power over the world, he could not give that power to secular princes," that the Pope had temporal power "but only so far as it [subserved] things spiritual" and finally that "The Pope [had] no temporal power over the Indian aborigines or over other unbelievers."[15]

In 1550, at the time of the trial of Valladolid, Francisco de Vitoria had died but there was another Dominican monk, namely Bartolomé de las Casas who defended the Indians. If Francisco de Vitoria is said to be the forerunner of international law,[16] Bartolomé de las Casas is often said to be the forerunner of modern human rights. In the trial, two conflicting views on the conquest and the status of the Indians were presented before The Council of Valladolid and Prince Philip, the son of King Charles. Bartolomé de las Casas was up against the royal historian and renaissance humanist Juan Ginés de la Sepúlveda who had just recently translated Aristotle›s *Politics* into Spanish. Sepúlveda enjoyed huge prestige and was backed up by different parties of interest. He spoke for one whole day and argued mainly, referring to Aristotle›s idea of natural slaves, that the Indians "are barbaric, uninstructed in letters and the art of government, and completely ignorant, unreasoning, and totally incapable of learning anything but the mechanical arts; that they are sunk in vice, are cruel, and of such a character that, as nature teaches, they are to be governed by the will of others."[17] Bartolomé de las Casas in turn spoke for 5 days, reading his *In Defense of the Indians* that was intended to show how Sepúlveda was wrong both in law and in fact.[18] Las Casas argued that native Americans were human beings, capable of reason and culture and that they lived according to a structured social order.

The text of *In Defense of the Indians* is an interesting hybrid of philosophical, theological, anthropological, and political arguments. In contrast with Vitoria and Sepúlveda, who never left Europe, Las Casas had made four extensive journeys in America; this and the fact that Las Casas was an exceptionally learned scholar contributed highly to the authority of the text. However, the controlling logic of the rhetoric in the text is political in the sense that it is oriented toward political action. Bartolomé de las Casas went through all the classical arguments about barbarism, but his interest was not philosophical—not even theological. His aim was to change the politics of the conquest. He did not, as Vitoria had done, question the papal bull but claimed that the Spaniards had corrupted and twisted the meaning of it.[19] According to

Las Casas, the papal bull was not meant to legitimize the "destruction of the Indies" but only to authorize the peaceful spreading of the Christian religion.[20]

Bartolomé de las Casas insist on the universalism of Christian religion to criticize or correct temporal power. He initiates his speech by addressing the young Prince Philip, reminding him of his subordinance to the faith of Christ: "you strive for immortal glory, not just with the imperial power but especially with the generous spirit and the wisdom that has been implanted in you by Christ."[21]Two pages later, he brings in the universalism of natural law as an argument against the military campaigns of the conquest:

What good can come from these military campaigns [...] how will that nation love us, how will they become our friends (which is necessary if they are to accept our religion) when children see themselves deprived of parents, wives of husbands, and fathers of children and friends? When they see those they love wounded, imprisoned, plundered, and reduced from an immense number to a few? When they see their rulers stripped of their authority, cursed, and afflicted with a wretched slavery? All these things flow necessarily from war. Who is there who would want the gospel preached to himself in such a fashion? Does not this negative precept apply to all men in general: "See that you do not do to another, what you would not have done to you by another"? And the same for the affirmative command: "So always treat others as you would like them to treat you." This is something that every man knows, grasps, and understands by the natural light that has been imparted to our minds.[22]

The reference for this universal feeling is the Bible (Matthew 7:12), but the argument is that this is a natural law: common to all men, no matter what religion they belong to. For Bartolomé de las Casas, the force of Christianity is not based in the power of the church but in the power of the universal message. Las Casas supports the papal bulls but makes it clear that the Pope is or has to be an incarnation of the general universalism of Christianity. Thus, when he explains that Sepúlveda has misunderstood the papal bull because it does not legitimize war on the Indians, he goes on to ask "For how would he [the Pope] permit something that conflicts with Christ's precepts and instruction and produces hatred of the name of Christ in the hearts of unbelievers and is utterly irreligious?"[23] This sounds like a warning to anyone who would dare to make war in the name of Christ, even a warning to the Pope himself.

However, for Las Casas, the universalism of Christianity is not only a set of axiomatic rules or ethical commands. Universalism can only be understood in its incorporation into differentiated living reality. This point becomes clear when Las Casas moves on to a discussion of what universalism is in relation to the understanding of the barbarian. Whereas Aristotle and Sepúlveda speak of natural slavery as an eternal state of a specific other, namely the barbarian, las Casas develops a flexible and multi-layered understanding of the barbarian. Las Casas takes his point of departure in the four categories of barbarians, as defined by Aristotle in *Politics* (books 1 and 3) and *Ethics*(book 7), and by Thomas Aquinas and "other doctors in various places".[24]

Let us look briefly at these arguments. Against the argument, that the barbarian is an "inhuman, wild, merciless" person, Bartolomé de las Casas argues that this kind of barbarianism is found in all cultures. Against the argument that barbarians are "people who do not have a written language that corresponds to the spoken one," this is not, Las Casas says, an absolute definition but a relative one, and he quotes Paul: "If I am ignorant of what the sound means, I am a barbarian to the man who is speaking and he is a barbarian to me."[25]

The third definition of barbarians is that they are people who have an evil character and live in barren regions and are stupid and strangers to reason. They are not governed by any law, do not cultivate friendships and do not have any organized community. These are barbarians in an absolute sense and according to Aristotle it is legitimate to try to subordinate them. Against this view, Las Casas argues that there can only be very few of these, since otherwise the creation of God must be considered bad, and Las Casas adds: "Who therefore, except one who is irreverent toward God and contemptuous of nature, has dared to write that countless numbers of natives across the ocean are barbarous, savage, uncivilized, and slow witted, when, if they are evaluated by an accurate judgment, they completely outnumber all other men?" writes Las Casas.[26] The sheer number of Indians makes it impossible for them to be barbarians. The person who had "dared to write that countless numbers of natives across the ocean are barbarous, savage, uncivilized, and slow witted" was Juan Ginés de Sepúlveda who here is turned into a blasphemous person—an intolerable position for a man who considered himself a true Christian and who heavily leaned on the decree of the Pope Alexandre VI who had given the Indies to Spain.

Finally, Las Casas argues that even if the Indians are evil, or their community is ruled by tyrants, you have to acknowledge that they have well-administered kingdoms with own autonomy that you cannot break. Las Casas goes on to argue: "Do you think that the Romans, once they had subjugated the wild and barbaric peoples of Spain, could with secure right divide all of you among themselves, handing over so many head of both males and females as allotments to individuals"? Here Las Casas comes close to the arguments of Francisco de Vitoria who had argued in favor of political autonomy of the Indian kingdoms, even in the cases when they were tyrannies, thus paving the way for the foundation of national sovereignty within international law.

Las Casas thus develops his arguments with strategic shifts between universalist and relativist perspectives. When confronted with relativist views (for instance that the Indians are different from us), he makes use of the universal argument of common nature, and when confronted with the universalistic argument of natural slavery, he opposes the relativistic view that the Indians have their own, independent culture.

This is also what we see in modern discussions on human rights. Boaventura Sousa-Santos for instance explains that the essence of human rights is that "We have the right to be equal whenever difference diminishes us; we have the right to be different whenever equality decharacterizes us."[27] Human rights are thus not just emerged in universal self-evidence, the very universalism itself will be negotiated in every new situation of application.

The persuasiveness of Las Casas' text depends on the flexibility of argument, but how did the King react to it? It was already an exceptional situation that the King had allowed the trial to put a halt on all expeditions. No ships were sent to America while Sepúlveda and Las Casas were talking and the commission worked on their procedures. But to understand all the political dimensions of this discourse, it has to be placed in its historical context.

BARTOLOMÉ DE LAS CASAS: A HUMANIST OR A BATTERING RAM FOR IMPERIALISM?

The direct outcome of the trial was relatively poor. Both Sepúlveda and Las Casas declared themselves to be winners, but the "court" was not able to reach a common decision. It was even difficult for the king to get the 14 members of the commission to write their opinions.[28] But it is generally assumed that Bartolomé de las Casas symbolically won the case in the long run. Even if the conquests did not stop, as Las Casas had wished, they became more pacific. The king forbade the use of the word "conquest." Instead the word "pacification" should be used, and the Spaniards were requested to try to persuade the aborigines to surrender by peaceful means.[29] Another significant indication was that the works of Sepúlveda were censored by the Inquisition while those by Bartolomé de las Casas were allowed to be printed, even the book *A Very Short Description of the Destruction of the Indies* (*Una brevísima relación de la destruición de las Indias*, 1552).[30]Bartolomé de las Casas had already begun writing the book in 1542, before the trial in Valladolid. The book gave a gruesome and detailed account of the horrors of the Spanish conquest. It told how the Spanish conquerors tortured and killed aborigines for the sake of winning gold, without reason, or for the sheer fun of killing. It can be regarded as an early example of "sensational journalism" or "atrocity tale."[31] Even if the Spanish conquest was very violent, the book is also exaggerating, but the sensational aspect was decisively underlined when it was re-published in 1598, containing horrific illustrations of torture scenes drawn by Theodore de Bry.

Theodore de Bry, Illustration for Brevísima relación de la destrucción de las Indias, 1598.

Copied from Wikipedia, http://en.wikipedia.org/wiki/File:De_Bry_1c.JPG, downloaded, Nov. 19, 2013, Commons, (582×509 pixels, file size: 385 KB, MIME type: image/jpeg). Free reproduction.

Bartolomé de las Casas' book was permitted publication in Spain and was not censored until more than 100 years later (in 1659).[32] Abroad it was one of the most published and read books. Between 1578 and 1648, 21 Dutch, eight Italian, six French, four German, two English, and two Latin translations were published. All in all 43 translations appeared in 70 years.[33] This book alone was enormously important in creating the Black Legend about the Spanish conquest, and it damaged the image of Spain abroad considerably. In an historical moment, when Spain was still the strongest imperial power in America, the idea that the Spanish conquest was cruel and inhuman was extremely valuable for the competing imperialistic nations, especially the Netherlands but also for France and England. According to Consuelo de Varela, in the hands of the British, the Dutch and the French, this legendary book turned into a "political weapon of the first order" ("un arma política de primer orden").[34]

The question is thus: why did the Spanish king allow such a damaging book to be printed? What was the political motivation? Can there be any national political motivation for the exposure of national responsibility for atrocities and "infringements" of human rights? As mentioned before, Lewis Hanke argues that the King was preoccupied with the Christian foundation of the conquest. There was an earnest ethical concern at play.

A reverse motivation could be that the critique made by Bartolomé de las Casas' of the violence of the conquest made it easier for the King to uphold political control over the conquerors. As Carl Schmitt has argued, political sovereignty is dependent on social order.[35] Fifty years after the Conquest, the problem of the king was not only how to gain wealth through the exploitation of the newly conquered land but also how to control the conquerors themselves. The King was extremely aware that the conquest was in risk of developing into pure chaos, if the conquerors were not kept in order. In this way, paradoxically, Bartolomé de las Casas' humanism served the King as yet a further tool in the imperialistic endeavors. Bartolomé de las Casas' extreme unpopularity among the conquerors also point in this direction.

As Daniel Castro has explained it in his highly critical study, Las Casas' critique of the violence and especially his wish to forbid the *encomiendas*[36]: "meshed perfectly with the crown's desire to limit the power of its subjects in the American kingdoms, thus Las Casas either advisedly or inadvertently once again ended up serving as the battering ram of an imperialist center."[37] In short, Bartolomé de las Casas' continuous critique of the conquerors' violence served as an excuse for the King to "remind" the *encomenderos* of the sovereignty of the king and the need to keep in order. This point of view is supported by the fact that Bartolomé de las Casas never made a critique of the conquest as such. He could not since he believed that it served the legitimate goal of christening the Indians. He just thought that the conquest should be enacted with peaceful means.[38]

Though Las Casas was later to condemn all means of force and insist on the voluntariness of conversion, there was no doubt about his ambition of converting the aborigines to the Christian faith. This is where the Christian mission departs from its own universal aspirations and an inner contradiction between the universal and the political appears. In Balibar's terms, this is an example of bad "politics of the universal" in the sense that it is about "propagating the right politics" or the right version of universalism, which is a logical self-contradiction.

In the historical situation, Las Casas' universalism seemed to serve the king's political goals, and therefore it is not a surprise that the King tolerated Las Casas' fierce critique of Spanish brutality. Yet, there may also be a third reason for the King's tolerance toward Las Casas', and this reason takes us to the heart of the politics of human rights. According to this line of thought, the King's apparent interest in the wellbeing of the Indians is really an interest in securing the foundation of sovereign power. Sovereignty is thus not seen (only) as a self-confirming, self-evident principle of power; in a paradoxical dialectic it is dependent on the subjects it represses. According to this line of thought, the King is preoccupied with the justice of the conquest because, ultimately, it is only the justice of the conquest that can logically legitimize the royal power and royal imperialism.

One could argue that the sovereignty of the King undermines this dialectics, since sovereignty is defined as the ability to rule as one pleases without asking anybody if it is legitimate or not; neither friends, nor enemies or subjects. In none of the historical discourses about human rights, discussed in this article, does any Indian interfere. The Indians do not speak for themselves. They are only represented. So the type of agency, conferred on the Indians here, is not direct agency and thus not political autonomy.

Yet, there is one way in which the Indians appear as if they had agency. This in the way that they are installed in the discourse as a possibly resisting subject. According to Balibar, even absolute power is dialectical, since it "presupposes a resistance" (17). And the renaissance and early baroque period in Spain, the period of the counterreformation, is dominated by a strong populism that presupposes the resistance that it tries to annihilate. In this specific sense, the Indians are seen as a people with agency.

As I wrote earlier: the use of human rights discourses in this early period is split down the middle: it serves both as a critique of power and as an extension of power, be that royal or ecclesiastic. The interesting thing is that "critique" and "extension" of power are part of the one and same discourse or dialectic. This raises a fundamental doubt about the status of human rights and the status of any humanism launched in the name of subjected people. Keeping Balibar's dialectics of universalism in mind, we must ask how the historical "de jure universalism" was used politically in the face of the undeniable evidence of the "de facto" discrimination of the Indians during the conquest, or how this bad politicization of human rights undermined the true politics of universalism.

UNIVERSALISM AND GLOBALIZATION TODAY

True politics of universalism demands autonomy of politics, as defined by Etienne Balibar. This means agency of the subjects involved in the political moment, and an avoidance of the victimization of the suppressed. One important step toward this is also a redefinition of power. In the essay "Toward a European 'Antistrategic' Policy", Balibar writes that we have to transform "the way we understand the concept of politics in relation with the idea of 'power'":

What I suggest is that we need to explore a completely different path, where *power does not predate action but is rather its result*, in a sense that depends upon the goals that one wants to achieve. It is action, or agency that produces the degree and distribution of power, not the reverse.[39]

This conception of power does not aim at constituting a new, great power, but at constituting a "*new type of power*, one that nobody can appropriate. [...] This type of power is essentially a new *correlation among the existing forces*".[40] The anti-strategic strategy of this new powerpolitics is meant to invite real interaction and collaboration that dissolves, or at least reinterprets the master–slave logic of power.

This vision of correlative, powerful action may be less utopian than it seems and in certain ways, it catches also the way that discussions about human rights and transnational legal culture proliferates itself through our global world. As Boaventura Sousa-Santos wrote already in 1995 about the transnationalization of the legal field:

Rather than being the product of an intellectual crusade by well-meaning jurists or philosophers, the transnationalization of the legal field is being promoted by practicing lawyers, state bureaucrats, and international institutions, as well as by popular movements and NGOs. Far from being a monolithic phenomenon, it is extremely diverse, combining uniformity with local differentiation, top-down impositions with bottom-up creation, formal declaration with interstitial emergence, boundary-maintaining orientation with boundary-transcending orientation.[41]

The international or rather global legal culture is thus a set of activities with a lot of different agents. The problem is that whereas peoples' lives and a lot of legal activity are border-crossing by nature: [the] legal protection of human beings seems to be much more territorialized than the legal protection of goods and services. [...] In a world saturated with an ideology of rights, and undergoing a period of intense globalization, the challenges posed by this "black hole" heavily underscore the sociological and political need to analyse the movements of people across national borders.[42]

Since World War II, human rights courts and human rights discourses have tried to bridge the gulf between independent nation-states. The Universal Declaration of Human Rights from 1948 proclaims the universal declaration of human rights "as a common standard of achievement for all peoples and all nations."[43] And the International Military Tribunal of the Nuremberg trials put forward in its charter that crimes against humanity legitimate a supranational or transnational interference in national sovereignty.[44]

However, if Boaventura de Sousa-Santos is right in his analysis, our problem is not only that of nations who claim to have a sovereign right to suppress their own people, it is also our problem that the legal system and vocabulary cannot fathom border-crossing reality. In that sense, the universalism of human rights will "always" come too late and there will always be a "black hole" to fill out. The solution, if there is one, is to turn the tables around, and start the discussion of human rights in living reality itself. As the historical example in this article shows, only flexible legal arguments that mix universal and relativist arguments may be able to catch up with the variability of reality. One first step in this direction is to stop treating human rights as if they were a valuable goal with imminent values in themselves. Human rights are only a means of achieving more justice, but if they are understood in a too rigid way with a stable vocabulary, as Balibar says: with too much pathos, they will not be able to work in living reality.

In recent uses of human rights discourses, it is obvious that human rights are seen not only as being related to individual rights, nor even to specific interests of class within a nation, but are used to support our sense of community in a global world. This is what Costas Douzinas has called the "Triumph of Human Rights" and he relates it directly to the post-ideological, postmodern global world that "unites left and right, the pulpit and the state, the minister and the rebel, the developing world and the liberals of Hampstead and Manhattan."[45]

However, this kind of triumph of human rights can only act at the most superficial rhetorical level. This is why I stated in the beginning that the question posed by Michelin Ishay: "Is globalization promoting or undermining human rights prospects?" should be turned around thus: "Are human rights promoting or undermining globalization,—meaning global community?" What kind of community is installed by a human rights regime? Since human rights discourses can be used equally well by the master and the slave—by sovereign power and suppressed people—human rights should always be analysed in their actual political setting. The question is always: who is speaking on behalf of whom, when we talk about human rights? What kind of subjectivity and what kind of liberation is at stake? Globalization holds the hope of universal community, and human rights seem to further such a community, but only if its politics is understood and acknowledged.

Seen from an historical and European point of view, there is no doubt that the first wave of globalization after the conquest of America promoted discussions on human rights and thus laid the ground for modern Europe.[46] Hence, Europe did not become modern because she invented human rights, Europe invented or developed the human rights because a global experience forced her to reflect on humanity and she did so not only out of a moral imperative, but also out of necessity and through violent social and discursive battles. However, in this early period of modernity, it is also clear that human rights discourses are never neutral as such. It is not only a battle for and against human rights; it is a battle about the right understanding of human rights and especially their role within a community. Human rights are promoted from different power-positions and with different political intentions that reinterpret the most basic sense of human, cultural and political community.

REFERENES

1. Micheline R. Ishay, *The History of Human Rights. From Ancient Times to the Globalization Era*(Berkeley and Los Angeles: University of California Press, 2008, 2004), 13.
2. Ibid., 13.
3. Etienne Balibar (for instance in *We The People of Europe* (Princeton: Princeton University Press, 2004)); and Ulrich Beck and Edgar Grande (for instance in *Cosmopolitan Europe* (Malden: Polity Press, 2008)) can be mentioned as significant examples.
4. Etienne Balibar, *Politics and the Other Scene* (London: Verso, 2002), 2. (First published as chapters in *La crainte des masses*, (1997) and *Droit de cité*, (1998).
5. Carl Schmitt, *The Nomos of the Earth in the International Law of the Jus Publicum Europaeum*, trans. G. L. Ulmen (New York: Telos Press Publishing, 2003), 15.
6. Susan Buck-Morss, *Hegel, Haiti, and Universal History* (Pittsburgh: University of Pittsburgh Press, 2009), 79.
7. Ibid., 80.
8. Balibar, *Politics and the Other Scene*, 3.
9. Ibid., 7.
10. Balibar argues that it must be so, seen from a logical point of view. "The proposition of equal liberty, as stated in revolutionary terms, has a remarkable logical form, which has, since the Greeks, been termed an *elegkhos* or, in other words, a self-refutation of its negation. It states the fact that it is impossible to maintain to a logical conclusion, without absurdity, the idea of perfect civil liberty based on discrimination, privilege and inequalities of condition […] just as it is impossible to conceive and institute equality between human beings based on despotism (even 'enlightened' despotism) or on a monopoly of power." (Balibar, *Politics and the Other Scene*, 3).
11. Ibid., 7.
12. Lewis Hanke, *The Spanish Struggle for Justice in the Conquest of America* (Dallas: Southern Methodist University Press, 2002), According to Hanke, the discussions on the problems of America reveal "both the highly developed individualism of the Spaniards and a deliberate, imaginative, and courageous attempt by the crown and the Spanish people to shoulder the heavy burdens placed on Spain by her political and ecclesiastical dominion in America" (10). Hanke states later that even when the "[i]mpatient conquistadores champed at the bit while intricate discussions were held concerning the applicability to the Indians of the Aristotelian doctrine of slavery." "The crown continued to listen to those idealists who had been responsible for the experiments [of making peaceful, farming settlements in America] and even for a time suspended conquest in America while its justice was being debated at Valladolid" (174).
13. In the first few years after the conquest, the line between the old and the new order was symbolically represented in the making of geographical and geopolitical demarcation lines between the old and the new world and the distribution of ownership according to these lines. This distribution of ownership was initialized by the Pope, Alexander VI, who in a papal bull *Inter Caetera* (from 1493) drew a geographical line from the North Pole to the South just west of Cape Verde. In the bull *Inter Caetera*, the Pope takes the position of a sovereign ruler, who by divine justice is able to decide upon the borders of the new geographical order, and decide who has the right to explore and conquest the new territories: And, in order that you may enter upon so great an undertaking with greater readiness and heartiness endowed with the benefit of our apostolic favor, we, of our own accord, not at your instance nor the request of anyone else in your regard, but of our own sole largess and certain knowledge and out of the fullness of our apostolic power, by the authority of Almighty God

conferred upon us in blessed Peter and of the vicarship of Jesus Christ, which we hold on earth, do by tenor of these presents, should any of said islands have been found by your envoys and captains, give, grant, and assign to you and your heirs and successors, kings of Castile and Leon, forever, together with all their dominions, cities, camps, places, and villages, and all rights, jurisdictions, and appurtenances, all islands and mainlands found and to be found, discovered and to be discovered towards the west and south, by drawing and establishing a line from the Arctic pole, namely the north, to the Antarctic pole, namely the south, no matter whether the said mainlands and islands are found and to be found in the direction of India or towards any other quarter, the said line to be distant one hundred leagues towards the west and south from any of the islands commonly known as the Azores and Cape Verde." http://www.catholic-forum.com/saints/pope0214a.htm (accessed March 25, 2012).

14. Hanke, *The Spanish Struggle for Justice*, 33.
15. Francisco de Vitoria, Section 3, Part 2, De Indis De Jure Belli, http://en.wikisource.org/wiki/De_Indis_De_Jure_Belli/Part_2 (accessed December 6, 2011).
16. See for example James Brown Scott, *The Spanish Origin of International Law. Francisco de Vitoria and his Law of Nations* (Oxford: Clarendon Press, 1934).
17. Bartolomé de la Vega, "Summary of Sepúlveda›s position", in *Bartolomé de las Casas*, trans. C. M. Stafford Poole (DeKalb, IL: Northern Illinois University Press, 1992), 15.
18. Bartolomé de las Casas, *In Defense of the Indians*, 28. Las Casas and Sepúlveda never actually met in the courtroom. They presented their pleas individually before the 14 members of the court. Las Casas' speech was so long that the court afterwards commissioned one of the members to make a resume of his main points.
19. Ibid., 26.
20. "Destruction of the Indies" is part of the title of his famous book *Brevísima relación de la destrucción de las Indes* that came out in 1552 but that he was writing already from 1542 and on. Regarding the misunderstanding of the papal bull, see Bartolomé de las Casas, *In Defense of the Indians*, 26.
21. Las Casas, *In Defense of the Indians*, 17.
22. Ibid., 27.
23. Ibid., 349.
24. Ibid., 28.
25. Ibid., 31.
26. Ibid., 35.
27. Boaventura de Sousa-Santos, *Toward a New Commons Sense. Law, Science and Politics in the Paradigmatic Transition* (New York: Routledge, 1995), 1059.
28. Lewis Hanke notes that as late as 1557, 6 years after the trial a note was sent to one of the members, Friar Melchor Cano, to ask him to immediately send his decision, Hanke, *The Spanish Struggle for Justice,* 129.
29. Hanke, *The Spanish Struggle for Justice*, 130–31.
30. Ibid., 129–30.
31. Giovanna Borradori, "Tiny Sparks of Contingency. On the Aesthetics of Human Rights", in *Philosophical Dimensions of Human Rights. Some Contemporary Views*, ed. Claudio Corradetti (Springer Science Press, 2012), 157–72, 156, http://www.springer.com/philosophy/value+theory/book/978-94-007-2375-7 (accessed October 4, 2012).
32. The Spanish Inquisition had been founded in 1480 by the monarchs Fernando and Isabella as an instrument not only for religious but also political control. Thus it did not only focus on the danger of Arabic and Jewish influence, it also served as a general political means of control in a period when Spain was establishing itself as a sovereign nation and an empire.
33. Consuelo Varela, "Introducción Biográfica y crítica" ("Biographic introduction and criticism"), in *Brevísima relación de la destrucción de las Indias* (Very brief account of the destruction of the Indies) (Madrid: Ed. Castalia, 1999), 50.
34. Juan Friede and Benjamin Keen, *Bartolomé de las Casas. Toward an Understanding of the Man and his Work* (De Kalb, IL: Northern Illinois University Press, 1971), 10ff.
35. Carl Schmitt, *The Nomos of the Earth in the International Law of the Jus Publicum Europaeum*, trans. G. L. Ulmen (New York: Telos Press Publishing, 2003).
36. The system of *encomiendas* secured the right of Spanish farmers to use Indians as slaves.
37. Daniel Castro, *Another Face of Empire, Bartolomé de las Casas. Indigenous Rights, and Ecclesiastical Imperialism* (Durham: Duke University Press, 2007), 153.
38. In his early critique of the laws of Burgos, created in 1512 to mitigate the fierceness of the conquest, Bartolomé de las Casas criticizes for instance the law that said that Indians must live in villages close to the Spaniards in houses with 12 people in them and that to avoid that they move back, the Spanish burnt their villages. He criticizes the fact that a pregnant woman could be sent to the mines and he protests against the law that permits the Indian to make a loan of one gold peso every year, ridiculing it by saying that for this amount of money, one could only get a couple of combs and a mirror. But Las Casas does not protest against the laws that were to Christianize the aborigines. Law number 4 said that all Indians should be rehearsed in their knowledge of Christ every 14 days, law number 10 said that all Indians must have a Christian burial and law number 17 that all sons of caciques who were under the age of 13 should go for 4 years to the Franciscans to learn about God. Andreas Wesch, *Kommentierte Edition und linguistische Untersuchung der Información de los Jerónimos, Santo Domingo 1517* (Commented edition and linguistic investigation of the rapports from los Jerónimos) (Tübingen: Gunter Narr Verlag, 1993), 48–68.
39. Etienne Balibar, *We, The People of Europe? Reflections on Transnational Citizenship*(Princeton: Princeton University Press, 2004), 221.
40. Ibid., 225.
41. Boaventura de Sousa-Santos, *Toward a New Common*

Sense, 252.

42. Ibid., 295.

43. See *Universal Declaration of Human Rights*, http://www.un.org/en/documents/udhr/ (accessed October 4, 2012).

44. Excerpt from Part II: "Jurisdiction and General Principles", *Nuremberg Trial Proceedings, Vol. 1, Charter of the International Military* Tribunal, 1945, "(c)CRIMES AGAINST HUMANITY: namely, murder, extermination, enslavement, deportation, and other inhumane acts committed against any civilian population, before or during the war; or persecutions on political, racial or religious grounds in execution of or in connection with any crime within the jurisdiction of the Tribunal, whether or not in violation of the domestic law of the country where perpetrated." http://avalon.law.yale.edu/imt/imtconst.asp#art6 (accessed October 4, 2012), See also Daniel Levy and Natan Sznaider, *The Holocaust and Memory in the Global Age*, trans. Assenka Oksiloff (Philadelphia, PA: Temple University Press, 2002, 93 and Beck, 2003), 34.

45. Costas Douzinas, *The End of Human Rights, Critical Legal Thought at the Turn of the Century*(Oxford: Hart Publishing), 1.

46. They were of course not human rights in the way we understand it today, but natural rights. However, for the sake of clarity I keep the term human rights all the way through. Mauricio Beuchot has argued that these early rights in Las Casas should be understood as proper human rights because they are rights for all human subjects and for all peoples. Mauricio Beuchot, *Los fundamentos de los derechos humanos en Bartolomé de las Casas* (Barcelona: Anthropos, 1994), 13.

CHAPTER 13

REFRAMING POST-MUGABE JUSTICE: A CRITICAL NEED FOR A TRUTH AND RECONCILIATION COMMISSION

Admore Tshuma

Keywords: Zimbabwe, Human rights, Injustice, Truth commissions, Reconciliation, Injustice, Redress, reparations.

INTRODUCTION

Those upon the margins of transitional justice's disciplinary boundaries are beginning to understand the need for an alternative approach in reconciling troubled and divided nations (Stanley, 2001, 2005; Hayner, 1998; Scharf, 1997; Laplante, 2008). This realisation is invariably prompted by society's failure to divorce with the past, particularly in countries where there have been human rights violations such as in Zimbabwe.

In the early 1980s, just as when many African nations were congratulating Zimbabweans for successfully executing the struggle for independence, the same revolutionary structure that had championed the liberation war began to come apart. The Patriotic Front comprising the Zimbabwe African People Union (led by Joshua Nkomo) and Zimbabwe African National Union (led by Robert Mugabe) - that had for two decades confronted the minority Rhodesian[1] government of Ian Douglas Smith started squabbling amongst themselves, leading up to unprecedented cases of human rights abuses (Nkomo, 1984).

Human rights concerns in Zimbabwe have been well-articulated, not only by local and international media, but also by Non-Governmental Organisations such as the Catholic Commission for Justice and Peace (CCJ), and the Legal Resources Foundation of Zimbabwe (LRFZ). Perhaps, the CCJ and LRFZ, (1999) correctly captures what went wrong in post-colonial Zimbabwe.

People have been tortured, seen their dead ones murdered or abducted, had their houses burnt. No efforts have been made to alleviate their plight and those who caused the damage have not been made answerable (CCJ and LRF, 1999, p30).

The conflict that ensued was fought seemingly without respect for Human Rights (Human Rights Watch, 2007). What happened were clear cases of violation of civil and political rights alongside social, economic and cultural rights. The Ndebele people of Zulu origin who supported the election losing candidate Joshua Nkomo suffered both physical and economic exploitation, with thousands of them skipping the country to neighbouring South Africa. More than 3.6 million Zimbabweans are estimated to have disserted their country, most of them living as economic and political refugees in South Africa, Britain, Australia, New Zealand (Human Rights Watch, 2007). Conventional wisdom dictates that there is something grossly imperfect with a political system that forces its citizens away from their country of birth.

With this in mind, the study advances an argument that the legacy of the 1980 disturbances may never go away unless an effective transitional mechanism that seeks to address a post-conflict ideological baggage is instituted. Although Critical thinkers such as Gibson (2004) and Hayner (1998) have not directly examined the Zimbabwean case, they contextually conceive the view that Zimbabwe desperately needs a forward-looking political strategy to prevent further socio-political fragmentation resulting from abuses of rights. The conception

Citation: Admore Tshuma, Reframing post-Mugabe justice: A critical need for a truth and reconciliation commission, DOI: 10.5897/AJPSIR2015.0804.

is that Zimbabwe's Human Rights record remains a "scar" that may impede processes of peace and stability if it is left unhealed.

A TRC can enable Zimbabwe to directly and thoroughly confront its atrocious past, as a means of shaping the future (Gibson, 2004). This could be a pragmatic approach in trying to construct a shared memory which is critical for the creation of a more reconciled society.

The focus is primarily on the new understanding of justice promulgated by truth commissions using the formula: *Truth + Redress = Reconciliation*. The aim is to put forward an alternative and effective framework for uniting Zimbabweans. A political discourse highlighting that recognising the truth about violations is imperative for the argument advanced in this study. The discourse also argues that instituting some redress policies may enable Zimbabweans to come into terms with their past, ultimately, reconcile. That way, Zimbabweans can at least begin to travel together on the road towards reconciliation and social cohesion.

What is a Truth Commission?

Truth Commissions are transitional justice mechanisms usually established during a transition to democracy to deal with human rights violations (Stanley, 2005; Hoffman, 2003). Transitional justice scholars, for example Minow (1998) have sought to define Truth Commissions in terms of philosophical standards of justice, while Allan and Allan (2000) define a truth commission as one of the institutions used in international law to investigate gross human rights violations within a specific country.

For Du Toit (2011), truth commissions are tools of transformative social action, which rests on the assumption that collective remembrance of the past will help prevent the recurrence of violence in the future. Du Toit (2011)'s views maybe critical for this analysis in terms of postcolonial abuses in Zimbabwe. Establishing a transformative mechanism may serve as a pragmatic approach in trying to address the legacy of post-colonial Zimbabwe injustices. Critical to this view is that social change in the wake of a culture of human rights abuses may require a shrewd transitional mechanism that is able to prevent the country from sliding into a civil war, hence it is posited that a TC can provide the required smooth transition of power. This is largely because victims who suffered grievously in the past may see an opportunity to engage in an orgy of revenge and retribution.

Characteristic of an effective Truth Commission

Efforts of establishing an effective truth commission should be guided by aspirations of the affected society (Scharf, 1997; Hayner, 1994, 2001, 2002). Critical to the premise of a TC are victims, survivors, bystanders and perpetrators as well. Consequently, TCs should seek to encompass many other causes of conflict with the hope of securing a peaceful post-conflict settlement (Hayner, 1998; Scharf, 1997).

For Freeman (2006), an effective TC should have five characteristics: be able to perform statement-taking, use subpoena powers, use powers of search and seizure, conduct public hearings, and be able to publish its findings in a final report.

Furthermore, TCs should provide assurances of non-repetition of repression or violence. For example, TCs can also been used against covert, state-sponsored crimes to reveal clandestine violence, establish the accountability of political and military leaders, and to publicly acknowledge the previously silenced stories of victims (Shaw, 2005). Public recounting of memories and testimonies about violence is also paramount. This may serve as a redemptive process of reconciliation and redress of injustice. The question of redress is imperative for post-Mugabe justice, for instance, one of the most divisive issues in Zimbabwe is the deployment of the Fifth Brigade (Gukurahundi) in Matabeleland and Midlands areas between 1982 and 1984 (Nkomo, 1984). The footprints of the Fifth Brigade are still vivid in Zimbabwe's socially-shared memory, and, perhaps more significantly, some perpetrators as well as the survivors can still be reached. The most productive approach maybe to redress victims and survivors as a means of paving way for reconciliation and unity.

Worldwide: Truth Commissions and Tribunals

This section examines the origins of Truth Commissions and explores how truth commissions have become increasingly popular transitional mechanisms in countries attempting to confront their past. The aim of this discussion is to demonstrate that the suggestion for a Zimbabwe TRC is a reflection of a wider world that is fast resorting to TCs; hence the idea is not a new one. It has been evolving for a long time. The main driver has been the search for social justice.

Citizens living under dictatorship that may have not only persecuted them, but also brought ravaged the economy are perhaps beginning to under-stand that poverty is both a cause and consequence of human rights abuse and lack of social protection (Fukuda-Parr, 2007). They now understand that extreme poverty which often is a consequence of controversial economic and political policies manifest as a violation of human rights, hence someone is morally responsible for their impoverishment (Pogge, 2003). Consequently, victims of violations must continue demanding redress for structural harms (Shaw, 2005). This new thinking, together with the desire for redress may have led to the formation of first TC in 1974 in Uganda under Idi Amin (Quinn, 2001).

For Scharf (1997), the first truth commission, the Carnegie Endowment for International Peace was set up in 1919 after World War I by allies to investigate alleged atrocities committed against civilians and prisoners of war during the Balkan Wars of 1912 and 1913. However, it is observed that the Carnegie Endowment for International Peace was not a national TC, but an international one. There is also a view that the first TC was the Bangladesh War Inquiry Commission appointed by the Pakistan president in December 1971 to investigate the killings of thousands of Bangladeshis (Government of Pakistan, 1974). The commission published its final report in 1974.

Nonetheless, much contemporary literature on transitional justice argues that the first conventional truth commission was formed by Idi Amin in Uganda in 1974 (Hayner, 2001; Brahm, 2007). The 1974 Ugandan Commission was established to examine accusations of disappearances carried out by the Ugandan military (Robben 2010; Quinn, 2001). Known as the Commission of Inquiry into the Disappearance of People in Uganda it was established by Amin's government in June 1974 to cover a period from 25 January 1971. However, TCs did not gain prominence until the 1980s in Latin America. Brahm (2005) suggests that this could have been because the Ugandan commission did not appear to have been a sincere attempt to rectify an atrocious past, but rather a flimsy effort to placate international pressure. Consequently, the Ugandan commission did not reach its potential. This resulted in a gap in the use of TCs with the second historic TC having been set up in 1982 in Bolivia.

However, from the 1980s to date, TCs have become popular mechanisms of transition from authoritarian regimes to democracy in many countries.

Early TCs in South America were charged with examining specifics of individual acts of violence according to the accepted norms of national and international jurisprudence (Grandin, 2005). Their main function was to address violations of civil and political rights. Apart from the Bolivia TC, amongst early truth commissions to be formed in South America were the Argentina Truth Commission in 1983. Grandin (2005) argues that political terror was one part of the early TCs' agenda to cultivate a notion that viewed the state as an executor of legal disputes and protector of individual rights. In this context, early TCs in Bolivia and Argentina were to be supplemented with prosecutions. Table 1 provides details about some of the South American truth commissions – the year they were formed and how they concluded their work.

[1] Before Zimbabwe became independent in 18 April 1980, it was known as Rhodesia named after British colonialist Cecil John Rhodes.

Table 1. Early commissions in South America

Country	Year	Commission	Result
Bolivia	1982	Commission of inquiry into disappearances	No report
Argentina	1983-1985	Commission on the disappearance of persons (Sabato Commission)	Nunca Mas report documented nearly 9,000 disappeared, analysed repression apparatus
El Salvador	1993-1994	Joint investigation committee on illegal armed groups	Reported many killings had political background; perpetrators mentioned in confidential appendix
Uruguay	1985	Parliamentary investigative commission on 'disappeared' persons	Report published, no details of individual cases
Honduras	1993	National commissioner for the protection of human rights	Report named those responsible for 1984 disappearances
Guatemala	1995	Commission of elucidation	Investigated human rights violations and acts of violence
Chile	1990-1991	National commission on truth and reconciliation	Extensive report documented 2,100 cases, analysed repression apparatus, many recommendations for reparation and rehabilitation
Chad	1991-1992	Commission of inquiry on crimes by ex-president Habre and others	Report said 40,000 were killed, details on 4,000 cases named perpetrators
El Salvador	1992	Ad hoc commission on the military	Confidential report recommended dismissal of 100 military officers for human rights violations
El Salvador	1992-1993	UN Commission of truth	Report said 60,900 killed, of which 5% by opposition; named perpetrators
Uruguay	1985	Parliamentary investigative commission on 'disappeared' persons	Report published, no details of individual cases

The Bolivian National Commission of Inquiry into Disappearances created days after the return to democracy in 1982 and the Ecuadorian commissions were disbanded before completing their work because the investigations became too politically sensitive (Brahm, 2005). Table 1 show that some TCs made their final report confidential; for example the El Salvador TC although it recommended the dismissal of 100 military officers for human rights violations. The focus of human rights was critical to the South African TRC. This shows a conceptual relationship between TCs and, as stated earlier highlights that TCs investigate human rights violations.

From the 1980s onwards, TCs have been used as a social function to unravel the truth about injustices and educate the public about those historical injustices in order to prevent their recurrence, while making recommendations of redress to establish peaceful democracies. For instance, in 1984 the Argentine commission investigated the truth about injustices of the past before recommending that reparations and compensation must be paid to families of the killed and disappeared to redress the past (Bonner and James, 2011). In 1992 the Chadian Commission of Inquiry explored socioeconomic deprivations, including how ordinary people were made homeless and destitute, and further explored the plight of orphans living on the streets (Hayner, 1998).

In 2003, the Peru TRC implicated socioeconomic injustice as a cause of conflict. In 2004, the Sierra Leone TRC concluded that there was a link between conflict and socioeconomic inequalities (Peru TRC, 2003). These examples demonstrate a trend in terms of shift towards redress and social justice.

Campbell (2000) observes that the concept of seeking justice emerged at the end of World War II with both the Nuremberg and Tokyo tribunals. She argues that these tribunals have become the standard by which all transitional mechanisms are measured. This view is relevant in the debate about appropriate transitional mechanism for Zimbabwe. This serves to contextualize the proposed Zimbabwe TRC with other historic transitional mechanisms, suggesting that the proposed TRC is not unique, but a developed duplication of other transitional justice experiments that have emerged since the end of the Second World War. The proposed Zimbabwe TRC can seek to address some various problems and obstacles encountered by many of the previous commissions, particularly those in Latin America (Campbell, 2000). This may mean that the proposed Zimbabwe TRC can improve over other experiments due to the nature of injustices and violations.

For example, the principle of crimes against humanity and systematic crimes against civilians set down by the Nuremberg Tribunals of 1945 which may apply to the Gukurahundi atrocities should be reflected in the mandate of the proposed Zimbabwe TRC but in a restorative format to help establish a human rights culture in Zimbabwe South Africa. A country which observes human rights may have lesser cases of crimes against humanity. As a result of the Nuremberg and Tokyo trials, 11 Nazis were sentenced to death and seven imprisoned at Spandau (Kaufman, 2010). In Tokyo, a military tribunal delivered retribution upon several prominent Japanese people. Two former Japanese premiers, Baron Koki Hirota and General Hideki Tojo, were hanged, as were five other Japanese generals (Kaufman, 2010). While in South Africa there is no record of death sentences resulting from apartheid crimes, a former apartheid police colonel in the counter-insurgency unit Eugene Alexander de Kock was denied amnesty after he was found by the TRC to have kidnapped, tortured, and murdered hundreds of anti-apartheid activists (Mahlangu and Pather, 2012). De Kock confessed his unit's crimes while testifying before the TRC and was in 1996 consequently tried and convicted on eighty-nine charges resulting in him being sentenced to 212 years in prison (Mahlangu and Pather, ibid). However, the South African TRC's main objective was not focused on retribution but on building a future free from it.

In the post-World War 2 period, a number of transitional mechanisms were introduced. For example, the Universal Declaration of Human Rights[1] (UDHR) adopted by the United Nations General Assembly on 10 December 1948 at Palais de Chaillot, Paris, was part of a concerted effort to find alternative and better ways of confronting past crimes. UDHR arose directly from the experience of the Second World War and represented the first global expression of rights to which all human beings are inherently entitled.

This section has explored the history transitional mechanisms, how tribunals relate to TCs, in particular has discussed ways how the proposed Zimbabwe TC can learn lessons from these to make its own improvements. The section demonstrated the concept of TCs marks a departure from relying on prosecutions alone as a means of transforming an emerging democracy. A shift of trend was outlined and a range of TCs and their history in the context of the social justice perspective was examined.

[1]The UDHR consists of 30 articles including the International Bill of Human Rights, the International Covenant on Economic, Social and Cultural Rights, and the International Covenant on Civil and Political Rights and its two Optional Protocols. The UDHR were used in the post-war period to attempt to address human rights abuses.

[1]The UDHR consists of 30 articles including the International Bill of Human Rights, the International Covenant on Economic, Social and Cultural Rights, and the International Covenant on Civil and Political Rights and its two Optional Protocols. The UDHR were used in the post-war period to attempt to address human rights abuses.

[1] Before Zimbabwe became independent in 18 April 1980, it was known as Rhodesia named after British colonialist Cecil John Rhodes.

METHODOLOGY

The section develops a critical methodology that underpins a transitional framework in trying to address the main research questions specified: *Is a TRC necessary for Zimbabwe?* To achieve this aim, the section details the approach used in gathering data. The approach seeks to identify underlying mechanisms in efforts to unite divided societies and conceives the potential of a Zimbabwe Truth and Reconciliation Commission (ZTRC) through different perspectives. The research design provides justification for the use of qualitative multiple methods while detailing the use of semi-structured questions, documents and statistical collection techniques. There were also seven sub-questions that were generated from the main research question: *Is a TRC necessary for Zimbabwe?*

1. Do you think there are human rights violations in Zimbabwe?
2. Do you think Zimbabwe needs a Truth Commission?
3. Should there be prosecutions for those who have violated human rights?
4. Are you proud of the independence of Zimbabwe which came in 1980?
5. If NO, explain why? If YES why?
6. What is your view on Gukurahundi?
7. How can Zimbabwe deal with tribalism and racism currently pervasive in the country?

This is a multiple-methods qualitative research divided into three stages, thus literature review, semi-structured interviews, statistical collection which involve secondary data and document collection (Denzin 2003; Harrell and Bradley, 2009).

The use of multiple-methods reflects an effort to secure some in-depth understanding of how a proposed truth commission can help solve Zimbabwe's record of human rights abuses. The aim is to identify an appropriate and effective strategy of uniting Zimbabweans following three decades of postcolonial black-on-black abuses.

Choosing appropriate methods in social science research has always been a challenge; hence, in this study, qualitative multiple-methods were perceived as methodologically sound. Denzin (2003) commend the use of qualitative multiple-methods, noting that the strategy adds rigour, breadth, richness and depth. Nonetheless, the approach was chosen in consideration of the nature of the phenomenon being investigated (Silverman, 1993). This perception is developed by Maxwell (2005) who argues that the key issue in choosing one research method over another is to ensure compatibility with the goals of research questions. Views from Maxwell (2005) and Silverman (1993) were useful in choosing the qualitative multi-method used in this study.

The approach was found to be appropriate and more pragmatic in an attempt to identify effective mechanisms of moving Zimbabwe forward as a nation against dramatic cases of violations.

While several other studies were examined, the main important studies that formed the mainstay of this study included Hayner (1994), Stanley (2005), Shcarf (1997) and Gibson (2004). Most of these studies were chosen because they focus on divided societies, reconciliation, redress and truth commissions in general. Arguments in these studies served well in conceptualising primary data gathered through semi-structured interviews.

A semi-systematic literature review was conducted to complement and interviews. Literature review sought to analyse the use of ideas as a means of justifying the approach used in this research. Hart (1999) argues that literature review should be conducted with some appropriate breadth, depth and rigour. Hart (1999) also states that literature review should reflect consistency, clarity and brevity. In Hart's view such an approach would provide effective synthesis and analysis. Furthermore, Webster and Watson (2002) argue that an effective literature review creates a firm foundation for advancing knowledge. They also argue that effective literature review facilitates theory development, closes areas where a plethora of research exists, and uncovers areas where research is needed.

Semi-structured interviews were conducted with exiled Zimbabweans including those residents in Zimbabwe. The interviews were carried out in Britain, South Africa and Zimbabwe between February 2010 and April 2010. A follow up study was done in January and February 2015. Semi-structured interviews were chosen because they often allow respondents to answer more on their own terms than standardised interviews permit. The choice of qualitative semi-structured questions was influenced by an understanding that semi-structured interviews could offer a flexible approach to different respondents while still covering the same areas of data collection (Ritchie and Lewis, 2003). The following interviews were conducted with Zimbabwe exiles that included asylum seekers, recognized refugees, academics, policymakers, and those still living in Zimbabwe. For instance, academics were asked questions such as a) *Do you think Zimbabwe needs a Truth Commission? B) In what way can Zimbabwe deal with tribalism and racism currently pervasive in the country?* Ordinary Zimbabwean asylum seekers, refugees and those still in the country were asked the following questions: *Are you proud of the independence of Zimbabwe which came in 1980? B) If NO, explain why? If YES why? C) What is your view on Gukurahundi?*

The interviews were tape-recorded to secure an accurate account of the conversations and avoid losing data since not everything can be written down during an interview. All the tape recordings were anonymised and numbered in order to avoid confusion at the analysis stage (Spencer et al., 2003). The interviews were conducted using a topic guide.

A thematic framework was used in the analysis of data which included familiarisation of raw data by listening to tapes, reading transcripts, and studying notes (Spencer et al., 2003). This entails identifying all the key issues, concepts, and themes by which the data were examined and referenced. Ritchie and Lewis (2003) state that the Thematic Framework is *a matrix based method for ordering and synthesising data* (p219). From the perspective of Ritchie and Lewis (2003), there are two key stages of the Thematic Framework, thus managing data and making sense out of it. This was achieved through descriptive and explanatory accounts.

Triangulation was achieved through the use of both quantitative (validation) and qualitative (inquiry) studies. This approach stems from Webb et al. (1966) who suggest that at least two measures are persuasive. Webb et al. (1966) state that:

Once a proposition has been confirmed by two or more independent measurement processes, the uncertainty of its interpretation is greatly reduced. The most persuasive evidence comes through a triangulation of measurement processes (p. 3).

Double measurement may be critical in ensuring credibility of a study of this magnitude. The approach may also help to clarify links between data, interpretation and conclusions within concepts such as validity, reliability, credibility (Spencer et al., 2003; Long and Godfrey, 2004).

The following section is based on a specific sub-research question that seeks to rationalise the purpose of this study - *Are there any unresolved violations in Zimbabwe?* Responses to this question serve as a basis of the study and bring up a diverse and rich responses, underscoring the need to deal with Zimbabwe's past.

ARE THERE ANY UNRESOLVED VIOLATIONS IN ZIMBABWE?

The purpose of this section is to examine the diversity of views on the research question: *Do you think there are human rights violations in Zimbabwe?* The aim is to try and understand the views of Zimbabweans on whether a truth commission will be necessary for problems bedevilling their country. What is of particular interest are their views on the human rights record of their country, and means of redressing violations.

The question being explored is complex in the sense that different respondents have provided diverse and rich answers. Despite differing and divergent views, there is an underlying moral case for social justice that calls for justice and unity. For example, when questioned whether there are human rights violations in Zimbabwe, Interview (21) stated.

When the 5th Brigade was deployed to Tsholotsho I was pregnant. They came over to our village and started beating up villagers including my parents. They rounded up every one and took turns raping me. The soldiers were so cruel and behaved like wild animals. I saw villagers, our neighbours including my friends being shot dead (Interview 21).

Interviewee (21) added:

I know one mass grave in which I personally witnessed people being buried alive after being ordered to get inside at gunpoint. Anyone who tried to escape was being shot dead. By sunset we had up to 10 dead villagers shot while trying to escape(Interviewee 21).

The claim of the presence of mass graves reflects the importance of a socio-political mechanism that could help investigate and find ways of identifying the victims for decent and "honourable burials". Interviewee (21) also reflects a pattern of systematic conduct by perpetrators which may have been a breach of the international law. The allegations can be criminalised in the light of Article 6 (c) of the International Military Tribunal developed by the United States and its Allies in the wake of Second World War crimes. Article 6 (c) defines crimes against humanity as *murder, extermination ...other inhuman acts committed against civilians*. Interviewee (21) can be conceptualised from the perspective of Article 6 (c).

Whenever such abuses happen, a TC maybe essential to construct an accurate memory of the past crimes. TCs can achieve this through archival and forensic truth-seeking processes complemented by interviewing of survivors and perpetrators (Boraine, 2000).

Interviewee (7) added:

Yes there were and there still are human rights violations to such an extent that I have lost count. I have personally seen people with decapitated limbs as a result of political torture (Interviewee, 7).

The quote highlights patterns of structural violence and scars of abuses, reflecting the need for some form of institutional response. What is remarkable is the interviewee's claim to have lost count of abuses. He however, states that he has encountered people with decapitated limbs, endorsing the much talked about claims of human rights violations in Zimbabwe.

Also responding to the question – *Are there human rights violations in Zimbabwe?* Interviewee (17) said:

Yes they have always been violations in Zimbabwe and there still are human rights violations to up to now. These violations include torture, murders and disappearances. We have lost many important relatives due to politics (Interviewee, 17).

The quote demonstrates an awareness of human rights violations in Zimbabwe by recounting the exact nature of violations, which in this case is torture, disappearances, and murder. This awareness endorses the view that a mechanism that can directly confront the legacy of abuses is vital for the post-Mugabe era. Addressing such bitterness may prepare a foundation for a stable and peaceful future.

However, interviewee (2) stated in response to the same question:

I guess human rights records are dependent on what is acceptable within that particular country. For example, instant justice maybe considered a human right violation in England, but accepted in Zimbabwe (Interviewee, 2).

While the quote attempts to highlight the instant justice discourse which might be a pervasive issue in developing countries; however, it is clearly not the case in Zimbabwe as the country has a Western adopted legal system and endeavours to replicate a Eurocentric - Western ideology of democracy. Although the Zimbabwe's justice system is based on Roman-Dutch law, it is clearly designed in a way that all crimes go through a structured and independent court system; hence, the claim of "instant justice" maybe contextually inappropriate. For instance, the post-colonial Zimbabwe constitution has always provided a right to a fair trial for any crime or cases (Judicial Service Commission Zimbabwe 2012). The country's judiciary system has attempted to rigorously enforce the right to a fair trial despite an unconducive environment.

However, claims of instant justice by interviewee (2) manifest in the 2002 findings by the African Commission which conducted a human rights fact finding commission. The African Commission (2002) stated that:

...there was enough evidence placed before the Mission to suggest that, at the very least during the period under review, human rights violations occurred in Zimbabwe. The Mission was presented with testimony from witnesses who were victims of political violence and others victims of torture while in police custody (African Commission, 2002, p4).

The AU statement is significant and adds value to claims of human rights violations in Zimbabwe, considering the legitimacy and role of the organisation in African continent. The AU succeeded the Organisation of African Unity (OAU) which played a vital role in the liberation of Zimbabwe. The AU has the mandate to prevent conflict, peacekeeping, peace-making and peace-building. The organisation was established to ensure continent-wide peace and security through its Peace and Security Council (Moolakkattu, 2010).

The AU Report added:

...The Government cannot wash its hands from responsibility for all these happenings...Government did not act soon enough and firmly enough against those guilty of gross criminal acts" (African Commission, 2002, p3-4).

The AU quote reflects a remarkable finding on human rights violations in Zimbabwe, consequently, reinforces the view for an alternative mechanism of dealing with rights violations. The quote also endorses claims of human rights violations and implicates the government of Zimbabwe for torture, stating that some victims were dying in police custody as a result of torture. Interviewee (4) echoes claims by the African Commission, stating:

In the first place, there have never ever been human rights in Zimbabwe (Interviewee, 4).

The quote suggests that the country has not installed a culture of human rights. This has a semblance of truth to a larger extent, considering what happened in Matabeleland and Midlands disturbances which left thousands of civilians dead soon after independence (CCJ, 1999).

The Matabeleland disturbances are further highlighted by interviewee (5):

Someone must be held accountable for Matabeleland massacres, it was a war I never saw but heard about in Matabeleland; the truth must come out (Interviewee 5).

The quote endorses the human rights paradigm of accountability whenever rights are violated (Hayner, 1994). In short, accountability highlighted by interviewee (5) serves as justice on its own. Consequently, it can be argued that a future government needs to ensure that the country upholds international human rights standards. This can be achieved by ensuring that perpetrators are brought to justice.

Interviewee (13) elaborates interviewee's views (4):

Yes, there have been human rights violations in Zimbabwe since 1980 up to now (Interviewee, 13).

Asked if he has forgiven those who committed atrocities, interviewee (13) said:

Reconciliation can never happen as long as the Shona people continue to discriminate Ndebele people and trivialise the Gukurahundi massacres. Restoration of Matabeleland Statehood would provide the best reconciliation that would be permanent (interviewee 13).

The above quote makes two important points, first, that there is a need to address tribal discrimination in Zimbabwe, secondly, there is a need to restore the historic Ndebele Kingdom which collapsed more than a century ago. Interviewee (13) provides evidence of pre-existing ethnic divisions which risks social conflict. Again, this points to ethnic divisions in Zimbabwe, requiring an institutional response.

Interviewee (13) added:

There must be reparations for Gukurahundi victims...and we should criminalise any trivialisation or of Gukurahundi massacres. We should also criminalise ethnic discrimination and nepotism and create an equal political system of sharing power between Shona people and Ndebele peoples (Interviewee 13).

The above quote highlights some critical issues in calls for justice. It states that there must be reparations for massacres committed during the Gukurahundi era. Claims for reparations following human massacres resonate with the aims of the International Criminal Court (ICC) 2004, which has provided victims of human rights violations the right to be redressed. The ICC notes that the right to reparation is a *well-established and basic human right that today is enshrined in universal and regional human rights treaties and instruments* (ICC, 2012, para.185).

This section has highlighted human rights violations in Zimbabwe which might need a TRC to move the nation forward. The section has demonstrated that Zimbabwe's past has not been addressed despite growing calls for justice and redress. The section has also shown that ordinary Zimbabweans are vying for a mechanism that will resolve divisive issues such as Gukurahundi massacres in Matabeleland. This pervasive view reflects unresolved black-on-black injustice which if not resolved risks repetition. Consequently, this calls for a TRC to deal with the past as a means of healing the society's psyche.

Nonetheless, views of research respondents highlight a critical need for a system of justice that focusses on the needs of survivors and victims. It is clear that such a system is needed to heal the society and restrain those who are in a habit of committing human rights crimes. The proposed TRC could enable victims and survivors obtain justice and redress, while promoting a post-conflict reconciliation project.

IS A TRC REALLY NECESSARY?

Reflecting on the achievements of the South African TRC, and based on narratives of flagged abuses in Zimbabwe, a proposed Zimbabwe TRC should serve as a response to victims' demands for justice and truth about why things happened the way they did? Who gave orders? What were the reasons behind it? Most importantly, a Zimbabwe TRC should serve as public acknowledgement of the suffering and victims. Victims would also expect a final report of the commission which should ideally recommend reparations and compensation for injustices.

Questioned if the Zimbabwe needed a Truth and Reconciliation Commission, interviewee (17) stated:

Yes the truth and reconciliation commission will be appropriate for Zimbabwe because there are a lot of unacceptable political crimes that happened after independence. What makes this more serious is that it happened after the Rhodesian war when everyone was thinking there is freedom and security (Interviewee, 17).

The above quote reaches beyond a simplistic idea of a mechanism needed to redress postcolonial injustices. The quote reflects a pregnant perception that is shaped by unresolved political crimes in post-colonial Zimbabwe. It is imperative for critical scholars to develop an explicit assumption that understanding the past will contribute to a more peaceful and democratic future (Gibson, 2004). This hypothesis has been comprehensively tested in South Africa by Washington University Scholar, Prof James Gibson.

In his seminal study, Prof Gibson concludes that 42 percent of South Africans have reconciled as a result of the truth and reconciliation Commission. That way, Gibson (2004) alludes that South Africa has attempted to come to grips with its apartheid history through its truth and reconciliation processes.

Moreover, the need for a truth commission in Zimbabwe has not escaped the attention of the United Nations High Commissioner for Human Rights, Navanethem «Navi» Pillay (NewZimbabwe.com, 2012). In her 2012 visit to Zimbabwe Pillay urged the Zimbabwean government to establish a TRC to deal with post-independence atrocities in Matabelaland and the Midlands as well as alleged abuses in successive elections.

In the context of Pillay, establishing a truth commission would be helpful in trying to document the truth about political crimes, hence help the country move forward. The logic is that all victims of Matabeleland and Midlands areas have the right to the truth. In general, there is a strong notion that victims of rights abuses have a right to the truth.

A truth commission will be vital for Zimbabwe because so many things that still angers a lot of people has happened after Mugabe took over power in 1980. We need these things to be properly clarified to enable the country recover from all this(Interviewee, 18).

The above quote demonstrates the desire for accountability for political crimes that may have occurred in Zimbabwe under President Mugabe's reign. The quote also reflects the desire to bury the past which however can only be achieved through a truth and reconciliation process.

A critical view of Hayner (2001) and Gibson's (2004) arguments reflect a consensus that truth commissions can be effective in addressing deep social and political dysfunction after periods of mass repression and violence. This view is further developed by a number of Transitional Justice scholars who have argued that truth commissions are a key bridge to sustainable peace, democracy and human rights (Scharf, 1997; Zyl, 1999). A link can be located between truth commissions and specific outcomes in post-conflict societies. This reflects a general understanding that truth commissions are appropriate for achieving peace and stability.

Interviewee (3) expresses the same notion:

We need a system like a truth commission to correlate information from both sides, that is, from victims and perpetrators. Although it will be hard to hold everyone to account such as tracking down the soldiers who committed Gukurahundi massacres, it may help with healing and closure (Interviewee, 3).

The quote clarifies an important element of truth commission, thus the investigative feature it has. The quote also reflects the potential of TCs and their ability to heal a divided nation.

While previous research has not adequately addressed the basis of the prosecution-to-truth commission paradigm shift, interviewee (3) shows the desire for system that is forward looking while at the same time healing the society. This view is critical, particularly from the perspective of growing calls for social justice (Varney, 2007; Schabas and Darcy, 2004). Interviewee (3) clearly shows a shift which is a result of a new social contract, both at domestic and international level - to bring justice and healing to people who have experienced violations (Graybill and Lanegran, 2004).

Hayner (1994) states that truth commissions may be ideal for such a task as they have an ability to transform an atrocious past into democratic politics. Hayner (2001) also observes that truth commissions focus on the past and in events that may have occurred in the recent past. Interviewee (19) shares this view:

Zimbabwe's past is a subject that has been ignored for too long. A lot of people have been scared by Gukurahundi and until it's addressed, there will never be true unity amongst Zimbabweans (Interviewee, 19).

The quote reiterates Hayner's views on the need to address the past. First, the quote is critical of lack of action on Gukurahundi atrocities and reflects a desire to deal with Zimbabwe's past. Secondly, the quote highlights that Gukurahundi has left a "scarred" society. It can be argued that the truth commissions' ability to investigate a pattern of abuse over a set period of time may be a suitable approach for post-Mugabe justice.

Consequently, there is a need for a new social contract which focuses on the country's turbulent history. Hoffman (2003, p302-303) talks of the need to *recognise the tragic experiences of others, and recognise ourselves in their experience. We cannot undo the past, or cure it, but we can perhaps – by small increments, and with sufficient awareness – derive from it the kind of insight that can be potentially reparative, and can begin to transform the potent forces of destruction into the energy of a more constructive vision.*

Hoffman shares the view of a forward-looking strategy, thus, processes of truth-telling. This stems from the view that a truth commission can provide a platform for recognition, in the process transform shame to pride. It is generally recognised that truth processes focus on forms of repair that are conducive to national healing and state building. The approach may help inform the formulation of redress such as policies of compensation and reparation.

More often, there are demands for justice, particularly in cases where crimes have been committed, and these demands may serve to shape the proposed TRC's mandate. Hayner (2009) shares this view, noting that *there is often a clear and vocal public demand to account for crimes of the war, part of a growing public perception that impunity is wrong* (p6).

However, Gibson (2004) notes that truth may not be the only route to reconciliation, but has since become a popular mechanism of those seeking to move beyond the past to a more peaceful and democratic future. Interviewee (3) echoes this viewpoint:

My view is that the best way is to allow the course of justice to prevail. It's up to the law to determine convictions or amnesties. Yes they should be prosecuted. This will set the record straight and a precedent so as to abate and curb any future similar behaviours (Interviewee, 3).

The quote conceives the idea of prosecutions, but leaves it open for the law to determine the course of justice. Interviewee (3) reflects the desire to use the court system in addressing political crimes that may have been committed. However, commissions have not only attempted to redress the past, but are also therapeutic in nature (Hayner, 1994, Gibson, 2004).

Scholars in the discipline of transitional justice have also noted that in many cases, truth commissions have provided society with an opportunity of positive and new beginnings (Laplante, 2008; Gibson, 2004). Whenever human rights are violated, questions of accountability are often brought to the fore (Hayner, 1998). In fact, a starting point in most post-conflict societies is accountability which may be accompanied by criminal prosecutions of those responsible for serious crimes, followed by redress (Freeman, 2006).

The view that accountability and prosecutions are necessary is shared by interviewee (21):

The commission cannot be used to bring legal justice. We may need commissions alongside tribunals. We cannot just for the sake of moving forward let people who have committed heinous crimes scot free. A truth commission must only be used to expose the truth and enable people to move forward (Interviewee, 21).

The quote argues that truth commissions are inadequate in trying to bring justice to victims. Interviewee (21) reflects a need for a retributive mechanism and views truth commissions as a mechanism that could also aid retributive justice. Moreover, these different viewpoints are closely linked to demands for justice on unresolved Zimbabwean abuses.

For instance, in concluding the report *Breaking Silence*, the Catholic Commission for Justice and Peace, and the Legal Resource Foundation of Zimbabwe point out concerns about the impact of violence in contemporary Zimbabwe.

There is great cause for concern in Zimbabwe when one considers the high numbers of survivors in the country. Many of these are survivors from the 1980s violence and the multiple impacts on people in physical, psychological and material terms have been enormous (CCJ and LRF, 1999, p30).

Moreover, the Catholic Commission for Justice and Peace, and Legal Resource Foundation have attempted to capture the more damaging and pervasive forms of post-violence in Zimbabwe, which by all means may require a truth commission. The above quote reflects the aims of this paper, thus the need to redress the past. The quote identifies harm caused by political violence in Zimbabwe and seeks to challenge lack of action in dealing with the harms.

While transitional societies have on many occasions used diverse strategies in dealing with their past, the idea of a TRC can be useful in confronting Zimbabwe's atrocious past. A TRC can unleash an effective and organised attempt to deal with crimes of the past placing an emphasis on redress through reparative justice to restore victims and survivors. The following section explores potential features for a proposed Zimbabwe TRC.

PROPOSED ZIMBABWE TRC

This section seeks to identify the characteristic of a proposed Zimbabwe truth commission. As stated earlier, it is imperative that a truth commission should reflect the aspirations of the affected society to achieve desired outcomes.

The proposed Zimbabwe TRC should also encompass therapeutic interventions for survivors of human rights abuses. This view is shared by interviewee (18).

We are a traumatised nation. The wounds and anger needs therapy, and this cannot just be ignored by politicians. There is no way the country can move forward with accountability and reconciliation (Interviewee, 18).

Kaminer et al. (2001) develops interviewee's (18) view, they suggest that truth commissions should be therapeutic in nature to help restore the victim's dignity.

This view stems from an understanding that abuses inflict injury which takes away dignity from the victim. For Lederach (1997), it is critical to create a space for victims to highlight their experiences as the approach allows them to validate their feelings, restore their dignity and assist them to re-enter society as equal partners. Furthermore, the proposed Zimbabwe TRC should be primarily aimed at addressing different grievances including political violence, murder, disappearances and inequalities that run on tribal lines with the Shona people of Mugabe's tribe being better off. This suggests a need to deal with black-on-black injustice. The truth commission should also seek to clarify what happened to Lockout Masuku[1], Josiah Tongogara[2], and the controversy behind the Bhalahwe mine[3] which is among other burning issues of Zimbabwe's post-colonial turbulent history. Among other issues to be addressed by the proposed Zimbabwe TRC is the 2008 political violence which marred the country's national elections, including "Operation Murambatsvina" which started in the Zimbabwe capital, Harare, and spread into a nationwide demolition and eviction campaign by police and the army.

Moreover, the idea of a TRC reflects a growing debate over the need for a more pragmatic approach in dealing with injustices of the past. The call for a Zimbabwe TRC should also encompass violations such as poverty and state sponsored crimes that may have caused perennial anger, suffering and divisions. It should recognise that violations include a number of socio-political situations, and some of these events may cause considerable suffering, not only to survivors and victims, but also for perpetrators as well. Critically to all this, a Zimbabwe TRC can help locate some of the graves of the missing such as Patrick Nabanyama[4] and clarify the murder of Strover Mutonhori[5]. It should also help construct a shared memory, which is useful for a country ready to move on.

Consequently, a proposed Zimbabwe TRC should reflect both historical and prevailing injustices. TRC should thrive to support "political paradigmatic" struggles for "recognition and redistribution" (Fraser, 1997). Thus, recognise injustices by unveiling measures that seek to prevent the past from re-occurring. This view brings into the fore political theories of recognition, developed by Nancy Fraser and others. These theories primarily focus on the role played by recognition in providing justice. This stems from the understanding that people who have been victims of human rights abuses lose something about themselves, hence restoration is critical. It is the "restoration" that the proposed Zimbabwe TRC should seek to achieve. That way, a more reconciled society can begin to emerge.

[1] Lieutenant General Lookout Masuku was commander the Zimbabwe People's Revolutionary Army, the militant wing of the Zimbabwe African People's Union, during the Rhodesian Bush War and served as the deputy commander of the Zimbabwe National Army until his arrest in 1982 for allegedly plotting to overthrow President Robert Mugabe. He denied the plot but was detained till his death in 1986.

[2] Josiah Tongogara was a commander of the ZANLA guerrilla. He had a lot of support from the guerrilla movement who may have heard different political opinions from Robert Mugabe.

[3] Bhalahwe mine is an old disused mine in Zimbabwe's Matabeleland South where it is believed there are thousands of dead Ndebele speaking people who were targeted by political hitmen.

[4] Patrick Nabanyama was an opposition election agent abducted in June 2000 election in front of his family and has not been seen since. Six war veterans were arrested but later pardoned.

[5] Mutonhori disappeared from the Omadu Hotel in Kezi, Matabeleland South and his remains were later found at Matopo Hills, outside Bulawayo.

RIGHTING ZIMBABWE WRONGS

Consequently, it can be argued that rectifying Zimbabwe wrongs can be achieved through a model propounded by Villa-Vicencio (2009) involving recognition which comes through compensation, reparation, restoration, apology and punishment for extreme criminal cases. This model can easily be achieved through processes of truth commissions as very few transitional mechanisms can afford to execute Villa-Vicencio's model. Villa-Vicencio (2009) argues that *both the material and subjective needs of victims and survivors of an oppressive past must be prioritised* (Villa-Vicencio, 2009, p106). This may imply that the proposed Zimbabwe TRC should recommend financial amounts to be paid out in reparations and compensation. The proposed TRC would be more informed to suggest pay-outs to the government as they would have met the victims and saw their plight. However, it can be suggested that there should be different pay outs especially for people whose relatives were murdered or disappeared as a results of politics. The government must also consider socioeconomic reparations for survivors such as free education and monthly financial entitlements. What maybe required is a comprehensive social welfare for victims and survivors. Being compensated and having reparations paid may create a notion of justice being done. Receiving compensation and reparations for the harm suffered is an essential step in their rehabilitation. Also needed is appropriate psychosocial support for victims in their pursuit of justice and reparation.

Dyzenhaus (2003) has proposed a framework that focuses on social development and preservation of human rights. He states that:

If one wants to build democracy after a period of severe injustice only a moral or justice-based justification will do(Dyzenhaus, 2003, p472).

For Dyzenhaus (2003), it is unlikely that rule of law and respect for human rights can be built in societies where injustices of the past have not been rectified. The onus is to build trust in state institutions as protectors of human rights violations.

TCs have provided a new framework for dealing with the past and in particular questions about human rights abuses. The TC thesis has established a new terrain for social, moral and political discourse about the need to right the wrongs of the past, through a truth-telling process. Transitional Justice experts such as Pricilla Hayner and Charles Villa-Vicencio have attempted to draw an attention to the challenging question of how societies can right the wrongs of the past. They concede that truth commissions are equipped with mandates to construct just institutions of recognition of wrongs and then recommend redress. This approach is essential for post-Mugabe justice, and is vital for reconciliation and progress.

CONCLUSION

This paper has attempted to investigate the relevance of the formula *Truth + Redress = Reconciliation* - from the perspective of post-Mugabe justice. The formula conceives that by revealing the truth about what happened under President Mugabe's reign, and then institute redress, the country is more likely to reconcile, consequently, move forward as one nation. If a truth commission succeeded in transforming South Africa to a stable democracy, perhaps it can be posited that a similar mechanism can work in Zimbabwe, considering the nature of violations committed in both neighbouring countries. The formula encompasses years of political, tribal and economic divisions that have caused harm, suffering and pain to millions of Zimbabweans. It also represent an approach used by Truth Commissions, which maybe critical for Zimbabwe where questions on why things happened the way they did remain unanswered.

Given allegations of the Fifth Brigade, killings and disappearances, a TC may be useful in revealing the truth while also seeking to unite the nation. The proposed TC must have the mandate to conduct public hearings which can also be televised. This is designed to serve as an acknowledgment for victims. Also, there is a critical need to focus on perpetrators as well to avoid creating a notion of one sided justice. Nevertheless, focusing on victims only has its disadvantages in healing societal harms that might have been inflicted during disturbances.

Consequently, the TC approach may provide recognition to victims of state crime who often suffer disadvantages that affect their ability to participate at par in the political economy.

This paper attempted to construct a model of the proposed truth commission from the perspective of the aspirations of Zimbabweans. For instance, it has been highlighted that the proposed Zimbabwe TRC may need public hearings which may be seen by many victims as therapeutic. Such an approach could be used as an abridgement of social distance between the perpetrator and victim.

Moreover, Zimbabwe may need to accompany a TRC with limited tribunals as some crimes committed maybe beyond human comprehension only requiring justice through a court system.

REFERENCES

1. Allan A, Allan MM (2000). The South African Truth and Reconciliation Commission as a therapeutic tool. Behav. Sci. Law 18(4):459-477.
2. Bonner M, James M (2011). "The Three R's of Seeking Transitional Justice: Reparation, Responsibility, and Reframing in Canada and Argentina", Department of Political Science, University of Victoria, The International Indigenous Policy Journal, Volume 2, Issue 3 Truth and Reconciliation, Article 3, August.
3. Boraine A (2000). Truth and recognition in South Africa: The third way In Truth v. justice: The morality of truth commissions, eds. Robert I. Rotberg and Dennis Thompson, 141-157. Princeton, NJ: Princeton University Press.
4. Brahm E (2005) Getting to the Bottom of Truth: Examining Truth Commission Success and Impact, Department of Political Science, University of Colorado at Boulder
5. Brahm, E (2007), Uncovering the Truth: Examining Truth Commission Success and Impact, International Studies Perspectives 8: 16–35, University of Nevada.
6. Campbell PJ (2000). The Truth and Reconciliation Commission (TRC): Human Rights and State Transitions. The South Africa Model, Afr. Stud. Q. 4: 3.
7. Catholic Commission for Justice and Peace (1999). Breaking the Silence, Building True Peace, A Report on the Disturbances, in Matabeleland and the Midlands 1980-1988, Catholic Commission for Justice and Peace, Legal Resources Foundation, Harare.
8. Denzin NK (1970). The Research Act in Sociology. Chicago: Aldine.
9. Du Toit F (2011). Take heed of Tutu tax, Reconciliation Barometer, South Africa Reconciliation Barometer, Accessed from http://reconciliationbarometer.org/volume-nine-2011/take-heed-of-tutu-tax/
10. Dyzenhaus D (2003). Judging the Judges, Judging Ourselves: Truth, Reconciliation, and the Apartheid Legal Order, Oxford: Hart Publishing.
11. Fukuda-Par S (2007). Human rights and National Poverty Reduction strategy: Conceptual framework for human rights analysis of poverty reduction strategies and reviews of Guatemala, Liberia and Nepal,
12. Government of Pakistan (1974). Cabinet Secretariat (Cabinet Division), Rawalpindi, 25 May.
13. Grandin G (2005), The Instruction of Great Catastrophe: Truth Commissions, National History, and State Formation in Argentina, Chile, and Guatemala, Am. Historical Rev. 110(1): 46–67.
14. Graybill L, Lanegran K (2004). Truth, Justice, and Reconciliation in Africa: Issues Cases Afr. Stud. Q. 8:1.

15. Hayner PB. (1994). Fifteen Truth Commissions - 1974 to 1994: A Comparative Study. Hum. Rights Q, 16(4): 597-655.

16. Hayner PB (1998). The contribution of truth commissions. In B. Dunér (ed.), An End to Torture: strategies for its eradication. London: Zed Books, 203-21.

17. Hayner PB. (2001). Unspeakable Truths: Confronting State Terror and Atrocity. New York: Routledge.

18. Hayner PB (2002). Unspeakable Truths: Facing the Challenge of Truth Commissions. New York: Routledge.

19. Hayner PB (2007). Centre for Humanitarian Dialogue, and International Center for Transitional Justice. Negotiating Peace in Sierra Leone Confronting the Justice Challenge. Geneva: Centre for Humanitarian Dialogue; International Center for Transitional Justice, Available at

20. Hoffman E (2003). Human Rights, Human Wrongs, The Oxford Amnesty Lectures 2001, Edited by Nicholas Owen, Oxford University Press.

21. International Criminal Court (2004). The Prosecutor v Thomas Lubanga Dyilo, Decision establishing the principles and procedures to be applied to reparations, No. ICC-01/04-01/06, 7 August 2012, para.185.

22. Judicial Service Commission Zimbabwe (2012). How the Courts Operate. Accessed from

23. Kaminer D, Stein DJ, Mbanga I, Zungu D (2001). Commission in South Africa: relation to psychiatric status and forgiveness among survivors of human rights abuses, Brit. J. Psychiatry, 178: 373-377.

24. Kaufman ZD (2010). The Nuremberg Tribunal versus the Tokyo Tribunal: Designs, Staffs, and Operations. John Marshall Law Rev. 43(3):753-768.

25. Laplante LJ (2008). Transitional Justice and Peace Building: Diagnosing and Addressing the Socioeconomic Roots of Violence through a Human Rights Framework. Int. J.Transitional Justice, 2(3): 331-355.

26. Lederach JP (1997). Building Peace: Sustainable Reconciliation in Divided Societies, UIP, Washington D.C.

27. Long AF, Godfrey M (2004). An evaluation tool to assess the quality of qualitative research studies, Int. J. Social Res. Methodol. 7(2): 181-96.

28. Mahlangu I, Pather S (2012). De Kock must rot in jail, January 29. Retrieved from:

29. Minow M (1998). Between Vengeance and Forgiveness: Facing History after Genocide and Mass Violence. Boston, MA: Beacon Press.

30. Moolakkattu JS (2010). The Role of the African Union in Continental Peace and Security Governance, India Quarterly: A J. Int. Affairs, 66(2): 151-165. June.

31. Nkomo J (1984). The Story of My Life, Methuen London, Sapes books, Harare 2001, p.1-4 "clown Herbert Ushewokunze, minister of home affairs".

32. Peru TRC Report (2003). Final Report of the Truth and Reconciliation Commission (Lima: Truth and Reconciliation Commission of Peru,), vol. 3.

33. Pogge TW (2003). Ethical and Human Rights Dimension of Poverty: Towards a New Paradigm in the Fight Against Poverty.

34. Quinn JR (2001). Dealing with a Legacy of Mass Atrocity: Truth Commissions in Uganda and Chile. Netherlands Quarterly on Human Rights 19 (4):20.

35. Ritchie J, Lewis J (2003). Qualitative Research Practice: A Guide for social science students and researchers, London, SAGE Publications Ltd.

36. Robben AC (2010), Transcultural Psychiatry 2010 47: 50, Processes During Transitional Justice, Commentary on Avruch: Group Dynamics in Social Reconciliation, DOI: 10.1177.

37. Schabas WA, Darcy S (2004). Truth Commissions and Courts: The Tension Between Criminal Justice and the Search for Truth, Kluwer Academic Publishers.

38. Spencer L, Ritchie J, Lewis J, Dillon L (2003). Quality in Qualitative Evaluation: A framework for assessing research evidence, London: Cabinet Office.

39. Stanley E (2001). Evaluating the Truth and Reconciliation Commission, Modern African Stud. 39(3): 525-546, United Kingdom.

40. Stanley E (2005). Truth Commissions and The Recognition of State Crime, Oxford University Press on behalf of the Centre and Justice Studies 45: 582-597 accessed on 19 April

41. Scharf MP (1997). The Case for a Permanent International Truth Commission, in Duke Journal of Comparative Politics and International Law, 7(2): 375-410.

CHAPTER 14

THE PROTECTION OF CULTURAL PROPERTY DURING PEACETIME AND IN THE EVENT OF ARMED CONFLICT: A HISTORICAL OVERVIEW AND A CASE STUDY, THE PLUNDERING OF LEBANON?S CULTURAL HERITAGE

Ahmad Hoteit and Issam Ali Khalifeh

Wars, confrontations and conflicts in general, between two or more opposing factions, have always represented a serious threat to the integrity of the cultural heritage located in their territories. Unfortunately, this threat most often materializes in the form of the destruction of significant amounts of cultural property (movable and immovable): monuments, religious sites, museums, libraries, archives, etc. Humanity is thus deprived of a shared and irreplaceable cultural heritage.

Although the practice has existed since ancient times, the destruction of cultural property has proved even more devastating since the introduction of aerial bombing and long-distance weapons [1].

Traditionally, the pillaging of cultural property proclaimed as "spoils of war" has been deliberately carried out by the victor. Separate from this practice of interstate plunder, there is individual pillaging made easy by the consequences of armed conflicts, especially if they are long-lasting and/or accompanied by a military occupation. These consequences include social and economic instability, poverty, weakening or even disappearance of the administrative authorities in charge of maintaining public order unless temporarily replaced by the occupying authorities [2].

A new threat to cultural property emerged after World War II, as non-international and/or ethnic conflicts increased. Not only do these conflicts fall outside of the scope of rules applicable to traditional interstate conflicts, but their goal is often clearly to destroy the adversary's or the opposing ethnic group's cultural heritage. In addition, this destruction is facilitated by the geographical proximity and mutual knowledge of the cultural sites and property, as well as the culture of the adversary.

This is exemplified by the destruction during the war in the former Yugoslavia, where cultural property that was not a military target was deliberately attacked by the opposing ethnic group, who sought to destroy the traces or symbols of the ethnic "enemy's" culture. Particularly significant examples include the bombing of the old town of Dubrovnik in Croatia and the destruction of the Mostar Bridge in Bosnia and Herzegovina.

These new challenges clearly show the need to improve protection of cultural property, particularly in the case of internal conflicts with an ethnic dimension.

THE STATE OF INTERNATIONAL LAW BEFORE THE ADOPTION OF THE 1954 HAGUE CONVENTION

The facts previously described remind us that the right to "spoils of war" of the victor, often associated with the destruction of cultural property remaining on the conquered site, characterizes most conflicts that have occurred since ancient times. If we look at this question from a legal standpoint, it was only from the 16th and 17th centuries onwards that the determination to protect artistic and cultural heritage appeared in international

Citation: Hoteit A, Khalifeh IA (2013) The Protection of Cultural Property during Peacetime and in the Event of Armed Conflict: A Historical Overview and a Case Study, The Plundering of Lebanon's Cultural Heritage, doi: 10.4172/2167-0374.S3-009

law. There are several historical reasons for this development. First, works of art were increasingly recognized as specific objects as opposed to "ordinary objects" from the Renaissance onwards. Second, private property was increasingly recognized as legally distinct from the property of the enemy state or power. This meant that private property could enjoy a different and more enviable fate.

Peace treaties are particularly demonstrative of the slow but undeniable progress of international law on this issue. Starting with the Treaty of Westphalia (1648), more and more treaties included clauses specifically referring to cultural property in the wide sense of the term as understood at the time) removed during the conflict, and often provided for its restitution [3].

However, this protection during wartime became substantial and consistent in international law only through the recognition, consecrated during international conferences (1899 and 1907), of the specific nature of cultural property and of the need to protect it. The two Hague Conventions (II of 1899 and IV of 1907) achieved this goal through a general codification of the laws governing war on land [4].

THE 1954 HAGUE CONVENTION AND ITS TWO PROTOCOLS (1954 AND 1999) BRIEF HISTORY

Following World War II and its damage to, and destruction of, cultural heritage on an unprecedented scale, the international community determined to prepare an international convention to anticipate, and, if possible, to prevent future destruction of irreplaceable historical and artistic treasures. On the initiative of the Netherlands, UNESCO, during the 4th session of its General Conference (Paris, 1949), adopted Resolution 6.42.

The Secretariat then undertook work, the results of which were presented at the 5th session of the General Conference (Florence, 1950), which adopted Resolution 4.44, authorizing the Director-General to "prepare and submit to Member States a draft for an international convention for the protection, in case of war, of monuments and other objects of cultural value....". This was transmitted to the Member States, and the responses of their governments were submitted to the 6th session of the General Conference (Paris, 1951). The draft was then reworked by the International Council on Monuments, Artistic and Historical Sites and Archaeological Excavations, then re-submitted to the governments and revised by the Secretariat following their comments. The final revision by a Committee of Governmental Experts produced three separate documents (a commentary, a draft Convention and draft Regulations for its Execution), which were submitted to the 7th session of the General Conference (Paris, 1952). Following the work of this session, UNESCO accepted the offer from the Government of the Netherlands to host an Intergovernmental Conference.

This Conference, held at The Hague from 21st April to 14th May 1954, led to the adoption on 14th May 1954 of the Convention for the Protection of Cultural Property in the Event of Armed Conflict, the Regulations for its Execution, its Protocol, and three resolutions [5].

The convention: The Convention represents the first international multilateral treaty with a universal vocation exclusively focused on the protection of cultural heritage in the event of armed conflict. The Convention covers both movable and immovable property, including architectural, artistic or historical monuments, archaeological sites, works of art, manuscripts, books and other objects of artistic, historical or archaeological interest, as well as scientific collections of all types.

The first protocol (1954): A protocol specific to movable cultural property and the difficult issues of its restitution was adopted with the Convention. The Protocol prohibits the export of such property from an occupied territory and requires its return to the territory of the State from which the property was exported. The Protocol prohibits the retention of cultural property as war reparations in that it specifically excludes the submission of cultural property to the regime of war reparations applicable to "ordinary" property.

The second protocol (1999): The acts of barbarism committed against cultural heritage during numerous conflicts that took place at the end of the 1980s and the beginning of the 1990s presented new challenges to the international community. Such conflicts and their repercussions were only partially taken into account during the negotiations of the Convention in the 1950s. Contemporary conflicts are often internal and of an ethnic nature, thus not within the scope of the international law applicable to classic interstate warfare. In addition, this type of conflict is often particularly destructive of cultural heritage. In this type of conflict, an aggressor often directly and deliberately targets a besieged ethnic group's culture and heritage with the ostensible intent of humiliating the target group by taking away privileged existence of its past, culture, and heritage.

Starting in 1991, a process of review of the Convention began, and led to the negotiation and adoption in The Hague in March 1999 of a Second Protocol to the Convention. This Protocol strengthens several provisions of the Convention concerning the safeguarding of and the respect for cultural property and conduct during hostilities. It creates a new category, "enhanced protection", for cultural property of the greatest importance for humanity. This category of cultural property is protected by adequate legal provisions at the national level and is not used for military purposes. The Second Protocol also increases the effectiveness by directly defining the sanctions due in the event that serious violations are committed against cultural property, and the conditions under which individual criminal responsibility applies.

This Protocol also establishes an institutional element: the Committee for the Protection of Cultural Property in the Event of Armed Conflict. The Committee consists of twelve States Parties, and is in charge of ensuring the implementation of the Second Protocol.

The Committee was elected for the first time at the first meeting of the Parties to the Second Protocol (UNESCO Headquarters, 26th October 2005). Following the elections of half of the Committee at the third Meeting of the Parties (UNESCO, Headquarters, 23-24th November, 2009), the Committee is composed as follows: six members whose mandate expires in 2011 (Cyprus, Finland, Greece, Lithuania, Japan and the Netherlands) and six members whose mandate expires in 2013 (Argentina, Austria, the Islamic Republic of Iran, Italy, Romania and Switzerland).

The most important current activity of the Committee to date has been to develop the Draft Guidelines for the Implementation of the Second Protocol. In addition, the Second Protocol sets up the Fund for the Protection of Cultural Property in the Event of Armed Conflict. The guidelines concerning the use of this Fund were also approved by the third Meeting of the Parties, and this Fund is currently open to receive donations.

The Second Protocol entered into force on 9th March, 2004 for its first twenty States Parties. Another important step in the international protection of cultural heritage has thus been achieved.

The status of the ratification of the 1954 Hague Convention and its two 1954 and 1999 Protocols can be consulted via the "Legal Instruments" page of the UNESCO Web site: www.unesco.org [1].

General Principles of the Convention and its two Protocols

The definition of cultural property: There is no universal legal definition of cultural property - it varies according to the applicable national legislation or international instrument. Each prescriptive instrument contains its own definition. The 1954 Convention (Article 1) and its two Protocols define cultural property, irrespective of origin or ownership, as follows:

- Movable or immovable property of great importance to the cultural heritage of every people, such as monuments of architecture, art or history, whether religious or secular; archaeological sites; groups of buildings which, as a whole, are of historical or artistic interest; works of art; manuscripts, books and other objects of artistic, historical or archaeological interest; as well as scientific collections and important collections of books or archives or of reproductions of the property defined above;
- Buildings whose main and effective purpose is to preserve or exhibit the movable cultural property defined in sub paragraph (a), such as museums, large libraries and depositories of archives, and refuges intended to shelter, in the event of armed conflict, the movable cultural property defined in sub-paragraph (a);
- Centres containing a large amount of cultural property as defined in subparagraphs (a) and (b), to be known as "centres containing monuments".

The states parties must principally adopt the following protective measures:

Mainly During Peacetime:

- Prepare for the safeguarding of cultural property situated within their own territory (Article 3 of the Convention). Article 5 of the Second Protocol also requires the preparation of inventories; the planning of emergency measures for protection against fire or structural collapse; the preparation for the removal of movable cultural property or the provision for adequate in situ protection of such property; and the designation of competent authorities responsible for the safeguarding of cultural property. It should be stressed that these measures often prove very useful not only in the event of armed conflict, but also in the event of natural disaster or as an effective method of fighting illicit trafficking in cultural property.
- Consider the possibility of placing a limited number of refuges, monumental centers and other immovable cultural property under "special" protection (Chapter II of the Convention and Articles 11 to 14 of the Regulations for its Execution) following an entry in the "International Register of Cultural Property under Special Protection". In addition, enhanced protection is provided for in Chapter 3 of the Second Protocol.
- Consider the use of the special distinctive emblem to facilitate identification of cultural property (Articles 6, 16 and 17 of the Convention and Article 20 of the Regulations for its Execution).
- Plan or establish, in peacetime within their armed forces, services or specialist personnel whose purpose will be to secure respect for cultural property and to cooperate with the civilian authorities thereon (Article 7 of the Convention).
- Widely disseminate the text of the Convention (Article 25) and that of the Second Protocol (Article 30).
- Remove, to the maximum extent feasible, movable cultural property from the vicinity of military objectives, and avoid locating military objectives near cultural property (Article 8 of the Second Protocol).
- Within the framework of their ordinary criminal jurisdiction, take all necessary steps to prosecute and impose penal or disciplinary sanctions upon those persons, of whatever nationality, who commit or order to be committed a breach of the Convention (Article 28 of the Convention). This obligation is reinforced by Chapter 4 of the Second Protocol concerning serious violations and other offences, as well as provisions in terms of penal procedure and legal cooperation.

During armed conflict: Respect cultural property situated within their own territory and the respective territories of other High Contracting Parties by refraining from directing any act of hostility directed against such property (Article 4(1) of the Convention). This obligation is reinforced by the provisions of Chapter 2 of the Second Protocol, and particularly by Articles 6, 7 and 8. These Articles provide for respect for cultural property, precautions in attack and the effects of hostilities. Respect for cultural property also applies to conflicts that are not of an international character (Article 19 of the Convention). Further, all the provisions of the Second Protocol are applicable to this type of conflict (Article 22).

- Refrain from directing any act of reprisals against cultural property (Article 4(4) of the Convention).
- Prohibit, prevent and, if necessary, put a stop to any form of theft, pillage or misappropriation of, and any acts of vandalism directed against, cultural property (Article 4(3) of the Convention).
- Take all necessary steps to prosecute and impose penal or disciplinary sanctions upon those persons who commit or order to be committed a breach of

the Convention (Article 28 of the Convention), and implement the penal measures laid out in Chapter 4 of the Second Protocol.

- Protect cultural property situated in occupied territory and, particularly, as far as possible, take the necessary measures for its preservation (Article 5 of the Convention). This obligation is reinforced by Article 9 of the Second Protocol which prohibits, in particular, all illicit export, removal or transfer of cultural property.
- After the hostilities: At the close of hostilities, return exported cultural property which is in its territory to the competent authorities of the territory previously occupied (Article I (3) of the 1954 Protocol).
- Prohibit the retention of cultural property as war reparations (Article 1(3) of the 1954 Protocol)).

On the Customary Value of these Principles

Like any other international treaty, the Convention and the two Protocols are legally binding on their respective States Parties only. However, the effect of these instruments is different if and to the extent that some or all of the provisions of the Convention and its Protocols have acquired value as international custom within the whole international community following repeated and constant practice by third-party States.

In 1946, the Nuremberg International Military Tribunal declared that in 1939 the rules contained in the Hague Convention (IV) respecting the Laws and Customs of War on Land were "recognized by all civilized nations and were regarded as being declaratory of the laws and customs of war...". This concerned, among other things, the obligations set out in Articles 27 and 56 protecting cultural property.

The 27th session of the General Conference of UNESCO (Paris, October-November 1993) adopted Resolution 3.5 on the Convention for the Protection of Cultural Property in the Event of Armed Conflict (The Hague, 1954) which, among other things, reaffirmed that "the fundamental principles of protecting and preserving cultural property in the event of armed conflict could be considered part of international customary law". This mainly concerns the principles contained in Articles 3 and 4 of the Convention regarding the safeguarding of and respect for cultural property.

In 2005 the Cambridge University Press published in English a twovolume study on customary international humanitarian law conducted by the International Committee of the Red Cross summarizing its rules related to the conduct of hostilities. The following rules are pertinent to the protection of cultural property in the event of armed conflict: Rules 38, 39, 40 and 41. Rules 38, 39 and 40 are applicable both in the event of both international and non-international conflicts and Rule 41 is applicable only in the event of international armed conflict [1].

THE PLUNDERING OF LEBANON'S CULTURAL HERITAGE

Just recently a resurgence of Phoenician studies started to circulate among various archaeological societies. Themes such as " The Emergence of the Phoenicians was one of the major themes of the 1988 meetings of the American schools of oriental research in Chicago, marking the first such presentation ever given in the U.S.A [1].

Why have Phoenician studies lagged so far behind? It was part the chance of excavation, part prejudice. A people who exist in the western world's religious consciousness as worshipers of Baal and Astarte, and who practiced infant sacrifice, and were of minimal interest to our archaeological forebears of the last century.

Slowly, however the tide has turned. Excavations at the overseas colonies, particularly in Cyprus and Spain, made it impossible to ignore the Phoenicians any longer. New excavations started around the Mediterranean following the sea trade routes of the Phoenicians, the first scholarly journal devoted to them "Rivista di studi Fenici " began in 1973. The first excavation dedicated to uncovering a homeland Phoenician port, Sarepta, got underway in 1969. Congresses have been held in Europe, and in 1988, "I Fenici ", the first major exhibit devoted to Phoenician and Punic arts and crafts, was held in Venice [6].

It is therefore a great tragedy that just when there was a modern revival of the Phoenicians, the war in Lebanon began. That the antiquities are suffering pales before the other suffering there, never the less, it is evident from the quantities of looted artifacts now available on the international market that Lebanon is being robbed not only of its present but also of its past [7]. For lack of a government authority in Lebanon, there is no one to certify that particular artifacts are stolen, so they are freely imported into United States and other countries. Local attempts to stop the looters often meet the response that "these people have to feed their families somehow "there is no answer to that. Soon scholars will have to decide whether it is more ethical to ignore those artifacts or to salvage what we can by studying and publishing material excavated under such circumstances.

Surviving on salaries made nearly worthless by war-driven inflation and working with almost no help from international archaeological community, a few courageous Lebanese and non Lebanese scholars have continued to do what they can locally. Camille Asmar, Leila Badre, Nina Jidejian, Issam khalifeh, Ibrahim Kaoukabani, Helene Sader, Hassan Salame-Sarkis, Helga Seeden, Fadie Stephan, Suzy Hakimian, and others are working under conditions few of us would tolerate for a week, let alone 15 years, their appeals to the rest of the world for funds to purchase such minor things as cement to consolidate crumbling mosaics, chemicals to treat frescoes, and wire to rebuild fences around endangered sites have for the most part fallen on deaf ears, yet these scholars continue to try to save what they can. They tried to contact U.N. forces asking to implement the Hague conventions of 1954 and other UNESCO declarations to safe-guard cultural heritage, hardly the U.N forces helped to install the signs of UNESCO to protect sites from bombing and pillaging. If scholars of the future have something left to study in Lebanon, it will be because of those local efforts [1,6] (Figure 1).

Figure 1: The Heart of Beirut (1983) [12]: Modern weaponry ruined historical architecture.

As Lebanon approaches the seventieth year of its existence as a state, its future is very uncertain. The historical and archaeological past of this land, created by a varied succession of cultures over the last million years, is being destroyed far faster than it can ever be retrieved. While the archaeological past of neighboring states is investigated by national and international scientific teams to construct a more coherent picture of their history, Lebanon lacks even a rudimentary map of its archaeological sites and remains. Building projects relentlessly remove surviving traces of the country's heritage while man-made destruction has ruined entire communities, adding haunting dead towns and villages to the landscape [8]

At the end of the twentieth century large cities are active models of site formation and transformation, where archaeological processes can be observed live and their causes and effects measured and recorded on the spot. Archaeological journalism would not be a contradiction in terms here. In Beirut, nature has reclaimed public squares and buildings, bomb rubble and subsequent dilapidation have made burial and settlement mounds out of once bustling market centers and historical architecture. Everywhere stand the horrifying man-made monuments to destruction of human life and effort [9] (Figure 1).

In this context illegal excavations thrived. Rampant inflation during the civil war has spurred clandestine digging rivaling gold rushes of the old days. Buried archaeological material is being robbed in every corner of this land in broad daylight. At no other time of its brief history have there been so many "excavations" in Lebanon. None of them is properly observed or recorded. The majority of Lebanese, though ignorant about their past, have understood that remnant bits and pieces of a broken up history have market value. While the soil of Lebanon is being plundered frantically, no museums are being built to tell the story of its people for future generations. Today there remains of Byblos only museum objects and their un-integrated catalogues, hardly anything has been published about Sidon, let alone the recent excavations in the 1990's. As for Baalbek, the world is scientifically still at the stage of knowledge reached by the German mission at the beginning of the twentieth century. Anjar, Shehim, Beit-Mery, Afqa, Faqra, and dozens of other sites of equal importance have no bibliographical record. Even Tyre is on the verge of disappearing from human memory [10]. Only efforts lately of the International Association to save Tyre attracted world's attention to Salvage the ruins of Tyre.

At Tyre, a small controlled test excavation revealed the remote part of the island and the old city. Another excavation at the Phoenician port of Sarafand brought evidence of a center for ceramic production from the second millennium B.C.

The work at Kamid el-Loz in the biqaa valley has also made a major contribution to the study of Lebanon's past. The treasures from the excavations are on a loan exhibition in Germany. The amount of information gained by the excavators from this one site is vast. However, very few Lebanese know of its existence or significance. The people of Kamid el-loz had asked that a museum be built for them in their village, but they were not heard. Today Kamid el-loz is being looted by people who learnt how to excavate well from the archaeologists who first uncovered the buried history of this ancient site [11].

In a recent spectacular exhibition entitled "I Fenici", luxuriously furnished, publicized and financed with Italian know-how and industry (1988), the legendary land of the Phoenicians, Lebanon, was represented by a large contribution in archaeological objects emanating entirely from Antiquities' Market! The few objects from museum collections, such as the American University of Beirut Museum pieces, did not originate from archaeological excavations either. In spite of its popular success, judgment of the exhibition was sadly divided. A portion of Italy's and Europe's scientific community engaged in investigating near eastern archaeology was absent from the exhibition in silent protest. To what avail? The circle seems closed and Lebanon remains one of the capitals of international antiquities' traffic [12].

In 1991, Robert Fisk a well-known (journalist investigates the plundering of Lebanon's Heritage, as correspondent for the London Independent, living in Beirut since 1978 deplores the fate of Lebanon's Heritage. After 15 years of war, Lebanon has fallen victim to the greatest pillage of) priceless artifacts ranging from the Bronze Ages to the Byzantine periods. Archaeological artifacts being illegally exported to Europe and U.S.A by Lebanese dealers and international middlemen while some of the most important archaeological sites in what was ancient Phoenicia have been destroyed by treasure-hunters [13].

Only now, with the prospect of peace at hand, have the Lebanese authorities started to stop such process of looting of the country's heritage. The scale of theft is staggering. For example, it has been revealed that several rooms full of excavated material from the Lebanese Department of Antiquities was stolen by militiamen from a store-house at Byblos [9] were shipped to European art dealers, some valuable treasures were discovered on public sale in Zurich. The AUB Museum was robbed in 1991 [8]. The National Museum was not saved, it was robbed and destroyed to a large extent, (Phoenician cemeteries east of Tyre are being dug up by amateur treasure-hunters, their contents of gold jewellery and pottery sold to Lebanese dealers and then shipped out of the country via Cyprus to Europe and U.S.A [8] (Figures 2-4).

Figure 2: Rockets hit AUB Museum (1989) shattering exhibition cases, and tower of AUB Post Hall.

Figure 3: Rescued objects and mosaics from clandestine excavations at Nabatiyyeh and Sidon.

Robert Fisk also laments the fate of Kamid el-loz which is one of the most important sites of Lebanon [14], the fruits of 19 years' work by German archaeologists, has been destroyed. The earth is still there, but it has been cut away with bulldozers and earth-diggers. Chunks of pottery have been thrown into a huge rubbish tip at one end of the tell, as if hurled away in frustration by the diggers, because the antiquities they were looking for were indeed largely elusive. the treasure which Kamid el-loz represented was historical rather than material [8] (Figure 5).

None of this was evident to the robbers. Nor to the two modernday armies whish briefly fought for Kamid el-loz in 1982. The site was the demarcation line between the Syrian and Israel armies [11]. Both armies fought to hold the site, and the warning sign of the UNESCO with the emblem comprised of white and blue triangles warning everybody including fighting armies that the premises are protected by the Hague convention of 1954 [12], and it should be safe-guarded in the event of armed conflict. Even this sign it didn't deter the fighting armies [12], such UNESCO signs were mounted on most archaeological sites in Lebanon, but it didn't deter fighting armies from bombing the sites, or stop the looters from plundering Lebanon's heritage.

Figure 4: Beirut National Museum devastated by bullets and shells in 1991, and a broken Roman sarcophagus outside the wrecked Museum.

Experts also blame the publicity afforded the " Sevso treasure " for the obsessive plundering. This multimillion dollar hoard of Roman period Silver plate of alleged Lebanese provenance made headlines in 1990 when it turned up in New York. The court case which followed had not been settled by mid-1992 [8]. specialists in such artifacts believe that the Sevso silver hoard did not originate in Lebanon, but was sold on the international market with illegally obtained Lebanese export papers. The " Sevso treasure " story gave people the idea that they could become millionaires by digging up the land. Bulldozers are at work all over the Biqaa ploughing through tells in the hope of finding treasures. They are destroying the archaeology of this land. It is another national tragedy [15].

Suzzy Hakimian in 1987 warned that the accumulated cultural heritage is today being rapidly destroyed and lost. She conducted a survey of illicit excavations, reported in the Lebanese press during the last decade of continued military action and break down of state control, shows the extent of these clandestine activities in Lebanon. When the sites reported are plotted anto a map, it becomes evident that no area of the country has been exempt from pillage which destroys all context information of artifacts obtained in this way. [14] (Figures 6).

Figure 5: Kamid El-Loz (1991) [4] Buldozers used to look (for hidden treasures, destroying one of the country's most important archaeological sites in Beqaa).

Figure 6: Objects rescued in (1991) from a clandestine excavation in Tyre, displayed in an exhibition at a bank in Beirut, and restored to the National Museum. Funerary jars and inscribed stelae with Phoenician letters.

What hope is there to break the cycle of ignorance which encourages the marketing of Lebanon's past? Only the careful creation of a common historical consciousness in present generations can encourage unity over opportunism in the future. Hence the importance of teaching a more comprehensive history for all Lebanese in the schools. Crediting the past is not simply collecting and selling precious artifacts made by our so-called ancestors. The past cannot survive in dismantled objects of art and trade, an endlessly broken record, a raped heritage. Lebanon's past can live only if it makes a contribution to the present, as a continuity of experience connected with life today. A people without a coherent past can only have an uncertain future [16].

Such attitude is strengthened if we expose the students at a certain level in their education to all of the UNESCO conventions on the protection of cultural heritage, in particular the 1954 convention and its protocols, which aim to ensure the survival and maintenance in situ no pillage or illicit export tolerated) of this heritage [1], The preamble of the convention reasserts that, damage to cultural property belonging to any people what so ever means damage to the cultural heritage of all mankind, since each people makes its contribution to the culture of the world [17].

REFERENCES

1. www.unesco.org
2. unesdoc.unesco.org
3. apps.americanbar.org
4. EU Commission - Working Document (2013) Panorama of EU industry 95/96. An extensive review of the situation and outlook of the manufacturing and service industries in the European Union. Archive of European Integration (AEI).
5. Bikai P (1990) Guest Editorial: The Emergence of the Phoenicians. BASOR 279: 7-8.
6. edmund2.hiof.no
7. ddc.aub.edu.lb
8. www.phoenicia.org
9. http://www.digiserve.com/mentor/frises/
10. Francioni F, Lenzerini F (2003) The Destruction of the Buddhas of Bamiyan and International Law. European Journal of International Law 4: 619-651.
11. http://www.oebh.at/
12. Robert F (1991) The biggest supermarket in Lebanon, a journalist investigates the plundering of Lebanon's Heritage. Berytus 39: 243-252.
13. Hakimian S (1987) Une Archeologie paralle'le: Les De'couvertes Clandestines et Fortuites au Liban. Berytus 35: 199-209.
14. www.today.az
15. http://www.kisbalaton.sziriuszstudio.hu
16. Gerstenblith P (2006) From Bamiyan to Baghdad: warfare and the preservation of cultural heritage at the beginning of the 2. Georgetown Journal of International Law. 37: Nbr 2.
17. Poliszczuk T, Broda D, Poliszczuk D (2012) Changes in Somatic Parameters and Dynamic Balance in Female Rhythimic Gymnasts Over a Space of Two Years. Polish journal of sport & tourism. 19: 240-245.

CHAPTER 15

PROSECUTING INTERNATIONAL CRIMES AT THE INTERNATIONAL CRIMINAL COURT: IS THERE A COHERENT AND COMPREHENSIVE PROSECUTION STRATEGY?

Kai Ambos and Ignaz Stegmiller

INTRODUCTION

The selection and prioritization of cases to be prosecuted before the ICC, while necessary and legitimate given the existing capacity constraints and the goals of the Court to prosecute the "most serious crimes" of the "most responsible", runs the risk to bring the Court into disrepute if not done properly, i.e., in a transparent and rational way. The selection of defendants is complex and essentially preceded by two main steps: first, it has to be distinguished between the primary selection of situations ("locations" where possible ICC crimes have taken place) and the subsequent extraction of cases (including one or more perpetrators) from these situations (cf. OTP Regulations 34 et seq.). Further, one must distinguish between the selection process of the Office of the Prosecutor (OTP) and the – lately very much criticised – referral procedure of the UN Security Council (SC) which so far has only been invoked with regard to Non-State Parties of the ICC (Darfur, Sudan and the Libyan Arab Jamahiriya). The ICC can normally exercise jurisdiction only in cases where the accused is a national of a State Party or when the alleged crime took place on the territory of a State Party.[1] Other scenarios can be referred to the ICC by the SC. The decision whether to refer a situation in a Non-State Party to the ICC – or not to refer it and thus not to trigger ICC jurisdiction – depends on eminently political considerations of the SC. The ICC has no bearing on this decision and may only, once a situation is referred to it, analyse the situation in light of its statutory criteria and decide whether or not to open a (formal) investigation.

This paper focuses primarily on the selection of cases, a core issue for prosecutorial coherence; yet it does not pretend to cover all questions that might arise during the complex selection process. As to this process different approaches are possible. One may choose cases on a first come, first serve basis, or according to the greatest ease of access to evidence, or based on formal criteria (Bergsmo, 2010, at 9 [8]). The last approach is an essential innovation of the ICC, where the OTP uses certain legal and policy criteria to rank cases in a coherent manner. The problem of selecting situations and cases was less important for other international(ized) tribunals, such as the International Criminal Tribunal for Rwanda (ICTR) and the International Criminal Tribunal for the Former Yugoslavia (ICTY), because their jurisdictional reach is far more limited in territorial and temporal terms in the first place. In other words, the *ad hoc*tribunals did not have to select their "situations" as these were already defined in their Statutes. The ICTR and ICTY could directly start off, selecting appropriate cases for investigation and prosecution. The ICC can, in turn, theoretically act on a universal scale. For these reasons, more difficult choices have to be made and selectivity plays an important role. The function of the court, and its legitimacy, stand and fall with such decisions. The authors will therefore concentrate on the ICC's selection strategy. As will be seen below, the OTP initiated a process of public consultations

Citation: Kai Ambos, Ignaz Stegmiller, Prosecuting International Crimes At The International Criminal Court: Is There A Coherent And Comprehensive Prosecution Strategy? DOI: 10.1007/s10611-012-9407-9.

to develop consistent selection criteria, quite different from earlier international criminal tribunals that did not address the issue in a public and transparent way. However, the debate on selection at the ICC is only just beginning. Many questions, such as the binding nature of those selection criteria and the exact choice of criteria, still remain and require further reflection and debate.

This paper focuses on the OTP approach laid down in its Prosecutorial Strategy (see Selection strategy at the ICC (OTP) section) and examines the four fundamental principles: focused investigations (see Focused investigations section), positive complementarity (see Positive complementarity section), interests of the victims (see Addressing the interests of victims section) and the impact of the OTP's work (see Maximising the impact: developing a coherent strategy at the ICC section). Only by means of certain improvements can the OTP's impact be maximised, primarily continued transparency is necessary; the publication of interim reports and the integration of all policy and strategy papers into one coherent strategy as a permanent model for case selection in the whole field of international criminal justice.

SELECTION STRATEGY AT THE ICC (OTP)

During the last years the OTP has consistently addressed key points of its selection strategy in several papers, albeit failing to develop a comprehensive approach. The Office dealt with the different problems as they arose publishing the respective policy and strategy papers outlined below.

Identifying Sources

According to OTP Regulation 14 (see Regulations of the OTP, 2009 [47]), the OTP, as already mentioned above, can make use of policy papers that reflect the key principles and criteria. Four fundamental principles lie at the core of the Strategy: (i) positive complementarity, (ii) focused investigations and prosecutions, (iii) addressing the interests of victims, and (iv) maximizing the impact of the Office's work (Prosecutorial Strategy, 2009–2012, at 4–7 [45]).

In accordance with OTP Regulation 14, the OTP have made various papers available to the public. First, key strategic issues are laid down in two strategy papers: (i) the Strategy 2006–2009 (Report on Prosecutorial Strategy, 2006 [48]),[2] and (ii) the Strategy 2009–2012 (Prosecutorial Strategy, 2010 [45]). Second, several policy papers of the OTP clarify other key issues, such as the "interests of justice", victim's participation and preliminary examinations. The latest draft version on preliminary examinations (Draft Policy Paper on Preliminary Examinations, 2010 [15]) will be further examined below. More policy papers on topics such as positive complementarity and case selection are in the consultation process and will be published in the future.

Lack of a Comprehensive, Overall Strategy

The OTP uses the terms "policy" and "strategy" indiscriminately. The strategy papers cover certain time periods (2006–2009 and 2009–2012) and clarify the strategic objectives for the OTP, while the policy papers address particular fundamental issues on which the Office wants to provide more clarity and transparency. In accordance with OTP Regulation 14 (1), however, it appears that the OTP shall develop a Prosecutorial Strategy as the overall guidance. In our understanding, OTP Regulation 14 (1) refers to one coherent prosecution strategy in one master document. The current practice of strategies for time-frames of approximately three years does thus not comply with the wording of the mentioned Regulation. This is not just a formal point. To have one main document with the overall general or specific goals of a prosecution strategy indicates the general direction for the Office and this not only for the interested public but also for the personnel working in the Office. It is also more practical to have the overall strategy in one document instead of in various documents which are produced at different times and focus on different topics. Only a master document can set out a *leitmotif* from which focused strategies can be developed and on the basis of which periodic reflection can take place.

Three-year plans are valid as working agendas for the Office. They set out the strategy and goals for a specific period. Similarly, the policy papers reflect the strategic objectives and form the basis of the strategy. They are subject to unlimited revision due to their policy nature and do not give rise to any rights of litigation (Policy Paper on the Interests of Justice, at 1 [34]). On the basis of these papers and the work of the Court to date, the Prosecutor should draw lessons learned and set out a clearer strategy (in a similar vein HRW, 2011, at 2, 46 [26]; HRW, 2011, at 3–4 [25]). The OTP has commenced a transparent dialogue with external actors, which should be continued. In fact, the Prosecutor is well advised to increase this process of mutual exchange to further the ICC's credibility and to avoid the appearance of inconsistency of its selection decisions. For example, the Prosecutor should publish (as in fact foreseen by the Prosecutorial Strategy, 2009–2012 at 10 [45]), interim reports that terminate or enable the OTP to monitor preliminary examinations of certain country situations.

Transparency through interim reporting enhances the ICC's legitimacy. It will further contribute to the institutional development of the ICC and strengthen the hand of the new ICC Prosecutor elected by the end of 2011 (HRW, 2011, at 4 [25]). This lessons-learned process involves a two-pronged approach to be taken by the OTP: first, developing a newly-arranged strategy paper in accordance with OTP Regulation 14 (1), and, second, a continuation of the consultation process with external actors to design prosecutorial guidelines that cover the situation and case selection process and its criteria (thereto Stegmiller, 2011, at 268–9, [63]). Such guidelines would have to integrate the existing (draft) policy papers on the "interests of justice", preliminary examinations, case selection, etc., thus harmonizing the papers and consolidating the selection criteria in the form of policy-oriented guidelines.

FOCUSED INVESTIGATIONS

One guiding principle of the OTP is that of focused investigations and prosecutions. The Office has chosen to focus on the most serious crimes and on "those bearing the greatest responsibility". While the latter terminology allows for certain flexibility, the ICC Prosecutor mainly selects the persons from the top of the (state) hierarchy for his cases. Others are left to national criminal justice systems, encouraging territorial and third states to take measures against those offenders and to close the impunity gap (see Positive complementarity section for further understanding). In line with this focused approach the OTP has originally adopted a sequential approach, investigating cases within a situation one after another and selecting them according to their gravity (Report on Prosecutorial Strategy, 2006, at 5 [48]; for critique see HRW, 2006, at 5 [23]; Ambos, 2010, at 38 [4]). Lately, the OTP has been more flexible in its approach and, for example in the Kenya proceedings, moved to simultaneous investigations, bringing two cases for prosecution at the same time (Case of the Prosecutor v. William Samoei Ruto, Henry Kiprono Kosgey and Joshua Arap Sang and the Case of the Prosecutor v. Francis Kirimi Muthaura, Uhuru Muigai Kenyatta and Mohammed Hussein Ali). Thus, while the OTP still mentions "focused investigations", the sequential approach is no longer explicitly contained in the Strategy 2009–2012 (at 10 [37]). This shows that certain flexibility is useful and that the Prosecutor must be able to adjust the strategy from time to time. Further, the Office's aim to shorten investigations and expedite trials is reflected in a selection of a limited number of the gravest incidents, representing the main types of victimization (Prosecutorial Strategy, 2010, at 6 [45]).

The focused approach adheres to practical realities and experiences from earlier international criminal trials. It is clearly impossible for the ICC to prosecute all potential perpetrators of international core crimes. The ensuing impunity gap can only be closed by prosecutions on the national level (Policy Paper, 2003, at 7 [33]). Thus, the success of the OTP's approach, with a view to the fight against impunity, depends on the strength of national systems and their integration into the international criminal justice system as a whole. On a different note, one must not confuse the OTP' *policy* choice to limit prosecutions to certain high caliber cases with the admissibility threshold as a *legal* barrier to bring certain cases (Rastan, 2010, at 97 [46]; Stegmiller, 2011 at 258, [63]). If the Prosecutor feels the need to take a broader approach, his policy may be adjusted accordingly, albeit always bearing in mind the need of coherence.

The OTP's Preliminary Examination

As stated at the beginning of this paper, the selection process of the OTP can be roughly divided into two stages: (i) the identification of situations, and (ii) the selection of cases. "Situations" refers to larger areas of conflict, in which the OTP investigates and builds up several case hypotheses. The situation selection is guided by the criteria of article 53 (1) ICC Statute, namely jurisdiction, admissibility and the "interests of justice" (Rules 48 and 104 RPE; further Stegmiller, 2011 at 209 et seq. [52]). Cases are selected according to similar legal criteria, either based on article 53 (2) ICC Statute or on a *mutatis mutandis* basis of article 53 (1) ICC Statute's factors.[3]

Before dealing with the question of case selection, the OTP must traverse the pre-investigation stage, during which the examination and selection of situations for further investigations takes place. This preliminary examination stage is an important and necessary innovation compared to the pre-trial procedure of former International Criminal Tribunals (the International Military Tribunals in Nuremberg and Tokyo, the ICTY and ICTR, the Special Court for Sierra Leone, the Extraordinary Chambers in the Courts of Cambodia and the Special Tribunal for Lebanon). Contrary to these Ad Hoc International Criminal Tribunals that all possessed jurisdiction over a specific situation, limited in temporal and territorial terms, the ICC does not have such jurisdictional limitations (Draft Policy Paper on Preliminary Examinations, 2010, at 4 [15]). Instead, the ICC must pre-investigate and select its own situations. Even in the case of *prima facie* pre-defined situations, by way of a SC or State referral (see next section), the ultimate decision whether to initiate a formal investigation rests upon the Prosecutor and the Judges, based on the criteria of articles 53 (1) ICC Statute (Draft Policy Paper on Preliminary Examinations, 2010, at 5 [15]; Stegmiller, 2011 at 113–4, [63]).

Overview of the Process

During the preliminary examination process the OTP assesses whether it opens a formal investigation into a situation. The analysis of a situation can be triggered through the following three mechanisms: (i) a State referral in accordance with articles 13 (a), 14 ICC Statute, (ii) a SC referral in accordance with article 13 (b) ICC Statute, or (iii) by *proprio motu* action of the Prosecutor on the basis of information received in accordance with articles 13 (c), 15 ICC Statute.

In general, all three trigger mechanisms are subject to the same analysis applying the same criteria. The initiation *proprio motu* only differs in two aspects: first, according to article 15 (3) ICC Statute the Prosecutor must submit a request for authorisation to the competent Pre-Trial Chamber, whereas in the case of referrals the Prosecutor can simply proceed with his formal investigation unless he determines that a reasonable basis does not exist (article 53 (1) ICC Statute); second, the assessment of information received under article 15 ICC Statute made it necessary to introduce a pre-filter mechanism. The "information received" (also referred to as "communications") shall be analyzed in accordance with article 15 (2) ICC Statute. This means that the information's "seriousness" is evaluated and crimes manifestly outside the ICC's jurisdiction are sorted out even before becoming formal "situations under analysis" (so called analysis phase 1, see Draft Policy Paper on Preliminary Examinations, 2010, at 18 [15]; HRW, 2011, at 4 [25]). The procedure under OTP Regulation 27 (a) arranges for an initial "pre-preliminary" check to filter out information that is unfounded on its face (according to the ICC website, by the end of May 2011 4,316 of a total of 9,214 communications received were considered "manifestly outside of the jurisdiction of the Court"; for an earlier report see Update on Communications, 2006, at 2–3 [64]). In any case, the "seriousness" filter is also applied to (State or Security Council) referrals (see Rule 104 (1) of the Rules of Procedure and Evidence (RPE). In fact, it is a procedural filtering mechanism invented by the OTP to manage the large quantity of information about possible crimes it receives.

In the following preliminary analysis, the OTP evaluates the criteria set out in article 53 (1) ICC Statute, namely jurisdictional issues, admissibility and the interests of justice. In the first years of the ICC, the OTP distinguished three analysis phases: (i) Phase I – Initial Review; (ii) Phase II – Jurisdiction and Admissibility Assessment; and (iii) Phase III – Advanced Analysis and Planning (Annex to the Policy Paper, 2003 [7]; Stegmiller, 2011 at 215 et seq. [63]). The working method of the OTP has recently been refined and the components of phase

II have been re-regrouped in the new phases two (jurisdiction), three (admissibility) and four (interests of justice), while giving up the former phase of advanced analysis and planning (Draft Policy Paper on Preliminary Examinations, 2010, at 18 [15]).

The differentiation of phases during the preliminary examination process was not foreseen by the ICC Statute and merely circumscribes the OTP's working process. On a statutory basis, two steps are distinguishable, which the OTP now clearly identified: first, article 15 (2) ICC Statute allows for an analysis of the "seriousness" of information received in order to identify communications that manifestly do not provide any basis for further action (see also RPE 104 (1). Second, the "reasonable basis" standard and the evaluation criteria must be examined. With regard to the three trigger possibilities mentioned above, it is most important to note that "reasonable basis" is applied in the same manner to all triggers according to articles 15 (3), (4), 53 ICC Statute, rules 48 and 104 of the ICC Rules of Procedure and Evidence (Stegmiller, 2011 at 213 [63]; Situation in Kenya, Decision pursuant to article 15 of the Rome Statute on the authorisation of an investigation into the situation in the Republic of Kenya, 31.3.2010, paras. 17 et seq. [57]). Jurisdiction, admissibility and interests of justice are thus the central criteria for the analysis and selections of situations.

Critical Evaluation of the Draft Policy Paper on Preliminary Examinations

The question of selecting situations and cases we apparent from the very beginning of the Court's work. Yet, in this starting phase practical necessities and administrative issues were on the top of the agenda rather than the development of a clear selection strategy. Furthermore, the situations of Uganda and the Democratic Republic of Congo (DRC), the first ones referred to the ICC in 2004 by the respective governments, were plainly of such gravity that a detailed weighting procedure did not yet present itself as a necessity. Only when the number of communications on potential situations increased, a policy with regard to preliminary examinations became a matter of urgency. At present, seven situations are under preliminary analysis (Colombia, Afghanistan, Georgia, Guinea, Honduras, Korea and Nigeria), and the OTP recently requested authorisation of an investigation regarding the Ivory Coast (Situation in the Republic of Côte d'Ivoire, Request for authorisation of an investigation pursuant to article 15, 23.06.2011 [58]), making it the second *proprio motu* request besides the situation in Kenya.

In October 2010 the OTP published a Draft Policy Paper on Preliminary Examinations which was widely circulated and invited critical commentary. This Preliminary Examinations Paper is largely based on an earlier (internal) draft paper on situation and case selection of 2006, which was also circulated, albeit not that widely, for comments among (external) experts. Other papers on key issues, such as case selection and positive complementarity, are still in the internal consultation process and have not yet been made available to the public. While it is certainly a major improvement, compared to the *ad hoc* tribunals, that the OTP interacts with NGOs and external experts, one wonders why the process of completing policy papers takes such a long time. Since early 2006 the OTP has been working on the strategic questions and postponed publication of those papers several times. From an outsider's perspective one can only speculate as to why the remaining papers have not been finalised. Give the increased activity of the Office, not least because of the (unexpected) SC referrals in the case of Sudan (Darfur) and Libya, it is quite likely that there are serious capacity problems. While there is no unit that deals exclusively with strategy or policy papers, most of the staff at the OTP are engaged in the pending situations and cases which involve complex, often new procedural questions which require priority treatment. Numerous legal challenges arise during on-going trial proceedings and deadlines pressure the OTP to find quick answers. Still, one wonders why the policy and strategy papers cannot be produced by the Chief Prosecutor and his immediate team, recently considerably reinforced by the appointment of additional advisors.[4] These advisors are not involved in the daily work of the Office and their function is, if any, to help the Prosecutor to develop a coherent strategy and policy. In any case, a transparent selection process is important for the future of the ICC and could save working capacity. It is also crucial for the common acceptance of the Court. Strategic questions must be prioritized and solved as soon as possible. The election of a new Chief Prosecutor in December of last year and her taking over by mid 2012 allows for a fresh start learning the necessary lessons from the various missteps and failures of the predecessor (Kaye (2011), at 118 et seq. [28]). The new Prosecutor should as one of his/her first actions clarify the overall strategy. Working groups should be formed to tackle this important issue, involving external experts. The selection strategy affects the ICC as a whole and shapes its future.

With regard to the Paper on Preliminary Examinations, some explanations given by the OTP require further clarification. Take for example the non-existence of a definite time period for the completion of a preliminary examination (Draft Policy Paper on Preliminary Examinations, 2010, at 17 [15]). While fixed time limits may prove too rigid in light of the complexity of investigations of macrocriminality, the complete absence of any rule and the lack of external control of the preliminary examinations creates legal insecurity and gives rise to tension between the state concerned, the OTP and victims. After all, international human rights law demands a speedy process and this also in relation to the investigation phase. Thus, with regard to the situation in the Central African Republic (CAR) controversy arose between the OTP and the Pre-Trial Chamber concerning the status of the situation since the OTP provided no information for more than two years. To avoid such altercation in the future, the Chambers should be entitled to request status information after a certain time of inaction, carefully balancing prosecutorial independence against necessary checks by the Chambers (for a new rule providing for a time period of 18 months Stegmiller, 2011, at 235, [63]).

The incumbent Prosecutor also introduced a practice of inviting so-called self-referrals, which, according to the OTP, was "explicitly contemplated during the negotiations in Rome" (Draft Policy Paper on Preliminary Examinations, 2010, at 16 [15]). It is, however, controversial if the "idea that a State might refer a situation against itself was ever contemplated" (Schabas, 2010, at 309–10 [53]); in any case, the wording of Art. 13 (a), 14 does not exclude this possibility (for a recent thorough analysis, including of the *travaux* Robinson, 2011, at

359 et seq. [51]). Moreover, the *policy* question whether such referrals are to be favored over the *proprio motu*trigger, which the OTP explicitly mentions in its policy paper with regard to DRC, Uganda and Kenya (Draft Policy Paper on Preliminary Examinations, 2010, at 16–7 [15]), is worth discussing. The Court is now working at full capacity and *proprio motu* investigations might be the better choice in some situations. The possibility of the perception of a biased Court conducting one-sided investigations must, however, not be underestimated. These denunciations can easily be propagated in communities where knowledge about the ICC is scarce; a self-referral policy facilitates the spreading of such rumors, although the subsequent case selection, prosecuting all sides of the conflict, may neutralize criticism. The OTP can also avoid or diminish criticism by its well-established outreach program, the re-definition of referred situations and by an increased use of the *proprio motu* power. The last-mentioned switch to the *proprio motu* mechanism could be facilitated by the pending situations of Kenya and Côte d'Ivoire that will necessarily entail the treatment and hopefully solution of some legal questions involved. Obviously, the decision whether *proprio motu* to be used as the OTP's last resort or as an equal and powerful trigger mechanism ultimately lies in the hands of the new Prosecutor.

Case Selection

Within those chosen situations the OTP must select cases for further investigation and prosecution. The determination of a case involves the following steps: (i) selecting regions, (ii) selecting incidents, (iii) selecting groups, and (iv) selecting individual perpetrators (Stahn, 2009, at 249 [60]; HRW, 2006, at 4 et seq. [23]; see also Regulation 49 of the Regulations of the Court which give guidance on what type of information the OTP needs to gather in order to start an inquiry). The Prosecutor has decided to select cases inside a situation according to *gravity* and prosecute only *those suspects who bear the greatest responsibility for the most serious crimes* (Prosecutorial Strategy, 2009–2012, at 6 [45]). The OTP implements the last-mentioned criteria in a discretionary manner (Stahn, 2009, at 251, 263 [60]). If applied in such a manner, the two criteria – "gravity" and "those bearing the greatest responsibility" – must be linked to the statutory basis that provides for prosecutorial discretion, i.e., article 42 (1) in general and article 53 (2) (c) in particular, including the broad "interest of justice" clause (Stegmiller, 2011, at 332 et seq., 355, 425, 428 et seq. [63]).

Gravity as a case Selection Criterion

The OTP stated in its policy papers that gravity is at the very heart of its selection procedure. According to OTP Regulation 29 (2), the following factors are to be taken into account: (i) scale, (ii) nature, (iii) manner of commission, and (iv) impact.

Before the adoption of the OTP Regulations, there had been an intense debate on the factors that should be taken into account when applying gravity. The Pre-Trial Chambers upheld the factors mentioned by the OTP and equally favoured a mixed qualitative-quantitative approach (Situation in Kenya, Decision pursuant to article 15 of the Rome Statute on the authorisation of an investigation into the situation in the Republic of Kenya, 31.3.2010, para. 62 [57]; Prosecutor v. Bahar Idriss Abu Garda, Decision on the Confirmation of Charges, 8.2.2010, para. 31 [37]). Prior to that, a very rigid interpretation of the gravity threshold by Pre-Trial Chambers I in the case against Lubanga and Ntaganda, establishing a legal threshold through a focus on senior leaders only (Prosecutor v. Lubanga, Decision on the Prosecutor's application for warrant of arrest, 10.2.2006, paras. 41 et seq. [39]), was reversed in appeal proceedings (Situation in DRC, Judgement on the Prosecutor's appeal against the decision of Pre-Trial Chamber I, 13.7.2006, paras. 1 et seq. [56]). In the Pre-Trial Chamber's view gravity is to be understood as a legal threshold limiting the admissibility of ICC cases to "senior leaders"; this, of course, seriously limits the scope of the Court's activities. Contrary to this view, we submit that gravity entails both a discretionary notion and a legal filter, the "senior leaders" focus belonging to the former concept of discretionary gravity. In any event, the floor for further legal arguments regarding gravity has been re-opened by the Appeals Chamber.

At present, despite this intense debate, the overall concept of gravity remains largely unclear (De Guzman, 2009, at 1401 et seq. [12]). In particular, it is unclear where the gravity determination can, in the Statute, be normatively grounded. For case selection, gravity could be taken into account under articles 53 (2) (b), 17 (d) ICC Statute and/or article 53 (2) (c) ICC Statute. Taking into account OTP Regulation 29 and the above-mentioned decision by Pre-Trial Chamber II in the Kenyan situation, it seems that the OTP and the Pre-Trial Chamber solely regard gravity as the second part of the admissibility test under article 17 (1) ICC Statute. The statutory basis would then be found in articles 53 (2) (b), 17 (1) (d) ICC Statute (Guariglia, 2009, at 213 [19]). However, the OTP's own understanding in its policy papers is different, suggesting a broader reading of gravity in the sense of a discretionary concept as mentioned above. In line with this understanding, Paul Seils, the former Head of the Situation Analysis Section of the OTP, argues that some form of discretion ("principle of opportunity") is taken into account when the Office reaches its gravity decision (Seils, 2010, at 73 et seq. [54]). The way gravity is applied by the OTP entails a relative assessment, comparing cases to one another and involving discretionary choices, thereby going beyond a purely legal determination. Such a discretionary approach differs from the legal (non-discretionary) determination of gravity under article 17 (1) (d) ICC Statute (Ambos, 2010, at 48–9 [4]). In our view, the OTP is not prevented by the law to use gravity in such a way, but the statutory basis for a discretionary understanding can be found in article 53 (2) (c) (not article 17) of the Statute. Therefore, if gravity is used by the Prosecutor as a case selection and prioritization factor, it should be labelled accordingly, i.e., the OTP must reveal whether it uses gravity as a legal minimum threshold under article 17 (1) (d) ICC Statute or as a case selection criterion that involves discretionary considerations. If the latter is the case, as it appears from the strategy and policy papers, the OTP's gravity determination is a matter of article 53 (2) (c) ICC Statute, subject to judicial control under article 53 (3) ICC Statute. As a consequence, any decision not to prosecute individuals based on discretionary determination of gravity – no matter whether the pending situation was triggered *proprio motu*, through a State referral or a Security Council referral – could be reviewed by the Chambers (Stegmiller, 2011, at 451 [63]). This clearly follows from the wording of article 53

(3) ICC Statute, although the ensuing power of the respective State or the Security Council to trigger such a review (pursuant to article 53 (3) (a)) gives rise to concerns for these parties normally decide according to political considerations. It is therefore to be welcomed that, under this provision, the Pre-Trial Chamber may only request the Prosecutor to "reconsider" his decision, i.e., the ultimate decision is with the OTP.[5]

Those Bearing the Greatest Responsibility

During case selection another important aspect is the OTP's policy of focusing on those suspects who bear the greatest responsibility for the most serious crimes. The question of whom to prosecute is one that concerns international crimes equally because the number of potential perpetrators is so large that is practically impossible to put everyone on trial. The related issue of avoiding impunity and prosecutorial gaps will be addressed below as a matter of positive complementarity, while at this point the implementation of the OTP's policy of focused investigations will be discussed.

The term used by the OTP ("those who bear the greatest responsibility") cannot be found in the ICC Statute, but guidance is given in the Preamble and in articles 5 and 17 ICC Statute (Policy Paper, 2003, at 6–7 [33]). The Prosecutor himself understands the criterion as a policy matter (Policy Paper, 2003, at 7 [33]). If it were to be understood as an legal requirement, a defendant could bring a challenge that he/she is only a minor perpetrator and as such would not fall under the *ratione personae* jurisdiction of the ICC or that his/her case would be inadmissible (in a similar context, the SCSL rejected a jurisdictional barrier; see Prosecutor v. Brima, Kamara and Kanu, paras. 282 et seq. [38]). In early jurisprudence, Pre-Trial Chamber I decided that, contrary to the OTP's view, a perpetrator must be among the "senior leaders most responsible" in order to comply with the admissibility requirement under the gravity threshold of article 17 (1) (d) ICC Statute (Decision on the Prosecutor's application for warrant of arrest, article 58, 10.2.2006, para. 51 [44]). This interpretation significantly limited the ICC's jurisdictional reach and was therefore correctly revoked by the Appeals Chamber. According to its view the Pre-Trial Chamber's approach would hamper the deterrent effect of the Court and it lacks a statutory basis (Situation in DRC, Judgement on the Prosecutor's appeal against the decision of Pre-Trial Chamber I, 13.7.2006, paras. 75 et seq. [56]). Consequently, the criterion is of a purely policy nature and cannot constitute a legal obstacle to the prosecution of certain persons (Guariglia, 2009, at 215 [19]). According to the OTP it is not a strict and precise threshold, but could even be interpreted as flexible as to include suspects below high-ranking officers (HRW, Courting History, 2008, at 59 [24]).

Given this flexibility it becomes apparent that this criterion cannot be associated with (legal) gravity under article 53 (2) (b), 17 (1) (d) ICC Statute, but must be located elsewhere. Indeed, a leadership requirement has not been treated by the OTP as a pure gravity notion (Schabas, 2008, at 745 [52]), but is certainly linked to it. According to Rod Rastan gravity "may have a broader function in guiding the exercise of discretionary powers in order to identify and prioritize the selection of cases" (Rastan, 2010, at 97 [46]).

While a certain level of flexibility with regard to the rank and role of suspects to be prosecuted is essential not only for the already mentioned reasons of deterrence but probably even more for very practical reasons, the implicit prosecutorial discretion in prioritizing certain suspects over others requires justification and reasons in order not to appear completely arbitrary.

The OTP itself has not yet made public its interpretation of this policy threshold, although factors related to gravity, such as the "manner of commission", give some indications as to the policy.[6] Nevertheless, the OTP has been very reluctant to link senior leadership to any statutory basis, except the very general reference to the preamble, articles 5 and 17 ICC Statute. In fact, the OTP claims always to have full discretion once the article 17 (1)(d) gravity threshold is passed but it should not be overlooked that article 53 (2) (c) ICC Statute provides for an adequate framework for the OTP's policy (Stegmiller, 2011, at 444, [63]). Article 53 (2) (c) ICC Statue comprises the three factors that are relevant for the adoption of a focus on those bearing the greatest responsibility: (i) discretion, (ii) gravity (as a policy matter), and (iii) the role in the alleged crime. The latter two factors are even explicitly mentioned in the relevant sub-paragraph of article 53 and cover the most important characteristics of the terminology used by the OTP: "those bearing the greatest responsibility" (= "role" in article 53 (2) (c)) for the "most serious crimes" (= "gravity" in article 53 (2) (c)). If the OTP combines these three factors, it can apply its policy focus accordingly and it finds a solid statutory basis for such a policy. The only argument that might speak against such a reading of article 53 (2) (c) ICC Statute - from an OTP perspective - is the fact that the Prosecutor cannot apply a free-standing discretionary policy, but is subject to checks and balances as envisaged by article 53 ICC Statute. In other words, the Prosecutor's choices might be reviewed by a Pre-Trial Chamber under article 53 (3) ICC Statute.

POSITIVE COMPLEMENTARITY

With regard to complementarity, the OTP correctly emphasises that the primary responsibility for conducting investigations and prosecutions rests with the territorial State (Report on Prosecutorial Strategy, 2006, at 5 [48]). The combination of the complementarity principle with the OTP's focus on the most responsible entails, however, the risk of impunity gaps if the territorial state, due to capacity or other problems, fails to bring those responsible for international crimes, but below the top level to justice.

Complementarity contains two conceptual approaches: (i) the admissibility principle that deals with competing jurisdictions, and (ii) a principle of burden sharing for the consensual distribution of caseloads (Rastan, 2010, at 83 [46]). Concerning the latter the OTP adopted a policy of coordinated action which has been labeled *positive complementarity* (Prosecutorial Strategy, 2009–2012, at 5 [45]; Rastan, 2010, at 112–3 [46]; Burke-White, 2008, at 61 et seq. [10]; Stahn, 2008, at 88 [59]; Pampalk/Knust, 2010, at 672–4 [32]). Positive complementarity rests, in the sense of the mentioned burden sharing, on a partnership-based approach (Stahn, 2008, at 93–4, 102 [59]). The ICC is not meant to "compete" with States for jurisdiction, but is guided by the principles of partnership and vigilance (Informal Expert Paper on Complementarity, 2003, at 3 [27]).

In practical terms, positive complementarity means that the Prosecutor will encourage proceedings at the national level rather than taking over a case himself. In other words, even if a case is admissible in terms of the complementarity test, i.e., the respective State is, in principle, either unwilling or unable to investigate and prosecute it (for more details see Introduction section), the Prosecutor might encourage this State to take own action with the assistance of the OTP, without being directly involved in capacity building (Prosecutorial Strategy, 2009–2012, at 5 [45]; also Stahn, 2011, at 192–3 [61]). However, this approach of constructive burden sharing has so far only been applied with a third state (namely Germany in the case of the prosecution of leading FDLR members, see Selection strategy at the ICC (OTP) section) but not yet with a territorial State. As to the situation of Libya, where the new State authorities claim that the national justice system is actively investigating the cases of Saif Al-Islam Gaddafi and Abdullah Al-Senussi, the ICC faces a dilemma. According to the official Libyan view, it must, in line with its positive complementarity approach, declare the cases inadmissible (Prosecutor v. Al-Islam Gaddafi and Abdullah Al-Senussi, paras. 3–4 [36]). However, the problem is that the ICC has not yet determined a firm strategy with respect to parallel proceedings at the national level and that the OTP's prosecutorial practice has been inconsistent (Stahn, 2012, at 332–3 [62]). While in some cases the Prosecutor gave priority to facilitating domestic proceedings (e.g. Colombia; cf. Ambos, 2010 [4]), regarding Libya it is apparently expected that it actively challenges admissibility. This makes plain that considerable uncertainties exist with regard to the determination of domestic investigations and prosecution strategies in line with the existing admissibility test (Stahn, 2012, at 335–6, 339–40 [62]). It remains to be seen to which extent the OTP applies positive complementarity in the future in light of the Libya experience. Of course, the deeper conceptual problems regarding the precise requirements of "positive complementarity" have to be clarified (Stahn, 2012, at 348 [62]). In any case, given the high caseload of the ICC, there is no alternative but to promote the exercise of domestic jurisdiction by way of positive complementarity. If the territorial State is not able or willing the ICC may also cooperate with third States.

Territorial States

A territorial State can render any ICC proceedings inadmissible if it complies with the requirements provided for by the complementarity principle. According to article 17 ICC Statute a three-pronged test applies: first, the Court examines whether the State has taken action at all (inactivity scenarios); second, the exceptions mentioned in articles 17 (1) (a) – (c), 20 (3) ICC Statute render a case inadmissible before the ICC, unless, third, the exception to the exception – the unwillingness/inability test – applies (Ambos, 2010, at 55 [4]). While the OTP recognizes, in principle, transitional justice mechanisms applied at the national level (Rastan, 2010, at 115 [46]; Policy Paper on the Interests of Justice, at 7–8 [34])), it has failed to provide guidance as to how transitional justice mechanisms are in compliance with statutory demands (Stegmiller, 2011 at 379, [63]). The Prosecutor cannot leave the ambiguous matter of alternative mechanisms entirely to States, but is supposed to monitor any crimes that are not investigated and prosecuted as far as these are related to the concrete situation or cases under investigation (too demanding Hall, 2009, at 227–8 [21] calling for a general monitoring function of the OTP). It is therefore an important task to develop coherent guidelines that specify the requirements for genuine investigations/prosecutions in territorial States. The Prosecutor must re-evaluate his Policy Paper on the Interests of Justice and propose his understanding of transitional justice mechanisms *vis-à-vis* the ICC Statute. The adopted narrow interpretation and the application of the "interests of justice" as a last resort (cf. Policy Paper on the Interests of Justice, at 3 [34]) does not exempt the OTP from developing a comprehensive approach. Despite the fact that each case varies and thus a case-specific approach is required, it is feasible and essential for the future work of the ICC to provide guidance on transitional justice mechanisms. From our point of view, the principle of complementarity even obliges the Prosecutor to recommend a proper framework which then may be accepted or corrected by the ICC Judges in a concrete proceeding. Otherwise, the territorial State cannot comply with (positive) complementarity as it can never be sure when its efforts are sufficient or not. It could only establish a mechanism in advance and then seek complementarity testing, with a high risk of failing the OTP's *ad hoc* standard. Positive complementarity, however, requires a mutual course of action in good faith. The OTP must therefore engage in a debate on measures that satisfy the complementarity regime.

While the latter task falls primarily within the sphere of the Prosecutor, the reform efforts concerning capacity building in the affected State do not. It is certainly necessary to foster national action to close the impunity gap, but significant progress in strengthening national justice systems is still lacking. The ICC itself lacks resources to become involved in national capacity building. It can potentially assist the territorial States by relying on its networks of cooperation, sharing certain information and databases etc. (Prosecutorial Strategy, 2010, at 5 [45]). The responsibility for strengthening the rule of law by providing technical and judicial assistance currently rests upon the international community (Rastan, 2010, at 121–2 [46]). During the stocktaking at the Review Conference in Kampala, the Assembly of State Parties committed itself to becoming a facilitator regarding the issue of complementarity and the strengthening of domestic jurisdictions (Resolution RC/Res.1 Complementarity, paras. 9–10 [50]. In our view, the Assembly of State Parties and the more powerful ICC Member States must take their responsibility more seriously and assist post-conflict States in their development of criminal justice capacity. While the ICC may leave cases in the hands of the territorial State based on positive complementarity, it cannot re-build this State's domestic judicial system.

These efforts notwithstanding, another key actor is the Security Council. It should not use the referral tool as an instrument to relieve pressure from itself. It has to "follow through" a referral, i.e., it has to actively support the ICC in the enforcement of the decisions resulting from the referral. Unfortunately, the current practice of the Security Council goes to the contrary leaving the Court alone once a referral has been made. This is most apparent in the case against Al Bashir who, far from being surrendered to the Court, instead contemplates his re-election and calls the charges against him "lies" and "fabrications" (BBC Hard Talk, 14 May 2011). Still worse, with regard to Muammar-al-Gaddafi, the same permanent Security Council members (France, UK and USA) which promoted the referral in the first place went on – before the final victory of the rebels – to initiate secret negotiations about a Gaddafi exit including an immunity deal (see Dicker, 2011 [14]; Ambos, 2011, at 6 [6]). All such political games undermine the credibility and legitimacy of the Court.

Third States

The international criminal justice system operates on three levels in the fight against impunity of international crimes: (i) the level of the territorial States exercising its territorial jurisdiction, (ii) the level of the ICC exercising supranational jurisdiction, and (iii) the level of third States exercising extra-territorial jurisdiction, normally pursuant to the principle of universal jurisdiction. Only a mutual burden sharing between these three levels may efficiently contribute to the closing of the existing impunity gaps.

In situations where the territorial State cannot fulfil its obligation to prosecute, the ICC or third States should take appropriate action. If a domestic justice system fails to hold perpetrators accountable due to unwillingness or inability, "the role of the international community becomes crucial" (Rastan, 2010, at 123 [46]). In this regard universal jurisdiction as a basis for third States to prosecute plays a significant role (Hall, 2010, at 201 [22]). The close cooperation between the ICC, Rwanda, France and Germany in the cases against those most responsible for crimes committed in Eastern Congo by the Forces Démocratiques de Libération du Rwanda (FDLR), resulting in three arrests, is a shining example for positive complementarity (Factsheet Situation in the DRC, Callixte Mbarusihmana, 2010, at 3 [16]). These FDLR members are being prosecuted before the ICC (Callixte Mbarusihmana) and before the German Higher Regional Court (*Oberlandesgericht*) of Stuttgart (Ignace Murwanashyaka and Straton Musoni). The OTP sees the legal basis for such an approach in the Preamble and article 93 (10) of the ICC Statute, as well as its policy of positive complementarity, and stressed that the DRC authorities have been inactive in relation to the investigations in the Kivu region (Prosecutor v. Mbarushimana, Prosecution's Submission on Jurisdiction, 14.10.2010, paras. 24–5 [43]).

The German authorities have conducted the trial against Murwanshayka and Musoni on the basis of universal jurisdiction as enshrined in § 1 of the German Code of International Criminal Law (GCICL, *Völkerstrafgesetzbuch*). This is the first time that universal jurisdiction under § 1 GCICL has actually been applied by German Courts. It should be noted that the Federal Prosecutor has previously used § 153f of the German Criminal Procedural Code (GCPC, *Strafprozessordnung*) in numerous cases, such as the one against Donald Rumsfeld, to suspend further proceedings (for an explanation of the relationship between § 1 GCICL and § 153f GCPC see Ambos, 2007, at 45 et seq. [1]; see also id., 2009, at 420 et seq. [3]). § 153f of the GCPC gives the Prosecution discretion whether or not to open a case based on universal jurisdiction, if certain conditions are fulfilled. The German Federal Prosecutor ceased its own preliminary investigations against Mbarushimana in accordance with § 153f (2) clause 1 no. 4 of the GCPC, which allows for a discontinuation if the offence is prosecuted by "an international court of justice or by a country on whose territory the offence was committed, a citizen of which is either suspected of the offence, or suffered injury as a result of the offence". Mbarushimana's Defence instantly brought challenges related to issues concerning complementarity, using the preliminary investigations and the decision to cease these measures by the German Federal Prosecutor as its legal footing against the admissibility of the case. Both challenges, (i) before the ICC, and (ii) before the German Federal Constitutional Court, were not successful, but are interesting to analyse against the background of article 17 ICC Statute and positive complementarity.

The Defence submitted to Pre-Trial Chamber I that information provided by the OTP under article 58 ICC Statute was incomplete and "prevented the Pre-Trial-Chamber from ruling on admissibility in such circumstances where the case would, undoubtedly, have been deemed inadmissible" (Prosecutor v. Mbarushimana, Defence Challenge to the Validity of the Arrest Warrant, 10.1.2011, para.16 [42]). In particular, the Defence argued that Mbarushimana was an actual suspect in criminal investigations in Germany as he was jointly investigated with Murwanshyaka, that such an investigation was still ongoing until the 3 December 2010 and that for these reasons genuine investigative proceedings in the sense of article 17 (1) (a) ICC Statute were being conducted in Germany at the date of issuance of the arrest warrant and would have rendered the case inadmissible (Prosecutor v. Mbarushimana, Defence Challenge to the Validity of the Arrest Warrant, 10.1.2011, paras. 9 et seq. [42]).

The Chamber dismissed the challenge because the arrest warrant was properly issued and the case had not been clearly inadmissible (Prosecutor v. Mbarushimana, Decision of the Defence Challenge to the Validity of the Arrest Warrant, 28.1.2011, paras. 10–1 [40]). The OTP thus succeeded with its submission that the arrest warrant was issued in accordance with article 58 and that the Office did not omit any information (Prosecutor v. Mbarushimana, Prosecution Reponse to the "Defence Challenge to the Validity of the Arrest Warrant", 27.1.2011, paras. 10 et seq. [41]). As a result, the Chamber did not even go into the merits of admissibility, but denied a profound analysis of the early arrest warrant stage. The admissibility evaluation will be undertaken at a later stage, although the Chamber's decision *prima facie* speaks in favour of admissibility, or at least against any apparent admissibility defects.

This notwithstanding, the Defence called into question whether investigations had already been undertaken by the German Federal Prosecutor in the sense of article 17 (1) (a) or (b) ICC Statute, which could render the case inadmissible at a later stage. As part of the forthcoming admissibility analysis, the case would then be inadmissible if "the case is being investigated by a State which has jurisdiction over it" or "has been investigated by a State which has jurisdiction over it and the State has decided not to prosecute the person concerned". The gist of the issue is whether article 17 (1) (a), (b) ICC Statute applies to third States at all. Only if this is answered in the affirmative, one would have to look at the nature of the proceedings in Germany. According to a literal interpretation, "a State which has jurisdiction" could also be a third State that exercises universal jurisdiction. In the context of the right to challenge admissibility under article 19 ICC Statute, Hall therefore includes those States that have provided their Courts with jurisdiction, even if based on universality, as long as they have established domestic jurisdiction (Hall, 2008, 649 [20]). Germany has implemented this jurisdictional basis in § 1 of the GCICL and would therefore, if one follows Hall, qualify as a country with the right to challenge admissibility. However, this interpretation is, for policy and practical reasons, not convincing. While it is clear that the ICC's jurisdiction only operates complementary to national jurisdictions, article 17 (1) (a), (b) ICC Statute is primarily meant to encourage States with a close link to the crime scene to take action (Ambos, 2009, 477 [2]). A teleological reading of complementarity therefore links article 17 (1) ICC Statute to the territorial State and the home country of the perpetrator or the victim, as recently correctly held by the German Constitutional Court following the first author of this paper (BVerfGE 2 BvR 1/11, 1.3.2011, NStZ 2011, at 354, para. 12 [11]). A double complementarity, implying that the ICC's jurisdiction is also subsidiary to universal jurisdiction, goes beyond the envisaged approach of complementarity (Kreß, 2000, at 625 [30]; van Heeck, 2006, at 172 [65]). The ICC only has subsidiary jurisdiction if the relevant national jurisdiction is based on the links expressed by the principles of territoriality, (active) nationality and or protection. With regard to the case of Mbarushimana, German authorities echoed a similar understanding of article 17 ICC Statute, stating that the ICC is the adequate forum to deal with the case and that they will assist the OTP's investigation (Prosecutor v. Mbarushimana, Prosecution Response to the "Defence Challenge to the Validity of the Arrest Warrant", 27.1.2011, para. 17 [41]; BVerfGE 2 BvR 1/11, 1.3.2011, NStZ 2011, at 353–4, para. 7 [11]).

In sum, *subsidiary* universal jurisdiction may play a decisive role to close the impunity gap, but it should only be subsidiary, i.e., be invoked only in exceptional cases as ultimate last resort. Third States can only exercise universal jurisdiction if (i) States with a stronger nexus are unable or unwilling to investigate or prosecute, and (ii) the ICC does not exercise its jurisdiction (Kleffner, 2008, at 284 [29]). For the first time, the cooperation between the ICC and Germany has touched upon this dimension of article 17 ICC Statute. Most likely, the issue will be examined in more detail once the Chamber conducts its admissibility assessment. It is though submitted that the course of action taken by the OTP was in accordance with complementarity to the extent that universal jurisdiction does not lead to subsidiarity of ICC proceedings. If one does not follow this understanding of article 17 ("a State which has jurisdiction"), one might have to examine more closely the actions taken by the German Prosecution authorities with regard to Callixte Mbarushimana. Irrespective of these questions, the OTP's enhancement of positive complementarity and the division of labour between the ICC and (third) States is to be welcomed as a matter of a wise and realistic prosecutorial policy. Indeed, only the close interaction with third States enables the ICC to close the impunity gap. Only increased cooperation between the territorial State, third States and the ICC brings us closer to world-wide accountability.

ADDRESSING THE INTERESTS OF VICTIMS

Another principle of the OTP's policy is that it will always take into account the interests of victims. The Prosecutor will seek their views during all stages of the proceedings, i.e. the preliminary examination, investigation, pre-trial, trial and reparation stage (Prosecutorial Strategy, 2010, at 6–7 [45]). This approach corresponds to OTP Regulation 16 which stipulates: "The Office shall, in coordination with the Victims Participation and Reparations Section (VPRS) of the Registry, as appropriate, seek and receive the views of the victims at all stages in order to be mindful of and take into account their interest." It is not yet an easy task to identify the needs of the victims and who speaks on behalf of victims (Bock, 2010, at 317 [9]). For this purpose, the OTP promotes direct interaction with victims and victims' associations (Policy Paper on Victims' Participation, 2010, at 1 [35]). Clearly the inclusion of victims' views in such strategies places the ICC and the OTP in a new, particular and innovative constellation.

In addition, victims may promote their interests themselves. Victims' participation is a statutory right, mainly grounded in article 68 (3) ICC Statute, but also in other provisions of the ICC's legal texts. It was an innovation of the ICC to grant victims a more active role in the proceedings (Bock, 2010, at 440 et seq. [9]). At the earliest stages of situation analysis victims may participate informally and pass information to the Prosecutor (Bock, 2010, at 277, 463 [9]). In contrast, article 68 (3) ICC Statute gives the victims a stronger, more formalized right to participate actively in proceedings if (i) the applicant qualifies as a victim under rule 85 of the Rules of Procedure and evidence, (ii) the applicant's personal interests are affected by legal or factual issues raised in the proceedings at hand (Situation in DRC, Judgement on Victim Participation, 19.12.2008, para. 45 [55]). The Appeal's Chamber further denied a general participatory right during investigations, which it deemed to be the exclusive province of the Prosecutor (Situation in DRC, Judgement on Victim Participation, 19.12.2008, paras. 51, 57–9 [55]; critically thereto Bock, 2010, at 453 et seq. [9]). Hence, the victims' rights of active participation have to be assessed on a case-by-case basis and do not apply during investigations. However, even the Appeals Chamber does not preclude victims' participation in judicial proceedings at the investigation stage of a situation (Situation in DRC, Judgement on Victim Participation, 19.12.2008, para. 57 [55] – see e.g. articles 56, 57 (3) ICC Statute).

Be that it may, the OTP is, in any case under various statutory obligations (articles 15 (3), 19 (3), 53 (1) (c) ICC Statute) to grant victims certain participatory rights through making representations, even during investigations, and to inform them of decisions accordingly (Bock, 2010, at 506 et seq. [9]). The OTP has acknowledged this responsibility and stated that it "ensures interaction through public notice of its preliminary examination and investigation activities" (Policy Paper on Victims' Participation, 2010, at 14 [35]). While the Prosecutor has continuously improved the providing of public information, especially through weekly updates on preliminary examinations on the ICC website, interim reporting can still be enhanced. It would be important to make the reports on the Office's assessment of article 53 ICC Statute available once the OTP dismisses a situation after preliminary inquiries. These reports could provide more insight for the victims and the interested public. Clearly such efforts to address victims and to include them in dialogue would be entirely undermined by a selection strategy which is felt to ignore them.

MAXIMISING THE IMPACT: DEVELOPING A COHERENT STRATEGY AT THE ICC

The last principle mentioned by the OTP is to maximize the impact of activities of the Office. Through monitoring of situations the Prosecutor seeks to deter future crimes (Prosecutorial Strategy, 2009–2012, at 7 [45]). Deterrence should be achieved through the creation and activities of the ICC, with the OTP being an important multiplier. During the first years of the ICC the Prosecutor has fulfilled some of his objectives. First of all, the Office is in place and functioning, investigating crimes world-wide. Such a watchdog function alone may, albeit difficult to empirically demonstrate, have a deterrent effect. It must not be overlooked though that the deterrence capacity of ICL and thus the ICC is generally seen critically in scholarly writings (see Francis/Francis (2010), at 58 et seq. [17]; Golash (2010), at 201 et seq. [18]; Mullins/Rothe (2010), at 776 et seq. [31]). In any event, clearly leaders cannot move as freely as without an ICC arrest warrant.

Other than that, the OTP has consistently improved its work through its own critical evaluation. However, the new Prosecutor should continue this initial work and intensify efforts with regard to the overall strategy. The OTP must, policy-wise, revisit goals and impact critically (Stahn, 2011, at 197 [61]). Many challenges await the next Prosecutor (Kaye (2011), at 123 et seq. [28]). In the past, the Prosecutors' selection choices have not always been consistent (HRW, 2011, at 8 [26]; HRW, 2011, at 3 [25]). For example, it seems that the OTP did not apply the above-mentioned criteria of "gravity" and "those bearing the greatest responsibility" in a comprehensive manner. Transparency and public access also bear potential for improvement. The more information the OTP provides on its selection choices the better understandable they are. However, such an open approach requires a solid strategy, in legal and policy terms. Only if prosecutorial selection is based on well-defined criteria, the Prosecutor's decisions will find support and gain legitimacy. Otherwise, negative implications and questions about the credibility and consistency of the Prosecutor's selection process will follow suit. The OTP should therefore foster efforts to develop comprehensible guidelines. These could be based on a comparative study on selection and prioritization of international crimes at the international (ICTY, ICTR and hybrid courts) and national level (for an initial survey see Bergsmo, 2010 [8]). While it is indeed difficult to learn from national models for ordinary crimes and even find models for international crimes (cf. Ambos, 2011 [5]), the ICC as an international court must explain its choices and is under greater pressure to justify selectivity. At least, a new strategy document, integrating the existing policy and strategy papers as well as drawing lessons learned, should be drafted with more clarity and precision. With regard to selection criteria, the Office must take definite positions. Moreover, the OTP's strategy should ideally be part of a broader prosecution strategy with regard to international crimes, making it clear which cases are to be pursued by the ICC and which ones are to be left to domestic jurisdictions. The impunity gap may only be closed or at least diminished through a comprehensive, well coordinated strategy. In any event, questions of prosecutorial discretion with regard to case selection and potential constraints remain the most significant issues in the near future of international criminal justice (cf De Guzman/Schabas, at 10–1 [13]). The OTP has also come under criticism for the fact that some situations have been under analysis for several years without any tangible results (HRW, 2011, at 7 [25]). It replied that no specific timeline governs the preliminary examinations (Draft Policy Paper on Preliminary Examinations, 2010, para. 84 [15]). While this is formally true since no specific time-frame exists in the applicable law, as already discussed above (III 1 b)), and preliminary examinations are the domain of the Prosecutor, the possibility for the Pre-Trial Chamber to intervene – at least in the form of asking for information on the status of the situation – should be included in the RPE (Stegmiller, 2011, at 233 et seq. [63]).

In sum, the OTP's strategy is still a work in progress. Issues of major importance, such as case selection and positive complementarity, are in the internal queue waiting for attention. Once the respective papers are published, the general ideas of prosecutorial selection are known and can thus be subject to public scrutiny. Some prosecutorial questions have already been consolidated by the OTP, while others remain disputed. In particular, the gravity criterion is far from settled jurisprudence and requires fine-tuning (Stegmiller, 2011, at 329 et seq. [63]). The whole selection process must lead to equal choices. If need be, a review mechanism for the Chambers could be established. Hitherto, the possible inclusion of judicial control under article 53 (3) ICC Statute has been carefully avoided due to the undefined use of discretion.

Finally, the understanding of discretion will shape the future of Court, especially the interaction and allocation of powers between the Prosecutor and the Chambers. Applying discretion in the selection process is certainly the Prosecutor's domain. However, as we have explained above, the ICC Statute does not provide for unlimited, free-standing discretion. The carefully drafted provision, dealing with selection choices, is article 53 ICC Statute. The Prosecutor must therefore adhere to the criteria of this provision, in other words, issues of (discretionary) "gravity" and "those bearing the greatest responsibility" are a matter of article 53 (1) (c) and (2) (c) ICC Statute. As such, a limited review power of the Pre-Trial Chamber may be exercised. Only checks and balances between the Prosecutor and the Chambers as well as a transparent selection strategy can ensure coherence of the ICC's future practice.

Footnotes

[1] Note that a declaration according to article 12 (3) ICC Statute triggers the ICC's jurisdiction and, in this sense, gives also rise to preliminary examinations. It will then be dealt with, however, under article 15 ICC Statute.

[2] See also the Report on the activities during the first three years, 2006 [49].

[3] According to OTP Regulation 33 the Prosecutor refers to the criteria of article 53 (1) ICC Statute regarding case selection, which seems to imply that article 53 (2) ICC Statute does not apply to case selection. Nevertheless, OTP Regulation 29 (5) mentions article 53 (2) in the context of prosecutions. As cases form the basis of a prosecution and are selected at a later stage, arising out of the specific situation, there is an argument that article 53 (2) covers case selection. Moreover, a limitation of article 53 (2) only to circumstances where the OTP decides to bring no prosecution at all in relation to a whole situation is not supported by literal and systematic interpretation: Article 53 (2) speaks of a "sufficient basis for prosecution", which is a higher standard than the one mentioned for situation selection ("reasonable basis") in Article 53 (1), and thus refers to a different stage. Systematically, both paragraphs 1 and 2 of

article 53 are phrased in negative terms ("no" and "not"), but they do not indicate that they only cover negative decisions not to proceed. Notwithstanding the review mechanism under article 53 (3) solely covers negative decisions ("*not* to proceed") and the Chamber's intervention depends on such a case-specific decision of the Prosecutor. Otherwise, the carefully drafted review mechanism under article 53 (3) would be undermined. In other words, as long as a decision under article 53 (2) with regard to a particular suspect has not been issued by the OTP, it is not-existent and thus non-reviewable.

[4] Special Advisor on Gender Crimes Prof. Catharine MacKinnon, Special Advisor on International Humanitarian Law Prof. Tim McCormack, Special Advisor on International Law Prof. José Alvarez, Special Advisor on Crime Prevention Prof. Juan Méndez, Special Council to the Prosecutor Benjamin Ferencz, and Consultant for the OTP Judge Baltasar Garzon (in the meantime in Colombia as advisor to the OAS mission MAPP-OEA). See also the debates by invited 'experts' at http://uclalawforum.com/.

[5] In contrast, a decision not to proceed in the "interests of justice" under article 53 (3) (b) ICC Statute must be confirmed by the Chamber.

[6] See the Draft Policy Paper on Preliminary Examinations, 2010, at 15 [15]: "The manner of commission of the crimes may be assessed in light of, inter alia, the means employed to execute the crime, the degree of participation and intent in its commission, the extent to which the crimes were systematic or result from a plan or organized policy or otherwise resulted from the abuse of power or official capacity, and elements of particular cruelty, including the vulnerability of the victims, any motives involving discrimination, or the use of rape and sexual violence as a means of destroying communities."

ACKNOWLEDGMENTS

The authors thank Dr. Rod Rastan (ICC-OTP), Prof. Robert Cryer and Dr. Marianne Wade (both Birmingham) for very useful and productive comments as well as Ousman Njikam (ICTY-Chamber) for a critical revision of the text.

REFERENCES

1. Ambos, K. (2007). International Core Crimes, Universal Jurisdiction and § 153f German Criminal Procedure Code: A Commentary on the Decisions of the Federal Prosecutor General and the Stuttgart Higher Regional Court in the Abu Ghraib/Rumsfeld Case. *Criminal Law Forum, 18*(1), 43–58.
2. Ambos, K. (2009a). § 1 VStGB, in: Münchner Kommentar, Strafgesetzbuch, Nebenstrafrecht III, Völkerstrafgesetzbuch, Wolfgang Joecks/Klaus Miebach (eds.), 461–485.
3. Ambos, K. (2009b). Prosecuting Guantánamo in Europe: Can and Shall the Masterminds of the "Torture Memos" Be Held Criminally Responsible on the Basis of Universal Jurisdiction? *Case Western Reserve Journal of International Law, 42*, 405–448.
4. Ambos, K. (2010). The Colombian Peace Process and the Principle of Complementarity of the International Criminal Court.
5. Ambos, K. (ed.) (2011a). Selección y priorización como estrategia de persecución en los casos de crímenes internacionales, Un estudio comparado, http://www2.gtz.de/dokumente/bib-2011/giz2011-0145es-estrategia-persecucion.pdf. Accessed 25 August 2012.
6. Ambos, K. (2011b). Geben und Nehmen, Frankfurter Allgemeine Zeitung, 11 August 2011 (spanish version, inter alia, in El Mundo, Madrid, 23 August 2011, 15).
7. Annex to the Policy Paper: Referrals and Communications, September 2003, The Hague. http://www.icc-cpi.int/Menus/ICC/Structure+of+the+Court/Office+of+the+Prosecutor/Policies+and+Strategies/. Accessed 25 August 2012.
8. Bergsmo, M. (2010). The Theme of Selection and Prioritization Criteria and Why it Is Relevant, in: FICHL Publication Series No. 4, Criteria for Prioritizing and Selecting Core International Crimes Cases, Morten Bergsmo (ed.), 7–14.
9. Bock, S. (2010). Das Opfer vor dem Internationalen Strafgerichtshof.
10. Burke-White, W. (2008). Implementing a Policy of Positive Complementarity in the Rome System of Jusitce. *Criminal Law Forum, 19*(1), 59–85.
11. B Verf GE 2 BvR 1/11, 1.3.2011, NStZ 2011, 353–354. http://www.bverfg.de/entscheidungen/rk20110301_2bvr000111.html. Accessed 25 August 2012.
12. De Guzman, M. (2009). Gravity and the Legitimacy of the International Criminal Court. *Fordham International Law Journal, 32*, 1400–1464.
13. De Guzman, M., & Schabas, W. (2011). Initiation of Investigations and Selection of Cases, in: International Criminal Procedure Expert Framework, Towards a Codification of General Rules and Principles of International Criminal Procedure, October 2011, 8–11.
14. Dicker, R. (2001). Handing Qaddafi a Get-Out-Of-Jail-Free Card, International Herald Tribune, 1 August 2011.
15. Draft Policy Paper on Preliminary Examinations, 4 October 2010, The Hague. http://www.icc-cpi.int/Menus/ICC/Strucutre+of+the+Court/Office+of+the+Prosecutor/Policies+and+Strategies/. Accessed 25 August 2012.
16. Factsheet Situation in the DRC, Callixte Mbarushimana, Office of the Prosecutor, The Hague, 11 October 2010. http://www.icc-cpi.int/NR/rdonlyres/DEB862E4-1E38-4C6E-9197-2953EC6D7EC9/282525/FactsheetENG2.pdf. Accessed 25 August 2012.
17. Francis, L., & Francis, J. (2010). International Criminal Courts, the Rule of Law, and the Prevention of Harm: Building Justice in Times if Injustice, in: International Criminal Law and Philosophy, Larry May/Zachary Hoskins (eds.), 58–72.
18. Golash, D. (2010). The Justification of Punishment in the International Context, in: International Criminal Law and Philosophy, Larry May/Zachary Hoskins (eds.), 201–223.
19. Guariglia, F. (2009). The selection of cases by the Office of the Prosecutor of the International Criminal Court,

in: The Emerging Practice of the International Criminal Court, Carsten Stahn/Göran Sluiter (eds.), 209–217.

20. Hall, C. (2008). Article 19, in: Commentary on the Rome Statute of the International Criminal Court, Second Edition, Otto Triffterer (ed.), 637–667.
21. Hall, C. (2009). Developing and Implementing an Effective Positive Complementarity Prosecution Strategy, in: The Emerging Practice of the International Criminal Court, Carsten Stahn/Göran Sluiter (eds.), 219–228.
22. Hall, C. (2010). The Role of Universal Jurisdiction in the International Criminal Court System, in: FICHL Publication Series No. 7, Complementarity and the Exercise of Universal Jurisdiction for Core International Crimes, Morten Bergsmo (ed.), 201–245.
23. HRW, The Selection of Situations and Cases for Trial before the International Criminal Court, A Human Rights Watch Policy Paper, October 2006. http://www.hrw.org/en/news/2006/10/26/selection-situations-and-cases-trial-international-criminal-court. Accessed 25 August 2012.
24. HRW, Courting History, The Landmark International Criminal Court's First Years, 2008, http://www.hrw.org/en/reports/2008/07/10/courting-history-0. Accessed 25 August 2012.
25. HRW, Course Correction: Recommendations to the ICC Prosecutor for a More Effective Approach to "Situations under Analysis", June 2011. http://www.hrw.org/en/news/2011/06/16/icc-course-correction. Accessed 25 August 2012.
26. HRW, Unfinished Business, Closing gaps in the Selection of ICC cases, 15 September 2011, http://www.hrw.org/reports/2011/09/15/unfinished-business-0. Accessed 25 August 2012.
27. Informal Expert Paper: The Principle of Complementarity in Practice, Office of the Prosecutor, The Hague, 2003. http://www.icc-cpi.int/Menus/ICC/Structure+of+the+Court/Office+of+the+Prosecutor/Network+with+Partners/. Accessed 25 August 2012.
28. Kaye, D. (2011). Who's afraid of the International Criminal Court? *Foreign Affairs, 2011*, 118–129.
29. Kleffner, J. (2008). Complementarity in the Rome Statute and National Criminal Jurisdictions.
30. Kreß, K. (2000). Völkerstrafrecht in Deutschland, in: Neue Zeitschrift für Strafrecht, No.12, 617–626.
31. Mullins, C., & Rothe, D. (2010). Ability of the International Criminal Court to Deter Violations of International Criminal Law. *International Criminal Law Review, 10*(5), 771–786.
32. Pampalk, M., & Knust, N. (2010). Transitional Justice und Positive Komplementarität, in: Zeitschrift für Internationale Strafrechtsdogmatik No. 11, 669–675.
33. Paper on policy issues before the Office of the Prosecutor, September 2003, The Hague. http://www.icc-cpi.int/Menus/ICC/Structure+of+the+Court/Office+of+the+Prosecutor/Policies+and+Strategies/. Accessed 25 August 2012.
34. Policy Paper on the Interests of Justice, September 2007, The Hague. http://www.icc-cpi.int/Menus/ICC/Structure+of+the+Court/Office+of+the+Prosecutor/Policies+and+Strategies/. Accessed 25 August 2012.
35. Policy Paper on Victims, 12 April 2010, Office of the Prosecutor, The Hague. http://www.icc-cpi.int/Menus/ICC/Structure+of+the+Court/Office+of+the+Prosecutor/Policies+and+Strategies/. Accessed 25 August 2012.
36. Prosecutor v. Al-Islam Gaddafi and Abdullah Al-Senussi, Application on behalf of the Government of Libya pursuant to Article 19 of the ICC Statute, 1.5.2012 (ICC-01/11-01/11-130).
37. Prosecutor v. Bahar Idriss Abu Garda, Decision on the Confirmation of Charges, 8.2.2010 (ICC-02/05-02/09-243). http://www.icc-cpi.int/Menus/ICC/Situations+and+Cases/Cases/. Accessed 25 August 2012.
38. Prosecutor v. Brima, Kamara and Kanu (AFRC trial), 22.2.2008 (SCSL-04-16-A-675).
39. Prosecutor v. Lubanga, Decision on the Prosecutor's application for warrant of arrest, article 58, 10.2.2006 (ICC-01/04-01/06-8-US-Corr., reclassified as public pursuant to decision ICC-01/04-01/06-37). http://www.icc-cpi.int/Menus/ICC/Situations+and+Cases/Cases/. Accessed 25 August 2012.
40. Prosecutor v. Mbarushimana, Decision of the Defence Challenge to the Validity of the Arrest Warrant, 28.1.2011 (ICC-01/04-01/10-50). http://www.icc-cpi.int/Menus/ICC/Situations+and+Cases/Cases/. Accessed 25 August 2012.
41. Prosecutor v. Mbarushimana, Prosecution Response to the "Defence Challenge to the Validity of the Arrest Warrant", 27.1.2011 (ICC-01/04-01/10-35). http://www.icc-cpi.int/Menus/ICC/Situations+and+Cases/Cases/. Accessed 25 August 2012.
42. Prosecutor v. Mbarushimana, Defence Challenge to the Validity of the Arrest Warrant, 10.1.2011 (ICC-01/04-01/10-32). http://www.icc-cpi.int/Menus/ICC/Situations+and+Cases/Cases/. Accessed 25 August 2012.
43. Prosecutor v. Mbarushimana, Prosecution's Submission on Jurisdiction, 14.10.2010 (ICC-01/04-01/10-12). http://www.icc-cpi.int/Menus/ICC/Situations+and+Cases/Cases/. Accessed 25 August 2012.
44. Prosecutor v. Ntaganda, Decision on the Prosecutor's application for warrant of arrest, article 58, 10.2.2006 (ICC-01/04-02/06-20-Anx2). http://www.icc-cpi.int/Menus/ICC/Situations+and+Cases/Cases/. Accessed 25 August 2012.
45. Prosecutorial Strategy, 2009–2012, 1 February 2010, The Hague. http://www.icc-cpi.int/Menus/ICC/Strucutre+of+the+Court/Office+of+the+Prosecutor/. Accessed 25 August 2012.
46. Rastan, R. (2010). Complementarity: Contest or collaboration? in: FICHL Publication Series No. 7, Complementarity and the Exercise of Universal Jurisdiction for Core International Crimes, Morten Bergsmo (ed.), 83–132.

47. Regulations of the Office of the Prosecutor, ICC-BD/05-01-09, Entry into force: 23. April 2009. http://www.icc-cpi.int/Menus/ICC/Legal+Texts+Tooles/. Accessed 25 August 2012.
48. Report on Prosecutorial Strategy, 14 September 2006, The Hague. http://www.icc-cpi.int/Menus/ICC/Strucutre+of+the+Court/Office+of+the+Prosecutor/Policies+and+Strategies/Report+on+Prosecutorial+Strategy.htm. Accessed 25 August 2012.
49. Report on the activities performed during the first three years (June 2003-June 2006), 12 September 2006, The Hague. http://www.icc-cpi.int/Menus/ICC/Structure+of+the+Court/Office+of+the+Prosecutor/Reports+and+Statements/. Accessed 25 August 2012.
50. Resolution RC/Res.1 Complementarity, ASP 9th plenary meeting, 8 June 2010, http://www.icc-cpi.int/Menus/ASP/ReviewConference/Stocktaking/. Accessed 25 August 2012.
51. Robinson, D. (2011). The Controversy over Territorial State Referrals and Reflections on ICL Disclosure. *Journal of International Criminal Justice, 9*(2), 355–384.
52. Schabas, W. (2008). Prosecutorial Discretion vs. Judicial Activism. *Journal of International Criminal Justice, 6*(4), 731–761.
53. Schabas, W. (2010). The International Criminal Court, A Commentary on the Rome Statute.
54. Seils, P. (2010). The Selection and Prioritization of Cases by the Office of the Prosecutor of the International Criminal Court, in: FICHL Publication Series No. 4, Criteria for Prioritizing and Selecting Core International Crimes Cases, Morten Bergsmo (ed.), 69–78.
55. Situation in DRC, Judgement on Victim Participation in the investigation stage of the proceedings in the appeal of the OPCD against the decision of Pre-Trial Chamber I of 7 December 2007 and in the appeals of the OPCD and the Prosecutor against the decision of Pre-Trial Chamber I of 24 December 2007, 19.12.2008 (ICC-01/04-556). http://www.icc-cpi.int/Menus/ICC/Situations+and+Cases/Cases/. Accessed 25 August 2012.
56. Situation in DRC, Judgement on the Prosecutor's appeal against the decision of Pre-Trial Chamber I entitled "Decision on the Prosecutor's application for warrants of arrest, article 58", 13.7.2006 (ICC-01/04-169). http://www.icc-cpi.int/Menus/ICC/Situations+and+Cases/Cases/. Accessed 25 August 2012.
57. Situation in Kenya, Decision pursuant to article 15 of the Rome Statute on the authorisation of an investigation into the situation in the Republic of Kenya, 31.3.2010 (ICC-01/09-19). http://www.icc-cpi.int/Menus/ICC/Situations+and+Cases/Cases/. Accessed 25 August 2012.
58. Situation in the Republic of Côte d'Ivoire, Request for authorisation of an investigation pursuant to article 15, 23.06.2011 (ICC-02/11-3). http://www.icc-cpi.int/Menus/ICC/Situations+and+Cases/Cases/. Accessed 25 August 2012.
59. Stahn, C. (2008). Complementarity: A Tale of Two Notions. *Criminal Law Forum, 19*(1), 87–113.
60. Stahn, C. (2009). Judicial review of prosecutorial discretion: Five years on, in: The Emerging Practice of the International Criminal Court, Carsten Stahn/Göran Sluiter (eds.), 247–279.
61. Stahn, C. (2011). How is the Water? *Criminal Law Forum, 22*(1–2), 175–197.
62. Stahn, C. (2012). Libya, the International Criminal Court and Complementarity. *Journal of International Criminal Justice, 10*, 325–349.
63. Stegmiller, I. (2011). The Pre-Investigation Stage of the ICC, Criteria for Situation Selection. Studies in International and European Criminal Law and Procedure, vol. 8.
64. Update on Communications Received by the Prosecutor of the ICC, 10 February 2006, The Hague. http://www.icc-cpi.int/Menus/ICC/Structure+of+the+Court/Office+of+the+Prosecutor/Reports+and+Statements/. Accessed 25 August 2012.
65. Van Heeck, S. (2006). Die Weiterentwicklung des formellen Völkerstrafrechts

CHAPTER 16

CHILDREN AND INTERNATIONAL CRIMINAL JUSTICE

Fatou Bensouda

Ladies and Gentlemen, Dear Colleagues, Let me begin by extending my deepest gratitude to the University of Georgia, School of Law for graciously hosting this important conference on children and international criminal justice, and for inviting me to address you here today. Thanks are also owed to the many sponsors that have made this event possible.

I would like to thank, in particular, my Special Adviser on Children in and affected by Armed Conflicts, Professor Diane Marie Amann for her commitment and her immensely valuable work in this area. I know that Diane, along with her hardworking team here at the law school, have worked tirelessly for the past few months to realize this event—I am grateful for their efforts and humbled by their dedication. They are certainly deserving of our utmost praise and a round of applause.

The Great Nelson Mandela once said: "We owe our children, the most vulnerable citizens in our society, a life free of violence and fear." These few simple but profoundly important words reflect the reasons and aspirations behind why we are all gathered here today. We must indeed pool our efforts, expertise, and energies to advance the rights of children and to shield them from harm in times of conflict. It is truly heartening to see such an impressive gathering of practitioners and academics, all committed to this worthy cause, and I feel privileged to be a part of today's rich discussions. The highly toxic effects of conflict and violence on children, both directly and indirectly is one of the gravest problems in need of redress today. In most armed conflicts, the recruitment of child soldiers, sexual slavery, attacks on schools, or forced displacement are regrettably common occurrences.

These heinous crimes are not only repugnant to our collective conscience but simply devastating to children's lives, and their families and communities—they should not be tolerated, but rather met with the full force of the law. Fighting impunity for crimes against children worldwide should be at the forefront of the global agenda. History has taught us that peace is simply a respite between wars. This new century alone has already witnessed countless conflicts erupt in different theatres around the world, with serious repercussions for children. While wars may be inevitable, we have an obligation to curb the destructive impact human conflicts can have on children.

My Office is firm in its commitment to stand against the commission of crimes against children during conflict. Where our jurisdiction permits, rest assured that we will robustly investigate and prosecute perpetrators of these crimes to the full extent of the law. We are also committed to respecting the rights of children with whom we interact in the course of our investigative and prosecutorial work, including their right to be heard and to have their best interests treated as a primary consideration. Ladies and Gentlemen, Dear Colleagues, Allow me to share with you our perspective from the Office of the Prosecutor of the International Criminal Court on how the Rome Statute, our founding treaty, can protect and promote the rights of children. In 1998, in part due to the efforts of a

Citation: Fatou Bensouda, Children and International Criminal Justice, http://digitalcommons.law.uga.edu/cgi/viewcontent.cgi?article = 2291&context=gjicl

robustly active NGO, the Children's Caucus, crimes against children was the subject of extensive negotiations at the Rome Diplomatic Conference, where States negotiated the provisions of what would become the Rome Statute. This served to highlight the important role that civil society plays in upholding the rights of children and other vulnerable groups. Thanks to very active actors, states and NGOs alike, the importance of the issue ultimately found legal backing in the provisions of the Rome Statute.

As such, charges regarding crimes against children are explicitly foreseen within each of the Rome Statute's core crimes. For instance, one of the five acts that may constitute genocide is forcibly transferring children of a protected group to another group. The Statute specifies that a crime against humanity of enslavement encompasses trafficking of children. Conscripting or enlisting children under the age of fifteen years into an armed force, or using them to actively participate in hostilities constitute war crimes.

Furthermore, the Rome Statute's sensitivity towards children's issues is clearly demonstrated in relation to the protection of victims and witnesses. Article 68(1) of the Rome Statute explicitly states that the Court must "have regard to all relevant factors, including gender and the nature of the crime, in particular, where the crime involves sexual or gender violence or violence against children." Addressing crimes against the most vulnerable members of society is a priority for my Office and the International Criminal Court. Article 54(1) of the Rome Statute thus requires that "the Prosecutor shall . . . take into account the nature of the crime, in particular where it involves . . . violence against children." When I assumed Office as Prosecutor in 2012, I categorically stated that in addition to focusing on "children who are forced to carry arms," we must also address the issue of "children who are affected by arms." This was a clear signal that the issue is critically important for me and my Office, and emphasized my pledge that such egregious crimes and their victims will not be ignored.

To this end, I have elevated this issue to one of the six key strategic goals in my Office's Strategic Plan for 2012–2015. Similarly, I have elevated fighting impunity for sexual and gender-based crimes to the same status, as it has become increasingly evident through my experience as Prosecutor that these acts in tandem create, perhaps, one of the greatest menaces to the security and welfare of our societies.

Furthermore, in order to reinforce our in-house expertise in this crucial area, in December 2012, I appointed Professor Amann as my Special Adviser on Children in and affected by Armed Conflicts. Professor Amann has provided and continues to provide my office with invaluable support since her appointment, including advising on the development of the Office's Children's Policy, and creating awareness on children's issues as they arise in situations involving war crimes, genocide and crimes against humanity. Ladies and Gentlemen, Dear Colleagues, It is important to recognize that the issue of children in armed conflict has also become a cornerstone of the ICC's early jurisprudence.

In our first case against Thomas Lubanga Dyilo, the former rebel leader in the Democratic Republic of Congo, we focused on charging him with the conscription, enlistment and use of children under the age of fifteen to participate actively in hostilities. This is a clear demonstration of the importance we attached to crimes against children from the inception of our work and we continue to do so. The guilty verdict against Mr. Lubanga in 2012 was a landmark decision for the Court and I believe for the whole Rome Statute system. Even before the verdict was pronounced, the Lubanga trial helped trigger much needed global debate on the recruitment of children into armed forces, including in Colombia and Sri Lanka.

The case also highlighted various issues, including the impact of crimes against children on whole communities, the specific issue of girl child soldiers, and the devastating effect that such crimes can have on the right of children to education. There can be no doubt that the crimes which Lubanga was convicted of, interrupted, delayed and denied education to children in the Ituri region of the Democratic Republic of the Congo.

For some children, denial of education took the form of recruitment as child soldiers. Young boys and girls were made to carry guns instead of their school books. Others were forced to work in the camps, or to be sex slaves for the commanders and soldiers. Families and entire communities suffered from the traumatic experience, with a constant threat and fear of being attacked, harmed or abducted. This was the reality for children living in the Ituri region of the Democratic Republic of the Congo. As a result, an entire generation of children was deprived of the right to education and an environment conducive to learning. What hope—we must ask ourselves—is there for such communities? The Judges of the Court recognized this fact in their comprehensive decision regarding the principles and procedures for victims' reparations.

They ruled that decisions granting compensation to victims must take into account lost opportunities, including those relating to employment and education. They also recognized that rehabilitation of the victims of child recruitment should include measures aimed at facilitating their reintegration into society, including the provision of education and vocational training. It bears noting that we have worked to expand the focus from the specific issue of child soldiers and to holistically consider the many different ways in which children are affected in situations of conflict.

This expanded focus is reflected in the way in which the charges were framed in the Second Arrest Warrant against Bosco Ntaganda, the alleged former deputy chief of the staff of the Forces Patriotiques pour la Libération du Congo. In June of this year, Pre-Trial Chamber II of the Court confirmed all the charges against Bosco Ntaganda. These charges include not only war crimes of conscription, enlistment and use of children, as in Lubanga, but also charges of sexual slavery and sexual violence against children who formed part of Ntaganda's own militia—this is a milestone decision.

During the confirmation of charges, the Office argued that the protections afforded by international humanitarian law extends to children generally and were not lost by those recruited into Ntaganda's own armed group. A Conviction in respect of these charges will represent an important, pioneering clarification of the protection international humanitarian law offers to children and the victims of sexual violence in situations of armed conflict. Nearly every charge against Bosco Ntaganda also speaks to the effects of armed conflict and related violence on children; for example, the war-crimes charges related to pillage and to attacks on protected objects, such as schools. Ladies and Gentlemen, Dear Colleagues, Our subject today is of critical importance. We all recognize the urgency with which we need to fight impunity for crimes against children worldwide. It is now the time to engineer a unified, cohesive, effective, global approach and implement the principle of complementary envisaged in the Rome Statute.

To that end, it is necessary to identify the many actors involved, at the local, the regional, and international levels in order to coordinate our efforts and maximize our potential. In the Rome Statute system, the national authorities of the Court's 122 States Parties form the first line of defense in addressing mass crimes, including those against children. They shoulder the primary responsibility for the investigation and prosecution of perpetrators of these crimes, through both individual efforts and mutual support.

As a Court of last resort, the ICC is only authorized to step in, in the event that a State is unwilling or unable to conduct genuine national investigations and prosecutions. This is one of the major strengths of the Rome Statute system: its capacity to contribute to the fight against impunity either directly through the Court's proceedings, or by incentivizing and mobilizing action at the national level. The work done by the Court can maximize the impact—including the preventative impact—of the work of other actors. For example, the former Special Representative of the UN SecretaryGeneral on children and armed conflict, Mrs. Radhika Coomaraswamy, capitalized on our Lubanga case, even before the completion of the trial, by using it to campaign around the world, to demobilize child solders, including in Nepal, which as you know is not a State Party.

This is an example of how the law can be employed to prevent crimes, and how the "shadow of the Court" can have an impact and reach beyond the contours of its jurisdictional limitations. Complementarity and prevention will be key aspects of my Office's new Policy Paper on Children for which consultations have already started. The Policy Paper on Children will be a comprehensive elaboration of how my Office handles, and intends to systematically approach children's issues in all aspects of its work.

It will address, not only issues relating to crimes against children, but also those relating to our interaction with children: for instance, taking into account their views, issues of protection and support of children who are witnesses and victims, as well as children of adult witnesses. I hope that this Policy Paper, once adopted, can also serve as a guide for States and other relevant actors in their work to combat crimes against children and to address children's issues in the judicial process. The rich discussions during this conference are extremely important and will feed into the drafting of this policy paper. I invite all those who are interested to provide input on this Paper once the draft is circulated for comments and suggestions.

Ladies and Gentlemen, Dear Colleagues, Allow me to conclude by observing that crimes against children in conflict destroy the individual, shatter the family unit, and tear violently at the social fabric of society. Indeed, they rob children of their innocence, childhood, and often, tragically, of their lives. They rob society of its future potential and of its greatest resource. These reprehensible acts must be confronted with a robust and unified response. We must join our efforts and work in concert to send a clear, firm, and consistent message that humanity stands united in its belief that crimes committed against children in conflict will neither be tolerated nor ignored.

Only with collective and unified action can we truly make a difference. Let us stay committed to the cause and do what needs to be done, no matter how formidable the challenges. History will judge us not by our words, but by our lasting conduct. The victims of these horrendous crimes will not find solace in our promises, but in what we manage to deliver in concrete terms.

Rest assured that my Office will certainly do its part, and we look forward to working with you in an integrated and coordinated fashion to achieve our common goal. A crime against a child is an offense against all of humanity; it is, to be sure, an affront to our basic tenets of human decency. We must end the scourge of violence against children during conflict, and I'm confident, together, we can. Thank you.

CHAPTER 17

THE FUTURE OF INTERNATIONAL LAW IS DOMESTIC (OR, THE EUROPEAN WAY OF LAW)

Anne-Marie Slaughter and William Burke-White

International law has traditionally been just that—international. Consisting of a largely separate set of legal rules and institutions,[1] international law has long governed relationships among states. Under the traditional rules of international law, the claims of individuals could reach the international plane only when a state exercised diplomatic protection and espoused the claims of its nationals in an international forum.[2] More recently, international law has penetrated the once exclusive zone of domestic affairs to regulate the relation-ships between governments and their own citizens, particularly through the growing bodies of human rights law and international criminal law.[3] But even in these examples, international law has recognized a clear demarcation be-tween domestic and international politics.

The classic model of international law as separate from the domestic realm rejects the traditional problems the international legal system sought to ad-dress, namely the facilitation of state-to-state cooperation and the treatment of one state's nationals by another state. Whether regulating the immunities of diplomats or the rights of ships on the high seas, the traditional purposes of international law have been interstate, not intrastate.

This foundation of international law rejects the principles of Westphalian sovereignty, often seemingly made up of equal parts myth and rhetoric. In this conception, the state is a de^a^ned physical territory "within which domestic political authorities are the sole arbiters of legitimate behavior."[4] States can be part of the international legal system to the degree they choose by consenting to particular rules. Likewise, they can choose to remain apart, asserting their own sovereignty and eschewing international involvement. For-mally, Westphalian sovereignty is the right to be left alone, to exclude, to be free from any external meddling or interference. But it is also the right to be recognized as an autonomous agent in the international system, capable of interacting with other states and entering into international agreements. With these background understandings of sovereignty, an international legal sys-tem, consisting of states and limited by the principle of state consent, emerged.

Today, however, the challenges facing states and the international com-munity alike demand very different responses from and thus new roles for the international legal system. The processes of globalization and the emergence of new transnational threats have fundamentally changed the nature of governance and the necessary purposes of international law in the past few years. From cross-border pollution to terrorist training camps, from refugee °owes to weapons proliferation, international problems have domestic roots that an interstate legal system is often powerless to address. To offer an effective response to these new challenges, the international legal system must be able to impudence the domestic policies of states and harness national institutions in pursuit of global objectives.

Citation: William W. Burke-White and Anne-Marie Slaughter, The Future of International Law is Domestic (or, The European Way of Law), http://scholarship.law.upenn.edu/cgi/viewcontent.cgi?article=1958&context=faculty_scholarship.

To create desirable conditions in the international system, from peace, to health to prosperity, international law must address the capacity and the will of domestic governments to respond to these issues at their sources. In turn, the primary terrain of international law must shift—and is already shifting in many instances—from independent regulation above the national state to direct engagement with domestic institutions. The three principal forms of such engagement are strengthening domestic institutions, backstopping them, and compelling them to act.

The most striking feature of this conception of international law is a direct emphasis on shaping or in fencing political outcomes within sovereign states in accordance with international legal rules. Even in 1945, the drafters of the U.N. Charter still maintained the classical position that international law and institutions shall not "intervene in matters which are essentially within the domestic jurisdiction of any state."[5] Today, however, the objectives of international law and the very stability of the international system itself de-pend critically on domestic choices previously left to the determination of national political processes—whether to enforce particular rules, establish institutions, or even engage in effective governance. By ensuring that national governments actually function in pursuit of collective aims, international law is starting to play a far more active role in shaping these national political choices. Assuming that current political, economic, and technological trends continue, the future effectiveness of international law will turn on its ability to innocence and alter domestic politics.

These functions of international law are already well known to the members of the European Union ("EU"). Indeed, in extending membership to ten new countries over the course of the past decade, the EU has relied on EU law as its primary tool of reform and socialization.[6] Even among the original member states, EU institutions continue to perform the types of backstop-ping, strengthening, and mandating functions described here. Europeans them-selves are coming to recognize these uses of law; a new generation of European policy thinkers has openly proclaimed the virtues of the European way of law.[7]

Some may, of course, argue that these new functions of international law have no applicability outside the European context in which they were [a]first embraced.[8] Yet each of the three means through which international law is coming to impudence domestic outcomes—strengthening domestic institutions, backstopping national governance, and compelling domestic action—is spreading beyond the Continent.

To the extent that what we describe as the "European way of law" is al-ready evident both within the EU and now in a growing number of other con-texts, this Article describes an important reorganization of the means and mechanisms through which international law operates. Our argument goes further, however, by suggesting that these new mechanisms of international law have the power to make the system as a whole far more effective. We there-fore move beyond description and prediction to prescription, are suggesting ways that the European way of law should become the future of international law writ large.

We also recognize, however, the potential dangers in current trends. As we emphasize in the conclusion, our vision of the principal future functions of international law assumes an intensive interaction between international law and domestic politics. But domestic politicians can manipulate international legal institutions and mandates to serve their own purposes, such as jailing political dissidents as part of complying with a Security Council resolution requiring domestic action against terrorism. More broadly, the basic positivist foundations of international law, requiring states to freely accept such interference in domestic politics, raise the possibility of manipulation and even imposition of such "acceptance" as a result of power disparities.

Part I of this Article identities a new set of global threats and actual and potential responses, including the EU's uses of law to transform new members "from the inside out." Part II argues that the future relevance, power, and potential of international law lie in its ability to backstop, strengthen, and compel domestic law and institutions. Part III examines the potential pitfalls and dangers of these new functions of international law. Finally, Part IV contrasts our analysis with other recent efforts to blur the boundaries be-tween the international and domestic spheres, noting that what is distinctive about our claim is not the intermingling of two kinds of law, but rather the impact of international law on domestic politics and vice versa.

NEW THREATS, NEW RESPONSES

Rules can reflect and embody aspirations for a better world. Alternatively, and equally likely, rules respond to concrete problems. The changing nature of international legal rules today responds to a new generation of worldwide problems. The most striking feature of these problems is that they arise from within states rather than from state actors themselves.

Examples abound: the terrorist attacks of September 11, 2001, were launched by a group of nonstate actors operating from within the territory of Afghanistan;[9] the massive ethnic crimes in Rwanda, Congo, and Sudan are, in large part, the product of rebel forces within states;[10] the most dangerous examples of nuclear proliferation can often be attributed to nonstate criminal networks such as those of A. Q. Kahn.[11] The 2004 Report of the Secretary-General's High-Level Panel on Threats, Challenges and Change identifies problems of intrastate origin such as "poverty, infectious disease and environmental degradation . . . civil war, genocide and other large scale atrocities nuclear, radiological, chemical and biological weapons, terrorism, [and] transnational organized crime" as among the core threats facing the international community today.[12]

More often than not, the origins of these threats can be addressed directly only by domestic governments that have the jurisdictional entitlements, police power, and institutional capability to act directly against them. Arresting criminals or terrorists, securing nuclear materials, and preventing pollution are within the traditional province of domestic law. The result is that the external security of many states depends on the ability of national governments to maintain internal security sufficient to establish and enforce national law.

Where states are strong enough to combat these internal threats directly, international law can and must play a critical coordinating role to ensure that governments cooperate in addressing threats *before* they span borders. Far too frequently, however, domestic governments lack the will or the capacity to adequately respond to these challenges. Since the early 1990s, the number of states unable to effectively govern their territories has increased.[13] As Francis Fukuyama affirms, "[s] ince the end of the Cold War, weak or failing states have arguably become the single most important problem for the international order . . . . Weak or failing states commit human rights abuses, provoke humanitarian disasters, drive massive waves of immigration, and attack their neighbors."[14]

Where national governments are unable or unwilling to address the origins of these threats themselves, international law may step in to help build their capacity or stiffen their will. This use of international law moves well beyond both its classical definition, as "the rights subsisting between nations,"[15] and its more modern conception, as, in part, regulating the conduct of states toward their own citizens.[16] Where human rights law identifies a set of clear prohibitions on government behavior, coupled with a set of positive aspirations toward economic, social, and cultural rights, these new international legal rules seek actively to shape not only domestic law but also the domestic political environment to enable and enhance domestic government action. The result is far more invasive, but also potentially transformative. For many countries, ranging from the United States to Russia, from the countries of the Middle East to those of Africa, this new use of international law is also far more frightening.

This new model springs from a conception of international law spreading outward from Europe. The Treaty of Westphalia, ending the bloody Thirty Years War with the principle of *cuius regio, eius religio*,[17] has given way to the Treaty of Rome, ending a century of bloody intra-European wars with a concept of pooled sovereignty that has steadily expanded and deepened in the contemporary EU. As the EU's legal system has evolved, the prime purpose of the European Court of Justice and even of the Commission has been less to create and impose EU law as international law than to spur national courts and regulatory agencies to embrace and enforce EU law as national law.

Moreover, as Mark Leonard writes in his provocative new book *Why Europe Will Run the 21st Century*, "Europe's weapon is the law."[18] He describes Europe's power in the world as "a transformative power,"[19] rooted in a strategy of democratization that is based on requiring candidate countries to "swallow all 80,000 pages of European laws and adapt their own legislation to accommodate them," as well as then accepting continual monitoring by EU officials to ensure that they are in fact living up to their new commitments.[20] The result has been a "rebuilding [of] these countries from the bottom up."[21] In-deed, "[t]he European model is the political equivalent of the strategy of the Jesuits: if you change the country at the beginning, you have it for life."[22]

Note the precise way that European law works in this equation. For all the 80,000 pages of regulations, the EU Council of Ministers and the EU Commission issue directives that specify ends rather than means. It is up to national legislatures and courts to decide precisely how the member state in question will fulfill a particular directive. Once those laws are passed, EU institutions—the Court and the Commission—look over national shoulders to ensure that they actually do what they commit to do. This European way of law is precisely the role that we postulate for international law generally around the world.[23]

Espen Barth Eide, a former state secretary in the Norwegian Foreign Ministry, writes that the "EU's 'soft' intervention in the 'domestic affairs' of EU member states is almost an everyday experience."[24] This is the hallmark of EU-style "post-Westphalian sovereignty," described so memorably by Robert Cooper, a top aide to Javier Solana, in *The Breaking of Nations*.[25] Eide and other leading European security strategists openly call for the extension of regional "integrative projects" based on the EU in Africa, Latin America, and Asia. The European Security Strategy, proposed by Javier Solana[26] and passed by the European Council in December 2003, fell short of openly embracing this vision, but recognized that the Association of Southeast Asian Nations (ASEAN), the Southern Cone Common Market ("MERCOSUR"), and the African Union "make an important contribution to a more orderly world."[27]

Spreading the European way of law beyond Europe, a process that is al-ready underway, requires a broader rethinking of the functions of international law. As in Europe, the focus of a growing number of international rules is no longer interstate relations; it is increasingly governments' capacity and will to act in prescribed ways toward their own peoples. The result is a growing interaction between international law and domestic politics, in ways that have lasting implications for both.

THE FUTURE FUNCTIONS OF INTERNATIONAL LAW

The all-too-often inadequate domestic response to transnational threats has three separate but related causes: a lack of domestic governance capacity, a lack of domestic will to act, and new problems that exceed the ordinary ability of states to address. International law has key leverage points to help improve the response of domestic governments in each of these three ways. International legal rules and institutions can enhance the capacity and effectiveness of domestic institutions. If properly designed and structured they can help backstop domestic political and legal groups trying to comply with international legal obligations. Finally, they can even compel or mandate action at the national level in response to a global threat. The following sections will examine each of these ways that international law can and in some cases is beginning to play a new role in domestic governance.

Strengthening Domestic Institutions

A primary limitation of the international system is the weakness of government institutions in so many states all over the world. Due to violence, poverty, disease, corruption, and limited technology or training, national governments all too often lack the resources, skills, and ability to provide adequate solutions to local and transnational problems. Examples are numerous: state failure in Somalia in the early 1990s, devastation from natural catastrophes like the 2004 tsunami, civil wars such as that in Angola from 1998 to 2003, or the rampant corruption all too evident in Russia in the mid-1990s. A 2004 report of the Commission on Weak States and U.S. National Security highlighted as a key national security concern the need to assist states "whose governments are unable to do the things that their own citizens and the international community expect from them: offer protection from internal and external threats, deliver basic health services and education, and provide institutions that respond to the legitimate demands and needs of the population."[28] Improving the capacity of government officials of all sorts— regulators, judges, and legislators—to actually govern is paramount.[29] Francis Fukuyama observes: "For the post–September 11th period, the chief issue for global politics will not be how to cut back on stateness but how to build it up."[30] International law has an important role to play in this process.

A critically important tool in strengthening the institutions of national governments is the formalization and inclusion of "government networks" as mechanisms of global governance. These largely voluntary networks link together domestic governmental officials from different countries in similar fields or spheres of responsibility. Such networks provide an effective means to harness national regulatory systems in the pursuit of common, international goals. Such networks can help harmonize national policies and can support the efforts of domestic official's vis-à-vis their own governments.

These networks of national government officials of all kinds are already operating across borders to regulate individuals and corporations operating in a global economy, combat global crime, and address common problems on a global scale.[31] They perform a range of functions that enhance the effective-ness of domestic governance. They build trust and establish relationships among their participants that create incentives to establish a good reputation and avoid a bad one. They regularly exchange information about their own activities and develop databases of best practices, or, in the judicial sphere, different approaches to common legal issues. Finally, they offer technical assistance and professional socialization to members—whether regulators, judges, or legislators—from less developed nations.[32]

If their existence and capacities were more widely recognized, government networks could do far more to strengthen domestic governance. Building the basic capacity to govern in countries that often lack sufficient material and human resources to pass, implement, and apply laws effectively is itself an important and valuable consequence of government networks. Regulatory, judicial, and legislative networks all engage in capacity-building directly, through training and technical assistance programs, and indirectly, through their provision of information, coordinated policy solutions, and moral support to their members. In effect, government networks communicate to their members everywhere the message that the Zimbabwean chief justice understood when he was under siege and commented, "I am not alone."[33]

The best examples of transnational networks strengthening domestic governance may be in the area of regulatory export. Kal Raustiala offers a number of examples of regulatory export in the securities, environmental, and antitrust areas. According to one securities regulator he interviewed, a prime outcome of U.S. Securities and Exchange Commission networking is the dissemination of "the 'regulatory gospel' of U.S. securities law," including: "strict insider trading rules; mandatory registration with a governmental agency of public securities issues; a mandatory disclosure system; issuer liability regarding registration statements and offering documents; broad antifraud pro-visions; and government oversight of brokers, dealers, exchanges, etc."[34] In effect, U.S. regulatory agencies make their own jobs easier by offering technical assistance and training to their foreign counterparts, because strong foreign authorities with compatible securities, environmental, and antitrust regimes will effectively extend the reach of U.S. regulators.

The EU has enjoyed similar advantages through the International Competition Network (ICN). As a result, a growing number of countries, particularly in Eastern Europe, are copying the EU approach to competition policy rather than the U.S. model.[35] The opening conference of the ICN, led by the head of the German competition agency, was held in Italy in 2002. The network describes itself as "a project-oriented, consensus-based, informal net-work of antitrust agencies from developed and developing countries that will address antitrust enforcement and policy issues of common interest and formulate proposals for procedural and substantive convergence through a results-oriented agenda and structure."[36]

Other examples of such networks strengthening domestic capacity in the economic arena include the Basel Committee on Banking Supervision[37] and the International Organization of Securities Commissioners, which have been inertial in enhancing the ability of national governments to regulate securities and maintain independent central banks.[38] The net result of these networks is twofold: first, convergence toward a set of standardized practices at the national level and, second, the creation of greater domestic regulatory capacity in participating nations.

It should not be assumed that regulatory expertise °owes only from developed to developing countries. At least in the judicial arena, European and Canadian courts have learned as much from South African and Indian courts as vice versa.[39] Among regulators, local experience with a wide range of problems can count for a great deal in the exchange of best practices.

Governments can do much more to strengthen domestic governance through government networks. For example: strengthening the International Network for Environmental Cooperation and Enforcement, composed of environmental officials; expanding the inclusivity and representativeness of global financial and leadership networks (such as expanding the G-8 to the G-20); creating a Global Justice Network of justice ministers; creating a Global Human Rights Network of the government officials responsible for human rights conditions; and bringing networks of legislators together under the auspices of the United Nations and other international institutions. Such networks must be pro-vided with both concrete tasks and the resources to accomplish them, enabling states to work together to strengthen both collective and individual governance capacity.

As the front line of authority, national government officials exercise an array of coercive and persuasive powers largely unmatched by international institutions. National governments, by operating through government networks, can bring these same powers to bear on behalf of international legal obligations. They can coerce, cajole, ªne, order, regulate, legislate, horse-trade, bully, or use whatever other methods that produce results within their political system. They are not subject to coercion at the transgovernmental level; on the contrary, they are likely to perceive themselves as choosing a specific course of action freely and deliberately. Yet, having decided, for whatever reasons, to adopt a particular code of best practices, to coordinate policy in a particular way, to accept the decision of a supranational tribunal, or even simply to join what seems to be an emerging international consensus on a particular issue, they can implement that decision within the limits of their own domestic power.

The international legal system could harness the power of trans govern-mental networks much more effectively than it does currently. For example, international law could more explicitly recognize the role of such networks and the soft regulations they often produce. Hard legal instruments could man-date or facilitate the creation of transnational networks in a range of areas of critical state weakness such as justice and human rights. Where the weak-ness of a particular government in a functional area poses a threat to international order, the U.N. Security Council could require state participation in such a network. Government networks offer an important tool to improve state capacity. Actors within the international legal system would be well served to partner with such networks and more directly integrate them into larger international legal frameworks.

Once again, the international legal system would be taking a leaf from the EU's book in this regard. Most EU law gets made and implemented through transgovernmental networks of EU officials, from ministers on down. In-deed, Mark Leonard describes the EU as "a decentralised network that is owned by its member-states."[40] Reaching outside the borders of Europe, the EU has sought to extend the network model to the Middle East and North Africa through the Euro-Mediterranean Partnership.[41]

Beyond government networks, Stephen Krasner suggests that international law and institutions can strengthen state capacity by engaging in processes of shared sovereignty with national governments. Such shared sovereignty "involves the creation of institutions for governing specific issue areas within state— areas over which external and internal actors voluntarily share authority."[42] Examples of these arrangements include the creation of special hybrid courts in Sierra Leone, East Timor, and, possibly, Cambodia, involving a mix of international and domestic law and judges. Similarly, a proposed oil pipeline agreement between Chad and the World Bank would involve shared control and governance.[43] Such shared sovereignty, Krasner claims, can "gird new political structures with more expertise, better-crafted policies, and guarantees against abuses of power" onto weak or failing states.[44]

Even within a more traditional framework, the international legal system can employ a range of mechanisms to strengthen the hand of domestic governments. Legal instruments and codes of international best practices can set standards to give national governments benchmarks for enhancing their own capability.[45] International institutions can provide aid and assistance specifically targeted for the domestic institutions of the recipient state.

International ªnancial institutions such as the International Monetary Fund (IMF) and the World Bank may play a particularly powerful role in building domestic capacity. Conditionality requirements give these bodies strong impudence over domestic outcomes. The IMF's success in enhancing the capabilities of domestic governments is much debated,[46] but the World Bank may have a better track record.[47] Part of the Bank's strategy in Africa has been to "put countries in the driver's seat" with a "platform of strong public capacity: capacity to formulate policies; capacity to build consensus; capacity to implement reform; and capacity to monitor results, learn lessons, and adapt accordingly."[48] Whatever their successes and failures to date, the IMF and the World Bank have significant leverage to enhance domestic government capacity. What they need is far more input from borrower countries, or at least reformers and political activists in borrower countries, about how best to achieve this goal.

Incorporating these types of mechanisms into future legal regimes as a means of promoting domestic capacity-building must be an ongoing priority. These mechanisms include building government networks, providing technical assistance, setting benchmarks and standards, or encouraging other forms of co-operation. Abram and Antonia Chayes have explained how this can be done through a "managerial model" of compliance.[49] According to this model, the task of maximizing compliance with a given set of international rules is a task more of management than of enforcement, ensuring that all parties know what is expected of them, that they have the capacity to comply, and that they receive the necessary assistance. To the degree Chayes and Chayes are cor-rect,[50] formal international legal regimes must recognize and promote the capacity-building needs of domestic governance through government net-works, technical assistance, benchmarks and standards, or other forms of cooperation.

More broadly, the success of many policies at the international level de-pends on political choices at the national level, for example, choices concerning the allocation of resources or the establishment of particular institutions. The effectiveness of international law may thus depend on its ability to shape political outcomes and institutional structures within states. At the same time, however, a feedback loop from domestic to international institutions becomes crucial for both accountability and effectiveness. Thus the various mechanisms canvassed above to strengthen domestic government institutions must be carefully designed.

Backstopping Domestic Government

A second means through which international law can foster more effective domestic governance is by backstopping domestic institutions where they fail to act. In some ways, this idea is not new at all, but rather follows from a long intellectual tradition. Without developed international institutions such as the International Criminal Court (ICC), cooperation among the criminal justice mechanisms of states provided a primitive form of back-stopping by ensuring that some state would prosecute an accused criminal even if the territorial state of the crime failed to act. Indeed, as early as 1625, Hugo Grotius recognized that the domestic courts of various states could backstop one another. Referring to an early form of the prosecute or extradite requirement, Grotius observed: "[I]t seems reasonable, that the State where the convicted Offender lives or has taken Shelter, should, upon Application being made to it, either punish the demanded person according to his Demerits, or else deliver him up to be treated at the Discretion of the injured party."[51] Centuries later, in the early 1920s, M. Maurice Travers developed the concept of "*la superposition des competences legislatives concurrences*," suggesting that the layering of overlapping jurisdiction of a number of states would allow national courts to reinforce one another.[52] What is new today is that international institutions—rather than the national courts of third states— are making a conscious effort to backstop their national counterparts. Structural rules that explicitly seek to further this backstopping function are now embedded in the very statutes of international tribunals and institutions.

The most obvious example of international law as a backstop is the complementarity provision of the Rome Statute of the International Criminal Court. The ICC is designed to operate only where national courts fail to act as a first line means of prosecution. Article 17 of the Rome Statute provides that the Court shall determine a case is inadmissible if "the case is being investigated or prosecuted by a State which has jurisdiction over it, unless the State is unwilling or unable genuinely to carry out the investigation or prosecution."[53] The ICC can step in and provide a second line of defense in cases where domestic institutions fail "due to a total or substantial collapse or unavailability of its national judicial system,"[54] or where a state is unwilling to prosecute "independently or impartially."[55] In other words, if the United States or Iraq were a member of the ICC and both states proved unable or unwilling to prosecute fully *all* members of the military involved in the abuses at Abu Ghraib, the ICC would have jurisdiction.

Other forms of international institutional design may similarly result in a backstopping function. In various human rights courts, the requirement that individuals ªrst exhaust local remedies gives states—and particularly their domestic courts—an incentive to reach conclusions acceptable to the inter-national institution so that the international court need not intervene to review the case.[56] Similarly, the dispute resolution mechanisms of the North American Free Trade Agreement (NAFTA) have served as an international backstop for domestic resolution of antidumping cases.[57] Under NAFTA, international arbitral panels are given the authority to review domestic administrative decisions and can remand decisions back to the issuing agency with guidance on acceptable outcomes. If the agency issues an acceptable ruling, no further action is taken. Yet, if the panels remain unsatisfied with the agency's response, they can issue a further ruling and remand the case yet again.[58] Like the Rome Statute's complementarity regime, this remand procedure gives domestic institutions within NAFTA countries an incentive to act first and to get it right. Where they fail to do so, the international process provides a backstop.

The actual effect of such backstopping provisions in international institutional design is twofold.[59] first, and most obvious, is the provision of a second line of defense when national institutions fail. Second, and potentially more powerful, is the ability of the international process to catalyze action at the national level. This second effect most often occurs when a domestic le-gal or political process exists that could be utilized, should the domestic government decide to do so, but government officials, or at least some powerful group of such officials, deem that the political or ªnancial costs of domestic action outweigh the benefits. In such cases the existence of an inter-national tribunal with concurrent jurisdiction can provide structural incentives that shift the cost benefit calculation and result in the use of a domes-tic process that would otherwise have been neglected. The political benefits of adjudicating matters domestically rather than giving jurisdiction to an international tribunal over which domestic officials have little or no control creates new incentives to act locally.

The ICC already appears to be having such a catalytic effect in two of the first situations it is investigating: the Democratic Republic of Congo, and the Darfur region of Sudan. In the wake of the ICC Prosecutor's 2003 announcement of an investigation in Congo, a range of efforts were initiated by certain elements within the Congolese government to reform the Congo-lese judiciary so as to be able to assert primacy over the ICC and undertake national proceedings.[60] Similarly, after the Prosecutor opened an investigation in Darfur, local courts, though of questionable legitimacy, were established to initiate domestic proceedings.[61] The ICC Prosecutor has himself suggested that complementarity may encourage domestic prosecutions. As he argued upon his swearing-in as the Court's first Prosecutor, "the absence of trials before this Court, as a consequence of the regular functioning of national institutions, would be a major success."[62]

International legal institutions operating as a backstop need not be limited to purely international courts. Adjudication in foreign domestic courts may likewise enhance the willingness of national judiciaries in territorial states to act themselves. The recent advances by Chilean courts toward the prosecution of Augusto Pinochet is, in part, due to the international community—acting largely through the Spanish and English judiciaries—getting serious about ensuring accountability for his crimes.[63] The prosecution by Spain and the proceedings in England[64]—though they did not result in a conviction—made clear to the Chileans that other options existed if they themselves refused to prosecute and may have bolstered the willingness of Chilean courts to hold Pinochet accountable.[65]

The backstopping effect of international institutions will take different forms and often be case specific. Sometimes, the international institution will generate incentives for domestic governmental authorities to act at home as an alternative to international prosecution. At other times, particularly where powerful actors within a national government lack the political will to act at home, the international institution may alter the balance in a domestic power struggle, strengthening the hand of those national officials who want to act. Alternatively, where the domestic government truly lacks the capacity to act, the international institution can backstop domestic courts by genuinely providing another forum. In any of these situations the international institution directly affects domestic government decisions, changing the incentives for domestic action and providing a second, international, forum for legal action.[66] It becomes a tacit actor in domestic political processes, pressuring national governments to reach specific political outcomes and helping to create the conditions to make them possible.

Compelling Action by National Governments

The effectiveness of international law in responding to new transnational threats will, to an ever greater degree, require the active cooperation of national institutions. Despite the proliferation of international courts and tri-bunals,[67] national governments have retained the nearly exclusive use of their instruments of coercive authority. In most cases, national governments alone can use the police power, a national judiciary, or the military—the tools necessary to address transnational threats before they grow and spread. In many cases, backstopping and strengthening domestic institutions will be sufficient to ensure that national governments use their power to address pre-sent and potential dangers. At times, however, domestic governments may be unwilling to use these institutions, either due to differing perceptions of national interest, a lack of political will, or infighting within governments themselves. In these cases, international law can be effective only by finding new ways to ensure that national governments actually use the tools at their disposal to address such threats before they spread.

International legal rules have long sought to constrain or mandate the behavior of states toward other states and toward other states' citizens. More recently, international treaties have required national governments to enact domestic legislation of various sorts, such as the domestic criminalization of certain transnational acts.[68] The type of compulsion described here, however, specifically directs domestic government institutions to go about what was formerly purely domestic business in particular ways. And it does so not by specific agreement on particular legal obligations that must then be domestically implemented, but rather by establishing general goals and requiring domestic governments to achieve them through a broad range of measures. EU directives work this way; in U.S. law, however, Congress is specifically prohibited from imposing broad general mandates requiring individual states to devise and pass specific legislation to achieve them.[69]

The use of international law to combat terrorism immediately after September 11, 2001, is a prime example of how specific obligations can be imposed on U.N. member states that they can fulfill only by directing domes-tic institutions to act in specific ways at the national level. U.N. Security Council Resolution 1373, for example, requires states to "prevent the com-mission of terrorist acts" and "deny safe haven to those who finance [or] plan. . . terrorist acts."[70] The resolution demands, among other things, the domestic criminalization of the ªfinancing of terrorism, freezing of terrorist as-sets by national authorities, use of domestic courts to bring to justice those involved in terrorist acts, and ratification by domestic authorities of relevant anti-terrorism conventions.[71] The White House describes Resolution 1373 as setting "new, strict standards for all states to meet in the global war against terrorism."[72] Likewise, the International Convention for the Suppression of the Financing of Terror-ism ("Financing Convention") and the International Convention for the Suppression of Terrorist Bombing ("Bombing Convention") require states to take concrete domestic action. The Financing Convention obliges states to "take appropriate measures . . . for the . . . seizure of any funds used or allocated for" the financing of terrorism,[73] while the Bombing Convention requires domestic criminalization of terrorist acts and the affirmative use of national judicial institutions to bring to justice the perpetrators of terrorist acts.[74]

Resolution 1373 links both the compelling and strengthening functions of the international legal system. Beyond merely mandating domestic action, the resolution establishes a Counter-Terrorism Committee that is tasked with monitoring the implementation of the resolution and increasing the "ability of States to ªght terrorism."[75] The Committee requires regular reporting by states of steps taken to comply with Resolution 1373 and provides expert advice on issues ranging from legislative drafting to customs requirements and policing.[76] Working jointly with international, regional, and sub-regional organizations, the Committee shares "codes, standards and best practices in their areas of competence."[77] In addition, the Committee makes available a database of technical assistance and a team of expert advisors to assist states in compliance.[78] By April 2005, at least one report had been received from all 191 member states; the Secretary-General has described state cooperation with the Committee to date as "unprecedented and exemplary."[79]

The Security Council's recent initiatives in the area of non-proliferation have imposed similar obligations on national governments and their respective sub-state institutions to take affirmative domestic action. Security Council Resolution 1540, for example, requires states to adopt national legislation prohibiting the manufacture or possession of weapons of mass destruction by nonstate actors and to establish export control regulations and physical protection regimes for weapons and related technologies.[80] While not going as far as the creation of the Counter-Terrorism Committee, the Security Council again recognized the importance of capacity-building in ensuring domes-tic action and invited states to offer assistance and resources to one another.[81] Likewise, functional international organizations such as the International Atomic Energy Agency (IAEA) have compelled states to act through their own institutions. IAEA Safeguards Agreements with nuclear states, for ex-ample, require a national system of materials controls and the use of particular accounting mechanisms.[82]

Admittedly, these new functions of international law may not always pro-vide sufficient leverage to produce desired outcomes of state behavior or consistent compliance with international legal obligations. Particularly where states have purposefully excluded themselves from international institutions or lack the will to comply (such as is arguably the situation with the alleged Iranian nuclear weapons program in 2006), resort to other methods—ranging from diplomatic isolation to economic sanctions and, in extreme cases, the use of military force—may be needed. In such hard cases, the best hope of international law is simply to push states toward participation in international institutions and the international legal system generally so that the functions of international law identified here can take hold and impudence state behavior and outcomes.[83]

To effectively respond to new international threats, international legal rules must penetrate the surface of the sovereign state by requiring governments to take specific domestic actions to meet specified targets. Sometimes simple backstopping of national institutions may be sufficient to accomplish this task. In other circumstances, assistance and the bolstering of weak state capacity may be an essential prerequisite. At yet other times, international law may have to actively compel state action. When it does so, it once again seeks to alter the political choices of national governments and to compel states to utilize their national institutions in new ways.

The most effective approach will often involve some combination of all three functions of international law. Leaders and legislators should then be held accountable by both their peers and their publics for whether and how their governments respond.

THE DANGERS OF USING INTERNATIONAL LAW TO SHAPE AND INFLUENCE DOMESTIC POLITICS

On one level, using international law to build the will and capacity of states to act domestically offers great opportunities to enhance the effective-ness of the international legal system. National governments will have new incentives to act. Domestic institutions will grow stronger, and can be harnessed in pursuit of international objectives. States can thus respond to transnational threats more effectively and efficiently.

Yet each of the new functions of the international system suggested here— backstopping, strengthening, and compelling—is a double-edged sword. Backstopping national institutions can be counterproductive to the degree

States may defer to an international forum as a less politically and financially costly alternative to national action.[84] Well-intentioned efforts to help, often through NGOs as well as international institutions, can end up weakening local government actors by siphoning off both funds and personnel. The process of strengthening domestic institutions, if not properly designed and implemented, can also squeeze out local domestic capacity.[85] Finally, and most dangerously, by compelling national action, the international legal system may undermine local democratic processes and prevent domestic experimentation with alternate approaches.[86]

The most significant danger inherent in these new functions of international law, however, lies in the potential of national governments to co-opt the force of international law to serve their own objectives. One of the modern limits to Westphalian concepts of sovereignty is the obligations imposed by international law—particularly human rights law—on the conduct of states toward their own citizens. Yet, by strengthening state capacity, international law may actually make states more effective at the very repression and abuse the interference challenge seeks to overcome. Similarly, by compelling state action, international law may give national governments new license to undertake otherwise illegal or unjust policies. Where critical values such as human rights and state security are seen to be in conflict, international legal compulsion of policies that favor one value may come at the expense of the other. This tension is particularly problematic where a repressive regime is able to use compulsion at the international level as a cover or an excuse to undertake its own domestic policies that may undermine legitimate opposition groups and violate citizens' rights.

Nowhere is this danger more apparent than in the legal compulsion of counter-terrorism activity. Mary Robinson, former U.N. high commissioner for human rights, observes: "Repressive new laws and detention practices have been introduced in a significant number of countries, all broadly justified by the new international war on terrorism."[87] Similarly, Kim Scheppele has documented the number of exceptions to international and domestic legal protections that states have invoked under the cover of fighting terrorism.[88] Among the worst offenders, according to Human Rights First, are Tanzania, Indonesia, Russia, Pakistan, and Uzbekistan, each of which has undertaken "draconian anti-terrorism laws" that compromise human rights and strengthen the hand of government vis-à-vis opposition groups.[89]

If these new purposes of international law are to be both effective and just, the goal must be to maximize the benefits of the backstopping, strengthening, and compelling functions while avoiding the dangers evident in the counter-terrorism case. The theoretical base of these new functions of international law is that domestic institutions can be used to further international legal objectives. Yet these same institutions can become sources of abuse by national governments. The challenge, then, is to design rules that will harness the strengths of well-functioning domestic institutions while targeting and restricting the reach of abusive ones.

One way of making such distinctions is for international law to consider directly the quality of domestic institutions. States with robust and independent institutions, strong constitutional frameworks, transparent political processes, and embedded systems of checks and balances are least likely to appropriate international law for their own purposes and engage or abuse their newfound power. In these states, domestic legal protections and other institutions within the national government can prevent abuse or counter-balance the strength of other institutions. Abuses will still occur in states with good institutional frameworks; however, the assumption built into institutions like the ICC is that when abuses do occur in a well-governed state, that state's own domestic system will provide an internal correction mechanism. It is these states with independent and transparent domestic institutions that should be most receptive to the new functions of the international legal system. European states, at least, largely bear out this prediction.

The problem, of course, is that it is often the states that lack institutional independence and embedded checks and balances that are most in need of capacity-building or compulsion to address threats and challenges at home before they spread. Where international law does target such states, international rules, regimes, and institutions will have to be designed to address both the capacity and quality of domestic governance. Checks and balances will have to be embedded into the system itself, pushing not only for particular substantive outcomes, but also for legitimate domestic processes to achieve those goals. Similarly, international regimes themselves will have to balance a range of competing values such as human rights and national security rather than focus on one particular goal when compelling state action.

Finally, as is already becoming apparent, both this overall conception of international law and the specific functions described here will meet with fierce resistance from states with very strong domestic legal systems, such as the United States, and from many states with very weak legal systems but strong political rulers. European states, as noted above, are accustomed to daily "soft intervention." Other states, however, will be far less comfortable with such intervention. The United States will not be alone here, but it may well find itself with a number of unsavory bedfellows. On the other hand, many European powers may find it more difficult than they expect to promote an EU-inspired model of pooled sovereignty among wary former colonies.

INTERNATIONAL LAW, DOMESTIC POLITICS

International lawyers and political scientists alike have long been fascinated with the blurring of the boundaries between domestic and international rules and institutions. In 1956, Philip Jessup made a hegemonic move, claiming for international lawyers not only the classic domain of international law, but also "all law which regulates actions or events that transcend national frontiers," which he dubbed "transnational law."[90] Forty-five years later, then-Justice Sandra Day O'Connor, a relative newcomer to the world of international law, observed: "[I] nternational law is no longer confined in relevance to a few treaties and business agreements. Rather, it . . . regulates actions or events that transcend national frontiers."[91]

In political science, James Rosenau has popularized the concept of the "domestic-foreign frontier."[92] On this frontier, "domestic and foreign issues converge, intermesh, or otherwise become indistinguishable."[93] In his conception, whereas a boundary is an imaginary line, a frontier is "a new and wide political space . . . *continuously shifting, widening, and narrowing, simultaneously undergoing erosion with respect to many issues and reinforcement with respect to others*[.]"[94] What Rosenau finds striking about relations along this frontier is that individuals work out a wide range of solutions to various problems through a mix of domestic and international rules, rather than "through the nation-state system."[95]

Our proposition is actually a quite different one. We endorse the division between domestic and international affairs, at least conceptually. Although it is quite possible, indeed likely, that international law is expanding to in-clude all sorts of rules and institutions that have a hybrid domestic-international character, as well as domestic rules reaching beyond borders, we suggest that traditional public international law, meaning treaties and custom operating among nations in their mutual relations, has a distinct identity and a distinct set of functions. We simply argue that those functions are changing fast.

Our claim "that the future of international law is domestic" refers not simply to domestic *law* but to domestic *politics*. More precisely, the future of international law lies in its ability to affect, influence, bolster, backstop, and even mandate speci ªc actors in domestic politics. International rules and institutions will and should be designed as a set of spurs and checks on domestic political actors to ensure that they do what they should be doing anyway, that is, what they have already committed to do in their domestic constitutions and laws.

In this conception, it is perfectly acceptable to continue to distinguish concretely between an "international" and a "domestic" sphere, even as we recognize that the boundary between them has blurred and that they intersect and even conflict in growing ways. Indeed, it is valuable for domestic political actors—the prosecutors trying to bring a former government official to justice, the judges seeking to resist executive pressure to decide a case a particular way, the parliamentary faction trying to fight global warming—to be able to point to a mandate, consequence, or spur from a distinct and separate political space. The result will be ever more elaborate two-level games,[96] but each game will remain on its own board, no matter how complex and dense the links between them.

What must change profoundly, however, is the legitimacy of allowing the architects of international rules and institutions to look within the domestic political sphere of all states actually and hypothetically subject to the rule or institution in question. This scrutiny cannot be undertaken with reference to speci ªc parties and actors in actual states, but rather must be based on data culled from history and the social sciences about the likely incentives of those parties and actors in varying circumstances. The critical question must be how the content of specific rules and the processes and procedures of institutions are likely to interact with, influence, or even change these incentives.

In consequence, the very concept of sovereignty will have to adapt to embrace, rather than reject, the influence of international rules and institutions on domestic political processes. A harbinger of this shift is the new doctrine of the responsibility to protect. The responsibility to protect first emerged from the International Commission on Intervention and State Sovereignty ("ICISS"), headed by former Australian foreign minister Gareth Evans and

Special Advisor to the U.N. Secretary-General Mohamed Sahnoun.[97] In December 2001 the ICISS issued an important and influential report entitled "The Responsibility to Protect," which essentially called for updating the U.N. Charter to incorporate a new understanding of sovereignty.[98]

In the Commission's conception, the core meaning of U.N. membership has shifted from "the final symbol of independent sovereign statehood and thus the seal of acceptance into the community of nations,"[99] to recognition of a state "as a responsible member of the community of nations."[100] Nations are free to choose whether or not to sign the Charter; if they do, however, they must accept the "responsibilities of membership °owing from their signa-ture."[101] According to the ICISS, "[t] here is no transfer or dilution of state sovereignty. But there is a necessary re-characterization involved: *from sovereignty as control* to *sovereignty as responsibility* in both internal functions and external duties."[102] Internally, a government has a responsibility to respect the dignity and basic rights of its citizens; externally, it has a responsibility to respect the sovereignty of other states.

Further, the ICISS places the responsibility to protect on both the state and on the international community as a whole. The ICISS insists that an individual state has the primary responsibility to protect the individuals within it.[103] However, where the state fails in that responsibility, a secondary responsibility falls on the international community acting through the United Nations. Thus, "where a population is suffering serious harm, as a result of internal war, insurgency, repression or state failure, and the state in question is unwilling or unable to halt or avert it, the principle of non-intervention yields to the international responsibility to protect."[104]

These shifts may seem dramatic; they are certainly bold. But in the view of a group of leading European policy thinkers asked to consider how the EU should respond to the U.N. Secretary-General's High-Level Panel Report on Threats, Challenges, and Change, EU states should go considerably further. They should "[p] romote 'the Responsibility to Protect,' while also reframing the sovereignty debate to cover a principle of both *enhancing* effective and legitimate sovereignty of weak states, (through international assistance) and *conditioning* sovereignty on state behavior."[105]

International law and the international community itself are thus coming to have not only the right but in many cases also the obligation to intervene in and influence what were previously the exclusive jurisdiction and political processes of national governments. By strengthening, backstopping, and compelling action at the national level, the international legal system has powerful tools at its disposal to alter domestic political outcomes. The future of international law ultimately depends on the future of international politics: the problems raised and the aspirations generated. If those problems and aspirations arise from within states rather than between them, international law must follow suit to shape and regulate domestic government institutions. But if it is simultaneously to remain a distinct body of *international* law, it must develop a whole new set of effective relationships with those institutions and with entire bodies of domestic law.

The EU is a great experiment with precisely this type of system, although one underpinned by a unique history and culture generating the necessary domestic political will and economic and social forces. The world is not likely to replicate this experience in terms of actual political and economic integration monitored by coercive supranational institutions. But to the extent that the European way of law uses international law to transform and buttress domestic political institutions, it is a model for how international law can function, and in our view, will and must function to address twenty-first-century international challenges.

REFERENCES

1. This approach is closely linked to the monist view of international law. Monists argue that interna-tional law and domestic law are part of the same system, in which international law is hierarchically prior to domestic law. Dualists, in contrast, claim that international and domestic law are part of two distinct systems and that domestic law is generally prior to international law. *See generally* J. G. Starke, *Monism and Dualism in the Theory of International Law*, 17 Brit. Y.B. Int'l L. 66 (1936). While both of these theories provide important linkages between international law and domestic law, for adherents of either approach the functions and institutions of international law remain largely at the international level. *See generally id.*
2. *See* Mavromatis Palestine Concessions (Greece v. Gr. Brit.), 1924 P.C.I.J. (ser. A) No. 2, at 12 (Aug. 30). Yet the decision of a state to espouse its citizen's claim is one of domestic politics—the state has no obligation to do so. International law does, however, regulate the right of the state to espouse an individ-ual claim, limiting such rights to cases of "close connection," usually in the form of "real and effective nationality" between the state and the citizen. *See, e.g.*, Nottebohm Case (Liech. v. Guat.), 1955 I.C.J. 4 (Apr. 6).
3. *See generally* Anne-Marie Slaughter & William Burke-White, *An International Constitutional Moment*, 43 Harv. Int'l L.J. 1 (2002).
4. *See, e.g.*, Stephen D. Krasner, Sovereignty: Organized Hypocrisy 20 (1999).
5. U.N. Charter art. 2, para. 7.
6. *See generally* Mark Leonard, Why Europe Will Run the 21st Century 43–46 (2005).
7. *See, e.g., id.*; Gráinne de Búrca, *Beyond the Charter: How Enlargement Has Enlarged the Human Rights Policy of the European Union*, 27 Fordham Int'l L.J. 679, 680 (2004) (arguing that a similar role of law is generating a "more general and comprehensive human rights policy" within the EU).
8. *See, e.g.*, Eric Posner & John Yoo, *Reply to Helfer and Slaughter*, 93 Cal. L. Rev. 957, 966 (2005) ("There is no reason to think that a court that works for Europe, where political and legal institutions in most countries are of high quality, would work for a world political community that lacks the same level of cohesion and integration. Whatever one thinks about the EU, it is nothing like the international community.")
9. S*ee generally* Nat'l Comm'n on Terrorist Attacks upon the U.S., The 9/11 Commission Re-port (2004).
10. S*ee, e.g.*, Josias Semujanga, Origins of the Rwandan Genocide (2003); Robert B. Edger-ton, The Troubled Heart of Africa: A History of the Congo (2002); Int'l Comm'n of Inquiry on Darfur, *Report of the International Commission of Inquiry on Darfur to the United Nations Secretary-General* (Jan. 25, 2005), http://www.un.org/News/dh/sudan/com_inq_darfur.pdf.
11. S*ee* William J. Broad & David E. Sanger, *Pakistani's Nuclear Black Market Seen as Offering Deepest Secrets of Building Bomb*, N.Y. Times, Mar. 21, 2005, at A7.
12. Secretary-General's High-Level Panel on Threats, Challenges and Change, *A More Secure World: Our Shared Responsibility* 2, U.N. Doc. A/59/565 (Dec. 2, 2004).
13. *See* Jeremy W. Weinstein et al., On the Brink, Weak States and US National Security: A Report of the Commission for Weak States and US National Security 9–12 (2004) (describing recent incidences of state failure); *see also* Stuart E. Eizenstat & John Edward Porter, *Weak States Are a US Security Threat*, Christian Sci. Monitor, June 29, 2004, at 9 ("In those states [Iraq and Haiti] and others like them—Afghanistan, Somalia, Liberia, and possibly Pakistan—where poor states lose control, it's often Americans who pay the price.").
14. Francis Fukuyama, State Building: Governance and World Order in the 21st Cen-tury 92–93 (2004).
15. Emmerich de Vattel described international law in the 1750s as "the rights subsisting between nations or states, and the obligations correspondent to those rights." Emmerich de Vattel, The Law of Nations Preliminaries § 3 (Joseph Chitty et al. trans. & ed. 1883) (1758).
16. *See generally* Slaughter & Burke-White, *supra* note 3. "Whose territory, his religion."
17. Leonard, *supra* note 6, at 35.
18. *Id.* at 5 (quoting Richard Youngs, *Engagement: Sharpening European In°uence*, *in* Global Europe Report 2: New Terms of Engagement 1, 5 (Richard Youngs ed., 2004)).
19. Leonard, *supra* note 6, at 45.
20. *Id.* Others have suggested that these changes are, at times, imposed instead from the top down, and may be indicative of a democratic de^acit in the EU. *See, e.g.*,

Giandomenico Majone, *Europe's Democ-ratic De®cit: A Question of Standards*, 4 Eur. L.J. 5 (1998) (observing that the "democratic de®cit . . . refers to the legitimacy problems of non-majoritarian institutions, i.e., institutions which by design are not directly accountable to the voters or to their elected representatives"); Jeremy Rabkin, *Is EU Policy Erod-ing the Sovereignty of Non-Member States?*, 1 Chi. J. Int'l L. 273, 273 (2000) (arguing that the EU is based on a "systematic program of eroding or recon®guring national sovereignty"). For a perspective on the EU that rejects the danger of the democratic de®cit and accords more closely with our vision, see Andrew Moravcsik, *In Defense of the Democratic De®cit: Reassessing Legitimacy in the European Union*, 40 J. Common Market Stud. 603 (2002).

21. Leonard, *supra* note 6, at 45–46.
22. Beyond the EU system, the European Court of Human Rights ("ECtHR") has repeatedly forced European governments to change their domestic laws governing issues from prosecution of criminals to admitting homosexuals into the armed services. Governments are all entitled to a "margin of apprecia-tion" in reconciling their domestic laws and practices with their treaty obligations, but the ECtHR is there to ensure that the margin does not grow too wide. *See, e.g.*, Handyside v. United Kingdom, 24 Eur. Ct. H.R. (ser. A) at 23 (1976) (applying the margin of appreciation to freedom of speech); Jersild v. Denmark, 298 Eur. Ct. H.R. (ser. A) (1994) (holding the margin of appreciation breached in the prosecu-tion of a journalist for racist speech); Lustig-Prean & Beckett v. United Kingdom, 29 Eur. Ct. H.R. 548, 587 (1999) (holding that the plaintiffs were wrongly discharged "on the grounds of their homosexuality" and requiring a change in UK policy toward sexual orientation in the military); Zana v. Turkey (No. 57), 1997-VII Eur. Ct. H.R. 2533 (holding that Turkey has a margin of appreciation in regulating incitement by Kurdish politicians).
23. Espen Barth Eide, *Introduction: The Role of the EU in Fostering "Effective Multilateralism," in* Effec-tive Multilateralism: Europe, Regional Security and a Revitalized UN 1, 1–10 (Espen Barth Eide ed., 2004).
24. *See generally* Robert Cooper, The Breaking of Nations: Order and Chaos in the 21st Century (2003).
25. Javier Solana is the Secretary-General of the Council of the European Union and the European Un-ion High Representative for the Common Foreign and Security Policy. Should the proposed EU Consti-tution eventually enter into force, he is expected to be appointed Foreign Minister of the EU. The Euro-pean Council is the "main decision-making body of the EU" and is composed of the ministers of the
26. member states for any particular subject area. *See* Council of the European Union, http://ue.eu.int/cms3_fo/showPage.asp?id=242&lang=EN&mode=g (last visited Mar. 23, 2006).
27. Javier Solana, A Secure Europe in a Better World—The European Security Strategy 9 (2003), http://ue.eu.int/uedocs/cmsUpload/78367.pdf.
28. Weinstein et al., *supra* note 13, at 6.
29. For a discussion of the importance of building state capacity, see Problematic Sovereignty: Contested Rules and Political Possibilities (Stephen Krasner ed., 2001).
30. Fukuyama, *supra* note 14, at 120.
31. *See generally* Anne-Marie Slaughter, A New World Order (2004).
32. For examples of this phenomenon among judges, see Kal Raustiala, *The Architecture of International Cooperation: Transgovernmental Networks and the Future of International Law*, 43 Va. J. Int'l L. 1 (2002); Anne-Marie Slaughter, *Judicial Globalization*, 40 Va. J. Int'l L. 1103 (2000). For discussion in the regu-latory context, see Slaughter, *supra* note 31.
33. Slaughter, *supra* note 31, at 99.
34. Kal Raustiala, *Rethinking the Sovereignty Debate in International Economic Law*, 6 J. Int'l Econ. L. 841, 843 (2003).
35. *35. See* Slaughter, *supra* note 31, at 175. Although the United States originally pushed the idea of a global network of antitrust regulators under the Clinton administration, the Bush administration has proven less enthusiastic. The lack of U.S. engagement in the process presently gives the EU considerable in°uence on global regulatory development.
36. International Competition Network, Memorandum on the Establishment and Operation of the International Competition Network, http://www.internationalcompetitionnetwork.org/mou.pdf (last visited Feb. 26, 2006).
37. *See* David Zaring, *Informal Procedure, Hard and Soft, in International Administration*, 5 Chi. J. Int'l L. 547, 595 (2005).
38. *Id.* at 561; *see also* International Organization of Securities Commissions, 2002 Ann. Rep. 22 (2002), http://dev.iosco.org/annual_report/PDF/IOSCO_2002.pdf.
39. For a general discussion, see Slaughter, *supra* note 31, at 65–103. For an example of cross-citation by the South African Constitutional Court, see State v. Makwanyane, 1995 (6) BCLR 665 (CC) (S. Afr.). For an example of borrowing by a developed country, see Regina v. Bow St. Metro Stipendiary Magistrate, *ex parte* Pinochet Ugarte (No. 3), [2000] 1 A.C. 147 (H.L. 1999), in which the English House of Lords cited to no fewer than twenty-one foreign judgments of countries including the United States, France, Israel, and Chile. The fact that such borrowing runs in both directions—from the devel-oped world to the developing world and back again—goes far to counter the criticism that such networks are merely a form of neo-colonial imposition.
40. Leonard, *supra* note 6, at 23 (citing Manuel Castells, The End of Millennium (2000)).
41. The Euro-Mediterranean Partnership, also known as the Barcelona Process, is a "wide framework of political, economic and social relations between the Member States of the European Union and Part-ners of the Southern Mediterranean" launched in Barcelona in 1995. European Union, Euro-Mediterranean Partnership/Barcelona Process, http://europa.eu.int/comm/external_

relations/euromed (last visited Mar. 9, 2006).

42. 41. Stephen D. Krasner, *Building Democracy After Con°ict: The Case for Shared Sovereignty*, 16 J. Democracy, Jan. 2005, at 69, 76.

43. posed oil pipeline agreement between Chad and the World Bank would in-volve shared control and governance.

44. 42. Such shared sovereignty, Krasner claims, can "gird new political structures with more expertise, better-crafted policies, and guarantees against abuses of power" onto weak or failing states.[44]Even within a more traditional framework, the international legal system can employ a range of mechanisms to strengthen the hand of domestic gov-ernments. Legal instruments and codes of international best practices can set standards to give national governments benchmarks for enhancing their own capability.[45] International institutions can provide aid and assistance speci^cally targeted for the domestic institutions of the recipient state. International ^nancial institutions such as the International Monetary Fund ("IMF") and the World Bank may play a particularly powerful role in build-ing domestic capacity. Conditionality requirements give these bodies strong in°uence over domestic outcomes. The IMF's success in enhancing the capa-bilities of domestic governments is much debated,[46] but the World Bank may have a better track record.[47] Part of the Bank's strategy in Africa has been to "put countries in the driver's seat" with a "platform of strong public capacity: capacity to formulate policies; capacity to build consensus; capacity to implement reform; and capacity to monitor results, learn lessons, and adapt accordingly."[48] Whatever their successes and failures to date, the IMF and the World Bank have signi^cant leverage to enhance domestic govern-ment capacity. What they need is far more input from borrower countries, or at least reformers and political activists in borrower countries, about how best to achieve this goal.

45. Incorporating these types of mechanisms into future legal regimes as a means of promoting domestic capacity-building must be an ongoing priority. These mechanisms include building government networks, providing technical assis-tance, setting benchmarks and standards, or encouraging other forms of co-

46. See generally id.

47. *Id.* at 70.

48. In the ^eld of judicial independence, the International Covenant on Civil and Political Rights provides a set of such benchmarks. *See* International Covenant on Civil and Political Rights arts. 9–11, Dec. 16, 1966, 999 U.N.T.S. 171. Additionally, the Rome Statute of the International Criminal Court offers further clari^cation and a potential legal testing ground. Rome Statute of the International Crimi-nal Court art. 17, July 17, 1998, 2187 U.N.T.S. 90 [hereinafter Rome Statute].

49. For two sides of this debate, see Randall Stone, Lending Credibility: The International Monetary Fund and the Post-Communist Transition 233–34 (2002) (arguing that IMF condi-tionality is appropriate and bene^cial) and James Vreeland, The IMF and Economic Development

50. 160–65 (2003) (suggesting that IMF conditionality may retard domestic development).

51. *See* Poul Engberg-Pedersen & Brian Levy, *Building State Capacity in Africa: Learning from Perform-ance and Results*, *in* Building State Capacity in Africa: New Approaches, Emerging Lessons 87 (Brian Levy & Sahr Kpundeh eds., 2004) (discussing the role of the World Bank in enhancing state capacity in Africa); *see also* Joel D. Barkan et al., *Emerging Legislatures: Institutions of Horizontal Accountability*, *in* Building State Capacity in Africa: New Approaches, Emerging Lessons 233–34 (Brian Levy

52. 48. Sahr Kpundeh eds., 2004) (discussing increased awareness across anglophone Africa of developments in peer legislatures as a possible result of World Bank initiatives).

53. Frannie A. Léautier & Callisto Madavo, *Foreword to* Building State Capacity in Africa: New Approaches, Emerging Lessons, at v (Brian Levy & Sahr Kpundeh eds., 2004).

54. Abram Chayes & Antonia Handler Chayes, The New Sovereignty 3 (1995).

55. This model is distinct both in underlying assumptions and in the resultant variables that govern state compliance from carrot-and-stick or norm-socialization approaches. *See, e.g.*, George W. Downs et al., *Is the Good News about Compliance Good News about Cooperation?*, 50 Int'l Org. 379 (1996) (offering a carrot-and-stick model); Ryan Goodman & Derek Jinks, *International Law and State Socialization: Conceptual, Empirical, and Normative Challenges*, 54 Duke L.J. 983 (2005) (linking compliance to state socialization); Harold H. Koh, *Transnational Legal Process*, 75 Neb. L. Rev. 181 (1996) (suggesting the importance of norm internalization). These alternate theories of compliance produce considerably differ-ent prescriptions for how international law may best alter state behavior.

56. 2 Hugo Grotius, The Rights of War and Peace 1062 (Richard Tuck trans., Liberty Fund 2005) (1625).

57. M. Maurice Travers, Le droit penal international et sa mise en oeuvre en temps de paix et en temps de guerre (1922). The key to Travers' argument is that concurrent legislative au-thority could, in turn, empower the judicial institutions of a number of states to act against any given criminal and thereby create overlapping judicial authority without the need for a formal international tribunal.

58. Rome Statute, *supra* note 45, art. 17(1).

59. *Id.* art. 17(3).

60. *Id.* art. 17(2).

61. Article 35 of the European Convention on Human Rights provides that "[t]he Court may only deal with the matter after all domestic remedies have been exhausted." European Convention for the Protection of Human Rights and Fundamental Freedoms art. 35(1), Nov. 4, 1950, Europ. T.S. No. 5, 213 U.N.T.S. 222; *see also* Organization of American States, American Convention on Human Rights art. 46, Nov. 22, 1969, O.A.S.T.S. No. 36, 1144 U.N.T.S. 123 (providing, "[a]dmission by

the Commission of a petition or communication lodged in accordance with Articles 44 or 45 shall be subject to the fol-lowing requirements . . . that the remedies under domestic law have been pursued and exhausted in accordance with generally recognized principles of international law").

62. The 1988 Canadian-American Free Trade Agreement and the more recent NAFTA both contain provisions for the creation of international panels to review the legality of administrative decisions with respect to antidumping and countervailing duty obligations. *See* Free Trade Agreement, U.S.-Can., ch. 19, Jan. 2, 1988, 27 I.L.M. 281; North American Free Trade Agreement, U.S.-Can.-Mex., art. 1904(1), Dec. 17, 1992, 32 I.L.M. 289 ("each Party shall replace judicial review of ªnal antidumping and coun-tervailing duty determinations with bi-national panel review"). Though not a traditional international court or arbitration tribunal, these panels act in a judicial capacity and issue decisions binding on state parties. Certain non-traditional aspects of the panels include the fact that domestic judicial review is not completely foreclosed. *See* Judith Goldstein, *International Law and Domestic Institutions: Reconciling North American "Unfair" Trade Laws*, 50 Int'l Org. 541, 546 (1996).

63. *See* Goldstein, *supra* note 57, at 551.

64. The potential for international institutions to produce these backstopping effects will often de-pend on the international institution having jurisdiction over the state in question or individuals within that state. After all, these effects often arise as a result of the threat of potential international adjudica-tion. Where national governments have refused to accept the jurisdiction of international courts, such effects will be limited.

65. Reform efforts to date have included attempts to reunify the divided judiciary through nationwide judicial conferences, establishing commissions on legislative reform, and launching a Truth and Recon-ciliation Commission. Interview by Yuriko Kuga, Leslie Medema, and Adrian Alvarez with Honorius Kisimba-Ngoy, Minister of Justice, Dem. Rep. Congo, in Kinshasa (Oct. 29, 2003). According to the Director of the Cabinet to the Minister of Human Rights, one "local commission [is] studying how to adapt the ICC to the DRC." Interview by Yuriko Kuga, Leslie Medema, and Adrian Alvarez with Olela Okondji, Director of the Cabinet to the Minister of Human Rights, Dem. Rep. Congo, in Kinshasa (Oct. 29, 2003). Similarly, "a permanent committee within the Ministry [of Justice has been established] for reforming the domestic law" and is "learning how to implement the ICC" crimes into domestic law. The Commission's formal name is the Commission Permanente de Réforme du Droit Congolais. *Id.* A Truth and Reconciliation Commission grew out of the Inter-Congolese Dialogue and is written into the new interim constitution. Constitution de la Transition, Journal Ofªciel de la République Dé-mocratique du Congo, 44 année, 5 Avril 2003, art. 154 ("*Les Institutions d'appui à la démocratie sont: . . .*

66. *La Commission vérité et réconciliation.*"). Despite the consideration of a number of draft laws, as of early 2004, an organic law for the commission has yet to be adopted. Interview with Dr. Kuye Wadonda, President of the Truth and Reconciliation Comm'n, Dem. Rep. Congo, in Kinshasa (Oct. 28, 2003). For a more

67. detailed discussion, see William W. Burke-White, *Complementarity in Practice: The International Criminal Court as Part of a System of Multi-Level Global Governance in the Democratic Republic of Congo*, 18 Leiden J. Int'l L. 557 (2005).

68. *See Sudan Insists Own Courts Must Try Darfur Crimes*, Sudan Trib., Jan. 10, 2006, http://sudantribune. com/article.php3?id_article=13485.

69. Louis Moreno-Ocampo, Chief Prosecutor, ICC, Statement at the Ceremony for the Solemn Under-taking of the Chief Prosecutor of the International Criminal Court (June 16, 2003), http://www.icc-cpi.int/library/organs/otp/030616_moreno_ocampo_english_ªnal.pdf. Similarly, an expert paper pub-lished by the Ofªce of the Prosecutor notes: "The complementarity regime serves as a mechanism to encourage and facilitate the compliance of States with their primary responsibility to investigate and prosecute core crimes." International Criminal Court, Ofªce of the Prosecutor, Informal Expert Paper: The Principle of Complementarity in Practice 3 (2003), http://www.icc-cpi.int/library/ organs/otp/complementarity.pdf.

70. The Chilean Supreme Court has recently ruled that Pinochet may stand trial domestically for international crimes against Chilean citizens committed during his rule. *See* David Sugarman, *Will Pinochet Ever Answer to the People of Chile?*, Times (London), Sept. 14, 2004, at 10.

71. *64. See* Regina v. Bow St. Metro Stipendiary Magistrate, *ex parte* Pinochet Ugarte (No. 3), [2000] 1 A.C. 147 (H.L. 1999).

72. For a discussion of potential problems this may pose for domestic democratic processes, see *infra* text accompanying notes 85–86; *cf.* Cutis A. Bradley & Jack L. Goldsmith, *Pinochet and International Human Rights Litigation*, 97 Mich. L. Rev. 2129, 2130 (1999) (discussing the "fundamental issue of whether any international criminal process is appropriate when a nation, like Chile, has addressed the human rights abuses of a prior regime through a domestic political compromise that facilitated a transi-tion to democracy"). One of the authors, however, has argued that such domestic compromises should not be given extraterritorial respect where they lack domestic legitimacy. *See* William W. Burke-White, *Reframing Impunity: Applying Liberal International Law Theory to an Analysis of Amnesty Legislation*, 42

73. Harv. Int'l L.J. 467 (2001).

74. Obviously, where the state in question has rejected the authority of the international tribunal or failed to ratify its Statute, such as the U.S. policy toward the ICC, none of these effects may materialize.

75. *See generally* Christian Tomuschat, *International Courts and Tribunals*, 1 Encyclopedia of Public International Law 92–99 (Rudolph Dolzer et al. eds., 1981).

76. For example, many treaties in the area of international criminal law require criminalization of certain behavior at the national level. *See, e.g.*, Convention on the Prevention and Punishment of the Crime of Genocide art. 5, Dec. 9, 1948, 78 U.N.T.S. 277; Convention Against Torture and Other Cruel, Inhu-man, or Degrading Treatment or Punishment art. 4, Dec. 10, 1984, S. Treaty Doc. No. 100-20 (1988), 1465 U.N.T.S. 113.

77. New York v. United States, 505 U.S. 144, 161 (1992) (quoting Hodel v. Virginia Surface Mining Reclamation Ass'n, 452 U.S. 264, 288 (1981)) (holding Congress may not "commandee[r] the legisla-tive processes of the States by directly compelling them to enact and enforce a federal regulatory pro-gram").

78. S.C. Res. 1373, ¶ 2(c)–(d), U.N. Doc. S/RES/1373 (Sept. 28, 2001).

79. *Id.* The White House, National Strategy for Combating Terrorism 13 (2003), http://www. whitehouse.gov/news/releases/2003/02/counter_terrorism/counter_terrorism_strategy.pdf

80. International Convention for the Suppression of the Financing of Terrorism, G.A. Res. 54/109, 8, U.N. Doc. A/RES/54/109 (Dec. 9, 1999).

81. International Convention for the Suppression of Terrorist Bombings, G.A. Res. 52/164, ¶¶ 5–7, U.N. Doc. A/RES/52/164 (Dec. 15, 1997).

82. Security Council Counter-Terrorism Committee, http://www.un.org/sc/ctc/ (last visited Feb. 26,2006).

83. CTC: About the CTC—How Does the CTC Work with States?, http://www.un.org/Docs/sc/ committees/1373/work.html (last visited Feb. 26, 2006).

84. CTC: Assistance to States—Working Together to Raise State Capacity, http://www.un.org/Docs/sc/committees/1373/capacity.html (last visited Feb. 26, 2006).

85. CTC: Assistance to States—How Can the CTC Help States?, http://www.un.org/Docs/sc/committees/ 1373/help.html (last visited Feb. 26, 2006).

86. *Id.*

87. S.C. Res. 1540, ¶ 2, U.N. Doc. S/RES/1540 (Apr. 28, 2004).

88. *Id.* ¶ 7. *See, e.g.*, Agreement Between the United States of America and the International Atomic Energy Agency for the Application of Safeguards in the United States, Nov. 18, 1977, 32.3 U.S.T. 3059.

89. This goal of inclusion re°ects Chayes and Chayes's recognition of the new sovereignty as a right to be included in international institutions, rather than the traditional right to exclude other states from interference. *See generally* Chayes & Chayes, *supra* note 49

90. One of the authors has described this as a moral hazard problem. *See* William W. Burke-White, Multi-Level Global Governance in the Enforcement of International Criminal Law ch. 4 (2006) (unpub-lished Ph.D. dissertation, University of Cambridge) (on ªle with author). The most obvious example of this is the government of Uganda's self-referral to the ICC concerning the Lords Resistance Army. Press Release, International Criminal Court, President of Uganda Refers Situation concerning the Lord's Resis-tance Army (LRA) to the ICC (Jan. 29, 2004), http://www.icc-cpi.int/pressrelease_details&id=16.html. In all likelihood, the Ugandan government could have addressed this situation domestically if it had not had the option of referring the situation to the ICC.

91. Fukuyama argues that "[t]he international community, including the vast numbers of NGOs that are an intimate part of it, comes so richly endowed and full of capabilities that it tends to crowd out rather than complement the extremely weak state capacities of the targeted countries." *See* Fukuyama, *supra* note 14, at 103.

92. For a discussion of the importance of such domestic experimentation, see Michael C. Dorf & Charles F. Sabel, *A Constitution of Democratic Experimentalism*, 98 Colum. L. Rev. 267 (1998).

93. Mary Robinson, *Shaping Globalization: The Role of Human Rights*, 19 Am. U. Int'l L. Rev. 1, 12 (2003).

94. *See* Kim L. Scheppele, *Law in a Time of Emergency: States of Exception and the Temptations of 9/11*, 6 U. Pa. J. Const. L. 1001 (2000).

95. Human Rights First, Imbalance of Powers: How Changes to U.S. Law and Policy Since 9/11 Erode Human Rights and Civil Liberties 76–79 (2003).

96. Phillip Jessup, Transnational Law 2 (1956).

97. Sandra Day O'Connor, Keynote Address at the Ninety-Sixth Annual Meeting of the American So-ciety of International Law (Mar. 16, 2002), *in* 96 Am. Soc'y Int'l L. Proc. 348, 350 (2002).

98. Rosenau observes that "[d]omestic and foreign affairs have always formed a seamless web . . . .[W]e can no longer allow the domestic-foreign boundary to confound our understanding of world af-fairs." James N. Rosenau, Along the Domestic-Foreign Frontier: Exploring Governance in a Turbulent World 4 (1997).

99. *Id.* at 5.

100. *Id.* at 4–5 (emphasis added).

101. *See id.* at 5–6; *see also* Mathias Albert & Lothar Brock, *Debordering the World of States: New Spaces in International Relations*, 35 New Pol. Sci. 69 (1996).

102. 96. *See generally* Robert Putnam, *Diplomacy and Domestic Politics: The Logic of Two-Level Games*, 42 Int'l Org. 427 (1988).

103. In September 1999, Koª Annan called on all U.N. members at the opening of the General As-sembly to "reach consensus—not only on the principle that massive and systematic violations of human rights must be checked, wherever they take place, but also on ways of deciding what action is necessary, and when, and by whom." Koª Annan, Two Concepts of Sovereignty, Address Before the U.N. General Assembly (Sept. 20, 1999), *in* Koª Annan, The Question of Intervention: Statements by the Secretary-General (1999).

104. Int'l Comm'n on Intervention and State Sovereignty, The Responsibility to Protect: Report of the ICISS (2001). The ICISS began from the premise that "in key respects .

. . the mandates and capacity of international institutions have not kept pace with international needs or modern expecta-

105. tions." *Id.* ¶ 1.11. More speci®cally, the ICISS argued that the intense debate over military protection for humanitarian purposes °owed from a "critical gap" between the immense and unavoidable reality of mass human suffering and the existing rules and mechanisms for managing world order. At the same time, it noted a widening gap between the rules and the principles of the Charter regarding non-interference in the domestic affairs of member nations and actual state practice as it has evolved since 1945. The ICISS frames the "responsibility to protect" as an "emerging principle" of customary international law—not yet existing as law but already supported both by state practice and a wide variety of legal sources. *See id.*2.24–2.27.

106. *Id.* ¶ 2.11.

107. *Id.* ¶ 2.14.

108. *Id.*

109. *Id.*

110. *See id.* ¶ 2.29.

111. *Id.* at XI.

CHAPTER 18 ADVANCING PEACE AND RESPECTING BASIC HUMAN RIGHTS? A NARROW MORAL APPRAISAL OF INTERNATIONAL LAW

Benoit Mayer

International lawyers and international relations scholars certainly have a role to play, along with moral philosophers, in debates on global justice. The expertise of international lawyers could most obviously help to characterize existing norms in international law, thus providing a factual basis for a moral reckoning of international law. International relations theories, on the contrary, may help us to envisage realistic steps toward a more just international law. Thus, while ethical reasoning is necessary in order to identify standards of justice (the end goal), moral philosophy alone is unlikely to lead to relevant proposals for incremental steps toward a more just international law. Some forms of interdisciplinary encounter are necessary to identify deficiencies in international law or windows of opportunities for reforms.

Therefore, *The Thin Justice of International Law: A Moral Reckoning of the Law of Nations* is to be welcomed as one of a few recent attempts by an international lawyer to contribute to global justice scholarship. While evidencing the relevance of international law to the debate, this work also reveals the difficulty of the enterprise: identifying relevant ethical standards for a moral reckoning of international law. Steven Ratner's methodology is based on the assumption that '[w]e can, without being circular, find justice in international law by applying a philosophical conception to legal norms, *but also see the corpus of international law as saying something about what is just in the first place*'.[1] Thus, Ratner purports to show that 'the core norms of international law … conform in major respects to a standard of global justice deserving of the name'[2]—a standard that he also calls 'decent'.[3] This standard—the so-called 'thin' justice of international law—is proposed as a 'moral minimum',[4] which is 'less dense, and certainly less demanding on individuals, than the justice needed for the governance of domestic societies'[5]—and, in fact, much less ambitious than virtually any global justice theory. Even though Ratner's monograph is a serious and interesting intellectual exercise, its conclusions rely entirely on an initial selection of 'core' norms of international law and of a particular standard of justice.

The thin justice standard proposed by Ratner consists of two consequentialist moral norms or 'pillars': the advancement of international and intrastate peace, and respect for basic human rights. On these bases, Ratner submits that, 'whether in changing an existing rule to meet the standard of thin justice or aspiring to a higher standard of global justice, we must remain aware of the risks to peace or human rights of alternative rules and not endanger what has been achieved to date'.[6] The thin justice framework is intended to take into account some of the main constraints of existing international law—most explicitly the existence of states with unequal power—in order to identify realistic ethical demands and paths of reform toward a more just international law. However, because the two pillars are drawn from a set of norms that Ratner considers central

Citation: Benoit Mayer, Advancing peace and respecting basic human rights? A narrow moral appraisal of international law, doi.org/10.3402/egp.v8.28925.

to international law,[7] it is unsurprising that most of these very same norms generally conform to this standard, resulting in what Anne Peters qualified of 'an ultimately overwhelmingly positive assessment of international law'.[8] Only a few of the specific norms discussed by Ratner are possibly incompatible with the standard of thin justice, for instance, the veto power of the five permanent members of the Security Council, the blanket ban on humanitarian intervention,[9] and certain aspects of sovereign immunity.

Besides developing a general theoretical framework, Ratner's monograph contains thorough discussions of prominent issues of international governance, such as humanitarian intervention or the liberalization of international trade, which could be read for their own sake. The present essay focuses however on the book as a whole, as a proposal for an innovative non-ideal theoretical framework which would serve to appraise the justice of international law in order to foster progress toward a more just international law (and the application of this framework). The following discussion first focuses on the relevance of the two pillars of thin justice; it then considers an alternative, in particular to broader standards of justice, which could serve to a moral reckoning of international law; and it finally considers the normative implications of the standard of thin justice.

PEACE AND BASIC HUMAN RIGHTS

Steven Ratner writes that 'it seems clear to [him], as [he] believe[s] it would be to any international lawyer, that the two basic values in [the] normative structure [of international affairs] are peace and human rights'.[10] However, the first reviews of Ratner's monograph confirm that not all international lawyers agree with this intuition.[11] Anticipating such challenges, Ratner acknowledges *mezza vocce* that different moral appraisals of international law could be based on alternative, ethically defensible standards,[12] and that there are after all 'many kinds of justice'.[13] This suggests that Ratner's theory does not depict *the* thin justice of international law, as something out there that could be documented following a nearly scientific method, but rather as *a view of some considerations of thin justice present in certain norms of international law*—a well-informed perspective, but hardly a compelling framework that could be transposed and reused in different contexts.

I leave to others to discuss whether peace or basic human rights are really standards of justice, rather than 'worthy goals that may be pursued through international law'.[14] What concerns me here is, more practically, whether these standards or goals are relevant for a moral reckoning of international law in general, as opposed to an analytical framework to think about some specific norms involving an arbitrage between peace and human rights. My inquiry is hindered by the lack of a consistent definition of each pillar—in particular, the second pillar is first defined as '*respect* for basic human rights'[15] (as an obligation of restraint), but Ratner then tends to give at least some weight to positive moral obligations, for instance when assessing whether states should have a legal obligation to intervene abroad on humanitarian grounds.[16] Indeed, international human rights law requires much more than non-interference with basic human rights, at least within a state's own territory; recent concepts such as a *responsibility* to protect and current debates on possible interventions in Syria or in the so-called 'Islamic State' reflect a growing expectation that states should also take some positive actions abroad.

More fundamentally, it is not always quite clear whether Ratner refers to basic human rights as legal entitlements defined in international conventions, which are subject to derogations for legitimate goals such as the protection of public order or national security, or as a broader political project promoting the protection of individuals in more general ways, thus requiring the pursuit of the same legitimate goals as an indirect way of advancing human welfare. The former alternative would hardly lead to anything more than a compatibility check between 'basic' components of the International Bill of Rights and the rest of the international law. But if the second pillar relates to the political project of advancing human welfare, it would certainly also include peace, and it is accordingly difficult to understand why peace should form a distinct pillar.[17] The advancement of interstate and intrastate peace is, for the most part (if not exclusively),[18] justified by the promotion of human welfare. While the author argues that warfare leads to 'unparalleled catastrophic consequences', he immediately acknowledges that more people die of hunger.[19]

Moreover, it appears throughout the book that the two pillars of thin justice do not readily apply to all norms of international law—far from that. It is granted that norms of coordination, for instance norms to avoid collisions of vessels at sea, have little moral value. Beyond, however, the author admits that many regimes of international law cannot really be assessed under a two-pillar standard of thin justice. For instance, peace plays little role in justifying international economic law.[20] Ratner further recognizes that the two pillars of thin justice do not provide a convincing basis for a moral reckoning of international humanitarian law, international criminal law, and international environmental law: 'their links to peace and basic human rights are elusive and seemingly unimportant for appraising their justice'.[21] One may also wonder whether the second pillar is really essential for a moral appraisal of the norms on the use of force, whose aim is before all to ensure a durable peace—systemic human rights violations could be viewed as a likely cause of war rather than an intrinsic goal.

The advancement of peace and respect for (basic) human rights appear therefore, at most, as a relevant basis for a moral reckoning of selected norms of international law, to which Ratner alludes as 'the core norms of international law'.[22] But some essential norms of international law are not within the purview of the thin justice framework—for instance, the norms identifying the sources of international law or asserting the sovereignty of states. The author admits that his 'choice of issues is somewhat selective and based on what [he] regard[s] as the major claims to date'.[23] The selected, prominent global governance issues that Ratner addresses relate, more often than not, with the adaptation of 'classical' norms, adopted no later than the mid-20th Century, to changing expectations at the turn of the 21st Century.[24] Thus, the prohibition of the use of force by the Charter of the United Nations has increasingly been challenged at the time of the 'global war on terror' (debate on the scope of self-defense),[25] in particular by the idea of a responsibility to protect (debate on humanitarian intervention).[26]Likewise, multiple fictions are arising between the classical emphasis on states' independence at the time of decolonization and the growing awareness of their interdependence, requiring adjustments in international economic law.[27]

Thus, in an explicit effort at abstracting a moral reckoning of international law from power politics,[28] Ratner oversees the role of changing expectations. The author recognizes that more or less demanding standards can be established when he briefly discusses an aspirational 'thicker' standard of justice in his last chapter (with a greater emphasis on positive efforts for the protection of all human rights). Nevertheless, the reader is likely to be under the impression that Ratner applies classical normative goals—which are now relatively well integrated in international law—to an assessment of present norms, thus systematically overseeing the inconsistency of these norms with *current* expectations.[29] Even within some of the debates selected by the author—from human rights considerations in international economic law to extraterritorial human rights obligations—the stakes are not just to ensure that international law advances peace and does not interfere with human rights protection. These debates, and many others, point to the need for international law to respond to growing expectations for something more deserving to be called 'global justice', including, in particular, demand for active human rights protection and, more generally, for the advancement of something such as sustainable development. Through an excessively narrow standard of thin justice, Ratner comes a bit too easily to the conservative conclusion that international law is not, after all, as unjust as it is often thought to be.[30]

THE POSSIBILITY OF A BROADER MORAL RECKONING OF INTERNATIONAL LAW

In the era of the Millennium Development Goals and the Sustainable Development Goals, a moral reckoning of international law that would reflect global expectations should certainly rely on more ambitious standards.[31] As noted before, Ratner outlines in his last chapter a 'thicker' standard of justice to which international law could progressively turn, as a form of 'aspirational theory'[32] situated somewhere between the standard of thin justice and an ideal theory of justice. Ratner suggests that, according to this thicker standard, 'the norms are just if and only if they advance the enjoyment of human rights without interfering with interstate or internal peace'.[33] More emphasis is thus put on human rights, including on their active protection.

Even if one interprets human rights as a general political project (essentially the promotion of human welfare) rather than as a set of individual entitlements defined by international conventions, this 'thicker' standard of justice remains quite under-inclusive. It still fails to apply, for instance, to international environmental law, and it does not comprehend academic discussions as well as civil society engagement in support of some degree of global redistribution. This aspirational, 'thicker' standard of justice does not even require that current generations take appropriate measures not to significantly hinder the environment—and perhaps even the possibility of existence—of future generations through massive greenhouse gas emissions. Essential moral considerations remain clearly outside of the discussion.

This leads us to wonder whether it is possible to imagine a *broader* moral reckoning of international law (as opposed to a *thicker* one), which would apply to a larger array of international norms. Ratner seems rather dismissive of such an endeavor, if only on practical grounds. In a later discussion of his book, the author put forward that '[t]he diversity of international law's norms makes it very hard to examine their justice through one framework that is not more complex that it is worth'.[34] Ratner thus seems rather to suggest that complementary appraisals of other fields of international law could be based on different standards of justice—for instance, considerations for non-human species in international environmental law,[35] or perhaps economic stability and prosperity to international economic law.[36] Likewise, when excluding considerations of global redistribution from the scope of international economic law, the author suggests that redistribution might better be undertaken 'by taking other, parallel approaches to economic development'.[37]

But attributing different objectives to different legal regimes (and excluding specific goals from the assessment of specific regimes) suggests an untenable vision of a fragmented and somewhat schizophrenic international law system, whereby the norms adopted in, say, international environmental law could be defeated by other norms in, say, international trade law. Just as Ratner emphasizes the need to balance peace and basic human rights, or also basic human rights and trade or investments, other important objectives—such as the protection of endangered species, environmental sustainability, some sense of international solidarity in addressing issues of human suffering, and even some measure of global redistribution—should, and tend to, be taken into consideration every time they appear relevant to a particular *norm*. There may be many different goals at play in the development of international law, and some goals might be more or less relevant to particular regimes, but confining specific values to specific regimes runs counter to our understanding of international law as a consistent normative system.

This suggests that the justice underlying international law may have much more than two pillars, and that all of these pillars could in principle be relevant in appraising any norm of international law—and, at any rate, for a comprehensive moral reckoning of international law. Concededly, some pillars might be more or less firmly established in states' practice, and some might be subject to controversies. Even a principle of sustainable development was agreed by states and civil societies only because it was sufficiently vague to support virtually decent normative claim. Overseeing the multiplicity of the ethical pillars of international law, or denying the diversity of views about what constitutes such pillars,[38] could contribute to legitimizing and encouraging the continued imposition of Western values over the rest of the world, while hindering reformative counter-projects toward a better representation of the Third World or a better gender balance in international law.[39]

NORMATIVE IMPLICATIONS

Perhaps, the most problematic aspects of the thin justice framework appears when Ratner turns from a purely descriptive moral reckoning of international law, to the production of normative suggestions about future evolutions of international law. Most obviously, there is certainly a risk that the rather apologetic account of existing international law, overlooking current expectations, would make international lawyers a bit too comfortable with the status quo, focusing on the (meager) past achievements of international law—rules that promote peace and do not interfere with basic human rights—while omitting current struggles, for instance, for the advancement of human rights, the promotion of development, and the protection of the environment.[40] More fundamentally, it is doubtful that the assessment of the goals that were pursued through international law could ever suffice to justify what goals international law *should*—or even *could*—pursue in the future.

Ratner submits that the reform of international law should aim 'to rectify those norms currently deficient as a matter of thin justice and to improve those norms that meet the standard but ought to do better, but to do so in a way that does not endanger their thin justice'.[41] One central aim of the theoretical framework of the thin justice is to indicate realistic and desirable reforms of international law.[42] Yet, Ratner's methodology does not enable him to 'advocate'[43] for thin justice, no more that it permits to identify 'the ways in which the law *should* and *can* change'.[44] It is one thing to identify certain prevailing ethical considerations (peace and basic human rights) throughout 'core' norms of international law; it is a totally different thing to argue that international law *should* further develop on these same pathways, or that it *could* realistically go further in the same direction.

Regarding the identification of desirable goals, Ratner's advocacy for international law reforms that would build further on international law's past achievements runs into the is–ought problem, once described by David Hume: a normative statement (here, about what the law *ought to be*) cannot be deduced only from a factual statement (here, about what the law *is*) without the adjunction of an additional normative premise.[45] Ratner cannot consistently turn from discovering 'decent' goals pursued by existing norms, directly to indicating that further reform projects should give priority to these same values, without making any intermediary normative claims in support of the desirability of pursuing similar justice standards. There is no obvious moral ground for reforms of international law to seek only to pursue those goals already best served by international law, rather than opening up to other, underrepresented 'pillars' of justice. On the contrary, consideration for all possible aspects of justice appear, *prima facie*, to be morally commendable.[46]

Regarding the feasibility of reforms, likewise, the past achievements of international law can only give a very rough notion of political opportunities for further developments. What international law has done best in the past is not necessarily what it could do best in the future. To the contrary, it might be that many of the low-hanging fruits have already been picked up for advancing peace or respecting human rights, while more opportunities for some 'decent' ethical reforms lie elsewhere—say, economic development and environmental sustainability.[47] Geopolitical circumstances are changing, and so are global expectations. One might suggest, for instance, that the displacement of the world's trade and economic centers of gravity toward Asia may lead Western values—such as a greater emphasis on civil and political rights—to lose weight in favor of 'Eastern' values—such as, possibly, economic development. Rather than international law, international relations theories (in particular the theory of norm entrepreneurship) would be helpful in assessing which ethical arguments are more likely to have a positive impact on the future of international law.[48] In the absence of such an analysis, Ratner's statement that '[i]nternational law lacks the capacity to guarantee the equality of individuals',[49] and hence to engage in global redistribution, relies entirely on pre-theoretical assumptions which, one might as well think, are increasingly likely to be challenged.

As a sketch of an agenda for the reform of international law, the framework of a thin justice is thus obstructed by a rather arbitrary determination of constants (e.g. the state-centeredness of international law, the impossibility of global redistribution) and variables (peace and human rights). Robert Howse criticized this dimension of Ratner's work by questioning 'the theoretical or practical value of simply assuming certain constraints on international legal normativity or ideal justice as immovable'.[50] Some of Ratner's proposed reforms to advance the thin justice of international law—most obviously the reform of the five permanent members of the Security Council—would face formidable political obstacles. On the contrary, ongoing evolutions (ranging from the progressive recognition of non-state actors, to the adoption of sustainable development goals) show the possibility of incremental changes in what Ratner considers as constants.

Way beyond the 'thin' nature of a non-ideal theory, the limitations of this theoretical framework results in a narrow view of what international law is trying to achieve, and in truncated consideration for possible and desirable reforms. The standards of peace and basic human rights are certainly relevant goals pursued through international law, but they do not provide a comprehensive picture of what is really at stake through international law. More is arguably lost than gained when the moral pursuit of international law is reduced to only two considerations, eclipsing hard-fought argumentative battles and opportunities for desirable reform beyond peace and (basic) human rights.

REFERENCES

1. Steven Ratner, *The Thin Justice of International Law: A Moral Reckoning of the Law of Nations* (Oxford: Oxford University Press, 2015), 6 (emphasis added).
2. Ibid., 2.
3. Ibid., 155, 216, 291 et passim.
4. Ibid., 90, citing Michael Walzer, *Thick and Thin: Moral Argument at Home and Abroad* (Notre Dame, IN: University of Notre Dame Press, 1994), 4–19.
5. Ratner, *The Thin Justice of International Law*, 90.
6. Ibid., 2.
7. Ibid., 65 and 408. Ratner claims to draw the thin justice principle from '[his] own set of observations about fundamental ideas permeating the normative structure of international affairs that includes international law', but it is far from clear how the 'normative structure of international affairs' differs from the 'core norms' of international law.
8. Anne Peters, 'Thin is beautiful—or are international lawyers anorectic?', *Blog of the European Journal of International Law*, http://www.ejiltalk.org/thin-is-beautiful-or-are-international-lawyers-anorectic/ (accessed June 2, 2015).
9. Yet, debates exist about the existence of this blanket

prohibition, some international lawyers arguing that humanitarian intervention is permitted without the Security Council's authorization under exceptional circumstances.

10. Ratner, *The Thin Justice of International Law*, 65.
11. See Frédéric Mégret, 'A Comment on Ratner on International Justice', *Blog of the European Journal of International Law*, http://www.ejiltalk.org/a-comment-on-ratner-on-international-justice/ (accessed June 4, 2015); and Robert Howse, 'Response to Ratner', *Blog of the European Journal of International Law*, http://www.ejiltalk.org/response-to-ratner-an-international-lawyer-has-got-to-dreamit-comes-with-the-territory/ (accessed June 4, 2015).
12. Ratner, *The Thin Justice of International Law*, 166.
13. Ibid., 406.
14. See Howse, 'Response to Ratner', second point.
15. Ratner, *The Thin Justice of International Law*, 73 (emphasis added).
16. Ibid., 306.
17. The relevance of ascribing a distinct pillar to peace was also critically discussed in Howse, 'Response to Ratner' (fourth point); and David Lefkowitz, 'Reflections on The Thin Justice of International Law: Peace, Justice, and Secession', *Ethics & International Affairs*, http://www.ethicsandinternationalaffairs.org/2015/reflections-on-the-thin-justice-of-international-law-peace-justice-and-secession-2/ (accessed June 3, 2015).
18. See Mégret, 'A Comment on Ratner on International Justice', suggesting an alternative first pillar consisting in 'an abiding concern with stability and order'. Yet, such concerns with stability and order might have less ethical than political value.
19. Ratner, *The Thin Justice of International Law*, 67.
20. Ibid., 322, 351.
21. Ibid., 383.
22. Ibid., 2.
23. See ibid., 268.
24. Thus, Ratner relies heavily on documents adopted or published decades ago, including the UN Charter, the writings of Hersch Lauterpacht, and a 1953 speech by UN Secretary General Dag Hammarskjöld. See ibid., 66, 107, 408. Despite their historical or legal importance, it is unlikely that any of these three sources would be expressed in exactly the same way today.
25. Ratner, *The Thin Justice of International Law*, 4.
26. Ibid., 292–312.
27. Ibid., 315–79.
28. Ibid., 414.
29. See Mégret, 'A Comment on Ratner on International Justice': 'one cannot help thinking that international law is being evaluated from the point of view of a standard of justice that is precariously thin because it is in fact conveniently derived from itself'.
30. See Ratner, The Thin Justice of International Law, 218 ('Sovereign equality thus turns out to be by and large thinly just—more just than many of its critics, whether from states or the academy, might think'); and ibid., 414 ('International law has indeed played a significant role in creating a more just world').
31. See Howse, 'Response to Ratner' (fourth point): '[e]ntire spheres of normativity are simply excluded ab initio by Ratner from the "thin" theory of justice'.
32. Ratner, *The Thin Justice of International Law*, 417.
33. Ibid., 417.
34. See Steven Ratner, 'A Response to the Discussants', *Blog of the European Journal of International Law*, http://www.ejiltalk.org/a-response-to-the-discussants/ (accessed June 5, 2015).
35. See Ratner, *The Thin Justice of International Law*, 405.
36. Ibid., 322.
37. Ibid., 379.
38. See Mégret, 'A Comment on Ratner on International Justice': 'the vast majority of Ratner's sources are taken from the aristocracy of (notably male) Anglo-American jurisprudence'.
39. See Prabhakar Singh and Benoit Mayer, eds., *Critical International Law: Postrealism, Postcolonialism, and Transnationalism* (Oxford: Oxford University Press, 2014); B.S. Chimni, 'Third World Approaches to International Law: A Manifesto', *International Community Law Review* 8 (2006): 3; and Hilary Charlesworth, Christine Chinkin, and Shelley Wright, 'Feminist Approaches to International Law', *American Journal of International Law* 85 (1991): 613.
40. See Howse, 'Response to Ratner', noting that Ratner's monograph 'is a technique of making the tension [between progressive ideals and the reality of international law] go away, rather than facing it squarely'.
41. Ratner, *The Thin Justice of International Law*, 407.
42. The normative conclusions are central to Ratner's project. See Ratner, 'A Response to the Discussants': 'I agree that it is possible to develop a one-pillar model based on human rights; I just think it's less convincing in terms of what global justice *should* entail and what standard of global justice should be used to appraise international law'. (emphasis added).
43. Ratner, *The Thin Justice of International Law*, 309.
44. Ibid., 142 (emphasis added).
45. See David Hume, *A Treatise of Human Nature* (Oxford: Oxford University Press, 1739) III.1.i.
46. Yet another element to consider, in a comprehensive normative theory of international law reform, is the need for international law to pursue particular goals. Some goals are more or less likely to be pursued by other means. Prima facie, states' individual interests might push them to avoid wars and protect human rights even in the absence of a clear international legal structure, while it is perhaps more difficult to imagine effective measures of global redistribution and protection of the global environment (e.g. climate change mitigation) without international law.
47. Thus, two kinds of normative arguments are typically made by international lawyers: productivist arguments,

which suggest to extend international norms by essentially prolonging existing lines, and the bandwagon arguments, which put emphasis on would-be precursory signs of new tendencies. These two arguments, however, are often in contradiction. See discussion in Benoit Mayer, 'Realizing Whose Utopia? The Structure of Normative International Law Arguments', *Leiden Journal of International Law* 27 (2014): 543.

48. On the theory of norm entrepreneurship, see in particular Finnemore and Kathryn Sikkink, 'International Norm Dynamics and Political Change', *International Organization* 4 (1998): 887; and Ian Johnstone, 'The Secretary-General as Norm Entrepreneur', in *Secretary or General: The UN Secretary-General in World Politics*, ed. Simon Chesterman (Cambridge: Cambridge University Press, 2007), 123.

49. Ratner, *The Thin Justice of International Law*, 419.

50. Howse, '*Response to Ratner*', (fifth point).

CHAPTER 19 AS INTERNATIONAL LAW GOES, THE EU IS A MODEL OF ACCOUNTABILITY AND DEMOCRACY

Katja Ziegler

Those advocating for a UK exit from the European Union claim that Britain would be "taking back control" from Brussels if it left the EU. But their arguments about sovereignty and "control" appear to conveniently forget that many laws exist internationally. Often, these laws are created in ways that are far less democratic than the way the EU makes its legislation.

While the chorus of those claiming Britain needs to get its sovereignty back gets louder, few would advocate a withdrawal from, say, the United Nations. This is for good reasons, among them the value of international cooperation. But the same reasons also apply to the EU, whose democratic and judicial accountability is actually further evolved than that of the UN and other international organisations. Undoing the EU as a more advanced system of international law would be a significant set-back for international cooperation.

Today, international cooperation spans a broad range of everyday life activities from travel by air, to trade and the internet. It also covers global issues such as environmental protection, terrorism, arms control and nuclear non-proliferation. Such cooperation happens through a complex web of international agreements, and has happened for a long time. International treaties predate the modern nation state and go back to antiquity, such as peace treaties of Ancient Greece or Rome or treaties conferring reciprocal privileges on foreigners or traders in a territory.

At the end of World War I in 1918, it was then-US President Woodrow Wilson in his famous Fourteen Points who proposed international integration to obtain "just and secure peace". The League of Nations was founded on these ideas, but it took another world war for states to face the reality that there was no alternative to cooperation. In 1945, in San Francisco, 50 countries founded the United Nations.

Since then, the legal framework established by international law, including specialised treaties and organisations has increased tremendously. Requirements of integration and changing perceptions about good governance and the rule of

Citation: Katja Ziegler, As international law goes, the EU is a model of accountability and democracy, https://theconversation.com/as-international-law-goes-the-eu-is-a-model-of-accountability-and-democracy-61042.

law have given rise to numerous human rights treaties since 1945 and which have put the individual more at the centre of international law. The Foreign and Commonwealth Office's database UK Treaties Online contains over 14,000 treaties involving the UK.

EU: a Lab for International Law

But the international legal framework remains rudimentary and incomplete in comparison to a country's domestic laws, both from the perspective of accountability – the rule of law – and of democracy.

There are two main consequences of this. First, an enforcement gap: international rules frequently cannot be enforced in the same way as laws within states. This means states and international organisations are less likely to be held to account if they breach the law. Second, a democracy gap: international law tends to be made by national executives, and the governance structure of international organisations tends to be less democratic than that of states.

On both counts, the EU and its law-making scrubs up much better than other international law and international organisations, including the UN.

The EU's legal framework holds to account both its own member states on the international stage and the EU itself – and empowers individuals to do the same. It is the most powerful but also the most accountable international organisation there is today and may even be considered as a model or "laboratory" for other areas of international law.

Such accountability contrasts sharply with the picture elsewhere in international law. UN peackekeepers have been criticised for human rights abuses. UN missions such as UN's Interim Administration Mission in Kosovo have extensive powers over individuals, but mechanisms to hold international organisations such as the UN to account either do not exist in the first place or are weak and only developing slowly.

In contrast, EU law has allowed individuals to review far-reaching interference with their rights. For example, people who were (at times erroneously) listed as terrorists have been able to review the restrictions imposed on them by EU – and indirectly UN law – such as the complete freezing of access to their bank accounts.

More than that, the EU has influenced the UN, which realised that it had to give individuals a means of challenging UN sanctions decisions made against them. This provided an impulse to create the Office of the Ombudsperson.

Questions of Legitimacy

In the context of decision-making on foreign policy issues, accountability is "thinned" out, although not totally eliminated. A government's action within the UN Security Council, for example, is made by representatives of its national government.

In contrast, through the EU treaties EU member states have createdsignificant mechanisms which are capable of conferring more direct democratic legitimacy – including a democratically-elected European Parliament and the involvement of national parliaments in legislative procedures. These mechanisms help to compensate for a general "loss of control" that occurs in foreign policy areas.

Although the procedures may not be perfect, the biggest challenge to democratic legitimacy results from the lack of participation of European citizens – one of the consequences of the picture painted of the EU by national governments.

The pro-Brexit argument that "taking back control" would "reinstate our sovereignty" is disingenuous. International interdependency and laws are here to stay, and need to stay, as two world wars have shown. We need cooperation both for peace and the environment, and for the more anodyne practicalities of our lives. It's also disingenuous because international cooperation in other contexts than the EU, such as bilateral trade agreements that have been proposed as an alternative to EU membership, would be far less accountable and democratic.

Leaving the EU and contributing to its potential downfall puts much more at stake than a few rules we don't understand or like and may want to legitimately criticise. Leaving threatens international integration as a principle and would cripple the most democratic and most accountable international integration project in recent history.

The EU needs to continue to provide a model of international cooperation in the future. For that it needs to be developed, not trashed.

CHAPTER 20 HISTORY OF PRIVATE MILITARY COMPANIES

"The mercenaries and auxiliaries are useless and dangerous, and if anyone supports his state by the arms of mercenaries, he will never stand firm or sure, as they are disunited, ambitious, without discipline, faithless, bold amongst friends, cowardly amongst enemies, they have no fear of God, and keep no faith with men," wrote Machiavelli in *The Prince*.

As Peter W. Singer says in his book, *Corporate Warriors: The Rise of the Privatized Military Industry* (ISBN 0801441145), «[T]he monopoly of the state over violence is the exception in world history, rather than the rule. The state itself is a rather new unit of governance, appearing only in the last four hundred years. Moreover, it drew from the private violence market to build its public power.»

And as Lt. Col. Tim Spicer says in his book, *An Unorthodox Soldier: Peace and War in the Sandline Affair* (ISBN 1840183497), «Mercenary soldiering has a long and honorable history...When something is both widespread and long lasting, there must be some fundamental reason for it. In the case of mercenaries, the reasons why they have continued to survive and prosper down the centuries can be reduced to just two: efficiency and technology.»

The War on Terror and the 21st Century

The modern private military company has evolved from a hybrid of the wild activities of rogue white officers, and their African recruits, often linked with intelligence agencies running around Africa, and their more legitimate counterparts working under contract from Cold War hero countries. This coupled with the risk advisory services offered to corporations by companies like Kroll, Inc. and CRG and the introduction of more legitimate players from the high ranks of big militaries have come together to offer security to companies doing business in hostile regions and to countries seeking to upgrade their militaries.

The war in Iraq and Afghanistan along with the promised long global war against terror has created a boom in the security and risk advisory market. Trained and experienced military personnel from Special Forces units in the US, UK, Israel and South Africa are retiring to take part. The same is true for the intelligence agencies as companies aiding business ventures in Iraq like GlobalOptions and Diligence see executives on the boards from the CIA, DIA, FBI, the Secret Service, FEMA and MI6.

Many companies are subsidiaries of larger firms. MPRI and Titan were bought by L-3 Communications which is traded on the NYSE. Defence Systems Limited was bought by Armor Holdings, Inc., renamed ArmorGroup than bought out by its board. Group 4 Securicor is a merger between Group 4 Falck and the Wackenhut Corporation providing services from armed prison guards to guarding embassies to supplying electronic surveillance. Computer Sciences Corporation acquired DynCorp.

Many of these companies, while paid with taxpayer money when working under government contracts, are often registered offshore somewhere, escaping tax on many profits from re-entering the representative, public Treasury.

Other companies provide specialized advice and training for maritime concerns such as Executive Solutions International, LLC (ESI). The threat to port cities where liquefied natural gas comes in on container ships could be severe. Pirating and other attacks on the high seas are a threat in many areas of the world. Companies are developing to meet the security needs of cities and companies subject to terrorist or other attacks on shipments.

The laws surrounding hired soldiers and civilian contractors is not clear and not well defined under international agreements.

This is a reason why increasingly the focus is regulation at the national level; e.g. as the licensing mechanisms used by the United States and South Africa demonstrate. Yet many of the hired soldiers are not American; they could be from the country of conflict, or flown in from Chile, El Salvador, or South Africa. Exactly what jurisdiction, aside from their employer, they are under is, according to some commentators, uncertain. [1]

This is true for American contractors as well. Civilian contractors working for Dyncorp in the Balkan wars were implicated by a fellow employee for indulging in a child prostitution and sale ring in the war torn country. [2] Those who turned in the employees were fired, and later the offending employees were fired, however not charged with anything.[3]

Some of the interrogators in the Abu Ghraib crimes were civilian contractors provided by Titan and CACI. They have yet to be charged for any crimes; however they are being sued as are the two companies. [4][5][6] All three companies have continued to receive large wartime contracts from the US government.

In 2006, the US Congress published an official report on US enterprises that had signed contracts with the State Department or the Defense Department so as to carry out anti-narcotics activities as a part of Plan Colombia. Most the private contract enterprises are under the responsibility of the Defense Department, but the largest contract (DynCorp) is in the hands of the State Department. [7]

Points of Interest

The Center for Public Integrity: Making A Killing: The Business of War:

- "At least 90 companies that provide services normally performed by national military forces but without the same degree of public oversight have operated in 110 countries worldwide." [8]
- "Arms dealers have profited from a massive unregulated sell off of low price surplus armaments into the most fragile, conflict-ridden states and failed states. The weapons, mostly from state-owned Eastern European factories, have found their way to Angola, Sudan, Ethiopia, Colombia, Congo-Brazzaville, Sri Lanka, Burundi and Afghanistan where conflicts have led to the deaths of up to 10 million people during the past decade." [9]
- «Since 1994, the U.S. Defense Department has entered into 3,061 contracts with 12 of the 24 U.S.-based PMCs identified by ICIJ, a review of government documents showed. Pentagon records valued those contracts was more than $300 billion. More than 2,700 of those contracts were held by just two companies: Kellogg Brown & Root and Booz Allen Hamilton. Because of the limited information the Pentagon provides and the breadth of services offered by some of the larger companies, it was impossible to determine what percentage of these contracts was for training, security or logistical services." [10]
- «The International Traffic in Arms Regulations Law (ITAR) requires PMCs to obtain approval from the State Department before selling their services to a foreign government. State's Office of Defense Trade Controls reviews contract proposals to ensure they do not violate sanctions or other U.S. policy. However, PMCs can also sell their services abroad through the Defense Department's Foreign Military Sales (FMS) program, which does not require any licensing by State. Under FMS, the Pentagon pays the contractor for services offered to a foreign government, which in turn reimburses the Pentagon." [11]

Outsourcing the Pentagon

The following is according to the Center for Public Integrity's Outsourcing the Pentagon:

- "In April [2002], the Army told Congress that its best guess was that the Army had between 124,000 and 605,000 service contract workers. In October, the Army announced that it would permit contractors to compete for "non-core" positions held by 154,910 civilian workers (more than half of the Army's civilian workforce) and 58,727 military personnel." [12]
- "In 2003, the IG [Inspector General] reported that out of 113 service contract actions reviewed (with an estimated value of $17.8 billion), at least 98 had one or more problems, including inadequate competition, lack of surveillance, or inadequate price reasonableness determinations." [13]
- "The Freedom of Information Act applies to "agency" records. Contractors, in this context, are not "agencies," even where they perform decisional roles. Similarly, government officials are subject to a body of conflict of interest provisions, pay caps, limits on political activity, and labor rules that do not similarly constrain contractors who perform similar, even the same, work." [14]
- «Between 1998 and 2003, the Pentagon awarded more than $47 billion in contracts designated for small businesses to companies that have each earned more than $100 million from Defense Department contracts alone during that six year period.» [15]
- «The homeland security industry is currently the fastest growing sector of the U.S. economy, predicted to grow from a $5 billion industry in 2000 to $130 billion in 2010, according to the Homeland Security Research Corporation, a private California think tank.» [16]

Corporate Warriors

In 2002, Peter W. Singer wrote the following in "Corporate Warriors: The Rise and Ramifications of the Privatized Military Industry" by Peter W. Singer. (Links to 91K/46 page .pdf file.)

- With the rise of the privatized military industry, actors in the global system can access capabilities that extend across the entire spectrum of military activity-from a team of commandos to a wing of fighter jets-simply by becoming a business partner.»? (pg. 1-2)
- Many PMFs operate as «virtual companies.» Similar to Internet firms that limit their expenditure on fixed (brick and mortar) assets, most PMFs do not maintain standing forces but draw from databases of qualified personnel and specialized subcontractors on a contract-by-contract basis.» (pg. 15)

- The unrestricted access to military services ushered in by the rise of the privatized military industry has clearly enhanced the role of nonstate groups which at one time had been at a disadvantage in a system dominated by states. PMFs provide these groups with new options and new paths to power not imagined until very recently.» (pg. 31)
- The ultimate problem with PMFs is that they diffuse responsibility. Questions about who monitors, regulates, and punishes employees or companies that go astray are still to be fully answered. That many of these firms are chartered in offshore accounts complicates the matter further.» (pg. 34)

Recruiting Candidates

In "Transfering Costs of War to Latin America is Morally, Politically Wrong" in *The Miami Herald*, January 29, 2005, Geoff Thale observes:

- "In El Salvador, the security firms are said to be pleased with the candidates they have found. Many of them served in the Salvadoran armed forces; they are highly motivated, because they are being paid several times what they could earn in the Salvadoran economy; and they are cheap, because even paying five times what an average Salvadoran earns means that the security firms are paying far less than they would have to pay to recruit U.S. civilians to do this work."
- "The U.S. military contracts out elements of security operations to U.S. companies, who recruit relatively low-cost Latin Americans to fill the jobs. The contractors keep labor costs down, thus helping their bottom line. The Latin Americans are poor, need the work and benefit from what are -- by their standards -- high salaries."
- "Latin America and other less-developed regions shouldn't serve as a cheap labor pool to recruit people for dangerous jobs that are part of the U.S. military mission in Iraq. It may be tempting to pay others to take risks for us. It may be particularly tempting to pay people from foreign countries such as El Salvador, Colombia or Chile, so that we don't experience the human cost of casualties or deaths ourselves. But it's not morally acceptable."
- "U.S. military and government officials are attempting to avoid paying the political cost in the United States of the war in Iraq by hiring poor Latin Americans to do part of the fighting and the dying in place of U.S. citizens. Whether one supports or opposes the U.S. war in Iraq, one can agree that it is the U.S. military that ought to bear the burden of fighting a war that the United States initiated. Allies may join in and send their own troops in support if they so choose. But U.S. contractors working for the Pentagon shouldn't be recruiting civilians in Latin America to bear the burden of carrying out a U.S. military mission."
- "When a U.S. soldier is wounded or killed in combat, his or her family, neighbors and community feel the weight of the war and ask themselves, *Is it worth it?* In a democracy such as the United States, it is important for citizens to share the burden related to military action abroad, feel the impact and make the judgment about whether it's worthwhile."

Creating Distance

The July 3, 2003 cover feature, *Soldiers of Good Fortune* by Barry Yeoman for *The Independent Weekly* makes the following assertions:

- Private military corporations become a way to distance themselves and create what we used to call ‹plausible deniability,›» says Daniel Nelson, a former professor of civil-military relations at the Defense Department›s Marshall European Center for Security Studies. «It›s disastrous for democracy.»
- The lack of oversight alarms some members of Congress. «Under a shroud of secrecy, the United States is carrying out military missions with people who don›t have the same level of accountability,» says Rep. Jan Schakowsky (D-Ill.), a leading congressional critic of privatized war. "We have individuals who are not obligated to follow orders or follow the Military Code of Conduct. Their main obligation is to their employer, not to their country."
- An analysis shows that 17 of the nation›s leading private military firms have invested more than $12.4 million in congressional and presidential campaigns since 1999.»
- In 2001, according to the most recent federal disclosure forms, 10 private military companies spent more than $32 million on lobbying.» More recently, «the ten largest contractors in the nation spent more than $27 million lobbying the federal government *in the last quarter* of 2009," according to a review of lobbying records. "The massive amount of money used to influence the legislative process came as the White House announced it would ramp up military activity in Afghanistan and Congress considered appropriations bills to pay for that buildup» [17].
- Federal law bans U.S. soldiers from participating in Colombia›s war against left-wing rebels and from training army units with ties to right-wing paramilitaries infamous for torture and political killings. There are no such restrictions on for-profit companies, though, and since the late 1990s, the United States has paid private military companies an estimated $1.2 billion, both to eradicate coca crops and to help the Colombian army put down rebels who use the drug trade to finance their insurgency.»
- The Pentagon has become so dependent on private military companies that it literally cannot wage war without them. Troops already rely on for-profit contractors to maintain 28 percent of all weapons systems."
- There are some weapons systems that the U.S. military forces do not have the capability to do their own maintenance on,» concedes David Young, a deputy commander at the Defense Contract Management Agency.»

ACCOUNTABILITY

Lt. Col. Tim Spicer makes the following remarks in his book, *An Unorthodox Soldier: Peace and War and the Sandline Affair*:

- "Another frequent allegation about PMCs is that they are "not accountable." Not accountable to whom? World opinion? Outside politicians? I can only speak for Sandline, but we are always accountable, to our own policies and ethos and to our client government, with whom we always have a binding contract."? (pg. 24)
- "[T]he majority of legitimate PMCs are quite capable of continuing to operate and grow without the introduction of a regulatory regime. PMCs will accept external regulation if it is manageable and adds to their commercial aspirations and operational effectiveness. [ ] I would suggest that since PMCs operate in an international setting and in high-risk, volatile situations, the sort of heavy-handed regulation employed in other areas of public concern might not be entirely appropriate." (pg. 27)
- "Any PMC must adhere to the law of armed conflict, as defined by the Geneva Convention, and show a respect for human dignity and human rights. Although our operatives are always enlisted in the forces of the governments who employ us, not least to ensure a clear chain of command, if one of our people were told, for example, to attack a village, an action which would unnecessarily endanger innocent lives, he would not do it." (pg. 53)

Trade Association View

Doug Brooks, president of the International Peace Operations Association, a representative group for PMCs makes the following statements:

- Contrary to various media reports, private security company (PSC) employees in Iraq are not becoming overnight millionaires. Sensational reports of $1500 or even $3500 per day salaries tax free float around in the media, but the reality is far different. Private security professionals with the highest qualifications and suffering the greatest risk may earn as much as $700 per day, far below the sensational salaries many experts have been claiming. [18]
- Skilled private contractors in Iraq are doing everything from rebuilding the education system and electrical grids to protecting fledgling democracy efforts. It is critical that the industry spearhead efforts challenging rogue companies and contractors who violate the public trust. [19]
- The reality is that every UN or regional peace operation in existence today requires and utilizes the services of the private sector. IPOA members have proven their effectiveness and value in these operations. [20]
- In a globalized economy, all transnational companies, whether their focus is manufacturing, mining, transportation or even security, look for employees with the required skill sets from local, regional, and international sources. [21]

INDEX

O

P

R

S

T

V

W